Dawning of the Cold War

Dawning of the Cold War

The United States' Quest for Order

Randall B. Woods & Howard Jones

The University of Georgia Press ■ Athens & London

Designed by Richard Hendel
Set in Sabon
The paper in this book meets the guidelines for permanence and durability of the Committee on Production Guidelines for Book Longevity of the Council on Library Resources.

Printed in the United States of America

95 94 93 92 91 5 4 3 2 1

Library of Congress Cataloging in Publication Data

Woods, Randall Bennett, 1944–
Dawning of the Cold War: the United States' quest for order /
Randall B. Woods and Howard Jones.
p. cm.
Includes bibliographical references (p.).
ISBN 0-8203-1265-7 (alk. paper). —
ISBN 0-8203-1266-5 (pbk.: alk. paper)
1. United States—Foreign relations—1945–1953.
2. Cold War. 3. World politics—1945–1955.
I. Jones, Howard, 1940–.
II. Title.
E813.W58 1991
327.73—dc20

90-10922
CIP

British Library Cataloging in Publication Data available

CONTENTS

PREFACE

On November 15, 1989, East German workers began punching holes in the Berlin Wall, the ultimate symbol of the Cold War. For a generation that ugly gash had marred not only the face of a graceful and historic city but the psyche of the entire Western world. Its demise came suddenly. Despite *perestroika* and *glasnost,* free elections in Poland, and the subsuming of the Hungarian Communist party within a broad socialist front, commentators had predicted only a week before the wall's opening that it would be the last symbol of the Cold War to go because its destruction would signal the bankruptcy of Communist rule in Eastern Europe. Berlin, they argued, would have to wait years for free access.

The abruptness with which the Berlin Wall was breached and the rapid onset of reform in Eastern Europe point above all to the extent to which the Communist regimes established in Europe following World War II depended on Soviet power. To Wojciech Jaruzelski in Poland, to Egon Krenz in East Germany, to Communist leaders in Hungary and throughout the Eastern bloc, Mikhail Gorbachev made clear that Soviet troops would not be sent in support of efforts to crush dissent. Given the overwhelming popular demand within their countries for political reforms and freedom of travel, the old guard in Eastern Europe faced the choice either of becoming reformers themselves or of relinquishing power.

What the world has witnessed during the past year is the destruction of the old order in Europe, a regime established during and immediately after World War II. This is true for the non-Communist as well as the Communist world. The advent of Gorbachev, perestroika, democracy, and national self-determination within the Eastern bloc has dramatically altered Western politics. It has made the United States, if not superfluous to European affairs, at least more peripheral. The question of German unification and the opening up of the East have dramatically altered plans for European integration. Held together for so long by a common enemy, NATO is threatened by the diverging interests of its members. Commitments and circumstances that have prevailed for forty years are changing with dizzying speed.

This book is about the establishment of the postwar order that is now disintegrating. Indeed, the end of the Cold War should not obscure the reality or the importance of that phenomenon as a historical subject. Between 1945 and 1950 the Soviet Union was an exhausted, brutalized nation, determined never again to be subjected to a holocaust such as that inflicted by Hitler and the Wehrmacht. The USSR was ruled by the iron-fisted and dictatorial Joseph Stalin and an entrenched *nomenklatura* dedicated to the perpetuation of its power. A totalitarian form of government, widespread devastation of the domestic economy, a sense of isolation, and a power vacuum combined to convince the Kremlin that it should project Soviet power into surrounding territories. American and British leaders perceived the Soviet Union as an expansionist, aggressive state bent on dominating as much of Europe and the Middle East as possible. The essentially conservative men who ruled Britain and the United States feared Soviet imperialism and felt threatened by Communism (insofar as they understood it) as a political and economic system. The clash between East and West from 1945 through 1950 was real, intense, and immensely dangerous. That the world is apparently entering a less confrontational, more pragmatic period makes the perceptions and events surrounding the dawning of the Cold War no less real or meaningful. We hope that this book contributes to an understanding of this most important historical phenomenon.

Although much of Europe lay in ruins at the close of World War II, those who had survived the rise and fall of Nazi Germany and Fascist Italy looked to the future with a good deal of anticipation. The war had spawned the Grand Alliance, a massive coalition of anti-Fascist powers presided over by Great Britain, the Soviet Union, and the United States. Not only had these nations succeeded in defeating the Axis, but they had joined together to form a new collective security organization, the United Nations. But popular hopes for a prolonged period of peace, democracy, national self-determination, and international harmony were to be dashed on the rocks of the Cold War.

The cement of the Grand Alliance, as has been the case with so many alliances of the past, was the common enemy, and once Germany surrendered, national aspirations and anxieties began to rend the alliance asunder. In the months following the Wehrmacht's invasion of Russia in 1941, the principal foreign policy goals of the Kremlin were first to stem the German tide and then to gain control of Poland and the Baltic states so as to protect the motherland from another invasion by an ambitious Central European power. Once the tide of war began to turn, however, Stalin's vision started to expand. Quite simply, the Soviet leader was prepared to project Russian power into as much of Europe as the capitalist democracies would allow. Militarily and politically he proved to be the ultimate opportunist. Winston Churchill was well aware of Stalin's intentions. As the prime minister saw it, his task was to hold as much of Europe as possible for capitalism and democracy and at the same time to preserve and strengthen what was left of the British Empire. Unfortunately for the United Kingdom, its power was ebbing rapidly, and as Churchill recognized, London could not realize its objectives without massive economic, military, and diplomatic support from the United States. Though he was committed to democracy and national self-determination for Europe, Franklin D. Roosevelt was loath to join in an Anglo-American alliance against the Soviet Union. He believed that the Grand Alliance could be maintained intact and that its preservation was the key to any success the United Nations might enjoy. Until his death in April 1945, he concentrated on disarming the Soviet Union by keeping Britain at arm's length while holding out the prospect of a massive postwar reconstruction loan to the Kremlin.

Though few in the West were willing to admit it, the Yalta accords of February 1945 sanctioned the division of Europe into two hostile camps. Stalin was forced to sign the Declaration of Liberated Europe, which committed each of the occupying powers to hold free elections in its occupation zone as soon as possible. But in fact, elections were held in Eastern Europe only after opposition parties had been outlawed and dissent suppressed. In essence, Soviet occupation authorities presided over plebiscites designed to legitimize local Communist regimes that the Russians had installed. Britain lacked the power and the United States the will to force the Soviets out of Eastern Europe.

The establishment of totalitarian, Soviet-controlled regimes in Hungary, Rumania, Poland, Bulgaria, and finally Czechoslovakia alienated a segment of the foreign policy establishment, the public, Congress, and the press in the United States. Upon his accession to office, Harry S. Truman assumed a hard line with the Soviets, but he quickly reverted to Roosevelt's "tripod" approach. Truman's secretary of state, James F. Byrnes, and a number of Roosevelt's advisers convinced the new president that by rejecting the appearance as well as the reality of a common Anglo-American front, and by wielding the stick of the atomic bomb and the carrot of a reconstruction loan, Washington could persuade the Soviets to act reasonably and responsibly. Throughout the summer and fall of 1945 Truman and Byrnes labored with Soviet and British diplomats to hammer out peace treaties with Italy, Germany, and their allies and to work out mutually acceptable occupation arrangements for these countries and Japan. They failed.

Following the London Foreign Ministers' Conference of September and the Moscow meeting in December, it became increasingly clear to all concerned that the Kremlin was not going to permit Western participation in the reconstruction of its sphere, and that the British and Americans were going to exclude the Russians from the occupation governments of Italy and Japan. Moreover, the Soviets appeared determined to expand their empire by annexing the northern half of Iran and converting the remainder of the country into a Soviet protectorate. In early 1946 the Labour government of Clement Attlee, which had come to power in Britain during the summer of 1945, hit upon the stratagem of confronting the Soviet Union within the framework of the United Nations. Whitehall perceived correctly that many Americans who tended to view London's attacks on Soviet imperialism as just another manifestation of power politics found those assaults acceptable within the context of and in the name of the United Nations. Finally, by early 1946, Senator Arthur H. Vandenberg had rallied the so-called presidential and congressional wings of the Republican party behind a campaign attacking the Democrats for being "soft on Communism" and for abandoning the peoples of Eastern Europe to Soviet imperialism.

Responding to events in Eastern Europe and the Near East, to continuing British pressure, and to attacks from a newly unified Republican party, the Truman administration gradually assumed a more confrontational posture toward the Soviet Union during the spring, summer, and fall of 1946. In March the president sponsored Churchill's iron curtain speech, an address that was a virtual call to arms to the non-Communist world. At the same time, Truman forced the Soviets to back down over Iran, and he and his advisers labored diligently throughout 1946 to maintain unilateral U.S. control over the atomic bomb. Though the former members of the Grand Alliance agreed at the Paris Peace Conference to sign peace treaties with Germany's wartime allies, the close of 1946 saw East and West bitterly divided.

As 1947 opened, the Truman administration perceived nothing less than the existence of a global campaign directed by the Kremlin to destroy self-determination, democracy, and capitalism, and to substitute in their place Communist totalitarianism. Washington's policymakers were convinced that areas with high unemployment, runaway inflation, and stunted production, which included much of Central and parts of Western Europe, were especially susceptible to Communist influence. According to Washington, the Russians were engaged in a "new kind of war," a total war embracing all fronts: economic, political, and social, as well as military. But the United States' sole possession of the atomic bomb dictated that

Soviet tactics would be indirect rather than direct. Utilizing infiltration, subversion, intimidation, propaganda, obstructionism, and proxies, Russian leaders would work tirelessly to draw non-Communist regimes into the Soviet sphere.

The White House countered with a policy of firmness that was grounded in flexibility and restraint. In seeking to contain Soviet aggression without escalating the Cold War into a shooting conflict, the Truman administration devised responses that were equivalent to the degrees of danger posed. Thus its strategy emphasized keeping means in harmony with ends while tacitly recognizing Soviet spheres of influence. American policymakers equated the national interest with the security of the non-Communist world and proclaimed the nation's welfare to be an integral part of that security. Such a commitment was global only in theory, however; practical considerations prevented automatic blanket commitments. The United States refused to act unilaterally, and it would not move unless the area in danger of collapse was subject to being saved.

The Truman Doctrine, the Marshall Plan, the Berlin crisis, NATO—all exemplified the Truman administration's efforts to contain perceived Soviet aggression by establishing order in the Near East and Western Europe. Economic and political instability plagued Greece and Turkey in the postwar era. To safeguard the eastern Mediterranean, the United States sent military assistance to Greece in an attempt to counter an insurgency mounted by a guerrilla army that received aid from neighboring Communist regimes. In the case of Turkey, Soviet armies waged a war of nerves along the two nations' common border; although the Communist troop movements never materialized into an invasion, the United States sent advisers and military aid as a precautionary measure. In Western Europe, where the problem was primarily economic, the Truman administration responded to joblessness, ever-rising prices, and low productivity with a massive aid program named after Secretary of State George C. Marshall. The goal of the Marshall Plan was to stabilize the Continent's economies and integrate them into a multilateral trade system. In the process, it was hoped, Communism would lose its appeal, and social democracy would reign supreme in areas still outside the iron curtain.

Throughout this period the German problem loomed as a major obstacle to international harmony. Indeed, Berlin was located at the crossroads of East and West and became the site of the first direct Cold War encounter between the Soviet Union and its wartime Western allies. During that crisis the White House went so far as to consider using the atomic bomb; but as in Greece and Turkey, the United States ultimately adhered to a measured response that was commensurate with the level of danger. In answer to the Soviet blockade of Berlin, the West countered with the airlift—accompanied by demonstrations of strength and Western unity that convinced the Kremlin that its tactics had merely unified and inspired its opponents. The Berlin crisis helped bring into being the defensive military alliance that Churchill originally called for at the close of World War II.

Thus did the Cold War dawn in Europe. Ironically, the emergence of mutually recognized spheres of interest has actually made possible the prolonged period of peace and relative stability that Europe and North America have enjoyed since 1945. The division between East and West seems to have been inescapable, given the two sides' mutually exclusive interests. Fortunately, the two chief Cold War antagonists—the United States and the Soviet Union—realized that an uneasy peace was preferable to a full-scale war.

In writing this book, we have attempted a synthesis of both older and more recently published works—indeed, a blending of orthodox, revisionist, postrevisionist, and corporatist scholarship. At the same time, this study is rooted in research in primary materials. Our survey of the origins of the Cold War in Europe is intended to appeal to both scholar and student. Though we have taken into account the latest contributions of various schools of thought on the origins of the Cold War, the thrust of our interpretation is clearly orthodox, or, to use another term, realist. Despite the Soviet Union's weakness at the close of World War II, the Truman administration, Congress, and a majority of the American people equated Communism with Soviet imperialism and perceived this totalitarian amalgam to be bent on world domination. That Stalin was a consummate pragmatist who did not want war with the West, and that the regime's aggressiveness in Eastern Europe and its repressiveness at home were as much products of domestic considerations as of other factors, does not alter the reality of that perception. Moreover, the Truman Doctrine, the Marshall Plan, the Berlin airlift, and NATO were measured responses designed to contain Communist expansion without provoking full-scale military conflict. Clearly the new scholarship made possible by glasnost is reinforcing the validity of this thesis.

■ ■ ■ ACKNOWLEDGMENTS

The making of a book is truly a group effort, and ours is no exception. We are deeply indebted to a number of people. For reading all or parts of the manuscript and offering numerous helpful recommendations, we wish to thank Robert A. Divine, Robert H. Ferrell, Melvyn P. Leffler, Forrest and Ellen McDonald, William W. Stueck, and two unidentified readers for the University of Georgia Press. Special recognition goes to the authors cited in the notes, whose fine studies have provided indispensable guidelines through this important period of history.

Others were vital to this study. Malcolm L. Call, the director of the University of Georgia Press, showed great interest in the project from its inception. Pauline Testerman of the Harry S. Truman Library located the illustrations. Our spouses and children again provided the faith and patience that empowered us to see this project to its finish.

Any merit that this book may have belongs in large measure to those listed above. The shortcomings we claim as our own.

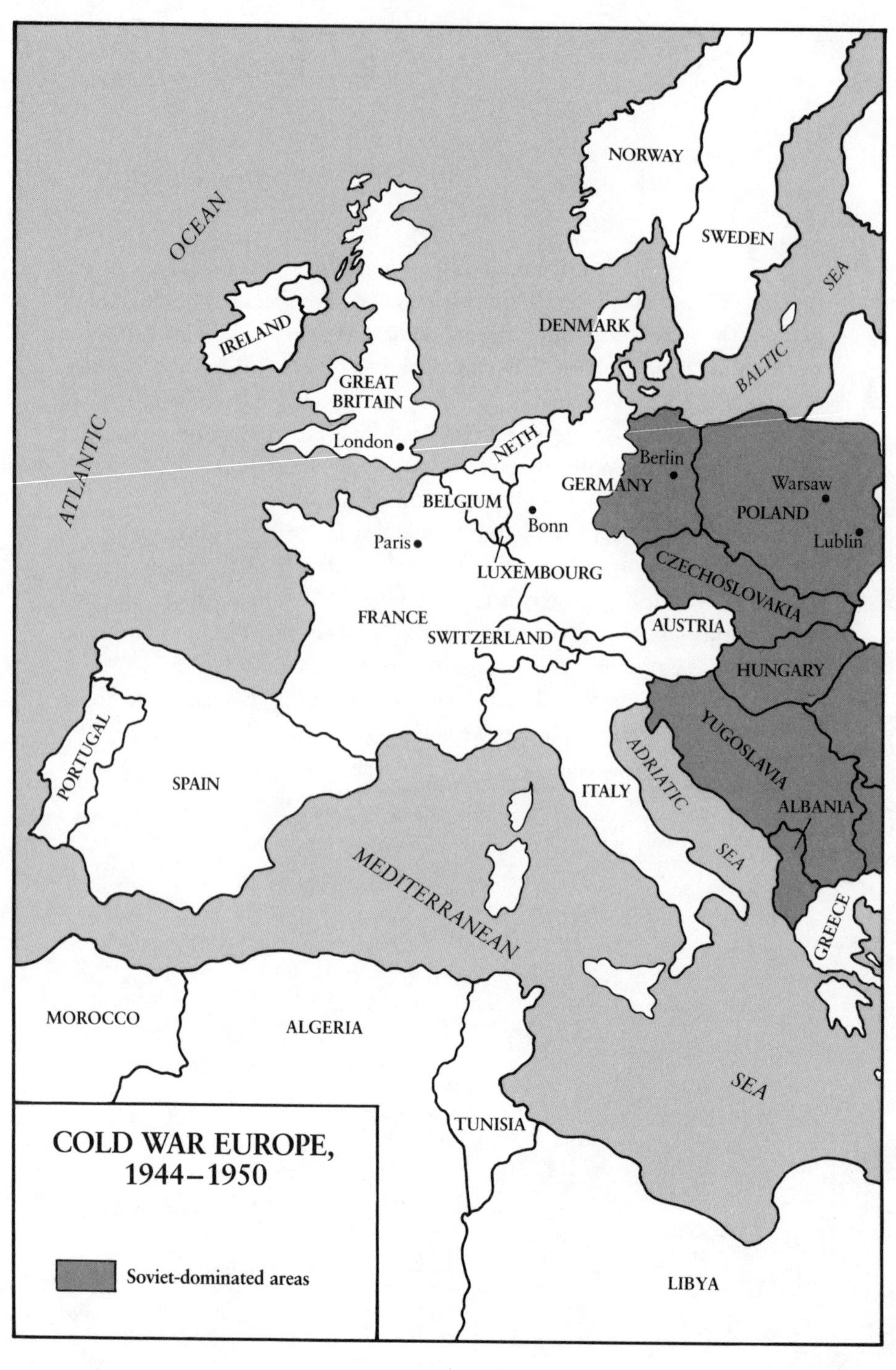
NORWAY
SWEDEN
OCEAN
SEA
DENMARK
IRELAND
BALTIC
GREAT
BRITAIN
ATLANTIC
London
NETH
Berlin
GERMANY
Warsaw
BELGIUM
POLAND
Bonn
Paris
Lublin
LUXEMBOURG
CZECHOSLOVAKIA
FRANCE
AUSTRIA
SWITZERLAND
HUNGARY
PORTUGAL
YUGOSLAVIA
ADRIATIC
SPAIN
ITALY
ALBANIA
SEA
MEDITERRANEAN
GREECE
MOROCCO
ALGERIA
SEA
TUNISIA
COLD WAR EUROPE,
1944–1950
Soviet-dominated areas
LIBYA

FINLAND
Leningrad
ESTONIA
Moscow
LATVIA
LITHUANIA
WHITE RUSSIA
SOVIET
UNION
ARAL SEA
Stalingrad
UKRAINE
RUMANIA
Yalta
CASPIAN
CAUCASUS
MTS.
BLACK
SEA
Ardahan
AZERBAIJAN
BULGARIA
SEA
Kars
Istanbul
Ankara
TURKEY
Teheran
AEGEAN
SEA
SYRIA
IRAN
LEBANON
IRAQ
MEDITERRANEAN
SEA
ISRAEL
JORDAN
Persian
Gulf
Suez Canal
SAUDI
ARABIA
EGYPT
RED SEA

■ ■ ■ PART I

Challenge

CHAPTER ONE

The Grand Alliance and the Road to Victory

Just as World War I would not have been possible without the Franco-Prussian War, nor World War II without the Great War, the Cold War was a product of the devastation wrought by six years of bloody conflict between the Axis and its enemies and, more specifically, by the politics of the Grand Alliance. Only the monumental threat to Western civilization posed by Adolf Hitler and his allies was sufficient to overcome American isolationists and the mutual distrust that existed between Anglo-America and the Soviet Union. As the tide of war began to turn against the Axis, national priorities gradually eclipsed the need for international cooperation.[1] As Great Britain, the Soviet Union, and the United States contemplated victory and began to make plans for the postwar world, they found themselves increasingly at odds.

British Prime Minister Winston Churchill feared that the United States intended to relegate his country to a position of undeserved and unrealistic inferiority while encouraging the disintegration of the British Empire, a trend that he fought with all his might. Churchill, a strong believer in the balance of power, assumed that the fate of Europe would continue to determine the fate of the world. He also assumed a basic conflict of interest between the Soviet Union and the West and therefore believed that Western Europe, especially France and Germany, ought to be rehabilitated as quickly as possible after the Nazis were destroyed. He was convinced that it was as much in America's interest as in Britain's to maintain a balance of power on the Continent and that, consequently, Washington should join London in rebuilding Central Europe and in resisting the expansion of Soviet influence.[2]

Throughout the war Soviet leaders proclaimed that their overriding goal in the postwar era was the physical security of Mother Russia. They were determined to construct a European order in which it would be impossible for another Napoleon or Hitler to ravage the Ukraine, the Caucasus, and the rest of European Russia. Accordingly, in 1942 Soviet Premier Joseph Stalin stated his nation's minimum territorial objectives: the full fruits of the Nazi-Soviet Pact of 1939, that is, annexation of Latvia, Estonia, and portions of Poland, as well as Lithuania and parts of Rumania and Finland (which the USSR had invaded shortly after the outbreak of war in 1939). The Kremlin further insisted that it would be politically necessary to establish "friendly" governments along the country's western flank. In practice, this meant Communist regimes. In sum, even as Hitler's soldiers drove relentlessly toward Moscow and Stalingrad, Stalin was a pragmatic expansionist who stood ready to seize every opportunity and utilize every tactic short of global war to expand Soviet power as far into Europe as possible.[3]

Until 1944 President Franklin D. Roosevelt favored a peace structure built around the concept of the "Four Policemen." Britain, Russia, America, and China would supervise their respective spheres of interest, preventing aggression and fostering democracy and self-determination of peoples. In 1944, in response to a popular surge of enthusiasm for Wilsonian internationalism, the administration ostentatiously announced that it favored the establishment of a new League of Nations, the United Nations, to keep the peace and work for global fair play and prosperity. In reality, Roosevelt never abandoned his affinity for the Four-Policemen idea, and as will be seen, the UN Charter, in establishing a Security Council with five permanent members (each of which had veto power) and in permitting regional defense arrangements, actually combined the concept of collective security with that of spheres of interest.[4]

Implicit in the Four-Policemen concept was a desire to protect U.S. interests and maintain a balance of power in Europe through a policy of *realpolitik*. FDR's ability to engage in hardheaded bargaining over boundaries, reparations, and political arrangements was severely circumscribed, however, by a combination of neo-isolationists and Wilsonian internationalists in the United States. Both groups were opposed to power politics, and they thought of bargaining over spheres of interest as exactly that. Intimidated by congressional and popular opinion, Roosevelt neglected to educate his nation about the realities of international politics in the postwar world, and he shunned concrete agreements until the Yalta Conference of 1945, when the Red Army was already in possession of much of Eastern Europe. Instead, the White House tacitly declared its independence of Britain and attempted to woo the USSR with the promise of a massive postwar reconstruction loan.[5]

■ ■ ■ When the United States joined the struggle against the Axis following Japan's attack at Pearl Harbor on December 7, 1941, Allied victory was by no means certain. A jubilant Churchill journeyed to Washington, where he met with Roosevelt and signed the Declaration of the United Nations. The UN Declaration pledged the signatories to wage all-out warfare until the Axis was defeated. But despite the optimism of the Roosevelt-Churchill communiqué, it was the Allies who met defeat on virtually every front in 1942. In the Far East Pearl Harbor was just a mask for Japanese amphibious landings in Southeast Asia. By the late spring of 1942 Thailand, Shanghai, the Dutch East Indies, and the Philippines had all been overrun. From their outposts in New Guinea Japanese forces threatened Australia, and from their positions in Burma they menaced India. In Europe Germany controlled virtually the entire Continent. In the spring of 1940 Hitler executed an adroit end run around French defenses, drove through Belgium and the Netherlands, and forced the emergency evacuation of the entire British expeditionary force from Dunkirk. France was left alone to face the German onslaught, and that beleaguered country surrendered within six weeks. For the rest of the year the Nazis harassed Britain with a barrage of bombs and rumors of cross-Channel, amphibious landings. But on June 22, 1941, Hitler threw all caution to the winds and invaded the Soviet Union. Following initial advances in the summer and fall of 1941, the Germans waited out the bitter winter and then drove north and south as the Russian snows melted in the spring. At the Wehrmacht's point of deepest penetration, it occupied most of European Russia. Meanwhile, in North Africa Field Marshall Erwin Rommel and the Afrika Corps threatened the Suez Canal from the west.

By the close of the year the Allies had halted the Axis advance. Royal Air Force night fighters inflicted heavy losses on the Luftwaffe in the Battle of Britain, and the long-feared Nazi invasion never materialized. British Field Marshall Sir Bernard Montgomery relieved pressure on Egypt and the Suez Canal by taking El Alamein. Then, in November 1942, British and American troops waded ashore at Oman and Algiers in North Africa. After putting up token resistance, troops loyal to Vichy France (the puppet government established by the Germans to rule central and southern France) surrendered, and the Allies thus secured a foothold from which they would launch successful attacks on Sicily and Italy in 1943. In a herculean effort, Soviet armies stopped the German advance at Stalingrad in late 1942 and early 1943. Meanwhile, in the Far East a makeshift U.S. task force had surprised the Japanese navy, sinking four enemy carriers at the Battle of Midway.[6]

With their immediate survival assured, Allied leaders turned their attention in 1943 to discussion of a strategy that would simultaneously win the war and provide for a lasting peace. Although fifty nations eventually signed the UN Declaration, the Grand Alliance was dominated by the Big Three: the United States, the Soviet Union, and the United Kingdom. As long as a common enemy threatened their existence, the partners displayed a modicum of cooperation, and a patina of congeniality overlay their discussions. Nevertheless, ideological differences, historical mistrust, and divergent strategic and economic objectives boded ill for the alliance. Geography, coupled with ties of language, history, and culture, meant that contacts between Britain and the United States were closer and more frequent than those between the Soviet Union and either of the other partners. In some respects the United Kingdom and the United States did fight as one. A series of combined boards assigned shipping and supplies to various Anglo-American theaters, and lend-lease provided Britain with a substantial portion of the matériel needed to fight the war. Churchill and Roosevelt had begun corresponding in 1939 as the situation in Europe deteriorated into war. With the former's accession to office in May 1940, the two communicated on an almost daily basis. British and American military leaders met continually to plan strategy for the Western European and Pacific theaters. And yet stresses and strains characterized the Anglo-American relationship.

Profound differences developed between London and Washington over strategy. To hold down Allied casualties, to redeem himself for the disastrous Gallipoli expedition of World War I, and to guarantee Anglo-American control of Central Europe in the postwar world, Churchill pressed for massive strategic bombing of occupied Europe, to be followed by an Allied invasion through the Balkans—the "soft underbelly" of Europe. The Roosevelt administration and its principal military planners, George C. Marshall and Dwight D. Eisenhower, rejected this approach as time-consuming and essentially diversionary. They won acceptance of a plan that called for massing troops in the British Isles and then launching a frontal assault on occupied Europe. Only after a series of bitter meetings did Churchill and his advisers reconcile themselves to OVERLORD, the code name assigned to the cross-Channel invasion. And the proud Britons succumbed then only because the United States' superiority in manufacturing plant, agricultural output, and manpower placed it in the position to dictate strategy.[7]

Other bones were lodged in the Anglo-American throat as well. The Roosevelt administration and many Americans blamed World Wars I and II on nationalism and colonialism. Among the promises made in the Atlantic Charter, a press release agreed to by Churchill and Roosevelt at Argentia in August 1941, was a pledge to work for the self-determination of all peoples. Whereas Churchill had in mind those Asians and Europeans enslaved by the Axis powers, Roosevelt intended for the Atlantic Charter to apply to the British and French empires as well. In short, World War II greatly accelerated the worldwide anticolonial movement, and Washington was determined to pose as leader even though British interests and sensibilities were threatened in the process.[8]

The United States also intended to compel Britain to toe the line on another Atlantic Charter promise: equality of economic opportunity and multilateral trade. Throughout the war the State and Treasury departments wielded the leverage provided by lend-lease and Britain's need for postwar economic aid to force a dissolution of the sterling bloc. They did so by insisting that Britain reduce empire preferences and eliminate exchange controls. To many Britons it seemed that their "cousins" were taking advantage of the global conflict to assume control of markets that were traditionally British.[9]

If the relationship between Britain and the United States was frequently strained, the Soviet-American alliance was at times downright rancorous. A number of factors contributed to mutual distrust. Though few Americans were aware of it, every Soviet schoolchild learned that U.S. troops, along with those of the French, British, and Japanese, had intervened in Russia in 1918–19 and, while evacuating war supplies, had skirmished with the Red Army. Russians were taught that the Allied landings were part of a Western conspiracy to stop the Bolshevik Revolution. The USSR's subsequent exclusion from the Washington Naval Conference in 1921–22 and the United States' refusal to extend diplomatic recognition until 1933 further deepened Soviet suspicions. Stalin and his associates in the Kremlin were convinced that the overriding goal of Western diplomacy from 1936 to 1938 was to turn Germany eastward by appeasing it with Czech and Polish territory.

Stalin and his minions remained suspicious of their allies even after Hitler launched Operation BARBAROSSA and Britain and the United States responded by furnishing the Soviet Union with munitions and nonmilitary supplies. In November 1941 the United States started shipping large quantities of lend-lease supplies to Russia via the northern ports of Murmansk and Archangel. A substantial portion of this matériel was sent to the bottom of the Arctic Ocean by marauding Nazi sub packs operating out of occupied Norway. Comparing the quantity of supplies that reached Britain with the volume received by Russia, Stalin insinuated that Washington was deliberately holding out on its Soviet ally.

Even more galling to the Russian leadership was Anglo-America's failure to launch a frontal assault on Axis-occupied Europe in 1942 and 1943. In May 1942 Soviet Foreign Minister Vyacheslav Molotov journeyed to London to sign a twenty-year treaty of peace and friendship with the Churchill government. Among other things, that agreement proposed to recognize the USSR's right to occupy the three Baltic states and the eastern third of Poland after the war. Decrying power politics and territorial transfers made without the consent of the peoples affected, the Roosevelt administration objected to the secret clauses of the Anglo-Soviet accord. Consequently, the Russian foreign minister and British Foreign Secretary Anthony Eden settled for a simple treaty of peace and amity. In the wake of his unsatisfactory negotiations in London, an angry Molotov journeyed to Washington and demanded the immediate establishment of a second front to relieve beleaguered Soviet armies in the east. Intimidated by Molotov's hostility toward U.S. "interference" in Anglo-Soviet negotiations and genuinely concerned at the mangling of Soviet units by the Wehrmacht, FDR promised a second front on the Continent before the year was out. But 1942 and 1943 passed without a major assault in the west. Not until June 1944 did British, American, and Canadian troops splash ashore at Normandy. With increasing bitterness the Soviets charged that the administration was putting Democratic Senator Harry S. Truman's advice into practice and letting Germany and Russia bleed each other to death. Indeed, Stalin never believed that OVERLORD would take place until it actually happened. When on June 5 Churchill cabled him that Western troops would be landing in France the next day, Stalin scoffed: "Yes, there'll be a landing, if there is no fog. Until now there was always something that interfered. I suspect tomorrow it will be something else. Maybe they'll meet up with some Germans! . . . Maybe there won't be a landing then, but just promises as usual."[10]

Americans had their own reasons for distrusting their Soviet ally. Most people, whether educated or unlettered, were more or less aware that Marxism-Leninism called for world revolution, abolition of private property, and elimination of organized religion. Not surprisingly, they found these objectives distasteful. To many in the United States, Communism equaled totalitarianism, and presumably, totalitarianism was what American GIs were then fighting against. In addition, Stalin seemed to be a brutal opportunist in his international dealings. In August of 1939 he had shocked the Western world by concluding the Nazi-Soviet Nonaggression

Pact with Hitler, and following Germany's invasion of Poland, he had seized the eastern third of that country as well as Latvia and Estonia.[11]

Tensions between the Soviet Union and its Western allies eased noticeably, however, with the establishment in France of a second front. Though Allied casualties from the Normandy invasion were heavy, Hitler's forces had become so weakened by losses in the east and by continual Allied bombing and shelling in the west that they could not repel the attack. Within a month, the supreme Allied commander in Europe, General Eisenhower, informed Roosevelt that the millionth Allied soldier had been put ashore.

No sooner had the Western democracies established a foothold in occupied Europe than a new Anglo-American rift developed over strategy. Because the 1943 Italian campaign would drain troops and supplies away from the buildup for OVERLORD, the Mediterranean operation had received only grudging support from U.S. military leaders. Nevertheless, in 1943 British and American troops successfully invaded first Sicily and then the Italian boot itself. Slowly and painfully, Allied troops inched their way up the peninsula. Finally, in mid-1944, as OVERLORD was unfolding, Rome surrendered. Churchill and his military chieftains wanted to continue into northern Italy and penetrate the Ljubljana Gap, a principal corridor into Central Europe. Such a strategy would protect at least part of Central and Southeastern Europe from Soviet occupation. Roosevelt, Eisenhower, and Marshall, however, insisted on an amphibious landing in southern France. This enterprise, code-named ANVIL, would lead to the capture of the Rhone Valley and facilitate a final attack on the heart of Germany. Because the United Kingdom's dependence on lend-lease gave him no choice, Churchill went along with ANVIL. The operation proved a great success, but its opponents claimed that much less of Central Europe would have fallen under Communist sway had the Italian campaign been continued.[12]

OVERLORD, ANVIL, and the fall of Rome marked the beginning of the end for the Axis in Europe. With Hitler's defeat assured, Allied officials turned their minds to the coming peace.

■ ■ ■ To a certain extent, the United States' conception of its role in world affairs at the close of the war was shaped by its relationship with Great Britain.[13] Members of the London government were aware of that fact and attempted to take maximum advantage of it. As early as 1944 Churchill believed that postwar security depended upon the Big Three. Inside or outside a revived League of Nations, he argued, the United Kingdom, the Soviet Union, and the United States should divide the world among themselves and police their respective areas. By the close of the year, however, it appeared that the USSR intended to encroach on part of Britain's bailiwick by absorbing not only Eastern but much of Central Europe as well. Despite the combined chiefs' choice of OVERLORD over Churchill's cherished plan for a thrust through the Balkans at the Ljubljana Gap, the prime minister remained convinced that the West could and should contain Soviet power through a combination of military force and hard bargaining. Committed to the idea that the nation that liberated a particular area of Europe should be free to occupy it and control its economic and political reconstruction, he adamantly opposed, for example, including Soviet representatives on the Allied Control Council for Italy. As German resistance crumbled in early 1945, Churchill was pressing Montgomery to work with Eisenhower in occupying as much of Europe as possible. At the same time he wanted to settle territorial and political issues with the Soviets before the Red Army and Anglo-American forces were cheek-to-jowl somewhere in Central Europe. The prime minister continued to assume, at least through the fall of 1944, that Anglo-American wartime cooperation would continue into the postwar period, and that the identity of interest between the countries in maintaining a balance of power in Europe was as obvious to Roosevelt as it was to him.[14]

To many within the right wing of the Conservative party in England, Anglo-American unity was an ideological as well as diplomatic necessity. Churchill and other High Tories, such as Lord Cherwell (Frederick Lindemann), Lord Beaverbrook (Max Aitken), and Brendan Bracken, not only saw the United States as a power source that would allow the United Kingdom to retain its great-power status, but also believed in the existence of an ideological community of interest between the nations. American aid to Britain would help preserve free enterprise in the United Kingdom, and a U.S. commitment to the security of Europe would contain international Communism. Britain was fighting for rugged individualism, private enterprise, and personal liberty. As a basically conservative country the United States would follow London's lead.[15]

Anthony Eden and a host of second-level officials in the Foreign Office and the Washington embassy initially expected a far less confrontational relationship with the Soviet Union than did Churchill. As of mid-1944 Eden still thought it possible to deal with the Soviet Union on a basis other than that of arms and power blocs. The foreign secretary argued that two schools of thought existed in the Kremlin, one a "collaborationist" faction that was preoccupied with the looming tasks of reconstruction and anxious to resume the government's interrupted program of internal development, and the other paranoid and aggressive, convinced that the

USSR should trust no one and should quickly acquire as much foreign territory as it could. Stalin, Eden advised his colleagues, belonged to the first group, and as of 1944, the collaborationists were still ascendant. The foreign secretary cited as proof conciliatory articles in *Pravda* and *Izvestia* published in June on the anniversary of the Anglo-Soviet treaty. They praised Anglo-American military operations in North Africa and Italy and contended that wartime collaboration among the Big Three would extend past the armistice. Britain, Eden argued, had to do everything possible to reinforce Stalin and the moderates.[16]

Eden and his liberal Conservative followers labored under no illusions, however. The devastation and suffering that would surely accompany the end of hostilities in Europe would make the Continent a breeding ground for totalitarianism, of either the Right or the Left. To counter this threat, Britain should assume the moral and political leadership of Europe. It was crucial to British interests, he argued, that as many European nations as possible should "seek our friendship and guidance and should give us their confidence." Because Britain's financial power was ebbing, Eden insisted, it would have to "compensate for that loss by winning the admiration of the European peoples for our way of life and for our achievements in social, economic, industrial, scientific and intellectual fields."[17] Britain's influence in Europe following the surrender of Germany, the foreign secretary advised, "will much depend upon whether, in attempting to restore order out of chaos . . . these countries adopt . . . methods and regimes such as would be likely to seek inspiration in Moscow, or whether they will model themselves on methods of Western democracies, and especially Great Britain." In turn, these decisions would depend on the perceived efficacy of British institutions and policies on the one hand and their Soviet counterparts on the other "in tackling the appalling social and economic problems of postwar Europe."[18] In short, Eden and his colleagues contended, Britain would have to couple a comprehensive program of full employment and social security with its democratic traditions in order to produce a progressive democracy that would serve as example to Europe. But as moderate and liberal Conservatives readily admitted, this British-led, progressive European bloc could not exist without massive U.S. aid.

Thus British cabinet officials from Churchill to Eden, career civil servants in both the Foreign Office and the Treasury, and the academic economists who had set up shop in Whitehall were all determined to use the United States to advance the national interest of the United Kingdom. Harold Macmillan, British minister resident in North Africa, aptly summed up his nation's strategy toward the United States in 1944: "We are like the Greeks in the late Roman Empire," he told a colleague. "They ran it because they were so much cleverer than the Romans, but they never told the Romans this. That must be our relation to the Americans."[19]

Unfortunately for British designs on American power, a broad consensus had developed in the United States by 1944 that Britain had not abandoned its imperial objectives and spheres-of-interest diplomacy and was conspiring to use America for selfish interests. Nearly every major political group disliked one aspect or another of British society and politics. Liberal New Dealers led by Henry Wallace and Eleanor Roosevelt considered Britain—even with the Labour party playing a prominent role in the coalition government—too anti-Russian, too concerned about preserving its empire, too little committed to internationalism. Fiscal conservatives in the United States could not forget that Britain had not repaid World War I debts. Moreover, businessmen believed that their counterparts in the United Kingdom were plotting a vast expansion of Britain's commercial and financial empire. For the typical English merchant, observed one U.S. industrialist, "the war is not something to be gotten over with; it is an event to be utilized for the sake of Britain's future."[20]

In addition, a "hard core of Anglophobes," as American newsman Edward R. Murrow told British MP Harold Nicolson, composed of Italian-, German-, and Irish-Americans, continued to rail against perfidious Albion. Traditional isolationists blamed John Bull for drawing the United States into World War I, a conflict that, they said, had no bearing on America's strategic and economic interests. And, of course, antiimperialism continued to flourish. During a speaking tour through the Midwest, Edmund Wilson, a State Department information officer, found the common people particularly concerned about British policy in Italy and Greece. Prevailing wisdom had it that His Majesty's officials were more concerned with propping up reactionary monarchies in both countries than with advancing democracy and promoting socioeconomic progress.[21]

A by-product of this Anglophobia, which observers on both sides of the Atlantic found more pronounced as the war approached its climax, was a pervasive desire in the United States to play a role in international politics independent of Great Britain. Reinforcing this tendency was the United States' logistical domination of the Anglo-American alliance. As the fourth year of the conflict in Europe drew to a close, U.S. predominance in men and matériel increased dramatically. By the end of October 1943 America was providing Britain with 77 percent of its escort vessels, 88 percent of its landing craft, 68 percent of its light bombers, virtually all of its transport aircraft, 60 percent of its tankers, all of its tank transporters and ten-ton trucks, and half of selected strategic materials such as magnesium. During 1942 alone, U.S. ground forces grew from 37 to

73 active divisions, and air combat units from 67 to 167. Until July 1944 the British Empire had more men in contact with the enemy than had the United States, but thereafter the balance shifted rapidly in the other direction.[22]

Britain's eclipse within the Anglo-American alliance was accompanied by an equally dramatic increase in Soviet power in Eastern Europe. The key to understanding Russian foreign policy during and immediately after World War II is Joseph Stalin. Faithful to the Leninist formula, Stalin thought in terms of minimum and maximum goals. When the USSR had its back against the wall in 1942, his objectives were the restoration of pre-June 1941 frontiers, the prevention of an anti-Soviet bloc in Europe, and the preservation of Communist outposts abroad. Anything in excess of these minimums remained wishful thinking until after the Battle of Stalingrad. The Red Army's ascendancy in the East by 1943 opened new vistas to Stalin. He briefly considered either concluding a separate peace with Germany, in which the two would divide Europe between them, or spreading Communism by force. He rejected both, however, and opted for the "orderly" growth of Communism from a base in Eastern Europe. Britain's constant and the United States' intermittent willingness to divide Europe into spheres of influence abetted Stalin's quest for power and influence; yet his exact goals remained fluid and subject to negotiation with the Western democracies.[23]

The second front profoundly changed Stalin's outlook, a change signified by his determination to seek a unilateral solution to the Polish question. The Anglo-American commitment embodied in the landings prompted Stalin to order his armies to move beyond the frontiers of June 1941 and conquer land that would eventually become part of the new empire. By the close of the year the Red Army was the most intimidating force on the Continent, attacking Germany with 13,000 tanks, 16,000 fighters and dive bombers, and 525 divisions totaling five million men.[24] As German forces retreated from eastern Poland, Rumania, and Bulgaria in 1944, the Red Army and its entourage of political commissars followed in its wake, establishing martial law and laying the foundations for provisional governments that would be friendly to the Soviet Union. Throughout this period the Kremlin evidenced a disturbing reluctance to define for the West the exact extent of its security needs.

In plotting the aggrandizement of the Soviet state and the expansion of Communist influence, Stalin was responding not only to the imperatives of Russian history and his own personal ideological beliefs but to domestic pressures as well. The Soviet premier was a ruthless and effective dictator, but he was not immune to pressure from various interest groups within the Soviet Union. In this case the two entities he had to placate and/or manipulate were the state bureaucracy, including the army, and the Communist Party of the Soviet Union (CPSU). Unfortunately, Stalin saw in an expansionist foreign policy a means to please both.

World War II witnessed a marked decline of the power and an atrophying of the organizational structure of the CPSU. Stalin had always been a statist; in addition, the need to prosecute the war efficiently resulted in a growth of the power and influence of the Red Army and the managerial class that organized and supervised the civilian aspects of the war effort. As 1944 dawned, Stalin looked upon these power centers with increasing alarm, viewing them as potential challengers to his rule. In the past, apparatuses of the state had been carefully manipulated by the Russian leader to increase his personal power. The wartime army and managerial class, however, had grown outside his direct control.[25] Not surprisingly, the Soviet Union's wartime managers were dedicated to the perpetuation of the bureaucracy that fed them, sheltered them, and accorded them special privileges. The military was also concerned with its own survival and aggrandizement and, like all military establishments, with the security of the state.

To contain and counterbalance these power centers, Stalin presided in 1944 and early 1945 over a revival of the Communist party. The leading figures in this renaissance were the Central Committee's professional propagandists. Geographically, the movement was centered in Moscow and in the Leningrad and Ukrainian party organizations.[26] The new party "enthusiasts" were doctrinaire Marxist-Leninists who accepted without question the notion that capitalism was rife with internal contradictions, that the United States would seek to supplant Great Britain as the world's leading imperial power after the war, and that this situation presented a golden opportunity to expand socialism. The ideologues also believed that capitalism, in its inevitable process of decay, would produce another world war within fifteen to twenty years.

There were differences over tactics between the statists on the one hand and the party on the other. The former favored a direct expansion of Soviet power through annexation of adjacent regions considered vital to the economic and military security of Russia, whereas the party enthusiasts, such as Molotov and Politburo member Andrei Zhdanov, advocated liberation of former Fascist and current capitalist areas through the subversive activities of indigenous Communist parties.[27]

Stalin was tempted in early 1944 to adopt a policy of annexationism toward Eastern Europe, but several factors dissuaded him. The first was the intellectual and political sophistication of the Comintern veterans in Moscow—men and women who still headed the most important Communist parties of the world. From Bulgaria there was Vasil Kolarov, from Germany Walter Ulbricht, and from Hungary Imre Nagy. The second factor was the collaborationist tactic Moscow had been urging on its sympathizers abroad since the Nazi invasion of Russia. Communists abroad had been told not to fight but rather to merge in popular-front fashion with the anti-Fascist forces. So successful was this tactic that in several cases European Communist parties were transformed from their anemic prewar selves to viable, popular movements. Many of them anticipated the triumph of socialism in their own countries rather than annexation to the Soviet Union.[28] The third factor, of course, was the growth in power and influence of the doctrinaire Marxist-Leninists within the revived CPSU.

As 1944 drew to a close, Stalin opted for tactics that would please both the statists and the party operatives. The goals of Soviet foreign policy would be to annex the Baltic states and the eastern third of Poland, to retain those portions of Finland and Rumania that Russia had seized in 1939–40, and to acquire military bases in the eastern Mediterranean and oil reserves in the Middle East. Soviet diplomats would at the same time negotiate agreements with other members of the Grand Alliance that would allow indigenous Communist parties maximum latitude for peaceful takeovers of their respective countries. In keeping with Soviet negotiating tactics, Stalin would conceal his objectives from the West for as long as he could, while persuading it either to sign agreements making their realization possible or to acquiesce in Soviet/Communist gains once they were achieved. The point here is that the dynamics of Soviet domestic politics, as well as other factors, impelled Stalin toward a policy of expansion through both annexation and subversion. As that Russian exponent of detente Maxim Litvinov told W. Averell Harriman in the spring of 1945, the "root cause" of the trouble between East and West was the "ideological conception prevailing [in Moscow] that conflict between Communism and capitalism is inevitable." There had been a change in policy, he said, and the wrong people were in charge of the Kremlin.[29]

Ironically, then, as 1944, the decisive year of the war, progressed and victory at last appeared on the horizon, Britain felt more and more crushed between the superpowers, both of whom seemed to be waiting in the wings, ready to fill the power vacuum created by German and Japanese aggression. "Political affairs—international ones, I mean—are not going very well," Sir Percy Grigg, secretary of state for war, wrote Montgomery in July. "I can't get out of my head the idea that the Americans and Russians are going to frame us in the end and that unless we make up our minds for a generation of hard work and self-denial . . . we shall be left in the position of the Dutch after Utrecht in 1713."[30]

■ ■ ■ While Whitehall and the war cabinet worried about mounting Anglophobia in the United States (as well as the expansionist tendencies in Soviet foreign policy), the Roosevelt administration attempted to make up its collective mind about what, if anything, it wanted to do in regard to Europe following Germany's surrender. There was no base upon which to build. Aside from the Good Neighbor initiative toward Latin America, the White House prior to 1939 failed to develop a distinctive foreign policy. Following America's entry into World War II, the president put forward the Four-Policemen concept as a solution to the world's problems. To old-line isolationists and newly converted internationalists, however, the Four-Policemen idea smacked of spheres-of-interest, power politics.

The Japanese attack on Pearl Harbor momentarily eclipsed but did not destroy isolationism in the United States. Taking their cue from GOP Senator Robert Taft and, in the House, Illinois Republican Jesse Sumner, these typically Republican and midwestern legislators continued to believe in the Fortress America concept and in the notion of U.S. economic self-sufficiency. Following the Republican gains in the midterm elections of 1942, those who had supported the Neutrality Acts and opposed the Lend-Lease Act of 1941 accused the Roosevelt administration of plotting additional global entanglements after the war. The isolationists continued to deny that the United States had a responsibility to confront aggression abroad. Though they acknowledged the relationship between poverty and war, they argued that the United States was under no obligation to assist the less fortunate nations of the world. America's first responsibility was to itself, and the war had grievously depleted the nation's natural and financial resources. Though isolationists such as Taft, along with Republicans Hugh A. Butler and Arthur H. Vandenberg, voted for lend-lease renewal, they were determined to see it cut off as soon as hostilities ended. And finally, they adamantly opposed stationing U.S. troops abroad following the defeat of Germany and Japan. Though it could be argued that the Four-Policemen concept was an extension of the Monroe Doctrine, the isolationists denounced Roosevelt's scheme as a stratagem sure to involve the United States in another foreign war.[31]

The internationalist movement in the United States that peaked in 1944 was more critical of the Four-Policemen idea than were Taft, Sumner, and their colleagues. Neo-Wilsonians vehemently denounced isolationism and called upon Roosevelt to commit the United States to a revitalized League of Nations. All countries, they proclaimed, had to surrender a portion of their national sovereignty for the common good, and the United States was no exception. In 1943 Congress had passed the Fulbright and Connally resolutions, which called for the establishment of a postwar collective security organization. In October of that year Secretary of State Cordell Hull journeyed to Moscow, where he persuaded a reluctant Eden and Molotov to endorse the idea of an association of nations capable of settling international disputes and keeping the peace. He was greeted upon his return to the United States with an outpouring of public support that deeply impressed Roosevelt and his confidant Harry Hopkins.[32] Republican internationalists were no less vehement in their attacks on power politics and enthusiastic in their paeans to a parliament of man than were their Democratic counterparts. In March 1944 twenty-four first-term members of the House who had voted for the Fulbright resolution put the administration on notice: "We believe that the great majority of the American people is badly confused by the seeming emergence of embryonic spheres of influence on a regional basis—the domination of small nations by great. Those who like ourselves have supported the efforts which . . . appeared to bear fruition at the Moscow Conference are now wondering whether they were being led up a blind alley."[33] True converts to world government were in a tiny minority in the United States, however. Congress and the average person applauded the ideas of President Woodrow Wilson and Wendell Willkie's *One World* without having any intention of limiting the nation's freedom of action within the context of a postwar collective security organization. Roosevelt shared that skepticism, and as the war drew to a close he searched for an alternative to pure internationalism on the one hand and spheres of interest on the other.

Sensing that the White House lacked confidence in Hull's internationalist schemes, the secretary's subordinates in the State Department worked behind their chief's back to devise a European policy that would be acceptable to Roosevelt and Hopkins. One group, including Adolf Berle, John Hickerson (chief of the Division of British Commonwealth Affairs), and the heads of the Western Europe, Eastern Europe, and Middle Eastern area desks, called for an updated version of President William Howard Taft's dollar diplomacy—the use of trade and investment for essentially political objectives. They no less than the White House believed that a permanent U.S. military presence in Europe following the war was politically out of the question. Equally inviable was a joint Anglo-American policy vis-à-vis the Soviet Union. The United States would have to act unilaterally to foster peace, to ensure the eventual establishment of "free and democratic governments" for both large and small nations, to promote liberal commercial policies, and to mold "a continent friendly to the United States."[34]

Again, politics was the dog, profits were the tail. According to Berle, "Commercial interests, though they are important in some respects, are incidental to the maintenance of the general moral and diplomatic position which we should have and which we will need, if we are not to be caught between the unresolved British and Soviet forces in respect of which there is no accommodation yet in sight."[35]

A small minority within the State Department headed by Assistant Secretary Dean Acheson displayed a strong skepticism toward both Wilsonian internationalism and dollar diplomacy. During his education at Groton, Yale—where W. Averell Harriman was his rowing coach—and Harvard Law, the tall, handsome, New England aristocrat developed the mental toughness and penchant for hard work that were to characterize his public career. A protégé of Felix Frankfurter and a former law clerk to Louis Brandeis, Acheson developed a skepticism toward panaceas and utopias and a commitment to pragmatic progress.[36] He argued that America's goal in Europe and the Middle East had to be stability even if it meant working with native monarchies and right-wing dictators such as Francisco Franco in Spain and Antonio Salazar in Portugal. "If chaos prevails there," Acheson insisted, "and the region becomes a military vacuum, tempting adventure, we shall face the same danger of war which accompanied the collapse of the Turkish and Austro-Hungarian Empires."[37] Acheson, of course, wanted to recognize Eastern Europe as a part of the Soviet sphere and work closely with Britain to rebuild Central Europe and maintain the status quo in the eastern Mediterranean and Middle East. His day would come, but in 1944 *realpolitik* was still out of fashion in the United States.

To placate the Wilsonian internationalists and to satisfy the smaller powers, Roosevelt in 1944 agreed to blend the Four-Policemen idea with the concept of a United Nations organization. The problem with this arrangement—or one of the most important problems—was that the Big Four were not equal in strength, nor did they agree on spheres of interest. As Churchill, Stalin, and the U.S. military recognized all along, China was a third-rate power that would in all probability grow weaker. Moreover, Britain seemed to be slipping from the ranks of the great, a development few had anticipated. Britain's decline and Japan's demise would produce a vacuum in Europe and the Far East. Differences of opinion existed among the Big Four about how those vacuums were to be filled. For example, it was becoming increasingly obvious that London's and Moscow's perceptions of their spheres of interest overlapped in Europe and the Middle

East. The greatest danger to peace in the postwar era, judged the U.S. Joint Chiefs of Staff, lay in either the USSR's or Great Britain's "seeking to attach to herself parts of Europe to the disadvantage and possible danger of her political adversary."[38]

The joint chiefs, the White House, and the State Department all agreed that the United States should act energetically to reduce friction and arrest tensions that could lead to another war in Europe. But how to play that role without intervening directly in the Continent's political and military affairs? FDR perceived correctly that the American people would be in no mood following the war to condone the permanent stationing of troops in Europe. Consequently, the White House rejected the role Churchill envisioned for the United States in European affairs. FDR wrote his British counterpart: "I am absolutely unwilling to police France and possibly Italy and the Balkans as well. After all, France is your baby and will take a lot of nursing in order to bring it to the point of walking alone."[39] The president later wrote Churchill: "'Do please don't' ask me to keep any American forces in France. I just cannot do it! I would have to bring them all back home. As I suggested before, I denounce and protest the paternity of Belgium, France, and Italy. You really ought to bring up and discipline your own children." Nor would the American people tolerate a common Anglo-American policy toward Europe. "It is clearly the policy of the Department to avoid as far as possible any situation in which the United States and the United Kingdom appear to have developed a party line," declared a State Department memo approved by the president.[40]

But what was left to FDR in 1945, the year in which he would finally have to endorse a special postwar order? Committed though he was to the Four-Policemen concept and to Acheson's *realpolitik,* the president decided that he could no more allow Churchill and Stalin to divide Europe into blocs or spheres in 1944 than he could in 1942. To maintain a working political consensus at home, the White House believed that it had to cultivate Hull and the internationalists. Roosevelt had to oppose regionalism and to support national self-determination. But dollar diplomacy and assertions of moral leadership promised to alarm both the Soviet Union and Britain without providing tangible benefits. The only alternative seemed to be to convince the Kremlin of the West's good intentions and trust Stalin not to destroy the independence of those nations occupied by the Red Army. Harriman recalled that the president thought he could explain to Stalin the positive world reaction he could expect from decent behavior, as opposed to the violent antagonism he would encounter if he seized certain territories. The "Kremlin's fear of public opinion," Roosevelt judged, "would restrain its actions."[41] More specifically, the White

House's plan of rapprochement called for internationalization of the land and sea approaches to the Baltic and of the Persian Railroad, as well as assumption of responsibility by the United States for the postwar reconstruction of the USSR. In addition, the West would require the Soviets to legitimize their occupation zones by holding plebiscites. Assured of economic and strategic security, the Soviet Union could assume its place among the Great Powers.

Above all, Roosevelt's strategy called for a harsh policy toward Germany. If Russian suspicion of the Western democracies were to be allayed, Moscow would have to be assured that Britain and the United States did not plan to breathe life into the German military machine and unleash it on the Soviet Union. Consequently, when Roosevelt met Churchill at the second Quebec Conference in September 1944, the president, using U.S. aid during Stage II (the period between Germany's and Japan's surrender) as leverage, persuaded his ally to initial the Morgenthau Plan. That policy recommendation called for the political dismemberment of the Third Reich and the destruction of the Ruhr and Saar. Designed to render Germany a land "primarily agricultural and pastoral," the plan interfered with the Churchill government's efforts to restore the European balance of power by de-Nazifying and rehabilitating its vanquished foe.[42]

Spurred by the specter of a permanently enfeebled Germany, Churchill attempted to work out a spheres-of-interest deal with Stalin that would establish and limit the boundaries of postwar Communism in Europe before the Red Army could advance farther. When the prime minister arrived in Moscow in October 1944, Soviet troops had penetrated Rumania and Bulgaria and had nearly completed their occupation of Hungary. The Germans were in retreat in Greece and fighting for survival in Yugoslavia. All five countries were experiencing intense internal turmoil. In addition to propping up the pro-British monarchy in Greece, the Churchill government was trying to engineer a workable accord between Josef Broz Tito's powerful Yugoslav partisan forces and the Yugoslav government-in-exile in London. Churchill had come to Moscow on a damage-control mission. In a now famous episode, the prime minister jotted down a proposed country-by-country division of power: Rumania, 90 percent for the Soviet Union and 10 percent for others; Greece, 90 percent for Britain "(in accordance with U.S.A.)" and 10 percent for the Soviet Union; Bulgaria and Yugoslavia to be divided evenly; and Hungary, 75 percent for the Soviet Union and 25 percent for others. Stalin seemed to approve—he told his English visitor to hold onto the paper.[43]

Churchill subsequently asked FDR to concur in his latest effort to delineate Soviet and Anglo-American interests in this volatile region. A tripartite agreement was necessary, he said, "so that we may prevent civil war from breaking out in several countries when probably you and I would be in sympathy with one side and U.J. [Uncle Joe] with the other." Roosevelt continued to believe that Soviet dominance in Eastern Europe was inevitable and, as he indicated in a letter to Ambassador Harriman in Moscow, was determined to take "such steps as are practical to insure against the Balkans getting us into a future international war." Nevertheless, although Roosevelt did not denounce the percentages deal, he refused to endorse it. He expressed hope that such spheres-of-influence arrangements should be only preliminaries to postwar settlements agreed to by the major powers.[44]

British leaders were stunned by the United States' foreign policy in the fall of 1944. Like the imp of the perverse, Roosevelt seemed determined not only to remove the United States from the postwar balance of power in Europe but also to keep Britain from establishing any arrangement that would protect its strategic interests. Alarmed by the shift of power in the Anglo-American alliance in 1943–44 and by signs in the United States that it intended to pursue an independent foreign policy, London had embraced the notion of a Western European Union as a means of ensuring its security in the postwar world. The United States then undermined the Churchill government's plans to restore non-Communist power bases in Central Europe by forcing Britain to approve the Morgenthau Plan. In desperation, Churchill had attempted to reach a spheres-of-interest understanding with Stalin, only to have Roosevelt withhold approval. The Churchill government seemed to have no choice but to stand by in anguish as Washington proceeded to conciliate the Soviet Union.

■ ■ ■ But allaying the Soviets' suspicions and satisfying their demands proved more difficult than Roosevelt had imagined. Having blocked Britain's efforts to lay the foundation for a strong Western European federation through the rehabilitation of Germany, the White House expected the Soviet Union to give up any plans to dominate Central and Eastern Europe. Those hopes were disappointed. The Warsaw uprising and the general Soviet policy toward Eastern Europe in late 1944 raised doubts about whether the Grand Alliance could be maintained into the postwar period and made it increasingly difficult for the president to justify stiff-arming the British and "disarming" the Soviets.

Poland was the first great blot on Roosevelt's blueprint for Soviet-American cooperation. The Soviet Union's brutal treatment of that country in the summer and fall of 1944 provoked a ground swell of anti-Soviet sentiment in the State and War departments and among Polish-Americans. In April 1943, after the Polish government-in-exile in London asked the

International Red Cross to investigate German charges that the Russians had massacred several thousand Polish officers at Katyn Woods in 1940, Moscow severed diplomatic relations with the London Poles. (Soviet historians recently unearthed and published documents showing the charges to be true.) Subsequently, the Red Army's victory at Stalingrad in early 1943 shifted the military balance of power on the Eastern Front and touched off a chain of events that would enable Stalin to impose his will on Eastern Europe.

Early in November 1943 Harriman cabled the White House that the Soviets not only would demand the right to annex the Baltic states and the eastern third of Poland but also would insist on having a "friendly" government installed in Warsaw. They regarded the London-based Poles as hostile. Above all, the Soviets were determined to prevent a resurrection of the old *cordon sanitaire* in Eastern Europe. Roosevelt's advisers agreed that the United States could do little to prevent Stalin from taking the territory he wanted. Through 1943 and 1944 the president's position therefore remained unchanged. Because Britain and the United States lacked the power and the will to prevent Stalin from having his way in Eastern Europe, Roosevelt maintained, London and Washington should concentrate on persuading the Soviet leader to be magnanimous while convincing Eastern Europeans that their interests could best be served by working with the Soviets.

At the Teheran Conference in late 1943 FDR made clear to Stalin that the United States would not fight the USSR over Poland and the rest of Eastern Europe. There were, however, six or seven million Polish-Americans in the United States, Roosevelt asserted, and as a "practical" man he did not want to lose their votes. He pressed Stalin for a pledge to hold plebiscites in the nations under his control, but the Soviet leader remained noncommittal.

Stalin was profoundly ignorant of the workings of the British and especially the U.S. political system. He thought of the capitalist West (and especially of the United States) as antagonistic, powerful, and treacherous. Paradoxically, he also viewed his adversaries as vulnerable, weak, and susceptible to Soviet manipulation.[45] He believed FDR's reference to the constraints imposed by congressional and public opinion to be disingenuous. In fact, Stalin's tendency throughout this period was to project his tactics and stratagems on the West. He viewed Roosevelt and Churchill as adversaries who would do unto him what he was willing to do unto them. In the spring of 1944 he told Tito's emissary, Milovan Djilas: "Perhaps you think that just because we are the allies of the English that we have forgotten who they are and who Churchill is. They find nothing sweeter than to trick their allies. During the First World War they constantly tricked the Russians and the French. And Churchill? Churchill is the kind who, if you don't watch him, will slip a kopeck out of your pocket. . . . And Roosevelt? Roosevelt is not like that. He dips in his hand only for bigger coins. But Churchill? Churchill—even for a kopeck."[46]

Thus Stalin welcomed Roosevelt's conciliatory stance at Teheran—FDR seemed to be asking merely for the trappings of democracy and self-determination in Poland—but he was convinced that the American position was merely a ploy to throw Russia off guard.

During numerous conversations with Polish Prime Minister Stanislaw Mikolajczyk in 1944, FDR advised the London-based Polish government to seek reconciliation with the Soviet Union. There were five times as many Russians as Poles, the president said, "and let me tell you now, the British and Americans have no intention of fighting Russia."[47]

Meanwhile, the Red Army had advanced beyond the Curzon Line and was nearing the outskirts of Warsaw. The Soviet government announced that the civil administration of liberated Poland was in the hands of the Committee of National Liberation, which was headquartered in Lublin and made up entirely of Polish Communists. In desperation, Mikolajczyk flew to Moscow. The day after his arrival the Warsaw uprising began. The Polish resistance movement inside the capital was generally loyal to the government-in-exile in London, but was nevertheless jubilant at the approach of the Red Army, which by July 31 had taken up positions within twelve miles of the city. Encouraged by radio broadcasts from Moscow, the people of Warsaw that day attacked German troops in the city. Anticipating the imminent arrival of Russian soldiers, the partisans faced tanks and machine guns with pistols, clubs, and bare hands. But the Soviet advance stopped the day the uprising began. For two months the Red Army waited outside the city while the Germans annihilated tens of thousands of potential rivals to the Lublin Poles.

Publicly, Stalin announced that he could not commit elements of the Red Army to the final battle for Warsaw because they needed to be held in reserve to counter possible German thrusts elsewhere. He termed the uprising a reckless undertaking. In reality, the delay allowed the Nazi occupation forces in Warsaw to destroy a Polish underground army that might have challenged Soviet dominance in Poland in the postwar period.[48]

Churchill wanted to aid the freedom fighters, but Roosevelt shrank from a confrontation with the Soviets over the issue. The most he would do was join Churchill in asking Stalin to permit British and U.S. planes to land behind Soviet lines after dropping arms to the Poles in Warsaw. After Stalin refused, Roosevelt told Churchill that there was nothing they could do.[49]

The Warsaw uprising was a turning point in Soviet-American and Anglo-American relations. It further aroused Polish-Americans against

Russia and caused them on the eve of the 1944 election to redouble their efforts to persuade the administration to stand up to Moscow. In addition, it turned influential individuals in the State and War departments and the American embassy in Moscow irrevocably against Stalin.

Since Harriman's appointment as ambassador to Moscow in 1943, he had grown increasingly resentful of Soviet complaints at delays in lend-lease deliveries. Nonetheless, he remained convinced that the United States and the USSR could cooperate and had become a leading advocate of a postwar reconstruction loan to the Soviets. Events in the fall of 1944 caused him to assign much darker motives to his hosts and to advocate a get-tough policy. "I have been conscious ever since early in the year," he wrote Hopkins on September 10, "of a division among Stalin's advisors on the question of cooperation with us. It is now my feeling that those who oppose the kind of cooperation we expect have recently been getting their way and a policy appears to be crystallizing to force us and the British to accept all Soviet policies backed by the strength and prestige of the Red Army." Calling on the White House to "materially change" its policy toward the Soviets, Harriman predicted that the USSR would become a "world bully" unless the United States stood up to it.[50]

Two months later, following the final collapse of Polish resistance in Warsaw, General John Deane, head of the American Military Mission in Moscow, denounced Soviet policy in a letter to Army Chief of Staff George C. Marshall. Wartime "generosity" toward the Soviet Union had been counterproductive, he argued. The United States should make no more concessions without Soviet pledges of cooperation in the political and economic sphere. Foreshadowing George F. Kennan's "Long Telegram" of fifteen months later (Kennan had joined Harriman's staff in the spring of 1944), this letter from Deane quickly circulated among Washington's highest officials. Russophobe James V. Forrestal, who had recently succeeded Secretary of the Navy Frank Knox, used the arguments in Deane's letter to facilitate his public campaign for a strong postwar U.S. military force and his private crusade for a tougher policy toward the Soviet Union. He wrote that the American who emphasized national security was "apt to be called a goddamned Fascist or Imperialist, while if Uncle Joe suggests that he needs the Baltic provinces, half of Poland, all of Bessarabia and access to the Mediterranean, all hands agree that he is a fine, frank, candid, and generally delightful fellow."[51] By September and early October 1944, then, a segment of the Roosevelt foreign policy establishment was arguing that the Soviets could not be trusted and would overrun Eastern and Central Europe if given the chance.

In November 1944 Hull, who was physically ill and emotionally distraught at his and the State Department's exclusion from day-to-day diplomacy, resigned as secretary of state. The man Roosevelt chose as replacement was a former General Motors head, Edward Stettinius, Jr. A handsome, well-meaning business executive, Stettinius was undereducated and inexperienced in foreign affairs. During his brief stint in 1943–44 as undersecretary of state, he had come to believe that the world could best solve its problems in the postwar era through the mechanism of an international collective security organization. One of his first jobs had been to supervise the creation of a task force under Leo Pasvolsky, which was given the title International Organization and Security Affairs. To Stettinius, power politics in Eastern Europe violated the spirit of internationalism and threatened to arouse the not-so-latent isolationism of the American people. If the United Nations were to become a reality, he was convinced, the Roosevelt administration would have to find some way to modify Soviet behavior. The new secretary's determination to be "hard headed" and "realistic" with Russia created an affinity between him and the anti-Communist element in the department.[52] And in fact, Stettinius reorganized the department in such a way as to maximize the influence of the hard-liners.

The former ambassador to Japan, Joseph Grew, assumed the post of undersecretary. A distinguished diplomat who had served in the American consulate in St. Petersburg before the Russian Revolution as well as in Tokyo between the wars, Grew was an outspoken critic of the Soviet Union. Nelson Rockefeller became assistant secretary for Latin American affairs; James C. Dunn was selected to oversee European and Far Eastern affairs. William L. Clayton became assistant secretary of state for economic matters. Acheson was assigned to congressional relations, a crucial post in light of the agreements that Congress would have to review during the months to come. At Hopkins's suggestion, Stettinius named career diplomat and Russian expert Charles E. Bohlen as liaison officer with the White House.[53] Bohlen's view of Stalin was typical of this group: "Historians," he wrote in his memoirs, "will argue whether Stalin was simply a realist with no moral values or a monster whose paranoia led him into senseless crimes. Judged by his actions, I believe he runs high on the list of the world's monsters."[54] The new regime in the State Department, supported by Harriman and Kennan in Moscow, was determined to assume control over foreign policy. Given the prejudices and perceptions shared by this group, that meant a harder line toward the Soviet Union, a softer one toward Britain, and confrontation with those who advocated appeasing Moscow.[55]

Roosevelt's and Hopkins's opposition to the rehabilitation of Germany, their denunciation of British colonialism, and their refusal to condone the October 1944 percentages deal would seem to have placed the White House and the new regime in the State Department on a collision course. But the president was still agile enough to keep from being associated with an unpopular policy. Instead of speaking out in behalf of rapprochement with the Soviet Union following the Quebec Conference, Roosevelt receded into the background, allowing liberals such as Secretary of Commerce Henry Wallace to take up the banner of Soviet-American friendship. As had so often happened in the past, the president assumed that his lieutenants would slug it out until a clear, popular consensus formed around one position or another. Then Roosevelt could step in and identify with the victor.

The focus of the struggle between Russophobes and Russophiles in late 1944 and early 1945 was the much-discussed reconstruction loan to the USSR.[56] Roosevelt and Hopkins had decided by late 1943 that a large postwar loan to the Soviet Union would do much to disarm Stalin and allay his suspicions of the West. Since early 1944 Admiral William Standley, Elbridge Durbrow of the Division of East European Affairs, and Harriman had been urging FDR to use lend-lease shipments to prevent the Communization of Eastern Europe. Roosevelt, however, resisted. During a conversation with a group of seven senators in January 1945, the president observed that "our economic position did not constitute a bargaining weapon of any strength because its only present impact was on lend-lease, which to cut down would hurt us as much as it would hurt the Russians."[57] In early October the president outlined to Donald M. Nelson, chairman of the War Production Board, the possible advantages of a Soviet loan. Roosevelt asked him to broach the subject with Stalin and Molotov during a forthcoming trip to Moscow to discuss postwar trade. On October 16 Nelson told Soviet leaders that the United States, with a surplus of industrial goods to export at war's end, wanted to aid in the reconstruction of the USSR. Could those products be purchased on credit? Stalin asked. In his personal opinion they could, Nelson replied.

Later that month Hull, who was in Moscow for the foreign ministers' conference, carried the loan negotiations one step farther. The United States wanted to help, he told Molotov, handing him a proposal for U.S. "cooperation in the rehabilitation of war damage in the Soviet Union."[58] The United States, he added, was prepared to begin preliminary discussions at once.

The White House's enthusiasm for a postwar credit to the Soviet Union both reflected and was reinforced by the views of Harriman. The ambassador, who frequently communicated directly with Hopkins and thus circumvented the State Department, told Soviet Trade Commissar Anastas

Mikoyan in November that the United States was interested in helping the USSR rebuild. Harriman explained that lend-lease assistance would have to terminate with the end of the war because Congress had so mandated. Although Roosevelt would interpret the law liberally, it would be unwise for him to go too far, especially in view of the forthcoming 1944 presidential elections. Harriman assured Mikoyan, however, that the American people wanted to help and that negotiations on a loan could begin immediately.

Harriman's motives at this point are not entirely clear. In his telegram to the State Department he emphasized the stimulating effect a credit would have on the United States' export trade in the postwar period. A loan, he wrote Hull, would be useful at home: it was in the "self-interest of the United States to be able to afford full-employment during the transition from a wartime to a peacetime economy."[59] But in addition, Harriman, who was increasingly irritated by Soviet intransigence in various negotiations, was already thinking of a loan as a means of pressuring the Soviets into a cooperative posture.[60]

Liberals such as Wallace and Secretary of the Treasury Henry Morgenthau were even more enthusiastic than Harriman about a credit to Russia. Morgenthau and his chief lieutenant, Harry Dexter White, were committed to Soviet-American cooperation for many of the reasons that motivated Hopkins and Roosevelt. During the 1930s White had been an outspoken admirer of the Soviet system; capitalism and Communism, he was convinced, could coexist. In addition, both Treasury leaders were of a mind that England, in the hands of ultraconservatives like Churchill and Beaverbrook, was a greater threat to peace, democracy, equality of opportunity, and U.S. interests than was the Soviet Union. Moreover, Morgenthau and, to a lesser extent, White still had high hopes that the USSR would participate in their schemes for an international stabilization fund and an international bank for reconstruction and development. As a result, in March 1944 the Treasury proposed to the White House that the United States extend "a credit of $5 billion to the USSR for the purchase of industrial and agricultural products over a five year period." The loan was to be repaid in full over thirty years, chiefly in the form of raw material exports.[61]

■ ■ ■ The opening weeks of 1945 witnessed a showdown within the Roosevelt administration between advocates of a large, unconditional loan to the Soviet Union—the Treasury leadership—and proponents of a smaller credit with a number of political strings attached—the new clique in the State Department. On January 10, 1945, Morgenthau and Stettinius met with Roosevelt at the White House to discuss the latest Soviet loan proposal. A week before, Molotov had summoned Harriman and presented a formal written "request" for a postwar credit. To help U.S. business and industry through the difficult reconversion and transition period, stated this request, "the Soviet Government considers it possible to place orders on the basis of long-term credits to the amount of $6 billion." The credit, to be repaid in thirty years at an annual interest rate of 2 percent, would include a 20 percent discount on orders placed before the end of the war. As a banker, Harriman was taken aback by the "unconventional character of the document and the unreasonableness of its terms," but he urged the administration to entertain the idea of a "generous credit," on the condition, of course, that it "should be tied into our overall diplomatic relations with the Soviet Union." Stettinius urged the president to heed the ambassador's advice. Morgenthau then stunned the others by proposing a $10 billion credit at 2 percent with an option for the United States to buy strategic materials from the Soviet Union. "This dramatic step," Morgenthau told FDR, "could . . . give you a powerful lever for use in the coming world negotiations *vis-a-vis* both Russia and other United Nations. Moreover, it is not an exaggeration to say that the consummation of such a financial agreement would be one of the most important non-military steps that could be taken at this time to shift the pattern of postwar international economic relations." In addition, Morgenthau told FDR that he wanted to be sent to Moscow "as your personal representative to fully explore these possibilities with the Soviet Government."[62] The loan should be free of political strings, he insisted.

Implying that the Treasury was naive in its assessment of the Russians, Stettinius argued that once the Kremlin received a loan, it would feel no compulsion to cooperate with the United States. Therefore, in accordance with Harriman's suggestion, the United States should demand that the Soviets make certain concessions beforehand. American negotiators should not, moreover, take the initiative on the loan question at the forthcoming conference at Yalta.[63] Roosevelt sided with the State Department. "Well, after all, we are not having any finance people with us and I will just tell them [the Soviets] concerning a loan we can't do anything until we get back to Washington. . . . I think it's very important that we hold back and don't give them any promises of finance until we get what we want."[64]

By January 1945, top officials in the State Department had compiled a list of demands to make of the Soviet Union in return for a loan: The USSR should accept membership in the Bretton Woods organizations and accord the United States a full role in the Allied Control Councils for Rumania, Bulgaria, and Hungary. Moreover, Moscow should place no obstacle in Washington's path as it sought to establish general economic relations with Poland, Czechoslovakia, and the Baltic States, and to participate in their reconstruction and development.

The president's decision to take Stettinius but not Morgenthau to Yalta reflected the outcome of the battle over Russian loan strategies. FDR accepted both the State Department approach and the rationale behind it; he told Senate leaders in January that it would be a mistake to communicate directly with Stalin or Molotov on the loan matter until and unless they brought up the question themselves.

Concerned that public disclosure of the proposed credit would destroy the loan's effectiveness as a diplomatic weapon, State Department officials went to great lengths to keep the matter quiet. Thus they were understandably upset when, shortly before the Yalta Conference, James Reston of the *New York Times* reported Molotov's formal request for assistance. The Treasury, which was fond of using the press in its battles with bureaucratic rivals and special interests, probably leaked the story. To counter Reston and proponents of unconditional aid, the State Department released a statement to the effect that requests for long-term loans had been received from a number of countries and that no action could or would be taken until the administration had fashioned a general foreign aid policy.[65]

Contrary to American hopes, Stalin did not ask about the status of the loan request at Yalta. Perhaps the Reston article put him off. Or he could have anticipated the administration's strategy. In view of their present domination of Eastern Europe and future plans to control parts of Central Europe, along with their intent to extract massive reparations from defeated enemies, the masters of the Kremlin may have believed that aid from the United States was unnecessary. In addition, there were within the Soviet leadership Marxist-Leninists who believed that the capitalist economy of the United States would once again plunge into depression following the war. The overriding need for foreign markets would then compel Washington to extend credits to the Soviet Union with no strings attached. The loan issue received some attention but at a secondary level. During a luncheon for the foreign ministers on February 5, Molotov told Stettinius that he hoped the United States would extend postwar credits. The secretary of state replied that his government was willing to discuss the matter at Yalta or later in Moscow or Washington. Molotov did not answer, and neither he nor any other member of the Soviet delegation made further mention of the matter during the conference.

Throughout the war Churchill had urged Roosevelt to join with him in securing specific agreements on postwar Europe while the Red Army remained within Soviet borders. Invoking the need to maintain harmony within the Grand Alliance, the president had refused. As 1945 dawned, however, victory over Germany was at long last in sight and Roosevelt could no longer postpone the inevitable. Yet by the time the Big Three gathered at Yalta in early February, the Kremlin acting unilaterally had taken giant strides toward redrawing the map of Europe.

By late July 1944 the counterattack that had begun after Stalingrad had completely cleared German armed forces from Belorussia and had reached the Vistula in central Poland. In August the Soviet offensive continued in the south, completing the liberation of the Ukraine. During the last week in August the king of Rumania decided that his country should change sides in the war. Immediately, the Rumanian army began driving elements of the Wehrmacht from its soil. By late September most of the lower Danube was in Soviet hands, and the battle of Hungary had begun. In the north, on September 3 and 4, Finland sued for peace and left the war. On September 5 a Soviet invasion of Bulgaria led to its collapse. And finally, by the opening weeks of 1945, only pockets of Nazi resistance remained in Poland. Since 1939, and especially since 1941, the Soviet frontier in Eastern Europe had been subject to negotiation. Now that frontier was solidly in Soviet hands; indeed, Moscow could extend it even farther. This solution of the frontier problem transformed Stalin's relationship with the Western powers from that of a client to that of an equal.[66]

Stalin did not want a cold war with the West. Second only to a hot war with his former allies, that was his last choice. What Stalin wanted was nothing less than a continuation of the relationship with the West that had been established during World War II—although, as his November 1944 speech indicated, he was not sure the "necessary preconditions" for the preservation of these ties could be obtained. But the entente Stalin desired was not the benign relationship so frequently depicted by revisionists. It was designed to foster Soviet control of Eastern Europe, whether directly (in the case of Poland, Rumania, and Bulgaria) or indirectly (in Hungary and Czechoslovakia); to expand Soviet influence in Western Europe, the Near East, and Asia; and to position the USSR for even greater gains when the next Western economic crisis struck.

This scenario was not so much a plan, with all contingencies taken into account, as a hope. In addition to these maximum goals, the Soviets had minimum aims (ensuring Communist hegemony over Eastern Europe and defeating, disarming, and extracting reparations from Germany) to which they could always retreat. The winter of 1944–45 was a period of optimism in the Kremlin. But even then Stalin had doubts and perhaps even moments of panic. The latent hostility of the capitalist powers was one cause for concern. The Soviet Union's own weakness was another.

Twenty million Russians would perish in World War II, and virtually all of European Russia from the Ukraine to the Caucasus lay in ruins by early 1945. There was still a war to be won. Nonetheless, Stalin's maximum goals seemed obtainable, at least until FDR died. The conference at Yalta in February 1945 offered an opportunity to test the scenario. The results must have been gratifying to Stalin.[67]

At Yalta, in addition to preliminary plans for the UN, the Big Three discussed four major questions: occupation zones for Germany, reparations, Poland, and the Far East. Roosevelt, Churchill, and Stalin, after awarding France a tiny zone in the western part of Germany, ratified the recommendations of the European Advisory Commission that divided Germany into three segments, the Soviet Union controlling the eastern third, Britain the northwest, and the United States the southwest. Berlin, situated in the Soviet zone, was to be a microcosm of Germany as a whole. Stalin, with support from Roosevelt, took a hard line on reparations, whereas Churchill took a soft line. After much wrangling it was decided that an Allied commission would meet in Moscow following the war and take $20 billion (half to the Soviet Union) as a basis for discussion. Both Roosevelt and Churchill pressed Stalin to broaden the Communist government he had installed in Warsaw and to hold free elections. Stalin finally agreed to include in a new Polish coalition non-Communist Poles from within the resistance and from the London government. The three leaders signed the Declaration on Liberated Europe, which committed the occupying powers to hold free and unsupervised elections in their zones at the earliest possible date. Finally, Stalin agreed to enter the war against Japan in return for Outer Mongolia, the Kurile Islands, the southern half of Sakhalin Island, and the opportunity to regain political and economic control of Manchuria.[68]

■ ■ ■ As the outcome of the Yalta meeting indicated, Roosevelt's foreign policy was paralyzed if not bankrupt by the opening weeks of 1945. Intimidated by isolationists and internationalists, FDR refused to educate the people of his country on the need to pursue a balance-of-power strategy in Europe. He clung to the hope that personal diplomacy could work a miracle, that it could simultaneously commit Stalin to "free" elections in areas under his control; preserve commercial, tourist, press, and diplomatic access for the United States to these areas; and secure a pledge of Soviet aid in the war against Japan. The only leverage he possessed, aside from personal charm, was the implied threat of withholding a large reconstruction loan to the Soviet Union. But Moscow proved unresponsive to this veiled economic pressure. Neither Stalin nor Molotov had broached the subject. Of the topics discussed at Yalta, substantive agreements were reached only on Germany, the Far East, and the UN.

Roosevelt, Hopkins, and Stettinius claimed to be much pleased with the Yalta Conference. The results proved, they asserted, that the Soviets were "reasonable and farseeing," as Hopkins put it, and that peaceful coexistence was a virtual certainty.[69] On March 1, 1945, the president, so sick and tired that he could not stand even with leg braces, addressed a joint session of Congress. Though not perfect, he told the legislators, the Yalta accords provided the foundations for a lasting peace. The Declaration on Liberated Europe had halted a trend toward the development of spheres of influence, and the compromise on Poland was the best chance the country had for freedom and independence.

But, of course, the administration was overly optimistic. Nothing had been done at Yalta to establish and protect the postwar economic and military security of Central and Western Europe. The events that had begun with the Warsaw uprising would continue into the spring and summer of 1945, souring moderate opinion and alarming the foreign policy establishments in both Britain and the United States. Roosevelt's policies did not die with him on April 12. Harry S. Truman would continue for a brief time to rely on Moscow's fulfillment of the Yalta agreements while dangling the carrot of a postwar reconstruction loan before the Soviet leaders and wielding the stick of the atomic bomb. He would, in addition, shun Anglo-American solidarity and struggle to avoid an association with British imperialism. But as had already become apparent to the State and War departments in the United States and to Eden and his moderate colleagues in Britain, the old Roosevelt stratagem was not enough to guarantee the economic and political security of those portions of Europe still untouched by the Red Army.

■ ■ ■ CHAPTER TWO

Harry S. Truman and the Policy of Mediation

For a brief period in the spring and early summer of 1945, British hopes that the United States might assume a more realistic stance toward postwar Europe and Soviet pretensions there rose dramatically. Frightened by Britain's isolation, offended by the treatment of its representatives in the Soviet Union, and shocked by the brutality of the Red Army, the various agencies and personalities responsible for making British foreign policy coalesced in favor of an all-out effort to persuade the United States to stand up to the USSR. FDR responded positively to Churchill's frantic arguments and to those of the hard-liners within his own foreign policy establishment by insisting that the Soviets live up to their "commitments" under the Yalta accords. Following Roosevelt's death, Truman, anxious to preserve continuity in foreign policy, determined to appear decisive, and momentarily swayed by the get-tough advocates in Washington, confronted the Soviet Union over its policy toward Eastern Europe. He insisted that Moscow broaden the Polish government and allow Westerners to participate in reconstruction of the Balkans.

The new president, however, quickly abandoned this initial attempt to prevent the formation of a closed Soviet sphere. Americans seemed as opposed to maintaining a permanent military force in Europe as always, and popular hopes for a rapprochement with the Soviets remained high. As the limits on U.S. power became apparent, Truman fell under the influence of those American liberals who favored a policy of conciliation. In cooperation with Anglophobes and Russophiles inside and outside the government, Truman attempted to pursue a "middle way" whereby the United States mediated between Britain and the Soviet Union in a tripolar world. Despite the experience of World War II and popular enthusiasm for the United Nations concept, Congress and the American people still longed for isolation from the vicissitudes of European politics. Under Truman the United States would develop strategic interests and attempt to project its power into Europe and the Near East,[1] but it would do so largely in response to the urgings of the United Kingdom and the perception of an expansionist Soviet Union. To the dismay of London, Truman and his new secretary of state, James F. Byrnes, clung to the belief that Moscow's desire for security and stability, along with the leverage of America's monopoly of atomic energy and reconstruction capital, would render Stalin reasonable if not pliant. Thus, throughout the summer and fall of 1945, Washington held Britain at arm's length while attempting to fashion understandings with Russia over occupation policy in Germany, Rumania, Hungary, Poland, and Japan.[2]

■ ■ ■ On that soft, sunlit day in Warm Springs, Georgia, when Franklin Delano Roosevelt died, Harry S. Truman was on the Hill hobnobbing with Sam Rayburn, Alben Barkley, and others of his legislative cronies. Indeed, he was in Rayburn's office having a bourbon and water when he received an urgent message to go at once to the White House. There he learned the news. After being sworn in as president of the United States, he told assembled reporters that he felt as if the stars and the moon had fallen on his shoulders. One of the reasons for Truman's feelings of inadequacy was his isolation from the various wartime conferences and from foreign affairs in general while he was vice-president. Roosevelt, who characteristically refused to confront the imminence of his own death, failed to give any on-the-job training to the man in line to succeed him. "He was an obscure vice-president who got to see Roosevelt much less than I did and who knew less than I did about United States foreign relations," Charles E. Bohlen recalled of Truman.[3]

Truman may have been shut out of meetings and conferences on international relations while serving as Roosevelt's second in command, but he came to the presidency with knowledge and skills in other areas. He had been an active member of both the Senate Appropriations and the Interstate and Foreign Commerce committees. And, of course, he had from 1941 to 1944 headed his own special committee to oversee the awarding of government war contracts. The Truman committee's self-proclaimed objectives were to ensure that the administration played no favorites and that the taxpayers got a fair return for their dollars. Truman was knowledgeable in such important areas as appropriations, the budget, the armed services, and executive-congressional relations. The activities of the Truman committee, moreover, had taught him a great deal about industry and the workings of the U.S. economy.[4]

Personally, Truman was a gregarious man, popular on the Hill; he was straightforward, unpretentious, and relatively candid. He was a skilled, methodical politician, schooled in the ways of compromise. The man from Missouri also had a short fuse and a bent for self-righteous indignation. After ten years in the Senate, he had put the Pendergast machine behind him, but he still came from a world of two-bit politicians.[5] Truman preferred mediocrity to brilliance in his friends and associates and was given to cronyism. He could be intensely partisan and was stubbornly loyal to those who had been loyal to him. He was never able to rid himself of a deep-seated inferiority complex. Always anxious to appear the hail-fellow-well-met, his diaries are full of attacks on stuffed shirts and "prima donnas."[6]

Truman was a New Dealer, but like his predecessor he tried to combine social justice with fiscal orthodoxy and the American creed of self-reliance and economic independence. He believed in a balanced budget. He distrusted theories and abstractions but took the position that the government had a responsibility to solve social and economic problems. Like most denizens of the American heartland he revered business and business people, but at the same time he distrusted concentrations of economic power. In brief, Truman was a well-meaning, decent man without intellectual depth, whose main point of reference was the world of big-city and then congressional politics.

Truman entered the White House confused, vulnerable, and insecure. His first and understandable reaction was to cling to the policies of Roosevelt in foreign as well as domestic affairs. That instinct immediately enmeshed him in the ambivalence that had characterized American policy toward the Soviet Union during FDR's last days.

In response to Soviet diplomacy, pressure from American Russophiles, and his own political instinct to compromise, Truman quickly adopted a more flexible posture toward the Kremlin. Throughout the summer and fall of 1945 the man from Missouri attempted to alleviate Soviet suspicions by seeing to it that both the United States and Britain lived up to their commitments under the Yalta accords, by participating wholeheartedly in the establishment and operation of a new League of Nations, by rejecting an Anglo-American alliance, and by continuing to press the British to dismantle their empire. At the same time, the United States under its new leadership would urge Moscow to fulfill its international obligations, including its "commitment" under the Declaration of Liberated Europe to hold free elections in areas under its control. As Truman moved into the first year of his administration, he relied more and more heavily first on the Soviet Union's perceived need for a reconstruction loan and subsequently on its putative fear of the atomic bomb to gain leverage with the Kremlin.

The new president's initial aggressiveness had as much to do with style as substance, however. Inexperienced in foreign affairs yet determined to assert his authority, Truman sought to convey an impression of efficiency and decisiveness that would contrast dramatically with the apparently random and dilatory style of his predecessor. As newsman Arthur Krock said of the new president: "His personality is that of a very charming man whose determination sticks out all over him."[7] No more soliloquies, Secretary of War Henry L. Stimson noted joyfully in his diary. Joseph Grew remarked after one early interview that he had gotten through fourteen items in fifteen minutes. This "dynamic" approach, however, was in part responsible for several hasty early decisions that made it seem as if the new chief executive had opted for confrontation with the Soviet Union.[8] Truman was initially much impressed with the arguments of the hardliners within the foreign policy establishment. Grew, Bohlen, and the new regime in the State Department, as well as Harriman, Deane, and Forrestal, had decided, like Churchill, not only that the Soviet Union would prove uncooperative in the postwar period but also that it was bent on domination of the European continent. Responding to their urgings, Truman during the first weeks of his presidency took a position so unyielding that it severely strained the Grand Alliance.

■ ■ ■ In Britain, not coincidentally, a rapidly growing consensus emerged in behalf of a policy of overt resistance to Soviet expansion in Eastern Europe and the Near East. Eden, Richard Law, Harold Macmillan, and their followers continued to favor every possible effort at cooperation with the Soviet Union, but this group was at the same time committed to the traditional British policy of seeing that no one power dominated the Continent. As Moscow consolidated its position in Europe following V-E Day, as local Communist parties successfully fished in troubled waters in France and Italy, as the apparently Communist-led revolutions in Greece and Iran (Azerbaijan) gained momentum, the Eden group's two objectives seemed more and more to be mutually exclusive. At the same time the reform Tories continued to believe that Britain could make up for its loss of economic and military power by exerting moral leadership and backing the forces of social democracy against totalitarianism of both right and left. All the while, Churchill, Cherwell, and their followers persisted in viewing Stalin as a reincarnation of Hitler, and Soviet Communism as another version of National Socialism. Despite their doubts about Washington's willingness to pursue a policy of *realpolitik* toward Europe, both the high and the reform Tories were driven back to the truth that their country would be hard pressed to maintain a balance of power in Europe without U.S. assistance.[9] Both groups of conservatives, it should be noted, continued to show little faith in the United Nations, viewing it largely as a placebo for internationalists in the United States.

In the weeks following the Yalta Conference, Anglo-Soviet relations had deteriorated sharply and British irritation with Roosevelt's conciliatory policy toward the USSR had grown into outright anger. The decline in Anglo-Soviet relations stemmed in part from a campaign of intimidation and repression launched by Moscow in the spring of 1945. On February 27 Andrei Vyshinsky, the chairman of the Allied Control Council in Rumania, descended upon Bucharest and demanded that King Michael replace the regime of General Nicolae Radescu with a "democratic front" government headed by a leftist peasant party leader, Petru Groza. When the king procrastinated, Vyshinsky gave him a two-hour ultimatum and, as he left, slammed the door so hard that the plaster on the ceiling cracked. The king gave in.[10] Vyshinsky's action was among the crudest examples of Soviet political meddling in Eastern Europe in the entire postwar period, a blatant violation of the Yalta agreements signed just a few weeks earlier.

Political intimidation in Eastern Europe was matched by widespread repression within the Soviet Union itself. Wartime patriotism gave way to intense governmental suspicion, particularly of Russians who had come in contact with the West. Surviving populations of regions once occupied by the Germans were rounded up and dispersed throughout the rest of the Soviet Union. Even former war prisoners, millions of whom had been exploited as forced laborers in Germany, were exiled to Soviet labor camps, the gulag that Alexander Solzhenitsyn has described in such chilling detail. At the same time Andrei Zhdanov set about purging Soviet drama, art, and literature of foreign, bourgeois influences. This leader of the party revival in the USSR presided over nothing less than a cultural reign of terror.[11]

According to one longtime student of Soviet affairs, the Kremlin's aggressive behavior in Eastern Europe and its brutal repression of its own citizens stemmed from the Soviet leadership's fear of the possible effects of contact with the West. Comparisons between the relative affluence and freedom to be found in the social democracies of Western Europe and North America and the low living standards, repression, and corruption extant in the Communist bloc were sure to generate discontent and even sow the seeds of revolution. That millions of Red Army soldiers had experienced life beyond the borders of the Soviet Union created great apprehension in the Kremlin. Too, Stalin did not want the United States and

Great Britain to realize the extent to which World War II had devastated his country. Perceived weakness might prompt the capitalists to launch a preemptive strike that would destroy socialism before it could spread any farther.[12]

The direction of Stalin's domestic and occupation policies was not readily apparent in the days following the Yalta Conference. Britain's initial reaction to the meeting had been positive, and on March 1 the House of Commons endorsed the Yalta accords by a vote of 413 to 0.[13] Harold Nicolson, man of letters, conservative politician, and friend of Churchill, reflected both this optimism and also the sense of foreboding and helplessness that underlay the vote when he wrote:

> We simply must practice appeasement toward the Soviets. And there is comfort in it. In appeasing Hitler we knew that we were appeasing an advancing tide, and that he would consolidate every position gained. But I do not think that the Russians are an advancing tide. I think that as in 1914, they will gradually recede. I pray to God that I am right in thinking this, because, if I am wrong, then the Balance of Power is permanently dislocated.[14]

Right-wing Conservatives, a faction that was still deeply entrenched in the Foreign Office, were of course extremely dubious about the possibility of an East-West rapprochement. They continued to assume that the Soviet Union was a totalitarian, expansionist power bent on establishing its hegemony throughout Europe. They were particularly disturbed by Moscow's hard line toward Germany, which they hoped to see quickly rehabilitated in order that it might form the cornerstone of a new *cordon sanitaire*. In addition, Russian uncooperativeness over Poland, and Stalin's charges that the West was plotting a secret peace with Germany, alarmed moderates and played into the hands of British Russophobes. It became obvious during March 1945, Permanent Secretary Alexander Cadogan wrote in his diaries, that the Soviet government intended to allow Britain and the United States very little say in Poland. In fact, the Soviet Ministry of Foreign Affairs refused to allow Western observers to visit Poland, all the while dealing with the Communist Lublin government exclusively. Later in March Moscow demanded that only the Lublin regime be invited to the UN Conference on International Organization in San Francisco. When Roosevelt and Churchill refused to exclude representatives of the London-based government-in-exile, Molotov announced that he would not attend. On March 16 several non-Communist political leaders from Poland journeyed to Moscow under written guarantee of safe-conduct to talk about the establishment of a multiparty provisional government. They disappeared without a trace. "How can one work with these animals," Cadogan snarled after learning of the arrest of the Polish delegation.[15] Then on April 5, to the outrage of the Churchill government, Stalin accused Anglo-American military leaders of holding talks with German agents in Berne, Switzerland, concerning the possibility of signing a separate peace in the West.

Hardening attitudes in Whitehall were reinforced by mounting Russophobia among British personnel who came in frequent contact with the Soviets. Diplomats and soldiers stationed in Moscow, Leningrad, Murmansk, and Archangel were alarmed not only by official Soviet policy but also by the suspicion and discourtesy they encountered on a personal level. Frustrated by months of bureaucratic red tape, electronic eavesdropping, rudeness, and ostracism by private Russian citizens fearful of reprisals if they were caught fraternizing with a Westerner, these soldiers and diplomats were portraying their host country in most unflattering terms by April 1945. After observing the Politburo at the opening session of the Supreme Soviet, Frank Roberts, Ambassador Alexander Clark-Kerr's deputy in Moscow, reported:

> The group at the back sitting with M. I. Kalinin are enough to make one shudder and fill one with considerable apprehension regarding future Soviet policy. Apart from Kalinin and . . . Voroshilov none of them, I think, are old party Bolsheviks. They are all tough, fat, prosperous individuals who might equally well have come to the top in any other ruthless, totalitarian society such as those we are defeating in Germany and Italy. Andrei Zhdanov in particular might be a plumper and perhaps more humane version of Hitler himself. Larrenti P. Beriya and George Malenkov at the back give the impression of being at worst perverts and sadists and at best reincarnations of medieval inquisitors justifying every action on the principle of the end justifying the means.[16]

Sir Orme Sargent, respected Foreign Office careerist, was partly responsible for Eden's loss of patience. He insisted that Soviet truculence stemmed from the establishment of the second front and the rapid advances of the Allied armies in the West. Convinced that Anglo-America was going to rehabilitate Germany "as we have undertaken to rehabilitate Italy so as to save her from Communism," the Soviets had decided to erect their own *cordon sanitaire* not merely against a revival of German power but also against the impending penetration of Central Europe by the Western allies. "In such a mood," observed Sargent, "they might not stop to count, in terms of Allied cooperation, the cost of destroying the last vestiges of bourgeois rule and sovereign independence in the countries to be sacrificed for this purpose." Now was the time for a showdown, the veteran diplomat advised. Until the opening of the second front, Britain's attitude had had to be defensive and almost apologetic. The prime minister had gone to great pains to establish a personal relationship with Stalin. But that time was gone; the Anglo-American armies were poised to fill the power vacuum in Central Europe. Continued kowtowing to Moscow would be taken as a sign of weakness.[17]

But it was Roberts, minister-counselor in the British embassy in Moscow, who articulated in the spring of 1945 what eventually came to be the Anglo-American policy of containment. He sensed that the foreign policymakers in London, having worked so long and so hard to establish a viable relationship with the Soviet Union, were becoming frustrated, and he perceived two emerging attitudes. One equated Stalin with Hitler and saw Soviet power to be as potentially dangerous as Germany's had been. The other accepted the argument that the country was simply immature and insecure, and advocated further patience in the expectation that Soviet aggressiveness would pass. Each of these options, Roberts thought, was based on fallacious assumptions, and both were equally dangerous. History, ideology, and the nature of the present leadership made the second course naive. As long as the Politburo was composed of "the tough, tricky and untrustworthy personalities" who then were in power, efforts to conciliate the Kremlin would be counterproductive. Nor should Britain forget that the Russian people were acutely conscious of past national glories; they identified Russian greatness with the power politics practiced by Peter the Great, Catherine the Great, and even Ivan the Terrible. Finally, Roberts observed, "there is a fundamental divergence between the Soviet political philosophy and totalitarian practices, and the way of life of the outside world." What was called for was a policy of reasoned firmness, a quiet resistance to Soviet expansion built on strength:

> We have, above all, to show that there is a limit beyond which they cannot go. We must also show them that we are not bankrupt in political and economic leadership and that the Western world, under our guidance and with the vast economic resources of the Anglo-Saxon world behind it, remains strong and healthy enough to resist Soviet pressure tactics. . . . Since Europe has been divided by Soviet action into two parts, we had better lose no time in ensuring that ours remains the better and with the support of the outside world, the stronger half.[18]

On April 3 Churchill addressed a conference of empire prime ministers. Relations with Russia, "which had offered such fair promise at the Crimea Conference," had deteriorated sharply in recent weeks, he announced. It was by no means clear that the empire "could count on Russia as a beneficent influence in Europe, or as a willing partner in maintaining the peace of the world." Yet the end of the war would see the Soviet Union in a position of "preponderant power and influence throughout the whole of Europe." Churchill told the prime ministers that the British Commonwealth had to unify and then utilize its superior statecraft and experience to match the power of the United States and the Soviet Union.[19]

Though increasingly pessimistic, the Churchill government did not give up trying to draw the United States into the European vacuum of power that would be created by Germany's demise. In March and early April 1945 Churchill bombarded the White House with telegrams generalizing from the Polish situation to all areas liberated by the Soviets and arguing that British and American troops must push into Central Europe as quickly as they could. Gradually, he began to make progress. Although there would be no race for Berlin—Roosevelt declared that he would not jeopardize Soviet-American relations for a few more miles of German rubble—by April Roosevelt's tone toward the Soviet Union seemed to be changing. He wrote Churchill that the West had to be firm with Stalin and leave no impression that it operated from fear.

On March 19, 1945, FDR agreed to a plan that called for Harriman and Clark-Kerr to send separate but identical statements to Molotov demanding again that domestic elements be introduced into the Lublin regime, that Western observers be allowed into Poland to oversee handling of U.S. POWs and war refugees, and that free elections be held throughout Eastern Europe as quickly as possible.

■ ■ ■ Though Harry Truman had not been privy to high-level discussions regarding wartime strategy and the politics of the Grand Alliance, he soon became aware that a shift in the direction of a firmer line toward the Soviet Union had developed in the last weeks before FDR's death. Anxious to appear decisive and to reflect the most recent trend in the policies of his predecessor, the new president set about making Moscow toe the line. On the day following Roosevelt's death, Harriman persuaded Stalin to reverse his earlier decision not to send Molotov to the San Francisco Conference on the UN. The Soviet foreign minister agreed to stop in Washington on his way to the conference to consult with the new chief executive. This arrangement gave Truman less than two weeks to decide how to deal with the Soviets, particularly over the Polish question, which, it was already clear, would be a major issue at San Francisco. Truman immediately closeted himself with Roosevelt's principal advisers on Soviet policy.

As luck would have it, Harriman was then in Washington for consultation. In private conversations with Truman, the ambassador bluntly warned that Soviet occupation of any country would resemble a "barbarian invasion" that would result not only in Russian domination of that country's foreign policy but also the establishment of a police state. What was called for, he argued, was a much firmer policy toward the Soviets.[20] Ignoring Stalin's silence at Yalta and the relative ability of the political leadership in a totalitarian society to disregard public opinion, Harriman told Truman that the Russians would not dare react violently to a tough approach from Washington because they still desperately needed U.S. economic assistance to repair their war-devastated economy.[21]

Other presidential counselors echoed Harriman's call for a harder line. The omnipresent Bernard Baruch, financier and self-styled "adviser to presidents," told Truman that the United States should strictly observe the provisions of the Yalta accords and should demand that the Soviet Union do likewise. Both General Deane and Admiral William D. Leahy, chief of staff to the commander-in-chief, declared that trust and a turn-the-other-cheek attitude toward the Soviet Union would achieve nothing. Deane and Leahy spoke not only for themselves but for a segment of the military bureaucracy as well. On April 2, 1945, War Department planners advised the Joint Chiefs of Staff that under the present uncertain circumstances, the United States could not afford to wait until the Soviet Union's policy was fully revealed before taking certain countermeasures in anticipation of another world war. The U.S. government would have to build a "West-European-American power system as a counterweight to Russia."[22] Of the hard-liners in the military establishment, Forrestal was the most strident. By February 1945 the navy chief had become convinced that the Soviets were determined to work outside the UN to establish puppet regimes in bordering countries. In addition, he was sure that Russia would attempt to dominate all Germany even to the extent of furnishing armed aid to pro-Soviet Germans. This situation, he argued, would most assuredly come to pass if Britain and the United States "gave marked evidence of indecisiveness" and if there was any indication of a resurgent isolationism in America.[23]

Truman's rhetoric began to reflect the influence of his Russophobe advisers. The Soviets were uncivil and untrustworthy, he proclaimed; their diatribes were "insulting." The Russians, he told Henry Wallace, were like people from across the tracks whose manners were bad. They did not keep their word. Moreover, the Soviets were wrong. Domination of other peoples against their will was immoral.[24]

By mid-April Truman's mind was made up: he would challenge Soviet efforts to dominate and, to use Bernard Baruch's phrase, "totalize" Eastern Europe. On April 17, after learning that the Soviets intended to sign a treaty of mutual assistance with the Lublin government, the president resolved to "lay it on the line with Molotov when he arrived in Washington." To Harriman and Leahy's delight, Truman talked to Molotov "as he had never been talked to before" in a famous interview on April 23. He sharply reprimanded the Soviet foreign minister for Moscow's failure to carry out the Yalta decisions on Poland. All that remained, said Truman, was for Stalin to keep his word.[25]

Encouraged by this tongue-lashing, the hard-liners within the foreign policy establishment set about trying to pry open the Communist clam in other parts of Eastern Europe and simultaneously to mobilize U.S. public opinion behind a get-tough policy. A week following the Truman-Molotov encounter, the State Department, while privately acknowledging that Soviet interests in Bulgaria and Rumania were more direct than those of the United States, demanded that the Soviets allow British and American representatives to participate in the political reconstruction of the two Balkan nations, and that Moscow open them to Western business people. Clearly reflecting the strategy suggested in 1943 by the now-departed Adolf Berle, Grew wrote Truman on May 1 that the department was determined to gain for the Rumanians and Bulgarians greater responsibility and freedom of action in their own affairs. The United States would then encounter no difficulty in securing removal of restrictions on the activities of U.S. personnel, obtaining equality of economic opportunity, setting up safeguards for American interests, and gaining access to public opinion, all of which "would serve our national interest and contribute to the general peace and security."[26]

That same day in San Francisco Harriman convened a secret midnight meeting of twelve leading journalists, among them Walter Lippmann, Ernest Lindley, Eugene Meyer, Raymond Graham Swing, Roy Howard, Anne O'Hare McCormick, H. V. Kaltenborn, and Blair Moody, to brief them on Soviet-American relations. He had come to the conclusion, Harriman told his guests, that on long-range policies irreconcilable differences existed between the United States and Britain on the one hand and the Soviet Union on the other. "The difference is this," he said: "Russia apparently intends to pursue a policy of Marxian penetration wherever she can to build up her own security system to protect her socialist conception and we want a world of free nations and peoples." Stalin entered into the Yalta accords in good faith, but something happened after he returned to Moscow from the Crimea. Security-conscious generals and the ideologues and gangsters in the Politburo had apparently gained the upper hand. The result, said Harriman, was the "unilateral setting up of governments" in areas falling under Soviet control.[27]

The United Nations Conference on International Organization opened with great fanfare on April 25, 1945. Stalin had been skeptical when in the fall of 1943 Cordell Hull had presented his plan for a postwar collective security organization. To Stalin, Hull's claim that a revived League of Nations would end war forever seemed utopian. Moreover, at first glance the U.S. plan appeared to be positively dangerous, since the USSR would be a minority of one in the world organization, with pro-Western votes stacked against it. But if the Americans insisted, Stalin eventually decided, the Soviets could learn to live with the United Nations, using skillful diplomacy and the Security Council veto to minimize the danger and even turn the project to Moscow's advantage.[28]

A great many Americans lauded the opening of the San Francisco Conference as the beginning of a new era in international relations. Ironically, the gathering about which so many Americans held such high hopes aggravated rather than alleviated international tensions, for it revealed to the American public the full extent of the differences between the Soviet Union and the West. No sooner had the delegates assembled than Molotov demanded that representatives of the Lublin regime be seated immediately; the official Polish delegation insisted that Secretary of State Stettinius publicly reject the Russian ploy. He agreed and subsequently told the assembled delegates that admission of the Lublin Poles would wreck any chance of approval of the UN Charter by the Senate. Then, on May 4, the Soviet government finally acknowledged that it had arrested sixteen Polish underground leaders after having promised them safe-conduct to come to Moscow and discuss broadening the Lublin regime. Leading American journals, primed by Harriman's briefing, opened up on the Soviets. Even the left-wing *New Republic* observed that the Soviet Union seemed to be acting more out of a desire to safeguard its own interests than out of any wish to make the UN work.[29] Not all press commentators blamed the growing East-West split on Moscow, but April and May 1945 did witness the first widespread press criticism of the Soviet Union since the Russo-Finnish War of 1939–40.

The U.S. delegation managed to block the seating of the Lublin government, but in the process it had to support admission of Argentina, whose right-wing government had broken with the Axis only weeks before the conference. Latin America was determined to preserve the integrity of the Inter-American System and to maximize its clout within the new international organization. Consequently, South and Central American delegations would agree to oppose the Kremlin's Polish strategy only if Washington sponsored Argentina for original membership.

Despite liberal-moderate criticism of the Argentine deal, Senator Vandenberg, in many ways the most influential member of the U.S. delegation, was delighted with the results of the conference. "I might sum it up for your private ear," he wrote Robert Taft, "by saying that we have stopped any possibility that San Francisco might become another Munich. I think the track is now clear for us to go ahead on the real job we have at hand. From my own personal standpoint, the situation in this respect is entirely satisfactory. I find widespread hospitality for the Republican point of view."[30] The Michigan senator's satisfaction, which was shared by fellow delegate John Foster Dulles, stemmed from three achievements: the Lublin Poles had not been seated; the United States had publicly confronted the Soviet Union; and the groundwork was being laid for an all-out political assault by the Republicans on what was becoming known as the Roosevelt-Truman administration's sellout at Yalta of Eastern Europe and the Far East.

But how could the Truman administration apply pressure on the Soviet Union? The Red Army continued to occupy Eastern Europe, and the president was no more ready for an armed confrontation with the Kremlin than FDR had been. Harriman was ready with a familiar suggestion: the United States should use its wealth and technological expertise to regulate the USSR's international behavior. At first he continued to argue that Washington should employ the Soviet Union's need for a postwar reconstruction loan to secure Stalin's cooperation. He acknowledged, as State Department commercial experts had been arguing, that the Russians, using their own resources, could regain their prewar level of capital investment by 1948. They could not, however, carry out their ambitious program of economic expansion without purchasing U.S. industrial equipment. Stalin had told both him and Eric Johnston of the U.S. Chamber of Commerce, Harriman pointed out to the department, that the Soviet Union planned to increase its annual steel production to sixty million tons, three times the annual prewar level, as part of a fifteen-year program of expansion in basic industries. For this, Russia would need American machinery. The United States, he told Grew, Stettinius, Truman, and the American columnists he met with on May 1, should parcel out the money in piecemeal fashion, extracting specific political concessions in return.[31]

By June, however, Harriman had decided that the United States could not trust the Kremlin in any sort of financial/political arrangement. Emerging from the war in possession of large quantities of gold, lend-lease stocks, and war booty, the Soviet Union would use U.S. assistance, if Washington were not careful, "to promote its political aims to our disadvantage."[32] The United States should therefore use its largesse to grant aid to countries "naturally friendly to us" and lend money to Russia only in return for "free elections and full access to occupied areas by western citizens." The United States, Harriman further advised, should accept only gold in repayment. He sympathized with the view expressed by Morgenthau and others that the United States needed to stockpile strategic materials such as manganese, chrome, and fuels, but he thought that Washington should acquire them from friendly nations and not from the USSR, lest the United States become dependent on the Communist world for vital supplies.[33]

Roosevelt had generally rejected the use of economic aid as a diplomatic weapon against the Soviet Union. Until the last six months of the war he had resisted the urgings of hard-liners such as William Bullitt and Harriman to use lend-lease to obtain concessions from the Soviets. In fact, the Roosevelt administration was generous with lend-lease materials and planned up through mid-1944 to manipulate the aid program to allow the Soviets to use it for postwar reconstruction. Roosevelt and Hopkins ordered a halt to shipments to the USSR for reconstruction purposes only after congressional critics attacked the Fourth Russian Supply Protocol, pointing out that lend-lease was intended to be purely a war-related program. Roosevelt reluctantly agreed not to take the initiative in offering a loan to the Soviets at the Yalta Conference, but he still had high hopes for Soviet-American cooperation and did not want to be accused by Moscow of engaging in blackmail.

Truman had no qualms about using economic aid as a lever to force diplomatic concessions from the Soviets. When Harriman briefed him on East-West relations in the days following FDR's death, he frequently mentioned economics and finance as areas in which Washington could exert pressure on Moscow. Truman was enthusiastic. He intended to be "firm" but "fair," because "the Russians need us more than we need them." During his confrontation with Molotov, Truman reminded the Soviet foreign minister that Congress would have to approve foreign economic aid, and he implied that Soviet conduct in Eastern Europe would largely determine whether approval was forthcoming.[34]

On May 9 Harriman suggested that in view of Germany's surrender, lend-lease supplies to the USSR be curtailed. Washington should continue to authorize shipments that facilitated Soviet preparations for war in the Pacific, he urged, but should closely scrutinize further requests with a view to U.S. interests and policies. Such a stratagem was "right down his alley," Truman told Stimson several days later. On May 11 the United States abruptly ended nonmilitary lend-lease to the Soviet Union. Foreign Economic Administration (FEA) chief Leo Crowley, acting on a State Department memo that had been approved by the White House, ordered U.S. ships laden with goods not destined for direct use on the battlefields of the Far East to turn around and head back to their home ports. Truman subsequently claimed that Crowley had overreacted, and the president moved to repair the damage caused to Soviet-American relations. He notified Moscow that "all allocations provided by treaty or protocol would be delivered."[35] Nonetheless, the president did intend to use U.S. aid to extract diplomatic concessions.

Nor did the Truman administration have any intention of allowing Russia to profit indirectly from U.S. aid to Germany. At Yalta the Big Three had agreed to establish a reparations commission that would meet in Moscow and take a figure of $20 billion, half going to the Soviet Union, as a basis for discussion. Truman and his advisers were determined to prevent a reparations settlement that would allow the Soviets to strip not only their occupation zone but also the British and American areas for their own reconstruction purposes. Such a policy would create a huge burden for American taxpayers, who would have to feed the German population. More important, the Russian option on reparations would ensure that a strong, politically rehabilitated, and prosperous Germany could not reappear to fill the power vacuum in Central Europe. To this end, the United States withheld its delegation to the reparations meetings in Moscow for as long as possible and then instructed its representatives to limit the removal of facilities and current production to a level that would permit the German people to support themselves without outside assistance.[36]

Despite Truman's tough talk to Molotov and his willingness to use economic leverage, there were obvious limits to the administration's confrontational strategy during these early, belligerent days. In reality, Washington was not willing to risk a military clash with the USSR. Truman's basic strategy was for the West to live up to its obligations under the Yalta agreements and then demand that the Soviets do the same. That this was Washington's approach became clear during the debate over how far Anglo-American troops should penetrate Central Europe in the last days of the war.

In early April, as German resistance collapsed in the West but stiffened in the East, Anglo-American troops faced an opportunity to occupy Berlin and its environs ahead of the Soviets even though the area was within the Soviet zone of occupation agreed upon at Yalta. Shortly before FDR's death, Eisenhower, as supreme Allied commander in Europe, announced his intention to stop at the Elbe River, a hundred miles west of Berlin, although his troops were in a position to move into the German capital and into Prague well ahead of the Russians. Eisenhower insisted that he wanted to work out a clear line of demarcation with the Soviet commanders, and thus prevent inadvertent clashes between his troops and those of the Red Army. Moreover, a simple thrust in the direction of Berlin might have exposed Eisenhower's flanks to German attack or allowed the last remnants of the German army to retreat to the "National Redoubt," a haven that U.S. intelligence claimed Hitler was preparing in the Alps. Either situation would prolong the war, thereby delaying the redeployment of American troops to the Pacific. Truman approved not only this decision but also a subsequent one in mid-April to have American and British troops withdraw from the Elbe to their designated occupation zones.[37]

Truman and Eisenhower stuck to this position over the violent protests of Churchill and the State Department. The Western powers, the prime minister told Truman, were missing a golden opportunity to occupy strategic areas in Central Europe. Eisenhower and British Field Marshal Sir Harold Alexander should seize as much territory as possible and not leave "until satisfied about Russian policies in Poland, Germany, and the Danube basin," he argued.[38] By the end of May Churchill was using the term "iron curtain" and insisting that no withdrawals take place until the whole question of future Anglo-American relations with the Soviet Union in Europe was settled.[39] Undersecretary of State Grew and the other hard-liners in the State Department echoed Churchill's advice: "The political importance of Czechoslovakia, the vital strategic location of Prague, and the high esteem of the American people for the Czech democratic system make it imperative that the agreement for cooperation between the US, GB, and the SU be carried out in connection with the liberation of Czechoslovakia rather than permit the SU to continue its exclusive control over this most important area in Central Europe," Grew wrote Truman. "The Department of State firmly believes that the interests of the US will best be served by the immediate occupation of Prague and supports the urgent request made to this effect by P. M. Churchill and For. Sec. Eden."[40] Truman ignored their advice, however, and by mid-June American and British troops had withdrawn from Czechoslovakia and from the Soviet occupation zone in Germany.

■ ■ ■ Indeed, by June 1945 Truman was beginning to soften his position on the Soviet Union. In the first place, a number of advisers and interest groups, alarmed by the influence that the hard-liners initially enjoyed with the new president, stepped forward to outline the implications of a confrontational stance toward the Soviets and the limitations on Washington's ability to get tough. The suspicion and dislike of the Soviet Union evidenced by some in the military and State Department in the spring and summer of 1945 were not shared by other influential members of the military's top command. Though determined to resist Soviet penetration of Western Europe, many service leaders showed little concern in April and May over Soviet domination of Eastern Europe. More broadly, these leaders still clung, though with diminishing confidence, to their hopes for Soviet participation in the Pacific war and cooperation in the crusade for world peace.[41]

The leader and chief spokesman for the military moderates was Henry L. Stimson, a traditional Republican nationalist in the Henry Cabot Lodge-Theodore Roosevelt tradition. He maintained that the primary concerns of U.S. foreign policy should be, first, the security of the Western Hemisphere and, second, peace and stability abroad. Maintenance of the Monroe Doctrine and the regional security system that had grown up around it was the key to the attainment of the first objective, Stimson argued. Allowing the Soviets to have their own sphere of interest in Eastern Europe might be the key to the second. "Some Americans are anxious to hang on to exaggerated views of the Monroe Doctrine and at the same time butt into every question that comes up in Central Europe," he told his deputy John J. McCloy. "Our position in the western hemisphere and Russia's in the eastern hemisphere could be adjusted without too much friction." He thought the Wilsonian impulse to export democracy was not only doomed to failure but actually dangerous to American interests. "I know very well from my experience with other nations that there are no nations in the world except the US and UK which have a real idea of what an independent free ballot is," he noted in his diary. "I learned that in Nicaragua and South America." In Stimson's opinion America's confrontation with Russia over Poland in 1945 stemmed from this misguided impulse and from personal pique. Harriman, Deane, and other members of the American mission in the Soviet Union who "[had] been suffering personally from the Russians' behavior on minor matters for a long time" were letting their feelings affect their policy recommendations. Stimson told Stettinius that despite "current problems . . . Russia [has] been very good to us on the larger issues. She [has] kept her word and carried out her engagements. We must remember that she has not learned the niceties of diplomatic intercourse and we must expect bad language from her."[42]

Eisenhower and Marshall shared Stimson's perspective. Much more than Marshall, Eisenhower recognized that all wars were fought for political ends, but he did not believe that eviction of the Soviets from Eastern Europe was a viable political goal. Given the manpower and matériel demands of the final stages of the war in the Far East, the United States could not afford a confrontation with the USSR over Eastern Europe. Indeed, if the United States wanted to protect Central and Western Europe and simultaneously demobilize, the best approach was for Washington to observe the Yalta accords while concluding agreements for four-power control of disputed areas with the Soviets. It should be remembered, finally, that the view of European relations and postwar conditions expressed by the joint chiefs in 1944 still prevailed among most military figures. They continued to believe that the peace of the world in the postwar era depended upon the maintenance of good relations among the Big Three; that the major disputes of the period would be between the Soviets and the British in the eastern Mediterranean, the Near East, and the Far East; that although the United States would always side with Britain in war, the two could never hope to win a military victory over the Soviet Union; and that therefore the United States should do everything in its power to mediate Anglo-Soviet disputes.[43]

In addition, a number of military leaders concerned primarily with the Pacific theater feared that despite the Quebec agreement of 1944, the British were going to allow the United States to bear the brunt of the final stages of the war and then, once Japan was knocked out, step in and reassert their claim to empire and influence in the Far East. General Douglas MacArthur was already openly pleading for an Asia-first policy after the war. He and others argued that imperialism constituted a severe obstacle to Asia's self-realization; if the West attempted to restore the status quo antebellum, it would create resentment and turmoil that would play into the hands of the Soviets. In mid-May General Patrick Hurley reported to Truman that the military, diplomatic, and commercial interests of Britain and the other nations with colonial interests in Asia were endeavoring to have Lord Louis Mountbatten appointed commander of all Allied forces in China. "Should Lord Louis or any other British admiral or general receive this appointment in preference to an American," Hurley asserted, "it would constitute an overwhelming victory for the hegemony of the imperialist nations and the principles of colonial imperialism in Asia. . . . Such an appointment would be a distinct setback for America and Democracy in Asia."[44] Some of the most Asia-conscious members of the military high command believed that much of the pressure for a hard line toward the Soviet Union came from those same Britishers who looked to the United States to fight their battles in the Far East. Moreover, from a simple strategic point of view, American planners wanted Russian help in the final assault on Japan.

Joining military moderates in urging a more flexible, realistic policy toward the Soviet Union was the coalition of individuals and publications that the British Foreign Office had labeled American liberal opinion. It included Henry Wallace and Eleanor Roosevelt, the *Nation* and *New Republic,* Raymond Graham Swing and Joseph E. Davies, and even Harry Hopkins. Liberals had been much alarmed by developments at San Francisco. Citing the drive to seat Argentina, they accused the U.S.-led Inter-American System and the British Commonwealth of ganging up on the Soviets and engaging in the worst type of power politics.[45] A real danger, liberals warned, was that the Soviet Union would be driven out of the UN, and no international organization could work without Soviet participation. Many saw an English Machiavelli behind the Soviet-American confrontation. "Harriman and Stettinius . . . are taking orders from London," one of Wallace's confidants wrote him, "and I'm dubious ABOUT LONDON WHEN LONDON TRIES TO LAY DOWN A FOREIGN POLICY FOR US."[46] Declared another Wallace correspondent: "Eden and Stettinius are Siamese twins out here—and the Russians know it." The brouhaha at San Francisco, wrote still another, was a product of Anglo-Soviet rivalry in Europe. But Britain, who had an alliance with the Soviets, was playing the United States for a fool: "We are the sonsabitches in the eyes of the Russians now by playing Britain's game."[47]

Many in this group continued to believe that the motive behind Soviet "aggression" was the Kremlin's fear of Germany. If America and England would join Russia in a pact to prevent the revival of German military and industrial might, they argued, then the Soviets would abandon power politics and participate in the United Nations.[48] Joseph E. Davies, wealthy Wisconsin businessman, former ambassador to the Soviet Union, and arch-proponent of Soviet-American friendship, wrote Byrnes in May that the Russian situation was deteriorating to a frightening degree. "It would be desperately tragic," he continued, "if after the Soviets had trusted us sufficiently to cooperate to win the war, they might . . . , from their point of view, be justifiably compelled to 'go it alone' in a hostile ideological and religious world, and to create a '*cordon sanitaire*' not only in Europe but in the Pacific because of some of the crazy militarists and prejudiced fools who preach the inevitability of war between Russia and the United States, and are 'sowing the dragon seed.'"[49] Presidential adviser Oscar Cox was so worried over the diplomatic situation and the influence of the hard-liners that he wrote an elaborate analysis of Soviet-American relations designed to show that no reason for conflict existed between the nations.[50] Former Undersecretary of State Sumner Welles, by then a widely syndicated columnist, declared that the Roosevelt stratagem of Soviet-American cooperation had been scrapped under the new administration, and that the United States now appeared to the Russians to be heading up an anti-Russian Western bloc. Walter Lippmann agreed. "Though the issue has apparently been drawn between the Soviets and ourselves," he wrote Byrnes following the San Francisco conference, "this alignment is not inherent in the nature of things. . . . There is a far deeper conflict between the British and the S.U. than between the USA and the Soviets." He added that the United States should seek once again to become the "moderating power which holds the balance."[51]

Stimson, Marshall, Hurley, Davies, Wallace, and other opponents of a get-tough policy made their views known repeatedly to Truman in late April and May and had much to do with the American decision not to take Prague. The president continued to be irritated with Soviet behavior, but he was also increasingly suspicious of British motives and fearful of an anti-Soviet backlash among the U.S. press and public that would tie his hands in dealing with the Kremlin.

Truman, no less than Roosevelt, tended initially to lump Britain and Russia together. Certainly no Anglophobe himself, the new president came from the section of the country least inclined to seek close ties with the British. He counted few friends among those intellectuals, financiers, and business people, most of whom resided along the eastern seaboard, who were traditionally Anglophile. Nor could he have been immune to the intense anti-British feeling that swept the United States in the months before his accession to office. The man from Missouri shared the midwestern progressive's fear of an international plutocracy, and he deplored colonialism. Even more than his predecessor, he was determined to give the United Nations a real chance to succeed, and Britain's traditional balance-of-power stratagem seemed antithetical to the whole idea of international cooperation. One of his principal tasks during the first weeks of his administration, he later wrote, was "to get Churchill in a frame of mind to forget the old power politics and get a United Nations organization to work."[52] To Eleanor Roosevelt he wrote: "I have been trying carefully to keep all my engagements with the Russians because they are touchy and suspicious of us. The difficulties with Churchill are very nearly as exasperating as they are with the Russians."[53]

Moreover, the American people, victims of their own government's propaganda, still regarded the Soviets as gallant wartime allies. A Princeton poll taken in May 1945 showed that 80 percent of the American people felt that the United States should continue to cooperate closely with *both* Britain and Russia after the war.[54] In addition, demobilization threatened to turn into disintegration following V-J Day, leaving America's armed forces in a dangerously weakened condition. Tough talk and direct economic pressure had not worked; why not, reasoned the president, try to build bridges to Moscow and, if necessary, put distance again between British and American policy? "Every time we get things going halfway with the Soviets," Truman confided to his diary the first week in June, "some smart aleck has to attack them. If it isn't Willie Hearst, Bertie McCormick or Burt Wheeler, it is some other bird who wanted to appease Germany, but just can't see any good in Russia. I'm not afraid of Russia. They've always been our friends and I can't see any reason why they shouldn't always be."[55] Truman managed to convince himself that Soviet leaders were no different from Western political leaders with whom deals could be struck. In effect, he decided to resort to the approach that FDR had clung to so tenaciously and that Lippmann was now espousing—mediation between Britain and the USSR.

In mid-May Truman took three important steps to try to reverse the decline in Soviet-American relations. First, he responded favorably to Churchill's pleas for another Big Three conference while rejecting his demand for an East-West showdown at that meeting; second, Truman decided to send the ailing Hopkins to Moscow for private talks with Stalin; and third, he asked Davies to talk with Churchill in London. Lord Halifax quickly perceived the meaning of Truman's moves. The administration, Halifax reported to the Foreign Office, was preoccupied with Soviet-American relations. The president was moving to counter "Liberal and Left-wing" criticism that he had been "maneuvered by Britain into an anti-Soviet bloc."[56]

During late May Davies talked with Churchill four times in London and at Chequers. The interviews were stormy, and neither man minced words. Davies openly blamed Britain for troubles within the Grand Alliance. He told Churchill that his recent public statements, particularly his May 13 victory speech, had reawakened Soviet suspicions of the West. The Soviet Union would naturally take steps to protect itself from a hostile Britain, particularly if the Kremlin sensed that the British and the Americans were ganging up on it. Truman's policy, Davies explained, was to establish a "balanced tripod of power." Only an approach that neither appeased nor isolated the Soviet Union, that placed Washington at an equal distance from Moscow and London, that, in short, made the United States a mediator in the age-old rivalry between Britain and the USSR, could sustain a lasting peace. Churchill was deeply offended by the term "ganging up." After delivering a long paean to the virtues of Anglo-American civilization, the prime minister asked Davies if he were trying to tell him that the United States intended to withdraw from European affairs. No president could keep troops in Europe indefinitely, Davies replied. If Truman ordered a precipitous withdrawal, Churchill declared, the steel curtain would descend over Western as well as Eastern Europe; Stalin would replace Hitler and the NKVD the Gestapo. What recourse did Britain have but to try to use American power to check Russia? Davies terminated the exchanges by accusing Churchill of secretly wanting to ally with Hitler to restrain the USSR.[57]

At this juncture there is every evidence that Truman liked and trusted Davies, and that Davies's views represented those of the president. Before the former ambassador departed for London, Truman had told him that both Stalin and Churchill were "trying to make me the paw for the cat that pulled the chestnuts out of the fire."[58] The president praised Davies's efforts in London upon his return and, more significant, appointed him one of the four principal members of the U.S. delegation to the Potsdam Conference. Davies's primary role at Potsdam, one writer has explained, was to symbolize by his very presence at the negotiating table the differences between Truman and Churchill.[59]

At Truman's request, Hopkins spent from May 26 through June 6 trying to convince Stalin of the president's genuine desire for cooperation and understanding between the countries.[60] Hopkins had a reputation as an advanced liberal, Truman observed to Davies, but not a professional one, "which I count the lowest form of politician." Hopkins had "horse sense" and knew how to use it. Although Hopkins was beginning to have serious doubts about Soviet-American collaboration, he still believed that German militarism posed a greater danger to world peace than the Soviet Union and that every effort should be directed toward ensuring no revival of that menace.[61] The American envoy apologized to Stalin again for the abrupt cutoff of lend-lease and proclaimed Washington's readiness to ensure that the Soviet Union obtained its fair share of reparations. When Stalin complained that the Truman administration had apparently abandoned its predecessor's support for the dismemberment of Germany, Hopkins denied the charge. But on Poland, Hopkins told Stalin, his government had to have something. Chicago was still the largest Polish population center outside Warsaw, and the American people in general identified with the Poles perhaps more than any other nationality victimized by the Nazis.[62] The United States would not support a policy in Poland that was directed entirely by the Soviet Union. But most important, Stalin had to promise to release the imprisoned Polish delegation that had been guaranteed safe-conduct.

His host, Hopkins reported, was conciliatory; he accepted the explanation of bureaucratic foul-up for the termination of lend-lease; he even endorsed the United States' open-door policy toward China, saying that America was the only power with the resources to aid China after the war; and he told his American guest that on May 23 the Supreme Soviet would pass a law demobilizing 40 percent of the Red Army in the West. (According to a 1960 article in *Pravda,* the 11,365,000-man Red Army had been cut to 2,874,000 by 1948.)[63] Moreover, before Hopkins departed, Stalin agreed to the U.S. position on voting in the UN Security Council. Finally, after listening intently to Hopkins's complaints about Poland, the Russian leader proposed a practical solution of the problem. The present Warsaw government would form the basis of the future Polish Provisional Government of National Unity, but representatives from other Polish groups who were friendly to both the Western Allies and the Soviets could have four or five of the eighteen or twenty ministries in the government. Truman subsequently endorsed this plan.[64]

Both Harriman and the British were skeptical about Stalin's promises and the ambassador told Truman so. Whitehall officials complained privately that Hopkins's mission demonstrated that the United States would be content with "papering over the cracks" in the alliance, not forcing the Soviets to live up to their agreements.[65] Churchill reluctantly concurred in the deal Hopkins had worked out with Stalin—"accepting the best Hopkins can get," he termed it. But Britain and the United States should not fool themselves: "All we have got is a certain number of concessions for outside Poles to take part in the preliminary discussion, out of which hopeful improvements in the Lublin Government may be made. I cannot feel therefore that we can regard this as more than a milestone in the long hill we ought never to have been asked to climb."[66] Truman and his advisers did not regard the Hopkins-Stalin encounter as the last word on Poland, but the president's acceptance of the deal indicated his realization that, short of military confrontation, the United States would have to rely on time and the pressure of world opinion to produce free Polish elections. As Bohlen, one of the original State Department hard-liners, put it, "The Hopkins mission was hardly a success, although it did show that the United States was prepared to go to considerable lengths to preserve friendship with the Soviet Union."[67]

■ ■ ■ For some weeks Churchill had been urging Truman to join him in convening a Big Three meeting to settle specific questions relating to boundaries, occupation policies, reparations, and colonies. "The retreat of the American army to our line of occupation in the central sector, thus bringing Soviet power into the heart of Western Europe," Churchill wrote Truman, should be accompanied by settlement of the host of important matters that would constitute "the true foundation of world peace."[68] The British, of course, wanted to meet separately beforehand with American military and political officials to work out a common strategy. This the president refused to do, but he did agree to attend a summit in mid-July. And in fact, it was Hopkins who broached the subject with Stalin. The Soviet leader answered that he would be glad to meet with Churchill and Roosevelt at a site in or near Berlin.

Churchill, with Clement Attlee in tow, arrived at Potsdam in an anxious and confrontational mood. He and his advisers had picked up on the changing mood in Washington and felt American power slipping through their hands. Jock Balfour, a member of the British embassy staff in Moscow, wrote Halifax in late May:

> Coming from Russia, I can't help thinking that every ounce of Anglo-American cooperation will be needed if the Bear is to be brought to a halt in the game of squeezing his Allies out of any say in the settlement of that part of Europe into which he had waddled. . . . It is therefore most aggravating to find that high-minded pundits like Lippmann and Raymond Graham Swing are showing signs of scuttling like rabbits for cover and persuading themselves that the behavior of the bear is largely the fault of the naughtily provocative British lion and that . . . it would therefore be best for Uncle Sam to adopt an attitude of "wise reserve" toward developments in Europe.[69]

J. C. Donnelley of the North American Department agreed: "The heresy of 'mediation' being preached by Lippmann and Swing has of course the appeal of the proverbial melody whistled in the dark." C. F. A. Warner, head of the Northern Department, termed it a new form of isolationism, observing that mediation was extremely popular with Americans because it was perceived as an alternative to placing their "boys" in "ugly situations."[70] Davies seemed to be saying, Sargent noted, that it "does not pay to be tough with the Soviets and it does pay to appease them." This was the language of 1938, and he hoped it did not reflect Truman's attitude; however, he observed pessimistically, "There is no smoke without fire."[71]

To Britain's dismay, Russia was well aware of America's vacillation and tried to take advantage of it. Why did the United Kingdom work so closely with the Americans? the minister-counselor at the Russian embassy asked Warner. They would only pull out of Europe as they always did. London would be much better served by making common cause with Moscow.[72]

The British made a halfhearted attempt to apply pressure on the Soviets unilaterally. In June the United Kingdom canceled further shipments of military goods to the USSR, but by then such aid was insignificant. A few considered drastic action—unleashing the "secret" Polish brigade on Soviet forces in Eastern Europe—but cooler heads prevailed. Again, Britain needed the United States. Though angry at American neo-isolationism, with its accompanying tendency to belittle British power and ignore the United Kingdom's interests, and pessimistic about their ability to convince the United States that its interests would always be bound up with those of Western Europe, the British decided to try again. If Britain could confront the Soviets and force their intransigence, unreasonableness, and aggressiveness into the open, the Truman administration would have no choice but to join London and the British and American embassies in Moscow in taking a tougher line.[73]

And, of course, the Hopkins and Davies missions both symbolized and confirmed Truman's intention to go to the next Big Three meeting and "come out with a working relationship with the Russians."[74] This attitude was shared by the man Truman named to succeed Stettinius as secretary of state in 1945, James F. Byrnes. Born in 1879, the son of Irish immigrant parents, Byrnes grew up in South Carolina. By the late 1920s he was a successful lawyer and an aspiring politician. He was elected district attorney and then in 1910 won a seat in the House of Representatives by the narrowest of margins. "I campaigned on nothing but gall," he boasted, "and gall won by 51 votes."[75] In 1930 he was elected to the Senate, where he remained until 1941. A New Dealer who retained his standing with southern conservatives, Byrnes grew to be a force in Washington. So impressed with the South Carolinian's loyal support of the New Deal was FDR that he appointed him to the Supreme Court in 1941 and the next year asked him to manage the mobilization effort at home by becoming director of the Office of Economic Stabilization (OES). Byrnes accepted, moved into the east wing of the White House, and told Hopkins: "There's just one suggestion I want to make to you, Harry, and that is to keep the hell out of my business."[76] First as director of OES and then as head of the Office of War Mobilization, Byrnes mediated feuds, established production priorities, and eliminated bottlenecks.

In many ways this southern politician-bureaucrat was a conservative. He was a Catholic who later converted to Episcopalianism and a man who counted Bernard Baruch among his closest friends. Byrnes frequently visited Baruch's South Carolina estate as a hunting guest. He opposed the wave of sit-down strikes in 1937 and gained a reputation as an opponent of "planning" and a guardian of free enterprise. Yet he campaigned vigorously in Congress in 1945 for passage of the Murray-Wagner full-employment bill. Above all Byrnes was a compromiser, a horse trader, a power broker. Leslie Biffle, secretary of the Senate, called Byrnes "the smartest, most effective and most unobstructive operator" he had ever seen in action: "One Senator reportedly remarked: 'When I see Jimmy Byrnes coming I put one hand on my watch, the other on my wallet, and wish to goodness I knew how to protect my conscience.'"[77] The new secretary of state looked forward to applying the negotiating techniques he had found useful in these jobs to the problems of foreign affairs.

Truman and Byrnes had one overriding objective at Potsdam: they wanted to clear up remaining wartime problems so that U.S. military and economic responsibilities in Europe could be terminated. Both men were able practitioners of the art of politics, acutely sensitive to the public's desire for a return to "normalcy" at home and abroad. At this point both tended to look upon the Soviets as fellow politicians, with whom a deal could be arranged. "The smart boys in the State Department, as usual, are against the best interests of the U.S. if they can circumvent a straightforward hard-hitting trader for the homefront," Truman confided to his diary. "But they are stymied this time. Byrnes and I shall expect our interests to come first."[78]

The president's optimism stemmed in large part from his faith in the efficacy of economic and atomic diplomacy. Even more than his predecessor, Truman believed that the USSR's need for a large reconstruction loan was real and compelling. This need, coupled with the fear induced by the soon-to-be demonstrated atomic bomb, would leave the Soviets no choice but to be responsive to Western diplomacy.

A week following FDR's death the State Department—not the Treasury, it should be noted—began to move on the loan issue. The State Department's plan, subsequently approved by Truman, conformed roughly to Harriman's suggestions. Emilio Collado, the head of the department's Office of Financial and Development Policy, recommended that following the San Francisco Conference the administration should offer Moscow a $1 billion loan (not $6 billion or $10 billion, as Morgenthau had originally proposed to Roosevelt in early 1945) through the Export-Import Bank at the bank's regular rate of interest, rather than the 2¼ percent proposed by the Soviets. In mid-July FEA chief Crowley asked Congress to raise the bank's loan ceiling from $700 million to $3.5 billion and to repeal the Johnson Act, which forbade loans to defaulting governments. In answer to a question from Senator Robert Taft, Crowley acknowledged that between \$700 million and \$1 billion of the new lending authority would be set aside for a loan to the Soviet Union. Taft criticized the request as an attempt to circumvent the congressional prohibition on the use of lend-lease for reconstruction purposes, but told Crowley that "\$1 billion was a fair amount to be used in the next year to finance trade with Russia."[79] Some members argued that the administration had been subsidizing Communist aggression in Europe with lend-lease funds and that the export-import credit would do the same thing. But at this point a majority in both houses of Congress supported the granting of credits to Russia and voted for the export-import bill. Russian intransigence was not yet apparent to the American people, and the United States still tended to associate internationalism with Soviet-American cooperation. The time was not yet ripe, Republican leaders felt, to open up on the administration regarding Eastern Europe.[80]

Armed with this new lending authority, Truman left for Potsdam in July for his first face-to-face meeting with Churchill and Stalin. The State Department advised Truman not to broach the matter of a loan unless Stalin first inquired. But as at Yalta, Stalin said nothing about his country's postwar reconstruction needs or an American credit. He concentrated instead on reproaching Truman for the abrupt cancellation of lend-lease in May. Thus Potsdam, like Yalta, ended without the Soviet loan issue playing any overt role.[81]

In selling Truman on the idea of using the Soviet Union's need for U.S. financial support to reconstruct and expand its domestic economy, Harriman apparently forgot to mention that Stalin had not risen to the bait at Yalta. Nonetheless, the Soviet state budget for 1945, released in May of that year, revealed that Russian leaders were indeed counting on an American loan. According to budget projections, U.S. aid, together with reparations from Germany, would account for one-fourth of the USSR's capital intake for the year. Stalin did not raise the issue at Yalta or Potsdam because Soviet leaders continued to believe that the United States' need for expanded export markets eventually would force it to extend a loan. Stalin in 1944 had told Eric Johnston that the gravest postwar problem the United States would face would be prevention of another major depression. When Molotov inquired about a loan in January 1945, he also made reference to an impending depression in the United States and the need for export markets. In addition, Harriman and Truman seemed to ignore the fact that the Soviet Union was a totalitarian society. The state was in a position to manipulate its own economy as well as those of its allies to achieve industrial reconstruction and expansion without making concessions to the West.[82]

Some historians have argued that the primary motive behind U.S. economic policy toward the Soviet Union during this period was the open door, that above all Washington wanted to pry open the markets of Eastern Europe for U.S. exports. And it is true that those markets were becoming increasingly closed to Western exports in the spring of 1945. Eastern Europe before World War II was predominantly agricultural and had carried on a large volume of trade with Western Europe—$1.75 billion in 1938, or 23 percent of inter-European trade. Eastern Europe also traded with other parts of the world, including the United States; indeed, in 1938 the region had accounted for 5 percent of the world's trade. Under Nazi control, Rumania, Poland, Bulgaria, and Hungary became more industrialized, primarily because the German war machine demanded huge quantities of manufactured items from them. This shift from agricultural production, together with the devastation caused by the war and the severe droughts of 1944–45, left Eastern Europe—once self-sufficient in food and other raw materials—in critical need of agricultural products, petroleum, and minerals. The Red Army happened to be on hand with the necessary transport facilities to deliver these items from the Soviet Union. In exchange, Moscow insisted that each nation sign a bilateral, restrictive trade agreement that tied up its industrial exports for years to come. In the trade pattern that developed, Moscow supplied raw materials to Eastern Europe while taking its finished products. The Soviets assumed a direct managerial role in key industries in occupied countries. These industries, of course, became nationalized, and throughout Eastern Europe foreign trade gradually turned into a state-controlled monopoly. Postwar Eastern Europe "had to choose between trade with the U.S.S.R. on the terms offered, or no trade at all," according to a British scholar. Europe's trade options were severely limited by the presence of the Red Army, but the Soviet Union was also the only nation that offered the region what it needed most—food and raw materials.[83]

Most senior American policymakers were not overly alarmed by the economic consequences of the Soviet trade initiative in Poland and the Baltic. The Roosevelt and Truman administrations were interested in opening Eastern Europe for political rather than economic reasons. In the first place, those concerned about depression in the postwar period wanted to acquire markets primarily for U.S. industrial goods. The economies of Eastern Europe had become competitive with, rather than complementary to, that of the United States and were not good prospective markets for

North American products. U.S. policymakers wanted the Soviet Union to allow Westerners to travel and trade freely in the area because they hoped that such contact would prevent the countries of Eastern Europe from becoming Soviet-dominated, totalitarian societies antithetical to Western values and traditions. Quite simply, Washington wanted to be in a position to compete with Moscow for the hearts and minds of the Eastern Europeans.

■ ■ ■ A postwar reconstruction loan constituted but one phase, the positive phase, of the carrot-and-stick approach the Truman administration took toward the Soviet Union in the spring and summer of 1945. The negative aspect of Washington's Russian policy was the implied threat of the atomic bomb. The overriding question that has absorbed diplomatic historians studying atomic diplomacy in 1945 is whether the bombing of Hiroshima and Nagasaki was necessary to end the war with Japan and, if it was not, whether the bombs were dropped primarily as a demonstration designed to intimidate the Soviets, with whom relations over Eastern Europe were deteriorating. The prevailing view among recent scholars is that Truman and his principal advisers were convinced that the bomb was militarily, politically, and diplomatically necessary to ending the war against Japan.[84] Since the inception in 1941 of the Manhattan Engineering District (the code name for the top-secret atomic development program), Roosevelt, Stimson, and their principal military advisers assumed that if an atomic weapon were developed before the close of the war, it would be utilized. If the American people and Congress had learned subsequently that the government had not used a weapon that would have brought the war to a close a year earlier than its actual end and would have saved the lives of thousands of GIs, they would have been outraged. Truman inherited Roosevelt's advisers and assumptions, and he anticipated the public reaction should it become known that he had the bomb and did not use it.

Although military and political considerations were controlling factors in the decision to use the bomb, the Truman administration perceived intimidation of the Soviet Union as a valuable by-product. As their actions demonstrated at the Potsdam Conference, Stimson, Truman, and Byrnes believed that the bomb would provide leverage in efforts to bend the Kremlin to Washington's will regarding Eastern Europe. Moreover, they hoped that the weapon's deployment would bring the war in the Far East to a speedy close, before the USSR could enter and claim the territorial and economic concessions it had been promised at Yalta. In short, the Truman administration was more than ready to employ atomic diplomacy in its dealings with the Kremlin; but the anticipated pressure that the bomb's use would bring to bear on the Soviet Union was not decisive in the president's decision.

By the spring of 1945 the Nazis were on the run on both fronts, and on May 8 Germany surrendered unconditionally. With the war in Europe over, the British and Americans were free to turn their attention to the destruction of Japanese power in the Far East. By May Japan was greatly weakened, its carrier fleet sunk or disabled and its air force reduced to a few squadrons of fanatical kamikazes. Not only had MacArthur recaptured the Philippines, but Okinawa and Iwo Jima had fallen to U.S. Marines in early 1945. Three options were available to the Truman administration for securing Japan's surrender.

The first and apparently the most viable and likely alternative was an invasion with conventional forces. The Combined Chiefs of Staff set in motion plans whereby the Japanese home islands would be enveloped in a giant pincer movement, with a task force under MacArthur moving up from the south and another assault group descending from the Aleutian Islands in the north. The task force, Truman's military advisers told him, would require a million men and would cost the Allies a minimum of a hundred thousand casualties. U.S. intelligence estimated that a million Japanese troops were still in Manchuria and another two million soldiers in the home islands. The military advised doing whatever was necessary to bring the Soviet Union into the war to tie down enemy troops in Manchuria. D-Day was set for November 1, 1945.

A second option available to Washington was to end the war through negotiation. Japan was suffering terribly by the early summer of 1945. Allied ships were shelling Japanese port cities at will, and U.S. bombers were devastating military-industrial targets in nightly raids. One incendiary attack on Tokyo killed eighty-four thousand people. A number of Far Eastern experts in the State Department, led by former ambassador to Japan Joseph Grew, argued that if the Allies would modify the doctrine of unconditional surrender and promise Japan that it could retain the institution of emperor, the government would surrender. Truman considered such a course but rejected it. The doctrine of unconditional surrender, announced by Churchill and Roosevelt in 1943, had wide political support in the United States and Britain, and there was no guarantee that if Emperor Hirohito and his heirs were declared sacrosanct, the military-dominated government would surrender. The closest Britain and the United States came to offering a negotiated settlement was the Potsdam Declaration issued at the Big Three meeting held in Germany in July 1945. The United Kingdom and the United States called upon Japan to surrender before total annihilation ensued. They promised not to dismember Japan or enslave the population, but they made no mention of the emperor. Tokyo did not even bother to respond.

The third means available to the new president for securing Tokyo's unconditional surrender was to traumatize Japan through utilization of the atomic bomb. Following a cabinet meeting on April 12, Secretary of War Stimson, in whose bailiwick the Manhattan Project fell, informed Truman of the existence of America's terrible new weapon. In late April the president asked Stimson to chair a special advisory body, subsequently dubbed the Interim Committee, to devise the best possible method for using the bomb to bring the war in the Far East to an end. The committee, which included Byrnes, Vannevar Bush, head of the Office of Scientific Research and Development, and Karl T. Compton, president of MIT, considered three options. Although they first thought of giving Japanese representatives a demonstration on some remote Pacific atoll, they rejected this scenario out of fear of a dud and because they believed that to the Japanese, Washington's unwillingness to use the bomb in combat would be a sign of weakness. The members next considered exploding an atomic device over a military-industrial target in Japan after first warning the Japanese so that they could evacuate noncombatants. Three considerations argued against this option. Once again the committee feared a technical failure. There were, moreover, some ten thousand American POWs in the home islands, and the authorities might well herd them into the blast site in an effort to ward off the attack. And finally, if the object of an atomic assault was to end the war through shock, then the more lives lost in the initial blast, the better. On June 6 Stimson informed Truman of the committee's recommendation: the United States should launch a surprise attack on "a vital war plant employing a large number of workers and closely surrounded by workers' houses."[85] The president subsequently approved this plan and, following the first successful detonation of an atomic device at the Alamogordo test site in New Mexico, ordered the War Department to select appropriate targets in Japan and drop one or more bombs at the first opportunity.

While the Truman administration struggled with the problem of how best to use the bomb to bring the Japanese to surrender, it simultaneously grappled with the question whether the United States should share atomic information with its Soviet ally or retain its monopoly and use the bomb to extract concessions from Moscow. During the course of the Manhattan Project, Washington had shown a marked reluctance to take not only Moscow but London into its confidence.

The Anglo-American partnership in atomic energy had been strained from the beginning. The threat of a German atomic bomb led to a hasty marriage of convenience in 1941 between British research and American resources. Britain had considered going it alone, but John Anderson (who would occupy wartime posts ranging from Lord Privy Seal to chancellor of the Exchequer) persuaded the cabinet to support a joint approach. Between October and December 1941 a consensus developed among those Americans concerned with the Manhattan Project that Britain should not automatically be made privy to atomic energy technology developed by the United States. James B. Conant, Vannevar Bush's deputy, listed three reasons for withholding information: the project had been transferred from scientific to military control; the United States was doing the lion's share of the development work; and security required absolute restriction of information distribution. Both Conant and Stimson believed that the British were primarily interested in atomic energy secrets for use on postwar industrial projects. In this context what right did Britain have to the fruits of American labor? On December 28, 1941, FDR had approved a policy of "restrictive interchange."[86]

When Truman entered office two agreements were in existence concerning the international control of atomic energy, both of them with Britain. At the first Quebec Conference, held in August 1943, Roosevelt and Churchill promised that neither the United States nor Britain would use the weapon against the other, or against the enemy without the other's consent, nor would either give atomic information without the other's consent to any third power. But cooperation in atomic diplomacy was hardly assured. The fifth point of the Anglo-American document signed at Quebec provided that information concerning all scientific research and development was to be shared, but that information concerning manufacturing know-how was to be communicated only if necessary to bring the Manhattan Project to a speedy culmination and if approved by a policy committee made up of three British and three U.S. members. Churchill had pressed Roosevelt to agree to complete pooling of information—including plant construction and weapons manufacture—but Bush, Conant, and General Leslie Groves, who officially headed the Manhattan Project, succeeded in maintaining the restrictive principle.[87] And in fact, Groves admitted that from the beginning he and his co-workers had shared as little information as possible with their British colleagues. Equally significant was the provision in the Quebec agreement that released the United States from any responsibility for sharing with Britain atomic information of economic value. "The British government recognizes that any postwar advantages of an industrial or commercial character shall be dealt with as between the United States and Great Britain on terms to be specified by the President of the United States," the joint communiqué read. "The Prime Minister expressly disclaims any interest in these industrial and commercial aspects beyond what may be considered by the President of the United States fair and just and in harmony with the economic welfare of the world."[88]

Not surprisingly, Churchill was uneasy with the concessions he had made, and he went to great lengths to keep them secret, especially from the Labour members of his government. The possibility of a political backlash once the Quebec agreements were published was real. Consequently, when Roosevelt and Churchill met at Hyde Park for further discussions following the second Quebec Conference in September 1944, the prime minister persuaded his host to sign a revised agreement, which read: "Full collaboration between the United States and the British Government in developing TUBE ALLOYS [the Anglo-American code name for atomic energy] for military and commercial purposes should continue after the defeat of Japan unless and until terminated by joint agreement."[89] But because American scientific and military personnel had not been collaborating and did not intend to do so, the Hyde Park document brought little change.

At Quebec and Hyde Park the president and the prime minister also confronted the issue of how the atomic bomb should be used to shape the postwar order. Anglo-America could use its possession of atomic secrets to initiate a diplomatic effort to work out a system for international control of atomic energy and weapons derived therefrom, or it could jealously guard its monopoly and wield it as a weapon if the Grand Alliance disintegrated. Churchill and Roosevelt chose the latter course. When Truman assumed office, the prevailing assumptions among Stimson and the other members of the Manhattan Project's top policy group were not only that the bomb would be put to military use if perfected before the war's end but that it would continue to be an Anglo-American secret, and that it constituted a prospective ace in the hole if East-West relations broke down during the latter stages of the war or afterward.[90]

In the wake of Harriman and the hard-liners' warnings about the Soviet-led "barbarian invasion" of Europe, the Kremlin's treatment of non-Communist Poles, and the exclusion of Westerners from the economic and political life of Bulgaria, Rumania, and other Soviet-occupied areas, Truman proved receptive to suggestions that he use the United States' atomic monopoly to make the Soviets more conciliatory. In May 1945 Stimson first suggested employment of the bomb as a bargaining counter in postwar negotiations with the Soviets; the president responded favorably. On May 28 Hopkins, then on a special mission to Moscow, cabled that there was reasonable expectation of compromise with the Soviets on outstanding problems and that, therefore, a summit conference was advisable. Truman proposed July 15, the latest estimated date for explosion of the first atomic device. According to one writer, by late May Stimson and Truman had decided that a fitting quid pro quo for taking the Soviet Union into the atomic partnership would be Western participation in the occupation of Poland, Rumania, Yugoslavia, and Manchuria, and meaningful non-Communist participation in the governments of those areas.[91]

There were those who argued to the foreign policy establishment that atomic threats would merely provoke intransigence from the Soviet Union and lead to more aggressive behavior. Chief among these was a group of atomic scientists working out of the University of Chicago and led by Leo Szilard and the famed Swedish physicist Niels Bohr. In May and June they objected that indiscriminate military use of the atomic bomb would undermine the possibility of achieving international control of atomic energy. The problem was to convince Stalin not that the atomic bomb was an unprecedented weapon that threatened the life of the world—his own nuclear physicists had undoubtedly alerted him to that fact—but that Anglo-America did not intend to wield it as a sword over his head. Stimson and Truman proved unwilling or unable to view an untried weapon as an effective diplomatic bargaining tool; on the contrary, they believed that its diplomatic value would grow out of its demonstrated military worth.

Between July 16 and July 21 reports on the successful test at Alamogordo reached the U.S. delegation at Potsdam, lifting spirits by heightening prospects for an early end to the war and for satisfactory agreements with the Soviets. After the plenary session on July 24, Truman "casually mentioned to Stalin" that the United States had "a new weapon of unusual destructive force."[92] The Soviet leader merely congratulated Truman and urged him to make good use of it against the Japanese. Clearly, if the Truman administration had even considered making a proposal to the Soviets at Potsdam on the international control of atomic energy, it had abandoned such a notion by the twenty-fourth. The record of talks between Soviet and Western diplomats contains no further mention of the bomb.

By July 23 the schedule for the atomic attack was settled. After consulting with Stimson and Byrnes, Truman gave the go-ahead for the specially trained B-29 crews of the 509th Composite Group to deliver the first bomb as soon after August 3 as weather permitted. By the time the Potsdam Conference convened and it became obvious that an atomic device would be available for use against the Japanese, the Truman administration had decided that Soviet participation in the last stages of the war in the Far East would be unnecessary and, indeed, counterproductive. U.S.

leaders hoped that the shock of the bomb would bring about a sudden Japanese surrender, averting a Soviet declaration of war and keeping Manchuria, the Kuriles, the southern half of Sakhalin, Outer Mongolia, and Port Arthur out of Communist hands. Such was not to be the case.

On August 6, 1945, the *Enola Gay* dropped a single atomic bomb that exploded two thousand feet above Hiroshima and instantly incinerated eighty-five thousand people. Two days later Ambassador Naotake Sato approached Molotov about the possibility of the Soviet Union's acting as a mediator between Japan and Anglo-America regarding peace negotiations, but he was told that a state of war would exist between Japan and the USSR the following day. Within two hours Soviet troops crossed the Manchurian border, and Russia thus became eligible to cash the Far Eastern check it had been issued at Yalta. On August 9 a second bomb was dropped, on Nagasaki, and Japan offered to surrender on condition that it be allowed to retain its imperial dynasty. Britain and the United States indirectly acceded to this request by declaring that Hirohito would be subject to the orders of the supreme commander of Allied occupation forces in Japan.[93]

Whether the demonstration of the atomic bomb or the refusal of the Western powers to put forward a proposal regarding the international control of atomic energy made the Soviet Union more or less pliable at Potsdam is probably unknowable. According to Nikita Khrushchev years afterward, the USSR had been spying on the Manhattan Project since 1941, and despite Stalin's bravado, he was scared to death at Potsdam. If so, Stalin gave no indication in either personal demeanor or negotiating posture.[94]

■ ■ ■ As a hedge against the failure of economic and atomic diplomacy, Washington belatedly embraced the notion of a rehabilitated Germany as a barrier to the intrusion of Soviet power into Central Europe. U.S. policy toward postwar Germany had been in a state of flux since Roosevelt's death. The army was initially prepared to implement JCS 1067, which incorporated Morgenthau's plan for dismemberment and pastoralization of the German economy.[95] But for a variety of reasons the State Department came to favor the quick rehabilitation of the Reich. Keeping Germany enfeebled and divided would perpetuate a power vacuum in Central Europe that, given Britain's weakness and the United States' determination to demobilize, the Soviets were sure to exploit. It was becoming increasingly apparent that the rehabilitation and hence stability of other war-torn Continental countries depended upon having the Ruhr and Saar operate at full capacity. Finally, if the Germans and their neighbors were not able to feed and clothe themselves, American taxpayers would more than likely have to assume the burden of doing so.

By the eve of Truman's departure for Potsdam, the military had swung to the State Department's position. Stimson asserted that he had never favored "repeating the mistakes" of Versailles and sowing the seeds of another war by crippling Germany economically. Partitioning Germany into several states would not break down "aggressive nationalism" there and "would tend to enlarge the field for the rivalries and political schemes of the European powers without compensating advantages," the joint chiefs advised the White House on June 26. They also recommended against internationalization of the Ruhr and Saar (the approach that JCS 1067 had substituted for the "dismantling" recommended by Morgenthau) because such a stratagem would eventually involve the UN, which event "could not but inject Russia into the affairs of Western Europe to an undesirable degree."[96] Truman proved responsive to his diplomatic and military advisers. In a conversation with State Department officials on May 10 he said that he "entirely disagreed" with Morgenthau's recommendation that synthetic oil plants in Germany be destroyed. Later he rebuked the Treasury secretary for wanting to dispense with legal procedures in meting out punishment to Nazi war criminals. Early in July, just before leaving for Potsdam, the president finally asked for Morgenthau's resignation. In his memoirs Truman claimed that he had always opposed the Morgenthau Plan.[97]

But the administration's decision to support rehabilitation made it imperative to work out a satisfactory agreement with the Soviet Union on reparations. If the Soviets were given free rein to take what they wanted, they would strip the industrialized areas of western Germany, producing the economic chaos that Washington wanted to avoid. But if the Soviets did not obtain a satisfactory settlement, they would cut off badly needed food shipments from their zone to the West, making it necessary for Britain and the United States to initiate a costly program to prevent starvation. That the USSR intended to use the leverage available quickly became apparent. On July 9 Marshal Georgi K. Zhukov notified his British and American colleagues on the Allied Control Council that they had to assume responsibility for feeding the German civilian populations in their respective areas. "Zhukov left no doubt that no resources east of the Oder-Neisse lines are available in the joint administration of German territory," reported America's political adviser in Germany.[98] Moreover, the Russians had already systematically stripped the areas under their control of heavy industry, railroad rolling stock, and agricultural implements, classifying this material as war booty rather than reparations.

Determined not to repeat the experience of the post–World War I era, Truman and Byrnes maintained a firm position on reparations throughout the Potsdam Conference. The final protocol provided that the reparations claims of each victor would be met by removals from the territory each occupied but that, in addition, the Soviets would receive from the Anglo-American zones 10 percent of "surplus" industrial capital equipment. The Soviets could collect an additional 15 percent of such equipment from the West in exchange for an equivalent value of food and raw materials from the Russian zone.

The British delegation saw eye-to-eye with Truman and his advisers on the German questions but quickly diverged over "enforcement" of the Declaration on Liberated Europe. It will be remembered that the British were of the opinion that Soviet security and ideological concerns were inextricably intertwined. The Kremlin, they had concluded, viewed capitalist nations as not only ideologically incompatible with Communist countries but overtly hostile to their very existence. In their search for friendly governments on their boundaries, which included potentially the entire world, Moscow would ally with and give aid to political elements that would inevitably be Communist. Moreover, the British came to Potsdam determined to reveal to the Americans the extent of Soviet ambitions and their techniques of expansion. As J. C. Donnelley of the Northern Department remarked: "The more intransigent they [the Soviets] are, the clearer it must be to the Americans that the Lippmann thesis is as absurd as it is dangerous."[99] Churchill believed that Yugoslavia was a good case in point. In Whitehall's view, Yugoslav leader Josef Broz Tito was a Kremlin puppet. Tito's occupation of Venezia Giulia, his claims to Fiume, Trieste, and areas in Greece and Austria, his suppression of criticism and opposition in areas under his control—all were tactics "too reminiscent of those of Hitler and Japan," Churchill wrote Truman.[100]

At the third meeting of the Big Three, Churchill brought up the Yugoslav situation in the context of the Declaration on Liberated Europe and insisted that the three powers act immediately and if necessary militarily. Stalin insisted that there was no proof of Tito's perfidy, and to Churchill's dismay Truman showed no interest in the matter. He had not come to Potsdam, Truman said, to judge matters that should eventually be decided by the UN. If they heard Tito, they would have to listen to Charles de Gaulle of France, Francisco Franco of Spain, and the others; he did not want to waste time listening to complaints. Churchill said that he wished to observe "with great respect" that the United States should be very interested in the carrying out of the Yalta agreement and that Potsdam was the place to hold the Soviets' feet to the fire.[101]

The Truman administration remained hopeful about Eastern Europe in general and Poland specifically and was angry with the British for trying to provoke a confrontation at Potsdam. In mid-June Harriman had held discussions with members of the Polish Lublin government whom Molotov had called to Moscow to talk about broadening their government. They expressed to the U.S. ambassador an almost "emotional" desire to include all political factions in the government and declared that Poland was in desperate need of massive economic aid from the United States. They complained bitterly that Britain was sponsoring and encouraging terrorist activities against them.[102] One British official saw great irony in all this. "Before the American election," he remarked, "we were popularly supposed to be more inclined than the Americans 'to sell the Poles down the river.' Now the tendency of American opinion is to want to make concessions to the Russians and to fear that we might cause difficulties by being less conciliatory."[103] As if to confirm this view, Truman, on the eve of the Potsdam Conference and after merely notifying Churchill of his purpose, recognized the new Polish government formed on the basis of the Hopkins-Stalin formula.[104]

Not surprisingly, the British at Potsdam showed themselves to be most concerned over their position in the eastern Mediterranean. They wanted simultaneously to keep the Soviets out of the area and to prevent a revival of Italian power that would threaten their transportation and communication lines running from the British Isles through the Suez to the Far East. The United States generally pursued a soft line toward Italy from 1943 on, moving quickly to restore authority first to Marshal Pietro Badoglio and King Umberto and then to the government of Ivanoe Bonomi. American officials argued that Italy ought to be rewarded for its military effort against the Germans and its furnishing of facilities and supplies for prosecution of the war against the Japanese, and consequently the U.S. delegation advocated the return of Libya and other areas to Italian control. The British, while supporting the non-Communist Badoglio, favored a harsher policy and in particular wanted Italy stripped of its colonies. At Potsdam Truman proposed that in view of Italy's recent declaration of war on Japan, the Big Three support Italian entry into the UN. Churchill refused, declaring that it had been Italy that had stabbed Britain and France in the back in 1940. No action was taken.[105]

Sensing an opportunity to take advantage of the rift between its Western allies, the Soviet Union pressed for a series of concessions in areas of critical strategic importance: the Dodecanese Islands, the disposition of the Italian colonies, control of the Turkish straits, and the continued presence of British troops in Greece. Specifically, the Soviets demanded a share in the administration of the Italian colonies and the right to build bases in the vicinity of the straits and in northeast Turkey.[106] At the same time they showed little interest in evacuating Iran. Britain wanted to exclude the Soviets in every case. According to Cadogan, "If we were to talk generously to the Russians this time about access to the wider oceans, I fear that they would only regard it as an indication that we had not been shocked by their demands on Turkey, and would proceed to make more and more demands on Persia and on other countries in the Middle East."[107] U.S. support for a common Anglo-American front against the Soviet Union over these points was almost completely lacking. In the end the Big Three agreed to the establishment of a Council of Foreign Ministers that would try to come to grips with these problems and would begin work on peace treaties with the former Axis allies.[108]

Though they had not realized all their goals, the Soviets emerged from the Potsdam Conference in a relatively optimistic frame of mind. The meeting ended with a series of specific deals. "Horse trading," to use Jimmy Byrnes's term, was a favorite Soviet device; Stalin and his negotiators had long been frustrated by the U.S. preference for moral and legal arguments. Stalin's chosen modus operandi was to lull the West with dreams of markets both in Germany and the USSR and with the prospect of peaceful coexistence. All the while he would consolidate his position in areas occupied by the Red Army and press his divided and confused adversary for military and economic concessions in areas not under the direct control of the Soviet military.[109]

U.S. officials left Germany with ambivalent feelings regarding the possibility of future cooperation with the Soviets. Davies was pessimistic, not because he believed that the Soviets were intractable and uncooperative, but because American hard-liners were getting closer to the president. "The whole entourage" at Potsdam, he lamented, was "highly critical" of the Soviet Union, and this mood had apparently affected even Stimson.[110] Davies was right. Stalin, Stimson warned Truman, wanted too much in return for entering the war against Japan. If his demands were met, the Bear would control Manchuria and close the door in China. Others who mistrusted Moscow were cheered by the conference. Leahy and General Lucius D. Clay applauded Truman's "toughness" regarding Germany and predicted that it would pay dividends in the form of East-West understandings in Central Europe. Byrnes was ambivalent. At one point he declared that the concessions reflected the realities of the situation in Europe and that the "horse trades" he had made on reparations and Poland would encourage further compromise. But to another confidant he was pessimistic. Somebody had made "an awful mistake" in permitting the USSR to emerge from the war with as much power as it wielded, and he expressed fear that there was too much difference in the ideologies of the United States and the Soviet Union to work out a long-term program of cooperation.[111]

Truman chose to be optimistic. Public opinion polls before the conference indicated that the American people thought Big Three cooperation was deteriorating at an alarming rate but that they very much wanted the Grand Alliance to continue. Truman found Stalin frustrating to deal with but manageable: "Stalin is as near like [Kansas City political boss] Tom Pendergast as any man I know," he said.[112] The president had not sided with the British, whom he regarded as openly provocative, and he had left the door open for compromise on virtually all issues. Despite the Kremlin's failure to respond to the implied threat of the atomic monopoly and the incentive of a postwar credit, the Truman administration's policy of mediation remained intact.

■ ■ ■ CHAPTER THREE

Walking the Tightrope

James F. Byrnes and the Diplomacy of the Middle Way

In July 1945 British voters went to the polls and by an overwhelming margin turned Winston Churchill out of office, electing a new Labour government. The election had remarkably little effect on British foreign policy, however. The party's center, composed of Prime Minister Clement Attlee, Foreign Secretary Ernest Bevin, and Chancellor of the Exchequer Hugh Dalton, proved to be as committed as any Tory government to the preservation of British strategic and economic interests. Alarmed by the rapid advance of the Red Army through Eastern Europe and by the police-state atmosphere in the Soviet Union, the Attlee government readily acknowledged the need to use the United States to redress the rapidly shifting balance of power in Europe. The new regime's determination to cling to its colonies and spheres of influence and to resist Soviet expansion served only to further stimulate Anglophobia in the United States and to confirm the Truman administration's conviction that steering a middle course between the United Kingdom and the USSR was the proper policy. Despite mounting suspicion of the Soviet Union within Congress and among certain members of the foreign policy establishment, the White House consistently declined to identify the United States' interests with those of Great Britain and to assume a confrontational posture toward the Soviets. Truman and Byrnes considered themselves consummate political brokers who could work out a deal that would satisfy the principals involved. Washington's determination to adhere to its tripod approach was brought home painfully to the British in 1945 by the Truman administration's refusal to form a common front against the Soviet Union at the

London and Moscow foreign ministers' meetings and by its decision to withhold atomic information not only from Moscow but from London as well.

■ ■ ■ British foreign policy was in shambles by late July 1945. Whitehall had goals both general and specific, but insufficient power to realize them. Britain was willing to take up sword and buckler against the Soviet menace to Western civilization, but its American steed kept trying to gallop off in the opposite direction. Russian intransigence at Potsdam triggered feelings of uneasiness in the minds of American officials, but their misgivings did not produce a stampede toward making common cause with the United Kingdom. The British found the meeting both disheartening and galling. Not only had the Americans refused to join them in confronting Stalin, they had held themselves condescendingly aloof from their Western partners in the Grand Alliance. Attlee, who accompanied Churchill and replaced him as head of the British delegation in mid-conference when the results of the general election became known, observed that U.S. officials were "inclined to think of Russia and America as two big boys who could settle things amicably between them." Foreign Office officials complained that their American counterparts presented them with proposals on a take-it-or-leave-it basis. One analyst remarked that the Americans were now in "one of their more irritating cockahoop moods."[1] In the week following Truman's return from Germany, Halifax reported that the idea was steadily gaining ground in the United States that Britain had come to occupy a position on the world stage distinctly inferior to those of its two major allies. Many Americans, conscious of the past quantities of lend-lease aid which had been shipped to the United Kingdom, had come to the conclusion that the former mother country was now dependent on its offspring for survival. Given that Americans historically were wont to equate material abundance with moral rectitude, relations with the United States were likely to be rockier in the future than in the past.

Confusion and uncertainty in British foreign policy in 1945 was a product not only of its ebbing power and its increasing despondency over an erratic United States, but also of the disintegration of the wartime coalition. Sizable segments of the British population had been dissatisfied with the patchwork government Churchill had put together. Its inability or unwillingness to address social and economic issues—a major achievement rather than a failure in Churchill's mind—rankled particularly with both blue- and white-collar Britons. What influence the Conservative party enjoyed by 1945 stemmed from its traditions and identification with the empire, its entrenched wealth and power, and Churchill as the embodiment of the coming victory. The right honorable member from Woodford had been able to establish by means of his broadcast addresses a remarkable degree of rapport with public opinion during the war. As a London tenant remarked to his housing manager during the Battle of Britain, Churchill "takes such an interest in the war doesn't he?"[2] What Americans seemed utterly unaware of was that few Britons considered Churchill an appropriate peacetime leader. He was perceived as insensitive to the social needs of the working class and ignorant of the complex economic and financial questions that would confront the nation in the postwar period.

By the opening months of 1945 all parties were busy preparing for the electoral contest that everyone expected would follow the defeat of Germany. Nevertheless, the sudden end of the war in Europe took many in British ruling circles by surprise. Churchill himself wished to postpone dissolution of the government until some eighteen months after the fall of Germany. He came under strong pressure from influential colleagues such as Beaverbrook, however, for a quick election that would take maximum advantage of his electoral appeal as the nation's great wartime leader. The prime minister overcame his doubts and offered the Labour party the choice of a July poll or continuance of the coalition until after the defeat of Japan. Attlee carefully put the pros and cons of these alternatives to Labour's National Executive Committee on May 19. It unequivocally instructed him to demand in return either an immediate end to the coalition or an October election. The latter course was unacceptable to the Conservatives, and on May 23 Churchill drove to Buckingham Palace and submitted his resignation. The election was set for July 5.[3]

In the ensuing campaign, Labour bested the opposition in both content and style. Whereas Labour promised housing, full employment, social security, and a comprehensive health service, the Conservatives dwelt on the "stark realism" of the present and tried to portray their opponents as hopeless visionaries. Party spokesmen accepted full employment and the Beveridge report while emphasizing the virtues of private enterprise. But the Conservatives relied too heavily on the personal stature of Churchill and the socialist bogey. In one famous address the prime minister confirmed the suspicions of many Britons that he was still, underneath the garb of wartime leader, an intemperate reactionary: he predicted that a Labour victory would usher in an era of totalitarianism with the prominent left-wing Labour leader Harold Laski as head of a British Gestapo. As one writer has put it: "The electors cheered Churchill but voted against him."[4]

Churchill and Attlee returned to London from Potsdam for the announcement of the election results. (Collection and tabulation of the soldier vote had required almost three weeks.) By midday on July 25 a Labour majority was assured, and Attlee set about forming a new government. Observers waited anxiously to see who his chief lieutenants were going to be. The leader of the party and Churchill's former deputy was not a charismatic man. "He remained ill-at-ease on the platform and in Parliament," one historian has said of him, "often giving an exhibition of feebleness or reducing great matters to the most meager aspect."[5] Attlee first offered the Foreign Office to Hugh Dalton, Labour economist and past president of the Board of Trade, but then changed his mind, giving foreign affairs to Ernest Bevin and offering the Exchequer to a disappointed Dalton. These three, together with Herbert Morrison, who became leader of the House of Commons, and Sir Stafford Cripps, who assumed Dalton's old post at the Board of Trade, constituted the inner circle that would rule Britain from 1945 to 1951.[6]

Attlee told Dalton that the principal reason he had changed his mind about the Foreign Office was the necessity of keeping apart Bevin and Morrison, who were bitter personal and political enemies. If one was concerned with the domestic scene and the other with foreign affairs, they would be less likely to be at each other's throats. But Dalton believed that Churchill had interceded with Attlee on July 26 and persuaded him to give the Foreign Office to Bevin.[7] The implication was that the tough-minded, pragmatic Bevin would be most likely to deal strongly with the Soviets and protect traditional British interests in the eastern Mediterranean and elsewhere, even if that meant utilizing balance-of-power tactics. And in fact, the careerists in the Foreign Office were much reassured by Bevin's appointment. "He's broadminded and sensible, honest and courageous," Alexander Cadogan remarked, "—the heavyweight of the Cabinet."[8] Bevin not only kept Cadogan on as undersecretary but retained Orme Sargent as well. Some of Bevin's antiestablishment colleagues complained at year's end that he had become very much devoted to the "Career Diplomat" and all the "Old Boys" in the Foreign Office.[9]

Attlee gave Bevin a free hand in foreign affairs, intervening only on specific issues and when the former Transport and General Workers Union leader needed support in the cabinet. As the prime minister put it: "When you've got a good dog, you don't bark yourself."[10] Bevin stood in sharp contrast to his elegant, well-educated predecessor, Anthony Eden. A short, fat man with a broad nose and thick lips, Bevin wore a perennially rumpled suit, and his speech was blunt and uncultivated. Rather than being a compromiser or bridge builder, he was a fighter. "Bevin did nothing to placate his critics," notes his principal biographer. "When he fought, he fought hard and to win. Conciliation was not in his nature, he was a 'good hater', as the *Express* said."[11] Increasingly, Bevin focused his formidable capacity for confrontation on the Soviets. Phrases like "resistance to aggression" began to appear in his speeches. He met Soviet intransigence with uncompromising logic of his own. His realism in dealing with the Soviets and protecting British interests was the product of years of experience at trade union negotiating sessions, of his fight against Communist infiltration of the trade union movement, of his intimate association with Churchill and the wartime coalition government, of his patriotism, and of a strong sense of where his country's interests lay. He was, declared one Soviet observer of British affairs scornfully, a member of the English "labor aristocracy." At the Labour party conference held in Blackpool in May 1945, Bevin told his fellow delegates: "Domestic revolutions do not change geography and revolutions do not change geographical needs."[12] Bevin reiterated his position that even though Germany could not be allowed to retain its war-making potential, sixty to eighty million Germans could not go hungry. He agreed with his colleagues that the Soviet Union had behaved in a "perfectly bloody way" at San Francisco.[13]

Bevin proved much more successful in manipulating the United States than had his predecessors.[14] Churchill later insisted that he would have broken up the Potsdam Conference before accepting the Byrnes-Molotov compromise, but his claim rings hollow. Britain's only sensible policy—as Attlee, Bevin, and Churchill knew—was to put Britain's complaints on record and then get back in step with the Americans. With one major exception (Israel), Bevin never strayed from that principle. Moreover, he believed even more than Churchill that it was essential to confront the Soviet Union—and to lead the United States into doing the same thing. Most important, he realized that unless Whitehall acted within the context of the United Nations, such a policy might rouse latent Anglophobia and isolationism within the United States. The Labour victory in 1945 had done much to dispel fears among American liberals concerning British imperialism and power politics.[15] But suspicion that Britain was ever ready to use the United States as a cat's-paw still lingered. Under Bevin, Britain became an enthusiastic participant in the UN, and his tirades there against Soviet totalitarianism and expansion had a telling effect in the United States.[16]

■ ■ ■ If any doubt existed within the new Labour government that Washington intended to pursue an independent course in world affairs, it was quickly dispelled when London attempted to influence the Truman administration's policy on atomic energy. Whereas Churchill saw an exclusive Anglo-American partnership as a key to maintaining economic and military power in the postwar world, Attlee and Bevin were more inclined toward a sharing of atomic information and the establishment of a system of international control of fissionable materials and weapons. The Labour government's stance on atomic energy was a reflection both of its belief that the bomb must be eliminated from international politics and of its fear that the United States intended to monopolize all aspects of atomic energy to the exclusion of not only the USSR but Britain as well. Leaders of the Labour party found out about the Quebec agreement of 1943 in late July after they assumed office. Military and strategic considerations aside, sputtered Dalton, "this astonishing sell out puts it in the power of the United States to refuse us any rights in the industrial application of atomic energy."[17] Despite the Hyde Park agreement, the Attlee government's ongoing suspicions of a conspiracy to maintain American atomic hegemony were well founded. The Truman administration proved unwilling to share atomic information with the Kremlin but at the same time, in conformity to the policy of mediation, opted for a unilateral rather than Anglo-American monopoly on atomic bombs, materials, and technology.

As World War II drew to a close in 1945, two alternatives were available to Washington concerning atomic energy: the United States could retain its monopoly over the bomb, including fissionable materials and technological know-how, for as long as possible; or it could turn over its weapons, uranium, and "secrets" to an international authority on the condition that future nuclear powers do the same. Because scientists advised that the U.S. monopoly would be temporary, the first approach threatened to precipitate a dangerous armaments race with the Soviet Union. Whereas international control might avoid such a contest, it would entrust atomic energy to a body in which Moscow would more than likely have the power of absolute veto.[18] The White House never considered forming an atomic consortium directly with the Soviets; as far as Truman was concerned it was either international control or monopoly. If the United States could appear to be internationalizing the bomb while retaining its monopoly, so much the better.

The Truman foreign policy establishment was at first polarized over how best to control atomic information and weapons. Stimson, supported by Vannevar Bush and other atomic scientists, favored an agreement with the Soviet Union that would halt work on bomb construction, impound existing weapons, and pledge the two powers not to use atomic energy for military purposes. At his last cabinet meeting in late September, the secretary of war even went so far as to argue for a direct approach to the Soviets, stressing that a distinction could be made between disclosures of basic scientific information concerning atomic energy and the technical secrets regarding the bomb. There would be no harm in sharing both, the former freely and the latter in return for concessions, Stimson insisted, because the Soviets would soon catch up in both areas. At that point there would be no secret to give away. Forrestal, the joint chiefs, and General Groves took the position that not only should the United States withhold information from the Soviet Union, it should also retain its freedom of action by continuing production and hoarding existing weapons. Byrnes argued that the United States ought to retain its monopoly, temporary though it might be, in order to gain immediate negotiating leverage with the Soviets.[19]

On October 8, 1945, Truman made his first comprehensive statement regarding atomic policy at Linda Lodge on Reelfoot Lake, near Tiptonville, Tennessee. In essence, he confirmed his adherence to a policy of exclusivity. The president distinguished among three types of secrets: (1) scientific knowledge, which was already widely known; (2) "know-how" or engineering secrets that the United States had but Britain might develop shortly; and (3) a combination of industrial capacity and resources, which the United States alone enjoyed and without which the first two types of knowledge were useless. Therefore, he implied, it was pointless to share information with anyone. In taking this position Truman ignored the advice of atomic scientists who indicated that the USSR could build a bomb within five years and instead accepted the counsel of Leslie Groves, who insisted that the Soviets had no uranium and that the United States' atomic monopoly would last two decades. Early in the war Groves had launched a clandestine operation, the Murray Hill project, to corner the world market on uranium and plutonium. By late 1945 he could report that the United States controlled directly or indirectly 90 percent of the world's fissionable materials.[20]

Despite the Murray Hill project and the fact that the United States was the only nation to have exploded an atomic device, the U.S. nuclear monopoly proved to be fragile and temporary. On September 30, 1945, Canadian Prime Minister William L. Mackenzie King informed Washington that his country's intelligence operatives had uncovered an elaborate Soviet espionage network that had transmitted an undetermined amount of information about the atomic bomb to the Soviet Union. Apparently in response to these revelations, Truman on October 3 told Congress that he was committed to the principle of international control. He announced that he would meet soon with Canadian and British leaders, and later on with other nations, in an attempt to work out an agreement among all actual and potential atomic powers to renounce the use of the bomb for military purposes.[21]

Congress's reaction to this announcement was overwhelmingly negative. The creation of the Special Senate Committee on Atomic Energy in October 1945 made clear that this was one field in which Congress intended to influence policy. Most legislators had reacted initially to news of the atomic bomb by insisting that the United States should not share the "secret." Such diverse figures as Tom Connally of Texas, Arthur Capper of Kansas, and Harold Knutson of Minnesota, as well as the ambitious Arthur H. Vandenberg of Michigan, called for retention of the atomic monopoly. Congressional fears that the Truman administration might share doomsday information with the Kremlin had reached near hysterical proportions on September 22 in response to newspaper accounts of the previous day's cabinet meeting, at which Secretary of Commerce Henry Wallace reportedly advocated such a course of action—the meeting in which Groves and Byrnes had taken a hard line.

Though Truman and Wallace denied it, the secretary of commerce had indeed argued for a full sharing of information and matériel with the Soviets. By the fall of 1945 Wallace was convinced that a conspiracy existed within the military-industrial complex to monopolize atomic information or, as he told Harold Ickes, that "a certain small group of industrialists, who in turn work very closely with the War Department, are trying the atomic energy thing in their own way."[22] At the cabinet meeting on September 21 when Stimson and other officials had staked out their positions, Wallace had lobbied for an immediate end to the American monopoly. The USSR had traditionally been the United States' friend, he said; the Soviets had nothing the Americans wanted, and the Americans had nothing the Soviets wanted. News accounts that were widely cited in Congress linked this attitude almost exclusively with Wallace's name. But Stimson, backed by his deputy, Robert Patterson, had taken almost exactly the same position. So had Dean Acheson, who was acting secretary and already on his way toward winning Truman's confidence.[23]

Advocates of an absolute and permanent U.S. monopoly on the bomb, such as Forrestal, Groves, and the new secretary of the Treasury, Fred Vinson, knew that if they linked internationalization exclusively with Wallace, the increasingly conservative Congress would opt for a policy of unilateralism. And they were right. A quickly arranged telegraph poll of congressmen taken the week following the cabinet meeting indicated that fifty-five of sixty-one responding senators opposed sharing knowledge of the bomb with any country. Two public opinion polls taken in August and November indicated that 70 percent of the public opposed turning over nuclear weapons to the United Nations.[24]

Truman's October 3 speech promising international control of atomic energy not only antagonized Congress but also failed to allay fears in Britain among press, public, and members of the Labour government that the United States intended to retain a monopoly over atomic weaponry and use that control indiscriminately and unilaterally. Although Halifax reported from Washington that "the bomb is doing more than Pearl Harbor to obliterate the last vestiges of the isolationist dream," he also warned that American nationalists were insisting that the United States retain the secret of the bomb in order to make other nations, especially the Soviet Union, behave.[25] Popular criticism of the administration's anticipated atomic diplomacy stemmed primarily from fear that a cataclysmic war with the Soviet Union might be the result. Whitehall was also worried about Armageddon, but in addition resented the United States' refusal to share atomic secrets fully with Britain for either military or commercial applications.

The bombings of Hiroshima and Nagasaki transformed atomic energy into a burning issue in Britain and riveted the Attlee government's attention. London officials were disappointed and angered by indications that the Truman administration had no intention of sharing with the United Kingdom a proficiency that had been acquired with the help of British scientists and research facilities. In October the British decided to set up their own atomic research plant at Harwell—in effect, a move to manufacture their own bomb. This declaration of nuclear independence was the result of a combination of security and prestige considerations, as well as sheer bureaucratic momentum. London still craved U.S. expertise, however, because it would make Britain's task easier and less expensive.[26]

Between August and September 1945 public and parliamentary pressure intensified on the Attlee government to define its atomic policy and to force the United States both to share knowledge about peacetime uses of atomic energy and to internationalize the bomb. "The explosion of the atomic bomb," declared one Labour MP, "had bludgeoned our imagination and bruised our souls."[27] Nearly all leading newspapers and weekly magazines adopted the view that atomic energy must be regarded as all humanity's heritage and that any temporary strategic advantage that might be gained by withholding the secret for the next few years would be more than offset by the antagonism this approach would arouse in Moscow. An editorial in the *Times* of London declared that the bomb should be, as Truman said in his speech, a "sacred trust," but cautioned that "it seems difficult to resist the conclusion that the United Nations Organization and its Security Council is in the end the right and natural repository and administrator of this tract."[28]

As a result of public pressure and his own concern, Attlee pressed Truman for a summit meeting on atomic policy. The day after Japan surrendered, the prime minister wrote Truman and suggested that the two heads of government issue directives to their respective officials to collaborate with each other on atomic energy matters in both military and commercial fields.[29] Receiving no meaningful response from Washington, Attlee wrote again a month later. He argued that although scientific and technical knowledge concerning nuclear fission was then confined to the United States and Britain, and the actual capacity for the production of atomic bombs to the United States, the very speed and success of the Manhattan Project meant that other countries with the necessary scientific and industrial resources could produce nuclear weapons in a matter of years. London and Washington had "gone a long way in securing control of" known sources of uranium and thorium, but new sources were coming to light all the time. Thus the United States' lead was temporary, its advantage feeble. It was imperative to begin developing an international control policy to head off an arms race. "Am I to plan for a peaceful or warlike world?" he asked Truman. Am I to "direct all our people to live like troglodytes underground as being the only hope of survival?"[30] Three days later Truman agreed on the need to consult but made no specific suggestions. In October Attlee complained that he was being subjected to heavy parliamentary pressure and could not put off demands for a policy statement much longer. "I need hardly say that I am prepared to come over as soon as convenient," he pled.[31]

The first concern of the Attlee government had been to persuade Washington to cut Britain in on America's military and commercial monopoly, but by November the prime minister's overriding preoccupation was the establishment of a plan for the international control of atomic energy. That goal reflected not only general fear of a nuclear holocaust but also a specific suspicion that the Soviet Union had either a nuclear device or the immediate capacity to produce one. More important than the Canadian spy case in creating this impression was an encounter Bevin had with Molotov in the hall of the Soviet embassy in London. Molotov, who had just downed several toasts, suddenly said to Bevin, "Here's to the Atom Bomb," and then added, "We've got it." One of his aides quickly led him away, but deliberately or not, the impression had been created. A few days later Dalton, Bevin, and other members of the Labour government huddled and agreed that the best course was to "tell the Russians all we know."[32]

Truman finally agreed to meet with Attlee and MacKenzie King on November 16 in Washington. By the time the three leaders sat down together the president was struggling to prevent Congress from seizing control of atomic energy policy and thus, among other things, tying his hands in dealing with the Soviets. With nationalism and Russophobia on the rise among the tribunes of the people, the president would not agree to Britain and Canada's demand that he either share atomic information directly with the Soviets or implement a plan for internationalization of atomic energy. But to gain British acquiescence on this point, Truman was willing to sign a pledge to share all atomic information, military or commercial, with the United Kingdom. On November 15 the three statesmen released a joint declaration announcing that they intended to keep detailed knowledge regarding the practical application of atomic energy to themselves and proposing the establishment of a UN commission to examine the problem in detail. The next day Truman, Attlee, and King signed a memo calling for "full and effective cooperation in the field of atomic energy" among the three nations.[33] No condition or reservation marred the terse communiqué; Attlee left Washington momentarily reassured that all difficulties in the way of collaboration had been removed and that his breaking of the American monopoly on atomic energy would placate Parliament. But, of course, his victory was illusory. The United States retained sole possession of the world's stock of atomic devices and a monopoly on the means to produce them.

The Truman administration's atomic diplomacy reflected a determination to pursue a foreign policy independent of Great Britain, to exert silent pressure on the Soviet Union, and to prevent U.S. foreign policy from becoming a prisoner of congressional opinion. Although Truman, by agreeing to pool atomic information with the British and the Canadians, had avoided direct provocation of Congress over the issue of sharing this same information with the Soviets, his deal with Attlee did nothing to halt the resurgent drive in the legislative branch to assert itself in foreign affairs.

■ ■ ■ By the fall of 1945 Congress, prompted by resentment at having been continually bypassed by FDR during the war, by real fear of Soviet imperialism, and by the GOP's desire to make political hay out of the Cold War, began to exert a major influence on foreign policy. In so doing, it sharply limited the Truman administration's freedom of action on both the atomic energy issue and the matter of a loan to the Soviet Union. More ominously, it was one of a number of factors that started the United States down the road toward a policy of confrontation with the Kremlin.

Soviet behavior in Eastern Europe had alienated many Americans, as had the uncompromising position of Soviet negotiators at San Francisco and Potsdam. The House Committee on Un-American Activities appeared to have died a timely death when its chairman and creator, Martin Dies of Texas, decided not to stand for reelection in 1944. But when Congress met in early January 1945, John E. Rankin of Mississippi succeeded in turning HUAC into a permanent standing committee of the House with broad investigative powers. In September it began its first postwar probe of American Communism. Shortly after V-E Day several other congressional committees began clamoring for the opportunity to evaluate Russian-American relations by visiting the Soviet Union.

One of these, composed of seven members of the House Select Committee on Postwar Economic Policy and Planning, toured the Soviet Union and thirteen other European countries in an effort to decide whether the United States should make postwar loans to foreign governments. On September 14, 1945, this delegation, led by committee chairman William M. Colmer of Mississippi, arranged an interview with Stalin. Colmer told the Soviet leader that he and his colleagues knew about the USSR's application for a $6 billion postwar loan from the United States and wanted to know what uses were to be made of the money, how repayment was to be made, and what concessions the United States could expect in return. Stalin acknowledged the request but said that Washington had never responded. The loan, he said, would be used to purchase American industrial equipment that Russia needed for reconstruction and would be repaid with exports of gold and raw materials. Surely the Soviet Union was a better credit risk than China or other nations to which the United States was considering loaning money, Stalin told the congressmen. But his explanations and arguments fell on deaf ears. The Americans were appalled by the police-state atmosphere they found in the USSR and by the fear of Soviet domination they uncovered in Eastern Europe. Colmer subsequently told Byrnes and Truman that the Kremlin was in "desperate haste to build up a system so powerful that it could support the flood of the Red Army and pour [it out] in the very near future." The United States, he declared, should end its "policy of appeasement."[34] The Colmer committee proved willing to endorse an American loan to Russia, but only if the Soviet Union met certain conditions, namely, reform of its internal system of government and abandonment of the sphere of influence it was constructing in Eastern Europe.

Congressional intrusion into atomic energy and economic policy resulted not just from Russophobia but also from the GOP's effort to offer an alternative to the Democrats in foreign policy. In searching for an option that it could sell to the American people and thus use to recapture the White House, the Republican party could not simply restate its traditional positions. Fiscal conservatism and economic nationalism, if properly masked, were in vogue, but political and military isolationism were not. If the American people were opposed to the permanent stationing of U.S. troops overseas, they were not averse to participating in a collective security organization. Vandenberg, Taft, and their colleagues were not ready to embrace military intervention, and certainly not Wilsonian internationalism. They could, however, rail at the menace of world Communist revolution and Soviet imperialism, portraying the Roosevelt-Truman administration as appeasers, and in the process appear to offer an alternative to Truman's tripod or mediation approach without alienating their conservative, isolationist constituents. Anti-Communism was the only kind of internationalism that conservative Republicans would buy because it was the only kind they could sell.[35]

Joining Congress in demanding a more intransigent policy toward the USSR in the fall of 1945 were planners in the U.S. defense establishment who embraced strategic deterrence as America's optimum defensive technique in the postwar era and who targeted the Soviet Union as the most likely threat to American security. U.S. military leaders reached speedy agreement on a strategy for postwar America when the joint chiefs and the service secretaries approved JCS 1496 and JCS 1518, respectively. Although the joint chiefs advocated the conventional goals of protecting the territorial integrity of the United States and its possessions, and enhancing the country's political, economic, and social well-being, they also defined a more ambitious aim, one not hitherto assumed: "the maintenance of world peace, under conditions which insure the security, well-being and advancement of our country."[36] This new role, coupled with advances in military technology, presented unique problems. Not only had the modern airplane and warship rendered America's geographical defenses obsolete, but there was an absence of strong allies to absorb the first blows of an aggressor. Recognizing the decisive role the United States had played in the first two world wars, any future enemy would not give it the time to mobilize its forces and productive capacity; the United States would be attacked first. The only counter available was for the United States to maintain an overwhelming deterrent force and to make plans for preventive war. In view of the military's ebbing confidence in the UN as a peace-keeping force, the joint chiefs' recommendation amounted to nothing less than a call for the United States to become the world's policeman and peacemaker.

At the same time, Army Intelligence, G-2, was drawing analogies between the Soviet Union's current policy and that of Germany in the 1930s. Both operated as totalitarian regimes, engaged in propaganda and subversion, and maintained a closed economy. Both also made temporary deals with their enemies to gain time—the Germans through the Nazi-

Soviet Pact in 1939, the Soviets by adhering to the UN Charter. And each shared the common goal of European domination.[37] Thus a facile equation between Nazism and Stalinism made the USSR appear to military intelligence to be an ominous threat and fostered an expectation that history would repeat itself in the form of a Soviet bid for Continental or world domination.[38]

Pressure from the defense establishment and Congress seemed to the Truman administration to point toward a firmer Soviet policy. But at the same time Congress and the American people were reluctant to pay the price—emotional and financial—for the policy of strategic deterrence envisioned by the joint chiefs. One of the requirements for implementation of their far-reaching plans was universal military service. But the United States was tired of arms and uniforms, of separations and the threat of sudden death. In the first year after V-J Day America's twelve-million-man military force shrank to less than three million. In October 1945 Truman called for the continuation of selective service and the institution of universal military training. Both proposals aroused strong opposition in a nation that had never known permanent conscription in peacetime. Moreover, with the war over many Americans hoped for relief from the burden of taxation required by a large military program. Congress, particularly its isolationist Republican members, reflected popular opinion; like the Republicans before the War of 1812, they simultaneously advocated frugality and confrontation with a powerful and dangerous enemy. Perhaps they believed that a continuation of the American monopoly on atomic energy would be enough. But judging from the London and Moscow foreign ministers' meetings in September and December respectively, the Soviet Union was no more willing to respond to atomic diplomacy than it had been at Potsdam.

■ ■ ■ Truman was vitally interested in foreign affairs, but he had no intention of being his own secretary of state. Unfortunately, he had filled that post with a man who duplicated rather than complemented his strengths and weaknesses: wisdom and experience in political and domestic matters but ignorance and inexperience in foreign affairs. Moreover, Jimmy Byrnes was a politician with an immense ego who came to the State Department with something to prove. He rather than Truman should have been sitting in the White House, Byrnes felt, and if FDR had not unfairly passed him over for the vice-presidency in 1944, he would have been. The South Carolinian, in short, was determined to be his own man as secretary of state and, indeed, the chief architect of U.S. foreign policy. As John Carter Vincent, one of the State Department's China experts, told B. E. F. Gage, the new head of the North American Department in the Foreign Office, it was Byrnes and not the department heads who made policy. In a now famous incident at the London meeting, the new secretary came across Theodore Achilles typing a report to be sent back to the department and asked, "What's this?" When Achilles explained, Byrnes exclaimed, "God Almighty, I might tell the President sometime what happened, but I'm never going to tell those little bastards at the State Department anything about it."[39]

Adding to Byrnes's problems as secretary of state was a misunderstanding between him and Truman over how much the South Carolinian knew about FDR's foreign policies. The president thought his new appointee was bright and honest, his only fault being a tendency "to look for hidden motives behind everything he was told." Truman later recalled that he had appointed Byrnes because Stettinius lacked ideas and because Byrnes had been cruelly treated by Roosevelt. But there was another reason. Roosevelt had pointedly taken Byrnes to Yalta. Truman, thinking Byrnes was privy to the various conferences and strategy sessions there, named him secretary in hopes of bringing some continuity and expertise to foreign policymaking. But as Byrnes's notes indicate, he was allowed to attend only those meetings that Roosevelt wished Congress and the public to hear about. Byrnes led everyone to believe that he knew more than he did. His ignorance also led him to portray the Yalta accords in a more favorable light than they deserved. When the truth emerged and the president began to uncover the nuances of the agreements, the revelation embarrassed both men and strained their relationship.[40]

Though Byrnes was committed to seeing that the Soviet Union lived up to the Yalta accords in regard to Eastern Europe—that is, that occupation authorities there permitted free elections and free access by Westerners—he was not a hard-liner. He was determined to be independent of the military and those who had influenced Roosevelt during his last days in the presidency and Truman during his first. In early August he remarked to a subordinate that Admiral Leahy still thought he was acting secretary of state, as he had been under FDR, but that he, Byrnes, would show him differently. The new secretary was also a close friend of Joseph E. Davies, former ambassador to the Soviet Union and champion of the policy of mediation. For Byrnes, diplomacy, like politics, was more process than substance. Diplomacy consisted of identifying respective positions and then negotiating a compromise. And like Roosevelt, Byrnes believed in personal diplomacy: Soviet-American differences could be worked out through dialogue between him and Molotov or him and Stalin. Unfortunately, Byrnes had no better luck than FDR with this approach.

The avowed purpose of the London Foreign Ministers' Conference, which was attended by representatives from the USSR, the United States, France, China, and Britain, was to draw up peace treaties for Germany's wartime allies: Finland, Hungary, Rumania, and Bulgaria. Moscow seemed willing to tolerate democracy in Finland and possibly Hungary, but American observers in Bucharest and Sofia accused Soviet occupation forces of trying to set up puppet governments there. Truman, Byrnes, and their advisers realized that the United States lacked the power to influence events in Rumania and Bulgaria directly, but they hoped that by delaying the signing of peace treaties and withholding diplomatic recognition, they could force the Kremlin to carry out its obligations under the Yalta accords. The Truman administration wanted specific pledges that Western correspondents would be admitted to both countries.

Byrnes went to London with the expectation that the Soviet Union's fear of the bomb and its need for a postwar reconstruction loan from the United States would be the hands that would part the iron curtain separating Bulgaria and Rumania from the West.[41] Late in August the secretary of state told John J. McCloy that at London he intended to negotiate with the implied threat of the bomb in his pocket, and on September 4 Stimson recorded in his diary a similar conversation with Byrnes. The strategy was not unanticipated in Moscow. During early conference maneuvering over procedural matters, Molotov asked Byrnes if he had an atomic bomb in his side pocket. "You don't know southerners," Byrnes replied. "We carry our artillery in our hip pocket. If you don't cut out all this stalling and let us get down to work, I am going to pull an atomic bomb out of my hip pocket and let you have it."[42] Both Molotov and his interpreter laughed. Several days later, at a dinner at Lancaster House, Molotov made a short speech in reply to a toast to his health in which he said: "Of course, we all have to pay great attention to what Mr. Byrnes says, because the United States are the only people who are making the Atomic Bomb." Remarks Byrnes made to Bevin during and after the London meeting indicated that the State Department was still considering a postwar loan to the Soviet Union and that economic policy was thought to be an important means for exerting pressure.[43]

To Byrnes's dismay, however, the Soviets proved to be more stubborn than ever at London. In his effort to guarantee Soviet security and protect his personal dictatorship, Stalin hewed to three main policy lines. First, the Kremlin sought to isolate its people from outside influences that might cast doubt upon the legitimacy and effectiveness of the Soviet system. This isolation would at the same time shield Soviet weakness from foreign eyes. Second, Stalin was determined to maintain pro-Soviet regimes in Eastern Europe. And third, the USSR wanted to play a major role in European politics.[44] The man charged with advancing these goals at London was Molotov, a formidable personality and an even more formidable negotiator.

Molotov had gained a reputation as a tough, nimble-footed survivor of the internecine wars that wracked the CPSU in the 1920s and 1930s. Fifty-eight years old in 1946, Molotov (a pseudonym meaning "hammer") joined a Marxist group as a youth and participated in the revolution of 1905. He rose through the ranks to become at thirty-five the youngest member of the Politburo. In 1939 he was appointed foreign minister. Milovan Djilas, a Yugoslav Communist and a contemporary of Stalin and Molotov, agreed with Churchill's characterization of the chief Soviet diplomat as "a complete modern robot." Molotov, Djilas noted in 1945, "looked upon everything—even upon Communism and its final aims—as relative, as something to which he had to, rather than ought to, subordinate his own fate. It was as though for him there was only a transitory and unideal reality which presented itself differently every day and to which he had to offer himself and his whole life."[45] As a negotiator, the chain-smoking Molotov became known, according to one writer, for "his apparently limitless capacity for intransigence."[46] According to Bevin, Molotov was "just like a communist in a local labour party. If you treated him badly, he made the most of the grievance, and if you treated him well, he only put his price up and abused you."[47]

When the delegates took their seats, the Soviet foreign minister repeated Stalin's Potsdam claim for his country's control of former Italian colonies in Africa. Moreover, Molotov backed the Yugoslavs' demand for Trieste. Both Britain and the United States favored continued Italian sovereignty over Trieste, but they differed over the issue of the colonies. Britain, still smarting from Italy's attacks on British and French troops in the early stages of the war, wanted to strip Italy of all colonial possessions and turn them over to the UN. The United States suggested that the colonies be placed under UN supervision. Molotov wanted great-power administration, with the Soviet Union being given the right to build a naval base at Eritrea.[48] Privately, Byrnes expressed the opinion that the Soviets wanted to gain a foothold in Africa in order to acquire deposits of uranium in the Belgian Congo. Molotov also accused the Americans of supporting anti-Russian elements in Eastern Europe, and asserted that the regimes in Bulgaria and Rumania were more representative than the British-sponsored government in Greece. He made clear his government's position: unless the British and Americans signed peace treaties with the Petru Groza government in Rumania and the left-wing regime in Bulgaria, both of whom were friendly to the Soviet Union, he would not accept the Anglo-American draft terminating hostilities with Italy.

In a series of private meetings with Molotov, Byrnes tried to break the logjam, but to no avail. Could not coalitions be formed in Eastern Europe that were simultaneously representative and friendly to the USSR? Molotov remained unmoved. In an apparent attempt to improve his bargaining position, Molotov called for the exclusion of France and China from further discussions of the peace treaties. Two days later he demanded establishment of an Allied Control Council in Japan, composed of representatives from the United States, the Soviet Union, Britain, and China, to supervise occupation policies. Byrnes refused to give in on either of these points, and after Truman issued a futile appeal to Stalin, the conference broke up in early October.[49]

The breakdown of the London Conference dealt a severe blow to Soviet hopes. Many within the Kremlin had taken Harry Truman at his word when he promised to continue unbroken the policies of his predecessor. Washington's newfound determination to draw the line caused deep disappointment. Through September 1945 the Soviet press had depicted the Truman administration as a progressive capitalist government forced to contend with reactionaries trying to poison Soviet-American relations. After London, Soviet writers increasingly identified American policy with that of the reactionaries. Between the fall of 1945 and the spring of 1947, the Soviet press portrayed a struggle in both Britain and the United States between two vaguely defined "tendencies": on the one hand, those "influential circles" who, with the support of "certain official circles," sought world domination for the Anglo-Saxon powers; on the other hand, "democratic forces" backing the efforts of "realistic statesmen" who were still willing to engage in authentic trilateral negotiation and to compromise.[50]

The London foreign ministers' meeting disappointed and angered Byrnes. He later informed the cabinet that Moscow had no intention of living up to the Yalta accords and was not to be trusted. He was particularly bitter at Molotov. On September 20, as the delegates packed their bags to leave London, Byrnes told one of his assistants that unless Molotov were ousted, he would lead the Soviet Union to the fate that had overtaken Germany under Hitler and Italy under Mussolini. Yet although frustrated, Byrnes was not ready to call it quits. When one of his advisers remarked that the United States was going to have to fight another war to prevent Soviet domination of Europe, Byrnes responded that war was out of the question. Moreover, though he despaired of Molotov, Byrnes still had hopes for Stalin. The only solution to the Soviet-American impasse, he declared, was to have another meeting in Moscow, where he could deal with Stalin personally.[51]

Back in Washington, Russophobes and Russophiles continued to bombard the key decision makers in the Truman administration with their recommendations. Congressional and military leaders were not displeased with what they considered to be Byrnes's firm line at London. Members of the Senate Foreign Relations Committee gave him a warm reception upon his return, and Navy Secretary Forrestal advised the president to speak out publicly against the Soviets in order to counteract growing pressure for demobilization. On October 27 Truman traveled to New York to deliver his aggressive and widely publicized Navy Day speech. After reviewing forty-seven fighting ships anchored along a seven-mile stretch of the Hudson River, he addressed a huge throng in Central Park. The United States would not, he said, recognize any government imposed by force upon its people. Moreover, he promised that America would maintain its military strength.

But like Byrnes, Truman had not given up hope of reaching an accommodation with the Soviets. Stresses and strains such as those that had appeared at the London Conference were bound to occur among allies who had fought a long war, he told himself. Serious differences existed, but they could be worked out if everyone was patient. On October 15 he met with Henry Wallace and told him that Stalin was "a fine man who wanted to do the right thing." Wallace argued that the primary goal of British foreign policy was to promote an "unbreachable break" between the Soviet Union and the United States. According to Wallace: "The President said he agreed. I said Britain's game in international affairs has always been intrigue. The President said he agreed. I said . . . we must not play her game. The President agreed."[52]

By mid-October Byrnes seems to have had second thoughts about the tough policy he had followed at the London Foreign Ministers' Conference. Even before departing for home he had announced America's willingness to recognize the government of Hungary pending the holding of free elections, and to consider Moscow's request for the establishment of an Allied Control Council in Japan. Shortly after Byrnes's return his close friend Davies praised him for keeping his head and his temper in London while others were losing theirs. Byrnes reiterated his view that Soviet stubbornness regarding Eastern Europe stemmed from the Kremlin's understandable feeling of insecurity, brought on by its conviction that Britain was trying to broaden its sphere of influence in the Balkans and the Middle East. Davies scoffed at American "perfectionists" who were trying to turn Soviet domination of the Balkans into a "moral issue" and who wanted the United States to go off tilting at windmills.[53] Byrnes, obviously flattered and impressed with Davies's arguments, told the former ambassador to Russia on October 9 that the United States had compromised on Poland, Finland, and Hungary, and would do the same on Rumania and Bulgaria.[54]

In mid-October Byrnes announced that he was sending a delegation headed by Mark Ethridge, editor of the Louisville *Courier-Journal,* to Rumania and Bulgaria to "ascertain whether the interim governments of those countries were broadly representative in the sense of the Yalta Declaration."[55] Ethridge returned on December 8 and reported that after interviewing more than three hundred persons in the two countries he had to report that they were not. "Furthermore," he wrote Byrnes, "I must say in all honesty that both governments are authoritarian and are dominated by one party, and that large democratic segments of the populations in both Rumania and Bulgaria have been forcibly excluded from representation in the government."[56] In effect, Byrnes ignored the Ethridge report. In an address before the *Herald-Tribune* Forum in New York he declared that the United States was fully aware of and sympathetic to the special security interests of the Soviet Union in Central and Eastern Europe. A British embassy report on the state of the Truman administration's Soviet policy in the fall of 1945 reported, accurately, that "all in all . . . and in spite of accumulating evidence of Soviet intransigence, there is a stubborn determination in responsible quarters to rationalize the actions of the Soviet Union wherever possible and to make conciliatory moves as and when the opportunity presents itself."[57]

On November 25 Byrnes suggested to Molotov that the council meet again in Moscow before Christmas. The secretary of state recorded in his memoirs that he had called the conference in part because he found it difficult to press for granting more authority to U.S. representatives in Rumania and Bulgaria while denying Soviet requests for a role in the occupation of Japan. Moreover, he realized that as long as the Rumanian and Bulgarian peace treaties remained unsigned, the Soviets would have an excuse to keep troops in these countries. In his proposal to Molotov, Byrnes deliberately excluded the French and Chinese, and even more astonishingly, he did not consult with Bevin beforehand or make the proposal simultaneously to London and Moscow. Indeed, Bevin first learned of the proposed meeting from the British ambassador to the Soviet Union.

The foreign secretary was hurt, angry, and incredulous. The British had been dismayed by the Hopkins and Davies missions and the Truman administration's willingness to embrace the Lippmann-Swing strategy of mediation, but the record since Roosevelt's death had not been entirely negative. Washington had striven, "at times even somewhat impetuously," to ensure fulfillment of the Yalta Declaration regarding liberated and other countries. At London Byrnes and Bevin had cooperated in blocking Molotov's demand for independent trusteeships over the Italian colonies. In addition, the British hailed Washington's determination to exclude the Soviet Union from the postwar administration of Japan and its refusal to recognize the Soviet puppet governments in Bulgaria and Rumania.[58] But Byrnes's sudden, independent action in calling the Moscow Conference obliterated the positive impression left by the London meeting.

In the first place, Bevin had chosen to make a major issue of Molotov's effort to exclude the French and Chinese from the London deliberations. In a policy address to the House of Commons on October 9 he had asked how Molotov's suggestion could be reconciled with the UN Charter, which "lays upon the five Powers as permanent members of the Security Council a special responsibility to maintain the peace of the world." He blamed the breakup of the meeting on Molotov's ploy.[59] Now Byrnes was proposing to meet on virtually the same issues without France and China. Bevin and the Foreign Office feared, moreover, that at the Moscow Conference British interests would become the sacrificial lamb in a new U.S. effort to appease the Soviet Union. The British foreign policy establishment, which had always viewed the Truman administration as more of a prisoner of congressional and public opinion than the Roosevelt regime had been, proclaimed that compromise was in the air. "Mr. Truman and his associates," Halifax wrote Bevin, "are disposed to chart their course in the manner best calculated to propitiate what they conceive to be the prevailing sentiments of Congress and of important pressure groups."[60] But Halifax mistakenly assumed that this sensitivity would produce appeasement and isolationism. Dalton offered a blunter evaluation: "I have the sensation that the Democratic Party in the U.S.A. is reverting to what it used to be before Roosevelt's time, with a strong Irish-American flavor, and not much sympathetic understanding towards us."[61] Byrnes was perceived as a shallow politician who was dedicated to compromise for compromise's sake, just the sort of person who would make concessions to the Soviet Union in areas of vital concern to Britain merely for the sake of an agreement. But one suspects that the most important element in the British reaction was a fear of being deserted during a period of weakness and insecurity. Bevin and the Foreign Office had not ruled out compromise with the Soviet Union, as Bevin made clear in his speech to the House. But Byrnes's independent action had hurt his official feelings and deepened Whitehall's sense of isolation.

On November 6 Ambassador John Winant cabled Byrnes from London: "Situation serious. Unilateral action deeply resented by both Bevin and Cabinet. Bevin refuses to talk tonight or attend conference Moscow." When Byrnes made no response, Bevin cracked first. Several days later Winant reported that the foreign secretary was "desperately anxious" to talk with Byrnes. If the secretary of state would stop in London on his way to Moscow and discuss an agenda, Winant advised, Bevin would probably attend. Byrnes rejected what he considered to be a proposal to gang up on the Soviets and implied that he was going to meet with Soviet leaders with or without the British.[62] Bevin and his colleagues knew that they would have to accept the impetuous American's initiative. If Britain stayed home it ran the risk of being cast in the role played by the Czechs at the Munich Conference. He and the cabinet consoled themselves with the thought that anything was preferable to U.S. isolationism.[63] Nonetheless, Bevin arrived in Moscow on December 15 in a foul mood. George F. Kennan, then minister-counselor to Harriman, recorded in his diary:

> Bevin looked highly disgusted with the whole procedure. It was easy to see from his face that he found himself in a position he did not like. He did not want to come to Moscow in the first place and was well aware that nothing good could come of the meeting. The Russians knew his position and were squeezing the last drop out of it. As for Byrnes, Bevin saw in him only another cocky and unreliable Irishman, similar to ones that he had known in his experience as a docker and labor leader. Byrnes, as the British saw it, had consistently shown himself negligent of British feelings and quite unconcerned for Anglo-American relations.[64]

After the opening session Bevin asked for a private conversation with Byrnes, and on December 17 they met at the American embassy. Bevin declared that the Kremlin was trying to undermine Britain's position in the Middle East, particularly in oil-rich and strategically located Iran.[65]

Bevin's fears seemed well-founded. Early in the war, for security purposes, Britain had occupied the southern part of Iran and the Soviet Union, the northern. At the Teheran Conference the Big Three had agreed to withdraw their troops from the country six months after the end of the war. But before that deadline passed, the Soviets, through a local organization subject to Communist control, the Tudeh (Masses) party, threw their weight behind a movement for autonomy for Azerbaijan, Iran's northernmost province.

The Tudeh was an ideal instrument of Soviet subversion. At its core was a group of leftist Iranian leaders whom Reza Shah had expelled in 1937 but who were granted amnesty by his successor in the fall of 1941. The membership included several thousand Azerbaijani Turks expelled from the Soviet Union in 1936, many Caucasians who followed the Russian armies into Iran in 1941, and leaders of minority factions who had crossed the border and organized nationalist groups friendly to the Soviet Union. Joining them were a handful of radical intellectuals and a number of the urban poor. As a longtime student of U.S.–Near Eastern relations has pointed out, Azerbaijan's substantial industrialization, its large wheat production, and its lack of natural physical barriers made it a good base for Soviet economic and political penetration.[66]

Though Stalin promised at Potsdam not to impinge on Iran's sovereignty, a revolt supported by Soviet arms and troops broke out in Azerbaijan in November 1945. It appeared to the British that the Soviets were at the least going to detach that region from the rest of the country and at the most going to include all Iran and its oil in a Soviet sphere of influence. Moreover, if Britain withdrew its troops from Greece as Moscow was demanding, the Communist-inspired and -led revolution would flare up again. Nor could the British government be indifferent to the Kremlin's recent demand for a base in the Bosporus. As in the past, London would act, in accordance with the Montreux Treaty of 1936, to protect Turkish sovereignty over the straits. The Kremlin, Bevin warned, was building a "Monroe area"—a sphere of influence—that would stretch from the Baltic to the Adriatic in the west to Port Arthur in the east.

What Bevin wanted was a common Anglo-American front to halt the Soviet advance. But it was not yet to be. Byrnes was determined to work out an agreement, and he saw not consensus but conflict in overt Anglo-American cooperation against the Soviets. Given U.S. coyness, Bevin decided that he had no choice but to approach the Russians alone. In discussions with Molotov on the eighteenth and with Stalin on the nineteenth, he and the Soviet leaders outlined their differences. Molotov and Stalin demanded that Britain remove its troops from Greece and permit free elections; Bevin insisted that his hosts do the same thing in Bulgaria and Rumania. Bevin asked Stalin when Soviet troops were going to be withdrawn from Iran. Not in the immediate future, the premier replied; he was worried about the security of the oil fields around Baku. The conversation shifted to Turkey, where the Soviets had asked not only for a military base in the Dardanelles but for annexation of the Georgian and Armenian provinces of northern Turkey as well. Bevin reminded Stalin that Britain had an alliance with Turkey, which had mobilized its army and deployed it along the Soviet frontier. Stalin promised that Soviet-Turkish differences could be settled through negotiation. But when Molotov and Bevin concluded their conversations, no important problem had been solved.[67]

The stage was now set for Byrnes to perform his political magic. The secretary of state came to Moscow determined to offer a proposal on the international control of atomic energy that he hoped would literally and figuratively disarm the Soviets and dispel much of the distrust that had been building in Soviet-American relations since the Yalta Conference. According to one writer, "Rather than approaching the Russians furtively with the atomic bomb in his pocket, as he had done at London, Byrnes meant to lay the bomb on the negotiating table at Moscow." Byrnes's proposal, which he had taken from Vannevar Bush, envisioned the following steps: ever-widening exchange of atomic scientists and scientific information; development and exchange of information regarding sources of fissionable raw materials; exchange of technological and engineering information on atomic energy; and safeguards against and control over the military use of the bomb. Progress in one phase of the program would not depend on satisfactory progress in another. Unfortunately and characteristically, Byrnes had failed to take either Congress or the president into his confidence. While Byrnes was en route to Moscow, the congressional Joint Committee on Atomic Energy, headed by Vandenberg, got wind of the Byrnes plan on atomic energy and paid Truman a visit. The legislators contended and the president agreed that Byrnes, in his passion for a Soviet-American accord, was jeopardizing the security of the free world. Truman had Acheson cable Byrnes, instructing him to make clear to the Soviets that negotiations could not begin on any of the first three stages until and unless agreement was reached on the last—the establishment of "effective and enforceable safeguards" over the manufacture and use of the atomic bomb.[68]

Fortunately for Byrnes's political position, but perhaps unfortunately for Soviet-American relations, Molotov had insisted that atomic energy be shifted from first to last place on the agenda. When he and Byrnes got around to the subject, Byrnes made a four-phase proposal for the control of atomic energy, the first three dependent upon satisfactory completion of the fourth. He also suggested that the UN establish a commission on atomic energy under supervision of the General Assembly. The Soviets called for separate and independent negotiations on each stage and the tying of any such commission to the Security Council, where it would be subject to great-power veto. In the end Molotov agreed to the U.S. position on the first three stages, and Byrnes acceded to the Soviet demand that the atomic commission be responsible to the Security Council.[69] The secretary must have realized, however, that Congress would never endorse even this trade-off.

Disappointed at the subversion of his plan to "lay the bomb on the table" at Moscow, Byrnes still perceived atomic diplomacy as a means to an end. The real issues at stake were the status of the provisional government in Rumania and Bulgaria and the makeup of a control commission for Japan.

In an effort to work out a final settlement of these matters, the South Carolinian met privately with Stalin on Christmas Eve. The Soviets had already taken a conciliatory posture toward the United States in the general sessions. Byrnes suggested that the powers compromise over Rumania and Bulgaria so that work on the peace treaties with Germany's former allies could begin; to his surprise and delight the premier gave ground. Stalin emphasized his country's determination to have friendly governments along its border. He then conceded that it might be possible to broaden the governments of both Bulgaria and Rumania in such a way as to "satisfy Mr. Byrnes." It was subsequently agreed that a three-power commission would go to Rumania and advise the government to take in two additional ministers. The Soviet government itself would take the initiative in expanding the Bulgarian regime. In return, the secretary of state agreed to token concessions on the issue of Japan. The United States would establish an allied control council made up of representatives of the United States, the British Commonwealth, China, and the Soviet Union, which would consult with and advise MacArthur on occupation policies.[70]

Byrnes was jubilant. He believed that he had ended the impasse created at the London Conference. But Stalin's concessions in Eastern Europe no more weakened Soviet influence in the area than Byrnes's gestures in the Far East undermined American authority in Japan. And when the secretary of state returned to the United States, he learned that a variety of powerful groups and individuals considered his "achievement" at best a superficial compromise and at worst an appeasement of a totalitarian power bent on world domination.

■ ■ ■ CHAPTER FOUR

Confrontation and Containment

From the Iron Curtain Speech to the Paris Peace Conference

In the fall of 1945 a series of events and forces converged to produce a dramatic reversal in American foreign policy and propel the Truman administration toward a policy of Anglo-American solidarity and overt resistance to Soviet expansion. Soviet intransigence at the London and Moscow foreign ministers' conferences led Truman and Byrnes to doubt the wisdom of a conciliatory approach, and subsequent Russian machinations in Iran drained the reservoir of goodwill Moscow had built up during the war. Meanwhile, the British Labour government adopted a new tactic that allowed the United Kingdom to resist Soviet aggression without incurring charges from the United States that it was playing spheres-of-interest, power politics. Attlee and Bevin, mindful of the restraining effect of both isolationism and the new internationalism on American foreign policy, confronted the Kremlin over Iran and other issues within the context and in the name of the United Nations. A stance Americans found provocative and anachronistic outside the United Nations they found not only acceptable but inspirational within.

But perhaps the most important factor responsible for the United States' rejection of the policy of mediation was the Republican party's decision in late 1945 and early 1946 to challenge the Democrats openly on foreign policy issues. Vandenberg was able to unite the presidential and congressional wings of the GOP behind a policy of overt resistance to the Soviet Union and criticism of the Truman administration as soft on Communism. His political fortunes already at a low ebb over domestic issues, Truman responded to the Republican challenge by sponsoring Churchill's iron curtain speech in Missouri and forcing the USSR to back down over Iran in March 1946. When public opinion polls and the debate over the British loan, approved by Congress in the summer, revealed widespread support for the hard line being advocated by Vandenberg, Dulles, and certain members of the administration, Truman and Byrnes confronted the Kremlin at the Paris Peace Conference and labored diligently to ensure that the United States retained its monopoly of atomic technology and materials.[1]

■ ■ ■ Between September 1945 and November 1946 Republican criticism of U.S. foreign policy approached pre–Pearl Harbor intensity. In October James Reston reported mounting GOP dissatisfaction with Byrnes's failure to ask advice from party leaders before formulating policy. Chief articulator of that dissatisfaction was John Foster Dulles, Wall Street lawyer and the Republicans' unofficial spokesman on foreign affairs. Byrnes had taken Dulles to the London conference but had not consulted him, and thus left the impression that Dulles was along to provide a Republican rubber stamp. Upon his return to the United States, Dulles reported to a closed meeting of the Council on Foreign Relations that the U.S. delegation had "set sail for the Conference without proper preparation and that the policy which it put forward at the meeting had not been discussed with the Foreign Relations Committee of the Senate or the Foreign Affairs Committee of the House, nor did it have a firm root in American public opinion."[2] Dulles's disaffection did not stem from personal pique alone. The New Yorker distrusted Byrnes's tendency to "compromise," and he favored a stiffer line toward the Soviet Union. As he told Republican Congressman Charles Halleck, the United States ought to make common cause with the other great powers by repudiating "great power domination of the world" and rejecting the thesis that world peace required the United States "to endorse alien doctrines or to abandon efforts to seek justice for the weaker peoples of the world."[3]

In addition, Dulles was a major player in the movement within the GOP to offer an alternative to Democratic foreign policy in 1946 and again in 1948, an alternative that would go beyond the Democrats in calling upon the United States to shoulder its global responsibilities. What made this movement so powerful was that it was supported by both the congressional and the presidential wings of the party. The congressional branch, which drew its strength from the West and Midwest, had been staunchly isolationist before Pearl Harbor and was fiscally conservative. The presidential wing was rooted in the East Coast business and financial establishment. It was more tolerant of governmental spending for social and economic programs and judged that the United States ought to play an active role in world affairs. To the Republican leadership's delight, however, GOP xenophobes from the heartland joined Dulles in criticizing Byrnes and Truman in late 1945. American policy toward the Soviet Union, Karl Mundt and Francis Bolton wrote the president, is "lacking on the side of firmness." They declared that the United States should approve in Eastern Europe and the Mideast only those Russian policies that conformed to an American standard of political morality. They even called for Harriman's replacement, since "he served as our ambassador during a period when the approved American policy followed the appeasement line toward Russia."[4] Herbert Brownell, chairman of the Republican National Committee, wrote his constituents in October 1945 that the London Foreign Ministers' Conference had been "a failure." He called for a clear and comprehensive statement of foreign policy by the administration, arguing that the survival of bipartisanship depended on it. "Particularly," he warned, "Republicans should be on guard against continuation of the secret personal diplomacy methods heretofore employed by the New Deal in international affairs."[5]

But the real leaders of the GOP revolt against bipartisanship were Robert Taft and Arthur H. Vandenberg. Taft was not as visible in the Senate on military and diplomatic as on social and economic matters, but he had definite views on Soviet-American relations and he expressed them. In a speech he prepared for delivery on the floor of the Senate, Taft predicted that if World War III—most certainly an atomic war—came, it would be due to mistakes in American foreign policy. Appeasement of aggression did not work in the 1930s, he pointed out, and it would not work in the 1940s or 1950s either. "Munich led to World War II," he wrote. "Yalta, Potsdam and Moscow may well lead to a war which may destroy civilization." He reviewed the situation in Poland—"a laboratory to test the results of this war"—and then spoke of Rumania, Bulgaria, and Yugoslavia, where "one form of terrorism has been replaced by another."[6]

The GOP foreign policy initiative in the fall of 1945 represented something of a personal and political triumph for Vandenberg. He had been trying to forge an alliance between the two wings of the party throughout the war. Republicans had been largely successful in shedding the isolationist albatross, but many believed that more was needed than the me-too approach of Thomas Dewey and Wendell Willkie. The advent of Truman and Soviet expansion in Europe and the Far East opened the door for a rapprochement between liberals and conservatives that the Michigan senator hoped would lead first to a Republican majority in Congress in 1946 and then to a Republican president in 1948.

Republican attacks on administration foreign policy came at a time when Americans were frightened and confused. As George C. Marshall told Halifax, "The American people are passing through an emotional crisis." They wanted to enjoy the fruits of victory, but events would not let them. The United States had learned the folly of appeasement and unpreparedness, but it wanted nothing so much as to be left alone to pursue the American dream of self-sufficient prosperity. The bomb made confrontation with the Soviets a terrifying prospect. Yet the existence of repression and totalitarianism in areas occupied by the Red Army could not be denied. "In articles that resemble nothing so much as the strophe and anti-strophe of a funeral dirge," the British embassy reported to Whitehall, "Lippmann and Dorothy Thompson have played Jeremiah and Cassandra to one another."[7] Truman and Byrnes's reassurances that the Soviets could be reasoned with, that peaceful coexistence was possible, were seductive, but what if the Republicans were right? Only with the greatest effort had Hitler been stopped; if the United States allowed Stalin to go too far, the democracies might not win a third world war. In desperation, the American people looked to the United Nations for an answer.

Instead of acting as a guard against dangerous East-West confrontations, however, the new world organization served as just another stage on which the burgeoning Cold War could be acted out. The Iranian question dominated the inaugural session. In mid-December 1945 Moscow Radio announced formation of an autonomous Republic of Azerbaijan in northwestern Iran. Government troops sent to crush the revolt were turned back by Soviet occupation forces. Bevin had confronted Stalin at Moscow with accusations of Soviet interference in Iranian internal affairs but had gotten nowhere. Byrnes had dissociated himself from those representations. Not only did he want agreement with the Soviet Union over Eastern Europe, but he also feared that if the United States identified itself with British interests in Iran—specifically its Iranian oil concessions, including the invaluable refinery at Abadan—Washington would sacrifice its influence in countries of the Middle East that were struggling against European imperialism. Ignoring advice from the United States and Britain to remain silent for the moment, the Iranian government formally charged the USSR at the UN meeting with instigating the Azerbaijanian revolt. Convinced that Whitehall was behind the Iranian move, the Russians retaliated by asking the Security Council to indict Britain for retaining troops in Greece. Bevin and Andrei Vyshinsky, Russia's delegate to the UN, minced few words in the terrific row that followed. Bevin took the high ground, asserting that there was a tremendous moral difference between a nation that kept its troops in a country against the government's will, as was the case with the Soviet Union in Iran, and one that stationed troops in a nation with the consent of its government, as was the case with Britain in Greece. The United States, hoping to spare the UN the stigma of a Russian or British veto, played its mediator role for what would be the last time. Byrnes worked out a compromise whereby Russia and Iran agreed to bilateral talks in Moscow.[8]

The period of mediation, which culminated with Byrnes's unilateral calling of the Moscow Conference and Washington's refusal to support the United Kingdom over Iran, plunged British officials into despondency and provoked a variety of theories about why the United States was again refusing to recognize that Anglo-American strategic and economic interests were inextricably intertwined. And, of course, it provoked an equal number of stratagems for getting the cousins to see the light. Some denizens of Whitehall fell back on the familiar and comfortable explanation that the Truman administration was basically midwestern and that midwesterners, Republican and Democratic, were parochial, agricultural, undereducated, introverted, xenophobic, and paranoid—in other words, unalterably isolationist. The head of the North American section of the Foreign Office, J. C. Donnelley, who had spent eight years in the United States, six of them in the Midwest, claimed that sibling theory was more appropriate than geography in explaining U.S. behavior. He argued that there was no real difference among regions of the United States in views on international relations generally and Great Britain specifically. "A leading psychologist told me the other day," he informed his colleagues, "that in his quite considerable experience of treating Americans, mostly persons of intellectual attainment, he had never found one who did not have a feeling of inferiority in relation to Europe generally and most acutely in relation to Britain." Britain, Donnelley declared, is the elder sister who inspires feelings of both close dependence and resentment. As long as the younger sibling perceived the elder as prosperous and strong, she acted with aloofness and even hostility. But when Britain faced serious difficulties, as after Dunkirk, "Americans feel sympathetic, rather conscience stricken and most anxious to help." The problem, he concluded, was how to bring out this more helpful side of the American mind without being obliged to stage an actual and dramatically obvious crisis.[9]

Jock Balfour, counselor in the British embassy in Washington, shared Donnelley's views. "Old attitudes of mind about the ability of the British to outsmart the innocent Americans in international negotiations still enter into the emotional makeup of this people," he wrote, "and we must consequently . . . make allowance for [a] latent inferiority complex in our dealings with them."[10] Others traced the "fickleness" of American foreign policy to the U.S. Constitution: it provided for too much public input into the decision-making process and too little cabinet responsibility. "My own theory is that 140 million experts on international affairs is too many even for the U.S.," Halifax wrote.[11]

Officials in the Foreign Office had not anticipated the confrontation at the UN, but they welcomed it. The positive reaction to the Bevin-Vyshinsky exchange from the American Congress and public reinforced the emerging view among British policymakers about how to handle Russia and the United States. Initially, British officials had despaired of America's apparent obsession with the United Nations, seeing it as a form of escapism. "There seems to be a tendency to regard the UN as a *deus ex machina,* which will relieve the U.S. of some of the responsibilities arising from her position in the world, rather than thinking of it as an experimental structure, which must be tested for strength before heavy burdens are laid on it," noted Foreign Office analyst Dennis Brogan.[12] But following extensive explanations by the Washington embassy, decision makers in London began to perceive that it was possible for those in charge of U.S. foreign policy to practice *realpolitik* only within the context of an international collective security organization. The United States' penchant for "universalizing" its "humanitarianism" had only increased with mounting international tensions, Donnelley noted.[13]

Taking up the cry, Balfour and Halifax repeatedly urged Whitehall to work within the UN at every opportunity. The UN Charter was the Truman administration's general authority from Congress to "involve or entangle" the United States in questions not hitherto regarded as American concerns. Moreover, by working through the UN and especially the Security Council, Britain could make the United States less apprehensive about appearing to "gang up" with it against the Soviet Union.[14] "Americans," Balfour told London, "are aware in their heart of hearts that the continuity of their country's moral values is inseparably bound up with the welfare of Great Britain."[15] By defending the charter and using it to indict Soviet imperialism, Britain could raise this sublimated truth to the level of consciousness. Indeed, following Bevin's speeches at the London UN meeting, Whitehall officials became positively euphoric for a time about the possibility of seizing leadership of the Anglo-American partnership. "In making a stand in defense of the fundamental principles of international conduct," observed Donnelley, "Mr. Bevin appears to Americans not just as a British statesman but as a champion of the Charter which is not only based on the same fundamental principles but is a declaration of American policy which both Houses of the American legislature endorsed with a degree of unanimity rare in their country's history." [16]

By January 1946 British officials noted that Americans were finally perceiving that in the "power and inscrutability of Russia, there may be a threat to the 'One World' upon which they had been relying in order to be free to continue their own secure, prosperous, and pleasant way of life." And despite their endless speculation on the Anglo-American equation, the British acknowledged that more important in determining American attitudes than what Truman or Congress or Whitehall did was what the Soviet Union did.[17] U.S. reaction to a speech delivered by Stalin on February 9 seemed to bear out Whitehall's analysis.

Stalin's speech, a "pre-election" address designed to inspire the masses to give his regime a 99 percent–plus mandate, dealt mostly with Russian affairs. The premier boasted about the wartime accomplishments of the Red Army, the rapid industrialization of the Soviet economy, and the unity of the Soviet Union's heterogeneous population. More ominous, however, was Stalin's declaration that both world wars had been caused by "contradictions" in capitalism and that until and unless these contradictions were eliminated, the world would continue to have wars. To prepare for any "eventuality," Stalin called for three consecutive five-year plans to increase the USSR's annual steel production from twenty to sixty million tons by 1960.

Stalin's "campaign" harangue fitted in perfectly with the Kremlin's stratagem for dealing with the West, an approach one student of Soviet-American relations has labeled "competitive coexistence." [18] By early 1946 it was apparent to Stalin that continuation of the Grand Alliance was no longer a viable option. Formally, the United States, the USSR, and Britain were still allies. But tensions were churning beneath the surface and beginning to boil up into public view. Competitive coexistence involved a moderate amount of tension coupled with almost continual negotiation. This arrangement had both defensive and offensive advantages as far as Moscow was concerned. It was safer than out-and-out conflict with an adversary who possessed overwhelming economic and military power. At the same time it promised gains in the form of concessions by opponents lulled into thinking that accommodation was still a possibility. Stalin's February address was an example of the rhetoric of competitive coexistence, intended to prepare the Soviet population for the sacrifices that the ensuing struggle would require and to frighten the peoples of the West into making concessions. Whether it motivated the Soviet people is not clear, but it certainly had the effect of hardening feelings in the United States.

Some Americans, such as liberal columnist Vera Michaels Dean, considered the speech merely a chauvinistic appeal to the Soviet people to make further sacrifices to complete Moscow's five-year plan. *Business Week* also cautioned against unwarranted panic. But journalists generally took a much more pessimistic view of the address. Eric Sevareid and Walter Lippmann argued that the Soviet leader had acceded fully to the "two camp thesis" and was saying that permanent peaceful coexistence was impossible. Noting with approval "Lippmann's new positive line," the British embassy reported to London that "there is no doubt that Stalin's speech has shocked a number of doubters and warners into a stiffer attitude toward Soviet aspirations."[19]

Indeed, in the aftermath of the Stalin address and Bevin's stand at the UN, Whitehall began to see public and press opinion in the United States as an ally rather than a parochial and adolescent enemy. "Provided only that leaders other than the President are found to enlighten public opinion," wrote Donnelley, "one can perhaps rely on public opinion to push even a weak President like Mr. Truman sooner or later into adequate action."[20] Such leaders did exist, and not only did their view of Stalin's speech correspond with that of Lippmann, they had had much to do with his changed perception of the Soviet Union and his rejection of mediation. H. Freeman Matthews, head of the State Department's Division of European Affairs, told Byrnes and Acheson: "Stalin's speech constitutes the most important and authoritative guide to post-war Soviet policy. It should be required reading for everyone in the Department. It will henceforth be the communist and fellow-traveler Bible throughout the world. It should be given great weight in any plans which may be in consideration for extending credits or other forms of economic assistance to the Soviet Union."[21]

But the most influential assessment of the Stalin speech was George F. Kennan's famous Long Telegram of February 22.[22] Kennan, a career foreign service officer with a reputation as a Kremlinologist, believed that the United States committed a dangerous error in not clearly defining its interests and wishes in Eastern and Central Europe. "Why could we not make a decent and definitive compromise," he wrote, ". . . —divide Europe frankly into spheres of influence—keep ourselves out of the Russian sphere and keep the Russians out of ours." In refusing to place any limits on Soviet expansion, the United States had confused the Kremlin's policymakers, "causing them constantly to wonder whether they are asking too little or whether it was some kind of trap."[23] Britain and the United States, Kennan wrote from Moscow, should give up their hopes of a permanent resolution of issues with the Soviet Union. Internal political necessity, not Anglo-American strategy, determined Stalin's foreign policy. The premier's complaint about an Anglo-American bloc was not an objective appraisal of Western policy; it was propaganda designed to keep Britain and the United States separated and to justify his repressive rule at home. To prevent a domestic uprising and undercut his rivals in the Politburo, in other words, Stalin needed a hostile Anglo-American bloc. Kennan concluded that the West must reject "one worldism" and accept the harsh reality of "two camps." Rather than continue the futile search for a postwar settlement with the Soviet Union, the Western democracies should move toward making their camp a model of liberalism and economic prosperity.[24]

Reaction in Washington to this explanation of Soviet behavior was, in Kennan's words, "nothing less than sensational." Truman read it, the State Department sent Kennan a message of commendation, and Secretary of the Navy Forrestal had it reproduced and made required reading for the entire upper echelon of the U.S. officer corps. As fate would have it, the telegram arrived just as pressures were converging from several other sources to take a harder line with the USSR. In the week following Stalin's speech, Matthews, Elbridge Durbrow, and Acheson met with Lippmann and other advocates of mediation, and used Kennan's arguments to persuade them that the Kremlin was implacably hostile to capitalism and democracy.[25]

The anti-Soviet trend in American attitudes was, then, a product of Soviet rhetoric, of the Republican search for an alternative foreign policy, and of the growing influence within the foreign policy establishment of a clique who had taken charge of the State Department in 1944 and whose views were shared by Harriman and his staff in Moscow. This faction was directly and indirectly cultivated by British diplomats. "With a weak presidential leadership, and oscillating public opinion and constantly harassed by pressure groups," Donnelley observed to his colleagues, "the task of the stubborn men in responsible quarters in evolving a consistent foreign policy suitable to deal effectively with the all important problem of the Soviets is no easy one."[26] With a little help from their British friends, however, these stubborn men might be able to succeed. Frank Roberts and Kennan, as has been noted, frequently exchanged views, and their opinions on Soviet foreign policy developed in parallel. Who was leading whom was not exactly clear, but the British felt that Bevin's stand in the UN and private contacts between British and American diplomats had been at least partly responsible for the new backbone apparent in American attitudes toward Russia. Responding to Kennan's Long Telegram, Roberts observed to his colleagues in London that for the time being the Americans seemed willing to take the advice of "the embassy here to eschew wishful thinking, and to take a more realistic line in regard to the Soviet Union."[27] Whether he meant the British or the U.S. embassy was not clear. What is clear is that the British foreign policy establishment no less than the Republican party and Soviet bellicosity played a role in Truman's decision to get tough.

■ ■ ■ As Soviet policy toward Germany, Eastern Europe, and Iran became more intransigent, and as bureaucratic and political pressure mounted on the White House to pursue a more aggressive policy, Truman became less and less happy with the results of the Moscow Conference and with Byrnes. Part of the difficulty with Byrnes was personal and part of it was substantive. During his brief tenure in office, the secretary of state displayed an almost public intention to act as an independent agent. Byrnes's reputation as a compromiser, which seemed to be borne out by the Moscow agreements on Rumania and Bulgaria, became not only a target for the GOP but also a matter of concern and discussion among members of the diplomatic corps and Truman's advisers. Admiral Leahy, who by late 1945 had come to regard almost anyone who would consider agreement with the Soviets as an appeaser, compared the Moscow accords with what Neville Chamberlain had done at Munich. Byrnes had, moreover, alienated both Harriman and Kennan at Moscow. Harriman complained that Byrnes was "stiff and unwilling to listen" to advisers, and Kennan noted that during negotiations Byrnes had not set objectives, was often unprepared, and relied instead on his mental agility.[28] Truman's resentment at being kept in the dark, coupled with congressional criticism of the tripod or mediation policy, drove a wedge between him and Byrnes and propelled the president into the arms of the hard-liners. More and more Truman relied on the advice of Acheson, whose views reflected the attitudes of the professionals in the State Department and in the embassy in Moscow.

Byrnes's decision to release the Moscow Conference communiqué before consulting the White House irritated Truman, who awaited the secretary's return from the Soviet Union in a stormy mood. Byrnes, who had instructed the State Department to arrange for a nationwide radio hookup so that he could report on the conference, was told not to speak before consulting with Truman and was in fact ordered to report immediately aboard the presidential yacht *Williamsburg*. Recollections differ about what took place. Truman recalled that he expressed emphatic dissatisfaction both with Byrnes's failure to communicate and with the substance of the Moscow communiqué. Byrnes later denied that he was reprimanded. Whatever Truman told Byrnes on board the *Williamsburg*, there is no doubt that the president disliked the Moscow agreements. After reviewing the negotiations, he put his thoughts on paper. He objected particularly to Byrnes's failure to secure "concessions" from the USSR on the international control of atomic energy and on the withdrawal of Russian troops from Iran. He charged that the Russians intended to invade Turkey and seize the Black Sea straits. Having just read the Ethridge report, Truman expressed his determination not to recognize the governments of Rumania and Bulgaria until their composition had been radically changed. It was unwise, he wrote, for the United States to attempt compromise with the Soviets any longer. Only one posture would work: firmness backed by military force.[29]

An arrangement whereby the Soviets would create the appearance of self-determination within their sphere of influence had seemed acceptable to Truman with regard to Poland in May 1945, but by December, when Byrnes agreed to similar compromises in Rumania and Bulgaria, public trust in Soviet intentions had badly eroded. Opinion polls showed that at the time of Japan's surrender, 54 percent of the people questioned in a national survey had been willing to trust the Soviets to cooperate with the United States in the postwar world. By the end of February 1946 the number had dropped to 35 percent. Truman realized the importance of this shift, especially in view of the clear indications that the Republicans intended to capitalize on it in the midterm elections of 1946.[30]

Opinion polls showed further that as popular distrust of Moscow increased, so did public disapproval of the president and his policies. Polls taken before Potsdam while Truman was still in his honeymoon period indicated an 87 percent approval rate for the way he was handling his job. A year later that figure had more than halved, dropping to 43 percent.[31] "Mr. Truman's present situation is distinctly unsatisfactory," noted an astute British observer of the American political scene. "Each unsuccessful new experiment naturally reduces the likelihood and the corresponding hopes that by his method of trial and error he will eventually learn how to provide the strong leadership which the United States obviously needs."[32]

Sensing that the time had at last arrived to seize the initiative in foreign policy, Vandenberg rose on the floor of the Senate on February 27, 1946, to deliver one of the most famous speeches of the Cold War era. "What is Russia up to now?" he asked. He went on to review Soviet activities in the Balkans, in Manchuria, and in Poland. Two rival ideologies, democracy and Communism, now found themselves face to face, he declared. Peaceful coexistence was possible only if the United States was as vigorous and firm as the Soviet Union in defending its interests. The United States should establish limits beyond which it would not compromise. Vandenberg went on to praise the work of every major participant in the Moscow Conference except Byrnes. The galleries gave the Michigan Republican a standing ovation, and his colleagues lined up to congratulate him.[33]

It should be noted that in calling for a policy of resistance to Soviet expansion, Vandenberg was not declaring his support for an Anglo-American alliance, tacit or otherwise. He wanted the United States, he said, to uphold the UN Charter and exert "moral leadership." The former isolationist made it plain that he would tolerate no power politics, no special relationships. The UN was the place and the means: "Mr. Vyshinsky," said Vandenberg, had used the Security Council to defend Russia's interest and Bevin had used it on more than one "eloquent and courageous" occasion.[34] Clearly, Jimmy Byrnes should do the same.

The Truman administration responded almost immediately. Speaking to the Overseas Press Club on February 28, Byrnes outlined America's new get-tough policy. Some observers saw this speech as a hastily prepared response to Vandenberg's address—the second Vandenberg concerto, one reporter dubbed it—but the press club speech was more than that. It marked the culmination of forces—political, bureaucratic, and diplomatic—that were impelling the Truman administration toward a policy of confrontation with the Soviet Union. Byrnes declared that any nation that kept troops on another nation's soil without its consent, that prolonged unnecessarily the peacemaking process, and that seized enemy property before a reparations agreement had been worked out violated the charter of the new world organization. Byrnes called upon the United States to perform its duty as a great power and act to ensure not only its own security but the peace of the world as well. The United States, he said, could not and would not permit aggression "by coercion or pressure or by subterfuges such as political infiltration."[35]

The "new departure" in American foreign policy did not have as its objective the eviction of the Soviet Union from Central and Eastern Europe. Although it could not admit so publicly for political reasons, the Truman administration was no more willing to challenge the USSR's domination of its sphere of influence in Eastern Europe than the Roosevelt administration had been. And in fact, matters appeared to be going as well there as they could. In mid-January, for example, Irving Brant reported to the president on a two-month trip to Poland. To be sure, the Polish government carefully avoided offending Moscow, he wrote, but there was "no indication of actual supervisory control, directly or through Polish communists." The government was nationalizing large-scale industry, but this movement had "extensive roots in prewar Poland," and the vast majority of its supporters were non-Communist. Criticism of the Polish government by Poles was "open and unobstructed." Antigovernment and Catholic papers were "increasing in numbers and gaining in freedom of expression."[36] Although Truman and Byrnes might, in response to mounting GOP criticism, rhetorically roll back the iron curtain, their real goal, as it emerged during the course of 1946, was to hold the line in Europe and to protect British interests in the eastern Mediterranean and Middle East.

As has been noted, by the summer of 1945 Middle East experts in Washington were intensely worried about a Soviet drive to seize control of the Bosporus. In July Joseph Grew reported to Truman that Russia was simultaneously making demands on the Turkish government for political and strategic concessions and massing troops in Bulgaria. His informants told him, Grew warned, that the Soviet Union was following the "time-honored formula of predatory states" and that the buildup of troops in Rumania and especially in the Bulgarian province adjacent to Turkey, and the construction of three pontoon bridges across the Danube, were calculated to "exert the necessary pressure to obtain Soviet military bases on the Dardanelles and elsewhere as well as to force governmental reorganization in Turkey favorable to the USSR."[37] By January 1946 Truman was writing of his conviction that the Soviets intended to invade Turkey and seize the Black Sea straits if someone did not stop them.

But even more alarming than Soviet pressure on the Bosporus was the situation in Iran. In a summary of his thoughts on international relations at this time, Truman was particularly critical of Russian activities in Azerbaijan—"an outrage if I ever saw one."[38] Here was a clear-cut case of Soviet expansion. In the economic sphere a Soviet-dominated Iran would tip the world's oil balance toward the USSR. Many American policymakers, including the president, had reached the conclusion by the spring of 1946 that Iran was part of a coordinated Russian effort to undermine British influence throughout the eastern Mediterranean and Persian Gulf area. And they concluded that, American antiimperialism notwithstanding, the United States could not afford to see the United Kingdom eliminated as the dominant strategic force in the Middle East. Even if the Truman administration had wanted to replace Britain as guardian of the oil sheikdoms, it could not have done so in 1946 because of public war weariness and the GOP-led drive for a reduction in government expenditures. The *Econo-*

mist (London) accurately posed the dilemma facing Washington in the spring of 1946:

> If they [the Americans] genuinely regard Britain as a valuable partner, they cannot afford to see a steady weakening of Britain's position in the world. They are traditionally blind to this point, until war and imminent collapse drive home the lesson. In wartime they recognize their own vital interest in British security. But in peacetime they are so obsessed with the need to "avoid playing Britain's game" that they run the risk of lending themselves to everybody else's game. Can they be persuaded to anticipate a little the last ditch and to realize that the Middle East is as vital to Britain as the Far East to America or Eastern Europe to Russia and that it is an American as well as a British interest to see that the position is not whittled away?[39]

The answer to the *Economist*'s question, given in Washington's response to the final stages of the Iranian crisis, was a resounding yes. The appointed day for Soviet troop withdrawals from Iran—March 2—came and went. Moscow announced that it would remove some of its personnel, but others would stay until the situation had been clarified.[40] The Soviets continued to insist on autonomy for Azerbaijan and the right to maintain troops in the north, but now they added a demand for the formation of a Soviet-Iranian Oil Company in which the USSR would own the controlling interest. Truman and Byrnes conferred on March 4. The next day the State Department charged Moscow with violating the Teheran Declaration and called for an immediate withdrawal of all Soviet troops. Instead, on the morning of March 6 the State Department received word from its vice-consul in Azerbaijan that "exceptionally heavy [Soviet] troop movements" were taking place, not toward the Soviet border, but in the direction of Turkey, Iraq, and the Iranian capital of Teheran. Byrnes was infuriated. The Russians had apparently decided to escalate from subversion and intimidation to outright aggression, he told an aide. When by March 12 no response had been received to Washington's demand for troop withdrawals, the department released to the press news that Soviet tanks were moving on Teheran.[41]

In mid-March Stalin complained to Ambassador Walter Bedell Smith that Washington was being particularly "unfriendly" in insisting on a United Nations confrontation over Iran, rather than letting the Soviets work out the situation on a bilateral basis. Stalin also contended that he had encountered "no objection" to the Russian proposals on Iran from Truman and Byrnes in advance. This exchange pointed to what had already become a classic pattern in the Soviets' diplomacy: to conceal their full intent, to take anything less than an absolute prohibition as an invitation to proceed, and then to condemn their rival's hostile reaction as a betrayal.[42]

Meanwhile the Soviet-Iranian negotiations had got nowhere, and with the encouragement of the United States, the shah's ministers made plans to submit the issue of Soviet troop movements to the UN Security Council, scheduled to meet again in New York on March 25. To dramatize the meeting and the Iranian issue, Byrnes represented the United States personally. When the delegates gathered at Hunter College, the Soviets tried to keep the Iranian complaint off the agenda. Finding that this attempt could not succeed, Andrei Gromyko stalked out of the meeting chamber. His departure was a parliamentary and propaganda ploy, but one that backfired in the United States. The American people took the UN seriously, and Russia seemed to be thumbing its nose at the last great hope of mankind. In a stunning reversal of events, the Iranian and Soviet governments one week later announced a formal agreement calling for the withdrawal of Soviet troops by early May and recognition of Iranian sovereignty over Azerbaijan.[43]

A recent biographer of Truman argues that the Soviets backed down in the 1946 Iranian crisis because the prospect of a breakdown in international relations so soon after a devastating war was too much for Moscow to contemplate. Another scholar maintains that either Truman or Byrnes, or both, verbally warned the Kremlin that there would be military consequences if it did not withdraw the troops from northern Iran. Specifically, between March 21 and March 23 Washington notified Stalin through Ambassador Smith in Moscow that the United States was transferring its Mediterranean fleet to the Persian Gulf.[44] Whatever the specifics of the warning, Truman decided in the spring of 1946 to resort to military action if necessary.[45]

As the Truman administration moved quickly and quietly to defuse the Iranian crisis, it simultaneously sponsored a bellicose speech by Churchill in an effort to test the American public's willingness to support a policy of confrontation with the Soviet Union and cooperation with Great Britain.[46] In October 1945 the president of Westminster College in Fulton, Missouri, learned that Churchill planned to visit the United States in the winter of 1946. Westminster had a fund to attract famous speakers, and the college decided to use the Missourian in the White House to lure the most famous orator of all. Truman endorsed the invitation and offered to introduce Churchill if he accepted. In November the former prime minister told Truman that he would indeed deliver an address at Westminster "on the world situation, under your aegis." He added, mysteriously: "This might possibly be advantageous from several points of view."[47]

Churchill arrived in Miami Beach for his North American vacation in January. The Westminster speech was not scheduled until March 5, but soon after arriving in Florida, Churchill wrote Truman: "I need to talk with you a good while before our Fulton date. I have a message to deliver to your country and to the world, and I think it very likely we shall be in full agreement about it. Under your auspices anything I say will command some attention and there is an opportunity for doing some good to this bewildered, baffled and breathless world."[48] On February 10 Churchill talked with Truman in Washington. Leahy commented on the meeting: "The subject of the address [Churchill's Fulton speech] will be the necessity for full military collaboration between Great Britain and the United States until the United Nations is able to keep the peace which will be at some time in the distant future."[49] The former prime minister traveled to Washington during the first week in March so that he and the president could make the trip to Missouri together.

The presidential train set out for Fulton on March 5. Truman had intended not to read Churchill's address, in order to be able to say that he had not seen it. He changed his mind once the trip had started and did read it, remarking, after he finished, that it was "admirable and would do nothing but good though it would make a stir."[50] While the official party drank whiskey and played poker, Churchill's press aides passed out copies of the speech to reporters and suggested a headline: "Churchill proposes Anglo-American alliance as Russian shadow darkens over the world."[51]

As both Churchill and Truman knew, the British leader's talk would be read by virtually every American with an interest in foreign affairs. The public was frightened and insecure. The shadow of the Soviet Union did indeed hang heavily over the world, and though the United States was sole possessor of the atom bomb, the very existence of a doomsday device seemed to make the shadow far more menacing than it might otherwise have been. Innate Anglophobia notwithstanding, Churchill was probably America's favorite foreigner. His defeat in 1945 had come as a profound shock, particularly to interventionist, middle-class Americans. English visitors were frequently asked to explain the strange ingratitude of the British people. The nation was flooded with cartoons and editorial tributes to what one paper called "this great Gladiator who bestrode the Continents like a Colossus."[52]

Thus it was that Truman introduced Churchill to a much wider audience than the students and faculty who were present at Westminster College on March 5, 1946. "I know," Truman said, "that he will have something constructive to say to the world." Churchill made the obligatory reference to Westminster and began. "War and Tyranny," he said, were threatening the world once again. An iron curtain had descended over Central Europe, and behind that curtain Soviet power was stamping out liberty and democracy. "It is not our duty at this time when difficulties are so numerous to interfere forcibly in the internal affairs of countries whom we have not conquered in wars," he declared. But he urged that Anglo-America had a right, indeed a duty, to defend Western civilization against further totalitarian incursions. He called for a strengthening of the "fraternal association" of English-speaking peoples as the surest safeguard against future wars. Anglo-America should not entrust the secret of the bomb to the international organization, he urged, and it should maintain a common military establishment, because there was nothing the Soviets respected so much as strength. He was talking not of balance of power and spheres of interest, Churchill said, but of the establishment of a common civilization based on democracy and liberty as a counterpart to Soviet totalitarianism. "If the population of the English-speaking Commonwealth be added to that of the United States," he asserted in conclusion, "with all that such cooperation implies in the air, on the sea and in science and industry, there will be no quivering precarious balance of power to offer its temptation to ambition or adventure: on the contrary, there will be overwhelming assurance of security."[53]

The response to Churchill's address in the United States was swift, and much of it was negative. "Why did you lend yourself today as a sounding board for Churchill to preach from?" Fred Arkin asked Truman. "Who on earth gives a good damn what British imperialists would like us to do?" he demanded, and added: "I keep telling myself you can't be as unenlightened and inane as you seem."[54] The National Union of Marine Cooks and Stewards passed a resolution denouncing the Churchill speech as "a definite call for a military alliance between the United States and Great Britain to wage war upon the Soviet Union, a member of the 'Big 3' and our valiant ally in the last war."[55] Others denounced Truman for supporting Churchill and his "UNO splitting tactics."[56] One correspondent asked Truman to describe the difference between British activities in Greece and Soviet policy in Eastern Europe, arguing that Churchill was just another calculating Britisher who should go home and mind his own business. Had he not been repudiated by his own people? another asked.[57] But those who were critical tended to be more outspoken than those who were not.

Anglophobia aside, Americans could not forget that Churchill had sounded the clarion call against Hitler. The prophet had spoken again, and though his vision was frightening, a large number of Americans felt that it should be taken into account. Among members of the press in the United States, only left-wing writers and broadcasters denounced the speech as warmongering and imperialistic. Even those declared that it was the "bad" rather than the "good" Mr. Churchill speaking. More moderate opinion proved willing to admit the validity of Churchill's statements regarding Soviet imperialism, the iron curtain, and America's global responsibilities, but recoiled from the remedy prescribed: an Anglo-American alliance. Asserting that no other statesman, American or foreign, could have got away with such a speech at so little cost, Halifax wrote Bevin that all but extreme Anglophobes and isolationists "concede that there is something wrong with the tooth in question; some are inclined to suspect that the condition may be grave indeed; but almost all shy with real or simulated horror from the idea of a drill and complain that the dentist is notorious for his love of drastic remedies, and that surely modern medicine had provided more painless methods of cure." The reaction in Congress was much the same, with Republicans and southern Democrats on the whole approving the attack on Communism and warning against appeasement while expressing varying degrees of skepticism about the prospect of an Anglo-American alliance. Liberal Democrats such as Claude Pepper attacked the speech as a disservice to the UN and a piece of reactionary imperialism. The only out-and-out support came from extreme right-wing, anti-Soviet legislators.[58]

Stalin treated Churchill's speech for what it was, an appeal to the non-Communist world to isolate the Soviet Union and its clients. On March 14, in an interview in *Pravda,* he labeled the Fulton address "a dangerous act designed to sow the seeds of discord among the allies and to undermine their collaboration." Churchill, Stalin said, was nothing less than a "warmonger"; he had "called for war with the USSR." The Englishman was no better than "Hitler and his friends." Whether Churchill would succeed in organizing the West for a war against world Communism Stalin claimed not to know, but he asserted that the West would lose any such contest. Stalin subsequently charged that the former prime minister was crying wolf to divert attention from domestic economic problems and imperial rivalries among the capitalist nations, while at the same time trying to intimidate Moscow. As one observer has pointed out, Stalin in this interview was projecting his methods and motives on Churchill. Stalin was playing the game he accused the Englishman of playing in his own war and peace propaganda: issue a call to arms in the name of peace, thus inspiring your own population and frightening your opponents while leaving open an avenue of escape.[59]

In Britain Churchill's iron curtain address provided a magnificent opportunity for critics of the government's foreign policy. Conservatives and Liberals sat back and watched with glee as Labour party members tore at each other. Left-wing Labour figures asked why a British Information Service official was with Churchill in the United States and why the BBC was translating the Fulton speech into German. When 105 backbenchers demanded a debate in Parliament on the speech, Herbert Morrison overruled them.[60] Attlee and Bevin went to great lengths to dissociate themselves from Churchill and his oration. Churchill had, Bevin told an American diplomat, shown poor judgment and had said the "right things at the wrong time."[61]

Truman and his subordinates were no less energetic than Attlee and Bevin in putting rhetorical distance between themselves and Churchill's Fulton remarks. After conferring with the president, Harry Vaughn, Truman's military aide, told all who inquired that "the President did not discuss with Mr. Churchill the subject of his speech nor did any of us see the speech until it was released to the press a few hours before it was delivered."[62] At his March 8 press conference Truman turned aside a reporter's attempt to elicit a clear statement of approval or disapproval. He merely defended Churchill's right as a private citizen to say whatever he wished. Byrnes went farther. On March 17, speaking to the Friendly Sons of St. Patrick, the secretary of state rejected the notion of a special relationship between Britain and the United States and stressed that American troops would be used only to enforce the Charter of the UN. Two days earlier New York City had honored Churchill with an afternoon parade and a gala dinner at the Waldorf-Astoria Hotel. Acheson, scheduled to deliver one of the introductory speeches, backed out twenty-four hours before the event.[63]

Such maneuverings, however, were designed to promote short-term political purposes. The Fulton speech served both the Truman and Attlee governments well. Halifax had read the speech in draft and had made no objection. Donnelley thought that given the history and strength of Anglophobia in America, the U.S. reaction to the speech was encouraging. "We have witnessed a remarkable demonstration of fundamental solidarity," he wrote: "If the Russians have any sense they will realize from what has been happening in recent weeks that if they did get involved in a war with the United Kingdom, once again and probably sooner than on the not dissimilar occasions in the past, the U.S. should range itself on the side of Britain." Foreign Office official Paul Mason, believing there to be no shrewder judge of American opinion than Churchill, argued that the former prime minister knew what he was doing. As Mason explained it, Churchill took an extreme position, painting the Soviet Union in the blackest of terms and calling for an Anglo-American alliance, knowing that the United States would accept neither his definition of the problem nor his remedy. But Churchill hoped that the United States would cease its drift, put an end to its uncertainty and divisions, and deal with the Soviets in a realistic and hard-nosed manner. In light of these intentions, the long-range impact of the speech might prove beneficial. "It is even possible now, while the dust is still flying," wrote Mason, "to see some indication that it will eventually settle . . . in the form . . . of American realization of the responsibility of world leadership which has fallen upon them."[64]

Truman and Byrnes had known what was in the speech, had approved, and had taken the political risk of associating themselves with it. On March 5 Henry Wallace and his wife attended a dinner given by the Achesons at which Charles E. Bohlen and Richard Casey, Australian ambassador to the United States, were present. "We then got to talking about Russia again," Wallace recorded in his diary, "and it was apparent that Bohlen, Acheson and Casey all think that the United States should run the risk of immediate war with Russia by a very hardboiled stand and being willing to use force if Russia should go beyond a certain point."[65] Soviet foreign policy was a dangerous amalgam of traditional Russian imperialism and Marxist/Leninist ideology, so the U.S. foreign policy establishment was convinced. Churchill could articulate publicly what Truman, Byrnes, Acheson, and Bohlen could say only privately. The administration could use Churchill to prepare the public for a course it had already decided upon, namely, the defense of British interests in the eastern Mediterranean and the Middle East. How better to gain public support for a policy than by using a surrogate who would absorb the political fallout? Truman had acted shrewdly to steal the anti-Soviet thunder of the political Right in the United States without exposing himself to attacks from Anglophobes on both the Right and the Left.

■ ■ ■ Despite grumblings about having to pull British chestnuts out of the fire, by mid-March 1946 the tide of public opinion in the United States had set strongly against continued efforts at Soviet-American cooperation. An opinion survey taken two weeks after Churchill's speech revealed that 71 percent of those polled disapproved of the policy that the Soviet Union was following in world affairs, and 60 percent indicated that the United States was "too soft in its policy toward Russia."[66] Buoyed by the hardening attitude of the U.S. electorate and anticipating the 1946 midterm congressional elections, Truman and Byrnes acted during the remainder of 1946 to confront the Soviet Union publicly as well as privately.

In the UN and in the Paris foreign ministers' meetings, over atomic energy and over Eastern Europe, the Truman administration labored to demonstrate its "toughness" to the American voter, to Congress, and to the Kremlin. If it did not succeed in rolling back the iron curtain in Central and Eastern Europe, Washington at least attained its objective of solidifying Western influence in Greece, Italy, and Turkey, preventing the spread of Soviet power into the eastern Mediterranean and North Africa, and preserving the United States' atomic monopoly.

At Moscow the foreign ministers had tentatively set May 1 as the opening date for a peace conference to draw up treaties with members of the Axis other than Germany. They also agreed to have their deputies meet in London beforehand to set the agenda. Meanwhile, Harriman reported that the commission on Rumania had failed to make the government of Petru Groza more representative, and subsequently Andrei Vyshinsky announced that owing to the extreme demands of the opposition parties, the Soviet effort to broaden the Bulgarian government had collapsed. From London the U.S. representative at the deputies' meeting informed Washington that he was convinced that the Soviets did not support the American goal of early treaties to ensure political and economic stability in Italy, Hungary, Bulgaria, and Rumania; rather, their objective was to procrastinate and thus allow the Red Army to remain in the Balkans and maintain the Kremlin's "puppet stooge governments" in power.[67] Byrnes thereupon decided to call a meeting of the Council of Foreign Ministers for April 15 in order to speed up preparation of the treaties and ensure that the peace conference did get under way in May.

The American secretary of state went to Paris determined again to pursue a carrot-and-stick strategy with the Soviets; but now he was determined to give wide public play to the stick while dangling the carrot in private. "The U.S. Government cannot expect the support of the American people in a policy of firm dealings with the Soviet Union," advised a top secret State Department study of Soviet-American relations, "unless it is willing to be as frank as possible with the public and to take the trouble to educate them as to the need for such a policy."[68] On April 17 Cyrus L. Sulzberger wrote in the *New York Times* that all sorts of officially inspired stories had been emanating from Washington indicating that the Truman administration intended to be tough with the Soviets. The United States, according to such stories, would insist that Italy keep Trieste and surrounding environs at the head of the Adriatic, that Greece be allowed to retain all the Dodecanese Islands, and that none of the great powers be allowed to seize colonies from their defeated enemies. As proof of the administration's intent, the State Department announced that

Vandenberg, now a symbol of the hard line toward the USSR, and Senator Tom Connally, chairman of the Senate Foreign Relations Committee, would be included in the American delegation.[69] At the same time, Byrnes privately invited the Soviet government to begin negotiations in May for a $1 billion loan from the Export-Import Bank.[70]

Byrnes made another significant decision before departing for Paris. On April 16 he officially notified the president of his decision to resign. He would stay on, he said, until the peace treaties were signed, but his decision was irrevocable. In his memoirs the South Carolinian cited an unfavorable doctor's report on his heart condition as the main reason for his decision to step down. It is likely, however, that his differences with Truman, his feelings of alienation from the State Department, and the buffeting he had absorbed at the hands of Vandenberg and Congress had more to do with his resignation than health. Certainly, his decision had nothing to do with any dissent regarding the decision to take a harder line with the Kremlin.

The first phase of the Paris foreign ministers' meeting opened on a hopeful note when Molotov, with an eye on the increasingly favorable political position of the French Communist party, conceded that all four powers, including France, should be allowed to frame treaties with all five of the European Axis powers. But matters quickly went from good to bad to worse. Byrnes and Bevin rejected the USSR's demands for $300 million in reparations from Italy on the ground that Germany's principal ally could not afford to pay. The Western powers were as reluctant in Italy's case as in Germany's to subsidize reparations to the Soviet Union by supporting the domestic economy of the debtor. Molotov agreed in principle to the transfer of the Dodecanese from Italy to Greece, but when he and the other ministers were unable to agree on the disposition of Italy's colonies, the Russian insisted that a decision be deferred until a later date. On the matter of Italy's overseas possessions, the Soviet Union demanded control of Tripolitania; the United States favored a UN trusteeship for all Italian colonies; and Britain pushed for immediate independence for Libya, including Tripolitania and Cyrenacia.[71] Tempers became frayed even further when the Western powers again rejected Yugoslavia's Soviet-backed demands for Trieste. When Byrnes proposed a twenty-five-year, four-power treaty guaranteeing German disarmament as a means of breaking the logjam, Molotov rejected it as unworkable. The ministers finally decided to end their deliberations without setting a date for a peace conference, to leave their deputies working in Paris, and to reconvene on June 15.[72]

The Truman administration's widely publicized decision not to make new concessions to the Soviet Union was reflected in its attitude toward the international control of atomic energy as well as in its negotiating posture at the various foreign ministers' meetings of 1946. In January Byrnes had named Dean Acheson to chair the secretary of state's committee on atomic energy. Other members were Leslie Groves, James Conant, Vannevar Bush, and John McCloy. Over Groves's objections, Acheson succeeded in persuading the committee to appoint a board of consultants headed by former Tennessee Valley Authority (TVA) chief David E. Lilienthal and made up primarily of nuclear physicists. By March the committee had developed and approved, again over Groves's protests, what came to be known as the Acheson-Lilienthal plan for the international control of atomic energy. Like the U.S. plan proffered at Moscow, the new scheme provided for transitional stages beginning with a freeze on the production of weapons and the inspection of atomic facilities in all affected countries. Under the Acheson-Lilienthal scheme, however, the "dangerous" or military uses of atomic energy would come under the jurisdiction of an international body, called the Atomic Development Authority (ADA), which would oversee the mining, refining, and utilization of the world's atomic raw materials. Atomic energy's so-called harmless uses—for commercial, medical, and purely scientific purposes—could remain safely in the hands of national governments after fissionable material had been "denatured" by the international authority and thus rendered useless for the secret manufacture of bombs.

The Acheson-Lilienthal plan was undercut, however, when in late March Truman named Bernard Baruch as the United States' delegate to the UN Atomic Energy Commission (AEC). A conservative financier himself, Baruch selected a group of conservative businessmen to advise him and obtained assurances from Truman that he was not in any way bound by the Acheson-Lilienthal plan. Baruch's appointment was indicative of the lengths to which Truman was willing to go to appease congressional conservatives: the president neither liked nor trusted his first representative to the AEC.[73]

Baruch's proposal for control of atomic technology and materials differed dramatically from that put forward by the secretary of state's committee. Under the Baruch plan, participating powers would halt atomic research and submit to inspection and to an audit of their fissionable materials. Responsibility for the mining and refining of fissionable materials would not be transferred to the ADA but would remain with private industry. Baruch accepted Groves's assurances that the Soviet Union had no uranium. In addition, no member of the ADA would have the right of veto. Finally, the United States would surrender its nuclear weapons to the international authority, but not until all other stages of the agreement had been completed. Thus the Baruch plan provided for the maintenance of the U.S. atomic monopoly through continued American control of fissionable materials. The scheme contained, moreover, the implied threat of an atomic attack on the Soviet Union if it violated the terms of the accord.[74]

Not surprisingly, the Soviet response to the Baruch plan was less than enthusiastic. On June 19 Andrei Gromyko, Russia's UN delegate, outlined his country's approach to the control of atomic energy. He called for an international convention prohibiting the production, possession, or use of atomic bombs. The Gromyko plan provided for neither inspection nor sanctions against violators at the outset. Instead, safeguards would be put in place concurrent with the sharing of atomic information and materials. Permanent members of the Security Council would retain their right of veto. If the United States was not willing to relinquish its atomic monopoly, the Kremlin was not about to become part of an agreement that blocked its own atomic research and development program. The Soviet-American confrontation over atomic energy culminated on December 31, 1946, when Baruch forced a vote on the U.S. plan. Although this scheme was approved by a vote of ten to two, the USSR's status as a permanent member of the Security Council and its power of veto ensured that the plan would never come to fruition.[75]

■ ■ ■ Anglophobia and one of its root causes—anticolonialism—had been driving forces behind Truman's policy of mediation. As late as March 26, 1946, Secretary of War Robert Patterson was writing that an Anglo-American coalition, formal or informal, was out of the question, because "if a member of the Big Five comes to feel that the others are ganging up on her by always acting in concert . . . the UNO is doomed." This would be a special problem, he observed, "if the 'affronted' nation were sensitive about encirclement to begin with."[76] That the American public and Congress had decided to suppress their historic distrust of John Bull and make common cause with the United Kingdom against the Soviet Union became clear when in the summer of 1946 Congress approved the Anglo-American Financial Agreement. The loan agreement that was signed at Washington on December 6, 1945, extended a total credit of $4.4 billion (including the final settlement of lend-lease) to Great Britain. The loan was not tied; that is, Britain could spend the money anywhere for anything. Although Britain was forced to pay 2 percent interest and to abolish the sterling area by accepting the free and full convertibility of sterling into other currencies within a year, the loan appeared to protect the United Kingdom from imminent bankruptcy. With American aid Britain could maintain its military outposts abroad, and the Attlee government would be able to make good on its promises of "Homes, Food, and Work" to the British populace.[77]

In the United States some initial sparring between opponents and supporters of the loan took place over the winter, but Congress did not take up the financial agreement officially until March 1946. William L. Clayton, Fred Vinson, and a score of loan supporters testified at length before the House and Senate Banking and Currency committees. Opponents of the loan were loud and persistent. Midwestern isolationists such as William Langer and William Knutson charged that the credit was an Anglo-American alliance in disguise and that, before long, the United States would again be pulling British chestnuts out of the fire. Fiscal conservatives maintained that the loan was the golden straw that would break the American camel's back. "There Will Always be a U.S.A.—If We Don't Give It Away" read the title of an antiloan tract widely circulated at the time.[78] A related criticism voiced with special eloquence by Illinois Republican Jesse Sumner was that the loan would advance the cause of socialism and regimentation on both sides of the Atlantic, in Britain because the Labour party would use the proceeds to finance its social experiments and in the United States because bankruptcy would destroy the free enterprise system. Still others argued that the loan was a bad business deal; Britain had never paid its World War I debts and could never be expected to live up to its obligations. Zionists such as Emmanuel Cellar declared that Congress should vote not a penny until the British allowed free immigration into Palestine. Many of these arguments were a cover for a surprisingly widespread and intense Anglophobia. "Among us, the common people," wrote one avid opponent of the loan, "there is no act our government could perform that would have higher acclaim than an outright declaration of war against the British Empire."[79]

In response, administration representatives mounted a coordinated counterattack that stressed the domestic and international advantages of a multilateral trading system. Following lengthy debates, the Anglo-American Financial Agreement passed the Senate by a vote of 46 to 34 on May 10 and the House by a vote of 219 to 155 on July 12.[80]

Given popular and congressional reservations about making common cause with Great Britain and about foreign aid in general, approval of the financial agreement was the product of mounting fear and distrust of the Soviet Union. The British had no doubt that deteriorating East-West relations were responsible. Events had served to bring America's fear of Russia, "a dominant but unadmitted emotion," to the surface and to make it the basis of U.S. policy, wrote J. C. Donnelley.[81] The notion that the loan was necessary to save Britain from Communism was introduced explicitly at the hearings on March 14 by Ralph Flanders, head of a machine tool firm, a member of the Boston Committee for Economic Development, and a future U.S. senator. The Soviet Union did not want war, Flanders said, but there would be an intense rivalry between the Russian socioeconomic system and Western, democratic capitalism. The criteria others would use to judge the two systems were living standards, and Britain was the first measure.[82] *Barron's,* a conservative financial journal that opposed multilateralism as "globaloney," declared early in the hearings: "At bottom what we are trying to do with that $3.75 billion is to assist the British because they are our allies. In other words the money is intended to help carry out the policies of Winston Churchill."[83] The *Wall Street Journal* warned that "without assistance Britain may have a very hard time holding her Empire together and she may lose strength and prestige to the extent that Russia will sweep over Western Europe and encompass the Mediterranean."[84] Harry Stanfill, a Kentucky Republican, summed up the feeling of Congress when he declared that the loan could not be justified to the American people as a business deal but that he had nevertheless supported it out of "enlightened self-interest," from the conviction that the British people were the "last barrier against communism."[85]

In the end, then, enough conservatives overcame their fiscal conservatism and fear of socialism, and enough liberals their abhorrence of British colonialism, to secure passage of the loan. Each group became convinced that both Communist ideology and Soviet foreign policy so threatened America's national security that a common Anglo-American front was inevitable.

While the House and Senate debated the merits of the British loan, the foreign ministers of the principal Allied powers converged again on Paris for the second phase of the council meeting. Byrnes left Washington aboard the presidential plane *Sacred Cow* on June 14, with Vandenberg and Connally in tow. To underscore the importance of the gathering, Truman saw the entourage off at the airport. Again the principal topics of discussion were Italian reparations and colonies, Trieste, the Dodecanese, peace treaties with the Balkans, and the timing of the general peace conference. In addition, Byrnes, Bevin, French Foreign Minister Georges Bidault, and Molotov struggled to reach a consensus on the outlines of peace treaties with Germany and Austria and to establish not only a date but procedural rules for the peace conference.

By the summer of 1946 U.S. officials had come to believe that the most effective negotiating technique in dealing with the Soviets was confrontation. A State Department paper on Russian diplomacy concluded that the leaders of the USSR were "fanatics" in the sense that one could talk to but not with them: "They won't 'reason' with you or come to a 'meeting of the minds' because they can't admit that we have any ultimate common purpose."[86]

Led by the United States and Britain, the council fought off Molotov's insistence on a generous reparations settlement from Italy while resisting the Kremlin's demands that Tito be given control of Trieste. Then, in line with a plan developed by Byrnes, East and West worked a trade-off on the two issues. Italy was forced to pay the Soviet Union $100 million in reparations, although Molotov did agree to grant Rome a two-year moratorium and a delivery period of seven years. The Council of Foreign Ministers then established Trieste as a free territory with a democratic government under control of the UN. The Security Council, after consulting with Italy and Yugoslavia, would appoint a governor for the area.

With the thorny Adriatic problem resolved, the foreign ministers turned their attention again to the fate of the Reich. A number of diplomats on both sides of the iron curtain had argued that the root of East-West tensions was Germany and that unless the victors could agree on a peace treaty with that nation, Europe would continue to be polarized. The Potsdam agreement on the economic unification of Germany had been a dead letter since its inception. Instead of receiving agricultural imports from the Soviet zone as anticipated, the United States found itself supporting the population of its food-deficient region to the tune of $400 million a year. In addition, the United States, Britain, and France had allowed some deliveries of capital goods and plant to the Soviets under the Potsdam proviso stipulating that the USSR would be entitled to 10 percent of the capital equipment that was "unnecessary for the German peace economy." To halt the dismantling of industrial plants and to pressure the Soviets into complying with the Potsdam accords, General Lucius D. Clay, military governor of the U.S. zone, had ordered a halt to further reparations shipments on May 3, 1946. At Paris, Byrnes insisted that the other ministers respond to his proposal for a twenty-five-year German disarmament treaty and that work begin at once on a German peace treaty. Molotov took the position that a twenty-five-year pact was inadequate. Germany had first to be totally disarmed, he argued, then reunified, and the Ruhr placed under international control, before negotiations on a peace treaty could begin. In the face of this deadlock, the ministers agreed to a special session of the council on Germany after the peace conference. Significantly, however, the United States and Great Britain began to lay plans for the financial and administrative unification of their two zones immediately after Paris.[87]

Before departing, the council members briefly considered a peace treaty for Austria, but the discussions foundered when Molotov demanded as a precondition the repatriation of 437,000 Russians and Ukrainians, members of the so-called White Guards, who had collaborated with the Germans following their invasion of the Soviet Union in 1941. The delegates set July 29 as the opening date of the peace conference, and on July 12 Bevin gaveled to a close the second session of the Paris Conference of the Council of Foreign Ministers.

Administration and congressional hard-liners such as Vandenberg regarded the meeting as a limited success. There had been no appeasement of the Soviet Union, Vandenberg reported to his Senate colleagues, and the prospects for peace treaties with Germany's five allies were bright. Most important, the former isolationist wrote Dulles, the U.S. delegation had refused "to compromise [its] moral leadership for the sake of agreements."[88]

The meeting that opened in Paris on July 29 was a somber affair compared to the euphoria and glamor surrounding the Versailles Peace Conference in 1919. East-West suspicion and confrontations, fueled by the Truman administration's decision to go public with its new tough approach to the Soviet Union, dispelled any illusions that Europeans or Americans might have had about a brave new world. The Continent was exhausted from six long years of war and polarized as never before. From Moscow Roberts wrote the Foreign Office that "the powerful Soviet propaganda machine" was drumming into the heads of the Soviet people the notion that "their major allies in the war are in fact reactionary and almost fascist countries." As long as this process continued, "the prospect of returning to even a semblance of Big Three collaboration are pretty gloomy."[89] The fifteen hundred delegates representing twenty-one nations who gathered at the Luxembourg Palace came with modest expectations indeed.

The delegation quickly divided into two rather consistent voting configurations. The Slavic bloc, headed by the Soviet Union, was filled out with Yugoslavia, Poland, Czechoslovakia, Byelorussia, and the Ukraine (at Potsdam the Soviet Union had been accorded three votes in the UN, one each for Russia, the Ukraine, and Byelorussia). The rest of the nations generally followed an Anglo-American lead. After a prolonged wrangle over procedure, the conference members agreed to make two types of recommendations to their home governments, those approved by a simple majority vote and those with a two-thirds majority. The vote, not surprisingly, was fifteen to six. The Russians announced that they would not be part of any recommendation supported by less than a two-thirds vote.

As the delegates prepared to ratify the Council of Foreign Ministers' proposals on Trieste, Italian reparations, colonies, and other issues, an incident occurred that strained East-West relations to the breaking point. For several weeks U.S. Army Air Transport pilots had been flying over the northwest corner of Yugoslavia. Belgrade first charged the United States with 176 separate violations of Yugoslav air space and then in August forced down two American planes, imprisoning the crewmen of the first and killing those of the second. Byrnes summoned the Yugoslav representative to the Paris meeting on August 20 and told him that his country had forty-eight hours to cease its aggression and release the captured pilots or Washington would take the matter to the Security Council. Tensions eased when Tito released his prisoners, and Byrnes had the pilot and copilot flown to Paris to see him.

During a brief recess in the peace conference Byrnes flew to Germany in an effort to reassure the citizens of that devastated and anxious country that the United States was committed to their political and economic rehabilitation. The secretary of state wanted to make America's position clear not only to Germany and the Soviet Union but also to France, who, out of a fear of revived German power, was demanding the right to annex the Rhineland and to control the production of the Ruhr and the Saar, the coal- and steel-producing heart of Europe. With Vandenberg and Connally by his side, the secretary arrived in Stuttgart in the U.S. zone on September 6. To the delight of his German audience and General Clay, Byrnes declared that although France had a right to the Saar, the Rhineland and the Ruhr were German territories and should be governed in accordance with the wishes of their populations. He also observed that it would probably be necessary to keep security forces in Germany for years to come. Clay hailed the speech as the first public declaration of America's intent to remain in Europe.[90]

Throughout the meetings of the Council of Foreign Ministers in Paris and the early stages of the peace conference, Byrnes had been buoyed by the belief that he at last had the support of the administration, Congress, and a majority of the American people. That confidence was shaken when Secretary of Commerce Henry Wallace delivered a now famous address on U.S. foreign policy in Madison Square Garden on September 12. Wallace was perhaps the most prominent member of America's liberal community and a long-time advocate of Soviet-American friendship. He believed that Truman and Byrnes's new firm approach was a betrayal of the Roosevelt legacy and a threat to world peace. He thoroughly agreed with Supreme Court Justice Hugo Black, another leading liberal, who observed in September that "the present foreign policy was not a Democratic foreign policy but a Republican foreign policy that had been forced on Byrnes by Vandenberg."[91] In his speech, which was billed as an important statement of administration foreign policy, Wallace denounced those who would confront the Soviet Union. Eastern Europe was crucial to Soviet security, he said, and Moscow had legitimate interests there. He called for Soviet-American cooperation and a common front against colonialism and Fascism.

Unfortunately for Truman, he had approved the speech without reading it. Had he looked at it, he would have realized that it was designed to force him to choose between confrontation with and conciliation of the USSR, between Byrnes and Wallace. The day following Wallace's address one of the secretary of state's lieutenants cabled him that its object was "to reverse American foreign policy and to humiliate and compromise you irretrievably."[92] FBI Chief J. Edgar Hoover advised the State Department that Wallace was nothing less than a tool of the American Communist party. From Paris Byrnes complained to the White House that Wallace's meddling in foreign affairs was undercutting America's bargaining position with the Soviets. On September 19 Truman cabled Byrnes to hold tight, and the following morning the president requested and secured Wallace's resignation.[93]

With these distractions out of the way, the peace conference was ready to get down to business. To speed up matters, the Council of Foreign Ministers decided to meet concurrently with the peace conference, as well as with the UN General Assembly. In an amazingly short time, given past differences, the conference had drawn up treaties for each of the five Axis powers except Germany. With some minor changes, the council's recommendations on Trieste, Italian reparations, and the Dodecanese Islands were accepted.

The Council of Foreign Ministers gathered in New York City on November 4 to meet concurrently with the UN General Assembly and either to ratify or to reject the work of the peace conference. The foreign ministers worked out the details of governance for the free territory of Trieste; set reparations payments from Italy to Albania, Greece, and Yugoslavia; and provided for a special conference on navigation of the Danube. Each of the peace agreements obliged the nations in question not to discriminate in their trade relations with foreign nationals and to keep trade barriers to a minimum. The State Department and Foreign Office again hoped to use economic access to Eastern Europe to retain political as well as economic influence there. Penalties for failure to comply were not spelled out in the peace treaties, however. The foreign ministers ended their New York conclave by instructing their deputies to prepare final drafts on the Italian, Balkan, and Finnish treaties and to submit these documents to the signatory nations in Paris on February 10, 1947.[94]

The peace treaties were perhaps the best that could be negotiated under the circumstances. The Soviets set out to weaken Western influence in Italy, and Britain and the United States did their best to diminish Soviet power in the Balkans. Both failed. The Kremlin proved unable to gain a toehold in the eastern Mediterranean and North Africa, and the West's efforts to keep open the economic door to the Balkans came to naught. The economic clauses of the treaties proved unenforceable. The Soviet Union received more in reparations than the United States desired but less than Moscow wanted.[95] The treaties merely ratified existing spheres of interest and as such finalized the process that had begun at the Yalta Conference.

■ ■ ■ By early spring of 1946 Americans inside and outside the foreign policy establishment had come to see in Soviet diplomacy a commitment to world revolution and a renewed determination to undermine capitalism. In August 1944 the Joint Chiefs of Staff had portrayed the Soviet Union as a war-devastated nation whose moves in Eastern Europe and the Far East were defensive in nature and based on an overriding desire for military security. By 1946 they were warning that world domination was the primary objective of Soviet foreign policy and that Moscow had come to see peaceful coexistence with the capitalist countries as impossible. "The USSR was concentrating therefore on building up its war potential and doing everything it could, short of open warfare to subjugate the satellite nations, to gain control of strategic areas, and to isolate and weaken the 'capitalistic' nations militarily," declared a JCS report to the president.[96] The Soviets were making frantic efforts to overcome the United States' lead in military technology and were receiving much help from French Communist scientists. They were openly trying to sabotage the UN and were busy undermining pro-Western governments from France to Indonesia.

During his first eight months in office, Truman had tried to treat America's wartime partners equally, to mediate between them, and especially to avoid giving Moscow the impression that there was a Washington-London axis directed against the USSR. The Soviets had proved intransigent and had clumsily provoked the United States over one issue after another, while under its new Labour government, Britain had shrewdly confronted Russia and defined its interests within the context and in the name of the United Nations. Meanwhile, the resurgent GOP, deciding that it had to offer an alternative to Democratic foreign and domestic policy, called for a get-tough policy abroad and retrenchment at home. Responding to both the political and the diplomatic environment, the Truman administration decided in the winter and spring of 1946 to pursue a harder line toward the Soviets. Like the interventionists in 1940 and 1941, Truman and his advisers concluded that it was better to deal with aggression on foreign soil and to act in concert with allies than to remain alone and isolated in the Western Hemisphere. That perception in turn led American policymakers again to identify Britain's strategic interests with those of the United States. The Soviet Union, B. E. F. Gage noted with delight, "is busily forging a . . . demand in the United States for a strong foreign policy and arousing universal sympathy for the British position, which many thinking Americans are beginning to have a comfortable feeling is their own."[97] In his Overseas Press Club speech Byrnes had denounced the Soviets for "gnawing away at the status quo." With the support of the president and a bipartisan coalition in Congress, the secretary of state spent the last year of his term in office trying to protect that status quo.

■ ■ ■ PART II

Response

■ ■ ■ CHAPTER FIVE

A Policy of Firmness

The Truman Doctrine and Global Strategy

By late 1946 the Truman administration had embarked on a course of firm resistance to perceived Soviet aggression. Events in the Near East and Eastern Europe, pressures from London, the demands of domestic politics, the controversy over atomic energy control—all had combined to convince the White House to drop its policy of mediation between Britain and the Soviet Union and assume the chief responsibility of stopping Communism. Some historians have argued that Stalin's demands exceeded his security needs and that his aggressive foreign policy was partly a response to growing dissidence at home. Others have insisted that his actions were vastly complicated by personal paranoia and vindictiveness. Whatever forces may have been guiding Stalin's actions, there can be little doubt that a major part of the explanation for the East-West conflict lies in each side's misperceptions of the other's intentions. According to some writers, Truman followed Roosevelt in a mistaken interpretation of Stalin's seemingly unreasonable behavior as deception, whereas Stalin, in turn, too simply regarded Roosevelt's efforts at friendship as deception (or illness) and Truman's hard-line approach as an attempt to deal with his country's domestic troubles. Thus Roosevelt's policy failed to win over Stalin, and Truman's encouraged the Soviet premier to adopt a stance even more conducive to confrontation. It seemed as if the two systems, capitalism and Communism, had come into conflict, and failure by the United States to adhere to a policy paralleling Britain's would assure the triumph of the Soviet Union and the demise of democracy and free enterprise.[1] Further, an Anglo-American coalition built on the principles of multilateral trade would simultaneously stimulate the U.S. economy and bring prosperity and stability to those areas of the world not yet behind the iron curtain. In sum, Americans had again come to identify their security with that of the British, and Washington was convinced that the Soviets' machinations compelled it to adopt a posture of confrontation.

The announcement of the Truman Doctrine in March 1947 set out the intent of the United States to pursue a global strategy aimed at combating the Soviet Union in what a *New York Times* correspondent in Greece described as "a new kind of war." The White House believed that in Greece and Turkey the Soviets hoped to establish their influence by indirect means. With the aid of neighboring Yugoslavia, Albania, and Bulgaria, Russian agents used terrorist tactics to spread Communism in Greece. And in Turkey the Soviets demanded joint control over the Black Sea straits and attempted to achieve that objective by engaging in a war of nerves along the countries' common border. The Truman administration attributed the insecurity and instability in both Near East nations to Soviet-inspired aggression and operated on the assumption that the crises, in turn, presented a danger to U.S. security. The threats to Greece and Turkey in early 1947, taken together with the Soviets' attempts during and immediately after World War II to expand into Iran, seemed part of a concerted effort to spread their interests into the "Northern Tier" of the Mediterranean. If successful, the USSR would cut British communications through the Suez Canal and gain access to the oil-rich Middle East.[2]

As the Truman administration saw events, its solitary possession of the atomic bomb was the primary reason why the Kremlin decided to rely on infiltration, subversion, propaganda, and the use of proxies in a campaign against pro-Western governments. Logic dictated that the Soviets seek control through any method short of war and that they choose targets that were economically and politically unstable and therefore susceptible to exploitation. Such soft-spot probing by the Soviets, as Washington saw it, prompted the United States to counter with a sophisticated policy capable of responding in kind to challenges posed by Communist aggression. A test of wills resulted, the outcome of which depended on convincing Moscow that it could not win. The White House had to devise a multifaceted strategy that was flexible and restrained, and thereby check the Soviets without provoking war. The Truman Doctrine exemplified the administration's approach.

■ ■ ■ After the resolution of the Iranian crisis of 1945–46, American-Soviet troubles in the Near East focused on Turkey. During the latter stages of World War II the Kremlin had attempted to win influence in Turkey in hopes of satisfying postwar interests in the eastern Mediterranean and Near East. The Soviets demanded joint control over the Black Sea straits, in 1936 assigned exclusively to Turkey by the Montreux Treaty.

They also wanted the cession of Kars and Ardahan, two Turkish districts bordering Soviet Georgia and Armenia. According to U.S. advisers, the Soviets had taken advantage of Turkey's economic and political problems in an effort to generate more internal trouble through diplomatic pressure. Molotov notified Ankara in March 1945 that the Kremlin would allow the long-standing Pact of Friendship between the countries to expire on schedule in November. Renewal of the pact, he made plain, was contingent on satisfaction of the Soviets' demands in the straits and along the border. Although U.S. and Turkish officials did not anticipate Soviet military action, they thought that the Kremlin sought bases in the Dardanelles as a first step toward expanding its influence into the Aegean and eastern Mediterranean and thus putting itself into position to challenge British economic and strategic interests in the entire region. As Soviet propaganda against Turkey intensified, the British and U.S. governments attempted to settle the matter by recommending international control over the waterways. Despite efforts at the Potsdam Conference of July–August 1945, the issue remained unresolved.[3]

Unrest in the Mediterranean was a source of mounting alarm as the White House came to interpret Soviet actions regarding Turkey in the autumn of 1946 as part of an effort to spread trouble throughout the world. Indeed, U.S. military leaders soon focused on Turkey's potential strategic value in the event of war with the Soviet Union. In a series of clashes in Paris at the Council of Foreign Ministers, Byrnes and Molotov traded bitter accusations that each was out to satisfy his own nation's imperial interests. An intelligence report from the Netherlands bolstered this American belief by warning that the Soviets were pursuing a "strategic offensive" that sought "world revolution in the Middle East" and ultimately "world supremacy." Conflicting territorial claims and ethnic rivalries in the Balkans aroused further ill feelings. Elsewhere, in Palestine Arab nationalists and Zionists were virtually in a state of civil war that threatened British interests and general political stability in the Middle East. Halfway around the world a similar conflict in China appeared imminent. Suspecting a Soviet hand in all these troubles, the White House concluded that the Kremlin's pressure on Turkey was part of a blueprint for global conquest. The U.S. ambassador in Ankara, Edwin C. Wilson, agreed; he warned that Turkey's collapse would lead to more Soviet encroachments.[4]

Anglo-American pressure temporarily eased the Turkish problem. In mid-August the White House joined the British government in urging the Turks to reject Soviet demands and in pointedly reminding the Kremlin that the Turkish government was responsible for the straits. The United States also made a show of force. The navy ordered to Istanbul a task force that consisted of the recently launched aircraft carrier *Franklin D. Roosevelt,* two cruisers, and five destroyers. Forrestal had wanted to send such a mission the previous February, but Byrnes had opted instead for dispatching the battleship *Missouri* to Turkey, ostensibly to return the ashes of the Turkish ambassador in Washington, who had died during the war. Pleased to see his idea finally becoming a reality, Forrestal seized the moment to announce that the U.S. naval presence in the eastern Mediterranean would continue. In October the Soviets relaxed their intimidation campaign against Turkey.[5]

Soviet actions in Eastern Europe and in the Middle East had led the president to instruct his legal counsel, Clark Clifford, to prepare an analysis of this new threat to peace. In September Clifford presented his report. Entitled "American Relations with the Soviet Union," it drew heavily on the ideas that Kennan had expressed in February in his Long Telegram warning that the Soviets were seeking expansion by direct and indirect means. According to the Clifford report the Soviets intended to "foment antagonisms among foreign powers" and bring down opposing governments by "discrediting their leadership, stirring up domestic discord, and inciting colonial unrest." In the UN Soviet representatives would attempt to obstruct any policy adverse to their interests. Greece and Turkey were the last barriers to Soviet expansion in the eastern Mediterranean and Middle East. Subversion, infiltration, propaganda—these were the weapons the Kremlin was using to menace the non-Communist world. The United States, Clifford urged, should adopt a firm policy against Soviet aggression that was "global in scope" and included "atomic and biological warfare." The report was so sensitive that Truman locked up all copies.[6]

The Clifford report helped focus a growing feeling within the administration that a flexible policy was necessary to combat Communism. Even though emphasizing that economic assistance to struggling nations would constitute "a more effective barrier to communism," the report urged the United States to enhance its military strength. Military assistance would be a proper response only "in case of attack" and as "a last resort." While the report was under consideration, Kennan (who had not seen it) likewise made a call for flexibility by advocating a multifaceted approach in foreign affairs. He exhorted colleagues in the State Department to pursue a "wise and unprovocative" policy that would "contain [the Soviets] both militarily and politically." Further, the Central Intelligence Group (forerunner of the CIA) favored a policy capable of adaptation to changing circumstances. According to the group's informants, the Soviets were pursuing indirect tactics to undermine capitalism and encourage the spread of Communism. Thus a variety of sources urged the White House to develop a policy adjustable to challenges. As Clifford put it, "When you are faced with that kind of crisis, you come up with whatever weapons you have—political, military, economic, psychological, whatever they might be."[7]

The White House perceived the recent wave of Soviet actions as aggressions that could lead to a clash between Communism and democracy. The United States' possession of nuclear weapons had caused the Kremlin to seek global objectives through means other than force; it was therefore incumbent on the United States to devise a policy capable of containing the threat without allowing a direct confrontation between the opposing powers. According to White House belief, the Soviets were challenging the right of self-determination on all fronts. Rebuffed in Iran and Turkey, they turned to Greece.

The Greek situation was exceedingly more complicated than that in Iran and Turkey. Internal dissension was exacerbated by long-standing economic problems, by widespread devastation stemming from Nazi occupation, and by competing regional interests in the Balkans. The most bitterly contested regional issue concerned Macedonia, a large and vaguely defined area in northern Greece coveted by Yugoslavia and Bulgaria.[8] U.S. observers feared that if those two Communist states acquired Macedonia, Greece would be weakened and the Soviets would wield such influence in the Aegean and the straits that Turkey would have to meet their demands. Further, successful Soviet aggression would dishearten nations dangling perilously between the non-Communist world and the Soviet bloc. The White House was caught in a dilemma. It wanted to avoid direct involvement in the Balkans, traditionally a labyrinth of troubles, but it could not concede a Soviet triumph. The West's sole inroad into the area was Greece, the only Balkan nation that was strongly anti-Communist.[9] Its collapse would have enormous psychological impact on Turkey, Italy, the eastern Mediterranean, and the Middle East.

The threatened outbreak of civil war in Greece during 1946 provided the basis for deepening U.S. concern about the region. The increased unrest in Greece was immediately attributable to indigenous problems—problems that had twice threatened to precipitate civil conflict during World War II. The first violence had occurred in late 1943 when the leading wartime resistance group in Greece, the Communist-led EAM/ELAS (the National Liberation Front and its military arm), tried to destroy its rival resistance organizations in an effort to end the Nazi menace and, with resulting popular support, seize control of the country. After a cease-fire in February 1944 was followed by Nazi withdrawal in October, the Communists attempted a second time to take over the Greek government in an uprising referred to as the December Revolution. In neither instance did the Soviets intervene—perhaps because of the secret percentages agreement in Moscow between Churchill and Stalin in October 1944, whose terms obliged the USSR to recognize British preeminence in Greece. In the December crisis of 1944, British military forces entered the conflict on behalf of the monarchical government of King George II (who was in exile in Cairo). Fighting raged in the streets of Athens until the British put down the uprising and the two sides agreed to an uneasy stalemate at Varkiza in February 1945.[10] But Greece was soon polarized again over the question whether the king should return to the throne. The EAM led the opposition to the king and worked with the Greek Communist party (KKE) in calling for the establishment of a "popular democracy." The British, as in the December Revolution, opposed the Communists and sought restoration of the monarchy. In the bitter general elections of March 1946, the Communists joined several leftist-socialist parties in boycotting the proceedings, thereby ensuring an easy victory for the Populist (or royalist) party in Parliament and for its standard bearer as prime minister, Constantine Tsaldaris. The government scheduled a plebiscite for September to decide whether the king should return to Athens.[11]

Civil war seemed imminent. On election eve a small group of guerrillas attacked a Greek gendarmerie post near Mount Olympus and set off what the KKE and others eventually heralded as the beginning of the war.[12] Sporadic violence soon broke out in other parts of the country, as Communist-led guerrillas raided villages, skirmished repeatedly with the gendarmerie, and threatened to establish a government of their own in the northern part of the country. By July the KKE had appointed a Communist and former member of EAM/ELAS, the ruggedly inspiring "General" Markos Vafiadis, as commander-in-chief of what would become known as the "Democratic Army." The most ominous sign of trouble was the increasing number of reports (later substantiated) that the guerrillas were being trained and equipped in Yugoslavia, Albania, and Bulgaria. Indeed, the Soviet Union and a number of Eastern European Communist regimes would soon provide the guerrillas with rifles, machine guns, antitank weapons, antiaircraft guns, land mines, clothing, and food.[13]

Events in Greece took on international importance by the summer of 1946, largely because the United States and the Soviet Union were engaged in what writers were already calling the Cold War.[14] The previous May, Byrnes had asked French Foreign Minister Georges Bidault what the Soviets wanted. The reply was "security through expansion." But the Soviets sought more than mere expansion, according to the State Department: they wanted to dominate the world. Recent events seemed to fit a pattern of behavior that rested on Soviet aggression. In a speech that the West probably interpreted out of context, Stalin appeared to add substance to Kennan's dire forecast about the growth of Communism by publicly insisting that the abyss between Communism and capitalism was too wide to be closed. Understandably, perhaps, U.S. observers were so caught up in the whirlwind of events that they failed to realize, as one writer suggests, that Stalin's mood was not offensive but defensive: he was attempting to counter derisive claims from the West that the Soviet industrial and collectivist programs were flawed, that the purges of the 1930s were brutal and unnecessary, and that the Soviet victory over Germany had not made the USSR into a power worthy of respect. Whatever Stalin's real purpose, in March U.S. attention was turned abruptly to the warning Churchill offered in Missouri (with Truman sitting on the speaker's platform) that the Soviets had lowered an iron curtain across Eastern Europe. In response, the War Department insisted that only the presence of British troops in Greece had dissuaded the Kremlin from making a more active attempt to establish Communist control over the government in Athens. The United States, it urged, had to hold the line against Communism in Greece.[15]

The Truman administration at first intended to help Greece by simply supporting the British lead, but by late 1946 the costs of two world wars had forced the government in London to adopt a worldwide retrenchment policy that thrust the United States to the front. As East-West tensions mounted, the British began preparations for pulling out of Greece the last of their fourteen thousand combat troops.[16] Not surprisingly, the fighting there intensified in mid-September as the process of withdrawal began.[17] The Greek government meanwhile placed pressure on the United States to intervene by formally taking the entire northern border issue before both the Truman administration and the UN. A Security Council commission investigated the alleged violations along the Greek border and recommended emergency economic assistance. The British refused to provide such help but hoped to persuade the United States to assume the task. Attlee and Bevin complained that the Americans for too long had evaded their international responsibilities.[18]

The Greek situation deteriorated in October as General Markos proclaimed over Communist radio the establishment of the Democratic Army in the northernmost Grammos and Vitsi mountains in Greece and ordered an escalation of terrorist activities. The Greek army (115,000 troops and 35,000 gendarmes) seemed large enough to defeat a force that could not have numbered more than 13,000. Indeed, the numerical and matériel advantages enjoyed by the Greek regulars appeared to guarantee the success of the government's strategy: chase the guerrillas, encircle them, and kill or capture them all. But the Greek soldier was neither well trained nor tightly disciplined, and he was poorly provisioned, largely unfamiliar with counterinsurgency tactics, deeply demoralized, and strongly opposed to taking the offensive. Although the few thousand British troops still in Greece did not fully compensate for these problems, their presence symbolized the West's commitment to Greece and left the implication that, in the event of trouble, more soldiers would come. Thus the British pullout would have as much a psychological as a direct impact on combat. According to British observers, the key to success in the war was an improvement, not an enlargement, of the Greek army, followed by a relentless attack that would flush the guerrillas from their strongholds in the north.[19] Whether the enemy was killed, captured, or driven out of the country, the results would be the same: the war would come to an end, and the government could reestablish domestic order.

In January 1947 the White House sent a special economic mission headed by Paul A. Porter to investigate the Greek government's requests for assistance. Porter seemed qualified for the arduous task. Before World War II he served as legal counsel for the Department of Agriculture and then for the CBS radio network, and during the war he worked with the Office of Price Administration (OPA) and later the Office of Economic Stabilization. After the war he became administrator of the OPA. The Porter mission returned to the United States a month later with a gloomy report showing that the country's economy was worse than anyone had imagined. Greece was nearly bankrupt, inflation was rampant, and blackmarketing and profiteering were widespread. Further, government interest in reform and investment in long-range reconstruction programs were virtually nonexistent, and political infighting and corruption riddled nearly every aspect of Greek life. The result was a nationwide sense of helplessness that the Greeks believed was capable of remedy only by a massive infusion of U.S. aid. Porter told Truman that the prognosis for essential economic changes was poor because the Greek government was "completely reactionary, . . . incredibly weak, stupid and venal."[20]

The U.S. ambassador in Greece, Lincoln MacVeagh, acknowledged the domestic political and economic dimensions of the trouble in Greece, but he also stressed the international scope of the problem. He enlisted the support of the new secretary of state in Washington, George C. Marshall, for the creation of a coalition government that would encourage economic reforms and thus resolve part of the issue. Marshall was receptive to these warnings. He had just become secretary of state in January 1947, having recently returned from a failed attempt in China to establish a coalition government that could avert civil war. Now, in Greece, Prime Minister Tsaldaris reluctantly resigned in late January, choosing to serve as vice-premier in a coalition regime headed by the new premier, Dimitrios Maximos. MacVeagh doubted that these changes would accomplish much. He did not agree with Porter that the problem in Greece was solely domestic, whether economic or political in nature. Much of the trouble, MacVeagh argued, came from outside the country. After considerable resistance, Porter finally conceded that the prerequisite to economic revival was resolution of the military problems along the northern border of Greece. The most immediate requirement, Porter now told the president, was military assistance. Otherwise, the economic rehabilitation of the country would have no chance for success.[21]

By late February the government in London heightened the anxiety in Washington by warning of an imminent end to British military aid to Greece and Turkey. The White House knew about the economic problems facing the British. Both in manpower and in industrial resources, they had suffered devastating losses in World War II that now combined with postwar needs, a heavy drain on sterling balances, overseas indebtedness, and poor crop yields caused by unusually bad weather to force London to reduce its role in international affairs. On Friday, February 21, the British embassy in Washington notified the State Department that on the following Monday the British ambassador, Lord Inverchapel, would deliver two notes: one explaining the cutbacks in Greece, the other focusing on those in Turkey. In accordance with diplomatic procedure, however, the first secretary of the British embassy forwarded copies of the notes that same Friday. They declared that British military assistance to both countries would end on March 31.[22]

The British notes accomplished their objective: the Truman administration had no choice but to assume the burden in the Near East and to draft an aid bill for that purpose. The two prime movers behind this new policy were Undersecretary of State Dean Acheson and the director of the State Department's new Near Eastern and African Affairs Division, Loy Henderson. Both men recognized the strategic importance of the Near East, and both were stern advocates of a hard-line stand against Soviet aggression. Marshall required no convincing. He was out of town when the notes arrived but had earlier reacted to a memorandum from Henderson about Greece by instructing Acheson to prepare an economic and military aid package for that country. The undersecretary of state now directed Henderson to work with his staff over the weekend in writing an aid program for Greece and Turkey that could be presented to Marshall on Monday morning. If the secretary of state approved, he would show the proposal to the president. Henderson recommended that Truman discuss the matter with numerous groups, including the army, navy, and Congress, before sharing it with the American people. Everyone must know "what's going on," Henderson declared. On Monday Marshall approved the draft and assured Henderson and others in the secretary's office that he would urge the president "to tell the world the truth." The president's chief of staff, Admiral Leahy, warned that such an aid program would necessitate the United States' "open involvement in the political and financial affairs of European Governments." Truman did not shrink from that prospect but maintained, "This is the right line."[23]

■ ■ ■ During the next few weeks the administration prepared for congressional consideration a Greek-Turkish aid bill that was part of a larger global strategy intended to halt Soviet aggression. Henderson chaired special committees whose membership included Kennan, Bohlen, and John Hickerson, all State Department advisers who shared deep suspicions of Soviet expansionist behavior and sought to bring it under control. The United States, the committee members agreed, had to assume the responsibility for safeguarding Greece and Turkey. Failure to do so would allow those countries to become "Soviet puppets," setting an example of unchallenged Soviet aggression that would encourage further Communist encroachments. The problems in Greece and Turkey, according to one committee's conclusion, should receive consideration "*as a whole*" because they were "*only part of a critical world situation confronting [the United States] today in many democratic countries.*" Although some advisers feared that economic involvement in Greece could develop into a military commitment and the ultimate assignment of U.S. combat troops, others argued that the continued presence of British troops would provide time for the assistance program to succeed before the issue could arise. The central question was how to convince a Republican budget-cutting and isolationist-minded Congress that it must approve an economic assistance program as one aspect of a new foreign policy that might entail extending aid to other troubled countries as well. Hickerson insisted that the administration had to scare both the American people and Congress into supporting the bill and the larger strategy it implied.[24]

The danger in an alarmist public relations campaign was that the White House would become trapped in its own declarations. Given the administration's assumptions about Soviet behavior, the global approach was inescapable. Further, the possibility that an initial economic involvement might escalate into military aid was implied by the administration's professed emphases on a flexible policy. Indeed, as one writer suggests, the United States' determination to define its interests as global in dimension dramatically raised the danger of overcommitment. The primary concern was Greece, for the situation there was much more complex and dangerous than that in Turkey. Greek economic needs were inextricably entangled with political problems, and both were immensely complicated by the military threat of guerrillas who were encouraged and assisted by neighboring countries. But the White House was confident that it could keep the situation under tight control and thus act with ample restraint. It intended to stay out of entangling regional issues and focus on "the reestablishment of internal order and the necessary political and economic stability to permit Greece to maintain her independence and the form of government desired by the majority of the Greek people."[25] The White House planned to react to individual problems with equivalent responses, designed to match the other side's aggressive action with a carefully constructed policy that would not allow the situation to escalate. Unexpected problems, of course, could interfere with the success of a well-reasoned policy. Such a strategy could slip out of control if policymakers had no time for cool reflection and reason gave way to irrationality or anger. Most important, they had to maintain the distinction between rhetoric and action without allowing the former to rule the latter. For the present, however, no such danger appeared to exist, because economic assistance seemed reasonable and sufficient.

But before the administration could approach Congress for help, the military danger suddenly worsened in Greece and convinced the Truman administration to shift its emphasis from economic to military aid. The ultimate objective, the economic rehabilitation of the country, remained constant; but prevailing sentiment in Washington was that the required economic reforms could not take place unless military stability was achieved first. In a paper written by the State-War-Navy Coordinating Subcommittee on Foreign Policy Information (FPI 30), the administration stated its central purpose: to "give support to free peoples who are attempting to resist subjugation from armed minorities or from outside forces."[26] The right of self-determination could not be guaranteed without the prior establishment of personal security.

To win support for the aid bill, the president met with congressional leaders from both political parties and then went before both houses in special session to call for economic and military appropriations for Greece and Turkey. In the cabinet room on February 27, Marshall explained the situation in the Near East to a bipartisan congressional delegation, but his stiff and dry presentation failed to convince listeners that the situation posed a serious threat to U.S. interests. Though ready since the fall of 1946 to confront the Soviet Union, at least in word, Republicans and southern conservatives were loath to risk dollars and possibly lives, especially in a

Clement Attlee, Harry Truman, and MacKenzie King issuing joint communique on atomic energy, November 15, 1945. Photograph from Matt Connelly scrapbooks; courtesy of Harry S. Truman Library.

President Truman and Secretary of State Dean Acheson in Oval Office, December 1950. Photograph by Abbie Rowe, National Park Services; courtesy of Harry S. Truman Library.

Presentation of Marshall Plan Album to George C. Marshall by Dean Acheson and Paul Hoffman in April 1950. Economic Cooperation Administration, Department of State photograph; courtesy of Harry S. Truman Library.

Winston Churchill, Harry Truman, and Joseph Stalin at Potsdam Conference in July 1945. U.S. Army photograph; courtesy of Harry S. Truman Library.

Tempelhof Airport in Berlin with planes ready for Berlin Airlift, August 1948. Courtesy of Harry S. Truman Library.

President Truman signing the North Atlantic Treaty on August 24, 1949. Photograph by Abbie Rowe, National Park Services; courtesy of Harry S. Truman Library.

what he'd do. He would make a statement of global policy, but confine his request for money right now to Greece and Turkey."[28]

Speaking before a joint session of Congress on March 12, Truman made no reference to the Soviet Union while insisting that a worldwide struggle was under way between two forces, one calling for self-determination, the other for totalitarianism, and both stemming from the age-old battle between Old World Europe and New World America. The governments in Greece and Turkey were in danger of falling before totalitarian aggression and had asked for U.S. help. Not only would the collapse of these two countries endanger order in the eastern Mediterranean and permit totalitarian forces to sweep into the Middle East, but the example of unchallenged aggression would send a message to the rest of the world that the United States' pledges to defend self-determination were empty rhetoric. The outcomes in Greece and Turkey were vital to the free world in both a geopolitical and a symbolic sense. Their fall, the president warned, would "undermine the foundations of international peace and hence the security of the United States."[29]

In a statement that capsulized what soon became known as the Truman Doctrine, the president paraphrased FPI 30 only slightly in declaring: "I believe that it must be the policy of the United States to support free peoples who are resisting attempted subjugation by armed minorities or by outside pressures." The assistance "should be primarily through economic and financial aid, which is essential to economic stability and orderly political processes." He asked for $400 million in emergency assistance, the bulk of it military and primarily for Greece. To implement the program, he called for civilian and military advisers to supervise the distribution of funds. Freedom was indivisible, Truman insisted: "If we falter in our leadership, we may endanger the peace of the world—and we shall surely endanger the welfare of our own nation."[30]

The president's address was of monumental importance. He was asking Congress to support a military and economic aid package that would, for the first time in the nation's history, involve it in Europe's political and military concerns during peacetime.[31] Further, he was calling upon the nation to assume the responsibilities for safeguarding the global peace bequeathed by World War II. Truman had referred only to Greece and Turkey, but he had made clear that they were examples of a broader threat to freedom. In the past, Americans had identified aggression with direct action engaged in by armies wearing uniforms or some form of national insignia. The present danger came from "armed minorities" and "outside pressures" that were nearly impossible to trace to national origins.

To listeners, however, the message was clear: the "minorities" were Communists and the "pressures" were those emanating from the Kremlin. In countering tactics that were as old as man but nonetheless new to the atomic age, the president advocated an assistance program that would provide a response equal to the danger posed.

Truman left immediately after the speech to vacation in Key West and await the nation's reaction. It came quickly. Although the opposition was vocal and included influential isolationist groups and leading political figures such as Robert Taft and Henry Wallace, it was no match for those who praised the administration for accepting reality. Taft warned of a deepening European involvement that could bankrupt the United States, and Wallace (still embittered by his dismissal from the administration the previous autumn) termed the Truman Doctrine a declaration of war on the Soviets and a "global Monroe Doctrine." But the *New York Times* hailed the end of the United States' "epoch of isolation" and welcomed "an epoch of American responsibility." James Reston spoke for many of the *Times*'s readers in declaring that the strategic interests of the United States included the safety of the Middle East. *Time* and *Newsweek* magazines defended the administration's pledge to protect freedom throughout the world. On the other side of the issue, the *Nation* and the *New Republic* joined liberal public leaders in criticizing the White House for adopting a policy that could lead to war with the Soviet Union. Columnist Walter Lippmann favored the assistance measure but insisted that the administration should first have worked through the UN to exert public pressure on the instigators of trouble, thus avoiding the accusation of U.S. imperialism.[32]

Kennan had meanwhile become disenchanted with the White House for embarking on what he feared was a dangerous and provocative crusade of global proportions that could culminate in disaster. Marshall, Bohlen, and Clifford conceded that the president's speech was strong, but they justified the approach as vital to securing congressional support. Kennan, however, insisted that the administration had devised a faulty strategy by failing to match the nation's objectives with its means for achieving those objectives. Although he supported a firm stand against Soviet aggression, he argued that the situations in Greece and Turkey were political and ideological in nature and that both problems could be resolved by economic assistance. Speaking before the National War College in Washington, Kennan declared that the Soviets had "taken care to shove forward Balkan communists to do their dirty work for them and to disguise as far as possible their own hand in Greek affairs." He admitted that failure to act would "confirm the impression that the Western Powers were on the run and that international communism was on the make." But he warned that the administration's emphasis on military aid was misguided and conducive to dangerous involvement. The president's speech before Congress was "grandiose" and "sweeping," he charged, bulging with commitments that the country could not and should not honor.[33]

Though Kennan and the White House seemed too far apart on policy to close their differences, both parties were in fact advocating the United States' global involvement. Kennan was not converted by the White House belief that the strong language in the president's speech was necessary to win congressional support. Nor was he confident about White House assurances that policymakers could control the temptation to escalate the amount and kind of aid if the intended results were not immediate. But like the White House, Kennan insisted that help should go only to countries that were both essential to U.S. security and capable of salvation. He also agreed with the president that the Kremlin was looking for "soft spots" throughout the world and that the United States had to contain Soviet expansion by shoring up weak areas. Finally, Kennan shared the prevailing perception in Washington that the Kremlin was instigating troubles on a global scale. Despite Kennan's charges, the Truman administration did not favor a blanket commitment to send assistance to any area of the world, regardless of its importance. The problem lay in defining the United States' interests. During the postwar era almost any area could be considered important either because of its physical resources or strategic location or because its collapse would symbolize Western weakness and hence encourage other peoples to make concessions to Communism. In this new kind of war, any threat to freedom was potentially worldwide in scope, and the only country capable of bringing such aggression to a halt was the United States.[34]

Both the Truman administration and Kennan believed in a flexible foreign policy, and despite their differences, they were largely in accord on the way the nation's objectives should be achieved. Both sought to checkmate Soviet advances by means short of war. Both thought that Greece was strategically and symbolically important to U.S. interests, and both believed the country capable of salvation. Their disagreements arose over their analyses of the causes of the unrest in Greece. Kennan insisted that economic palliatives were sufficient; four decades afterward, he still maintained that the real Soviet threat in 1947 was "ideological-political" and not military. The White House, however, was convinced that underlying economic problems had become so serious that they had taken on military dimensions. By this argument, the United States' interests were at stake and conditions were susceptible to correction—the "remedy" at that time being military in nature.[35]

■ ■ ■ Congressional hearings on the Greek-Turkish aid bill began a week after the president's message. Acheson and an impressive array of administration spokesmen appeared before the House and Senate committees on foreign affairs to defend the need for assisting the two countries. The White House anticipated success and, in expectation of reimbursement, had already extended interim assistance to Athens and Ankara from the Reconstruction Finance Corporation. In addition, by early April Washington had sent a number of "surplus property credits" that included a patrol boat, a landing ship dock, nearly three dozen training planes, fourteen aircraft engines, and nineteen minesweepers, along with the same number of landing craft. Eventually the list would include gasoline, airplane parts, motor vehicles, food and clothing, mules and horses, and weapons and ammunition. Secretary of War Robert Patterson insisted that although many Americans feared that the assistance program would lead to direct military involvement in the Greek war, the aid bill contained a safeguard—the U.S. military figures would serve "in an advisory capacity only"—that would establish the necessary limitations on the United States' role.[36]

Acheson confronted several explosive issues in defending the administration's requests. He answered the most frequently voiced criticism of the aid proposal by insisting that the UN did not have either the money or the authority to resolve the Greek-Turkish problem. To those who suspected that cynical U.S. oil barons were behind the nation's concern for the Middle East, Acheson admitted that oil was an important consideration but declared that the White House would have pursued the same policy regardless of its presence. Oil, he argued correctly, was only a single component of the nation's overall strategic interests in the area. In defense of Acheson's stance before the committees, several facts eventually became clear. Byrnes, Forrestal, and Leahy had all gone on public and private record in declaring that Middle East oil had been integral to success in World War II and would continue to grow in importance in the period afterward. Although the United States had more than enough oil at war's end, that surplus would diminish as needs arose; a temporary sufficiency in no way lessened the importance of the massive reserves of the Middle East (40 percent of the world's supply). Further, recent studies show that the economic objectives of U.S. oil companies paralleled, not dictated, the policy of the United States in the Middle East.[37]

The most touchy issue, however, was a fear of war caused by the possible dispatch of U.S. soldiers to the Near East. The bill's provisions, Acheson emphasized, "do not include our sending troops to Greece or Turkey. We have not been asked to do so. We have no understandings with either Greece or Turkey, oral or otherwise, in regard to the sending of troops to those countries." When pushed on whether intervention would provoke an incident leading to all-out conflict, Acheson told the hushed audience: "I was going to say—no possibility it would lead to war." After a brief hesitation he conceded: "I don't think it could lead to war."[38]

The aid program, Acheson gravely maintained, was intended to protect self-determination wherever endangered, but it did not entail an automatic commitment on a worldwide basis; each request for aid would receive individual consideration solely on its merits. Most important, Acheson declared, countries inside the "Russian sphere of physical force" would not be eligible for help. Vandenberg discerned the conditions that must precede U.S. assistance and sought to clarify the point: "In other words, I think what you are saying is that wherever we find free peoples having difficulty in the maintenance of free institutions, and difficulty in defending against aggressive movements that seek to impose upon them totalitarian regimes, we do not necessarily react in the same way each time, but we propose to react." Acheson concurred. Vandenberg's words, Joseph Jones later declared, highlighted the "test of practicability" and hence defined "the global implications of the Truman Doctrine."[39]

If the White House was confident that its involvements in Greece and Turkey would not get out of hand in either military or global terms, it nonetheless recognized that advisory functions alone might not be sufficient to resolve problems. The administration's repeated calls for flexibility and open-endedness in the program underlined the need for keeping all options open. If the British pulled out the last of their troops from Greece, the United States would have to decide whether to forsake its commitment or to expand it to include at least a token combat force in order to symbolize the West's continued protection of the right of self-determination. Given the United States' massive postwar demobilization, a large contingent of soldiers was out of the question. By June 1947 the United States had reduced its armed forces, from twelve million in June 1945, to one and a half million. In Europe the nation's troops had been slashed from three and a half million to a bare two hundred thousand. The Soviet army was much larger. Though cut from its high of eleven million in May 1946, it still maintained nearly three million men by early 1948. Only a major mobilization in the United States could provide the men required in Greece, and the administration could not afford to make such a politically unpopular move. Washington decided that it would have to convince the British to postpone military withdrawal. In an effort to ease this growing concern, Brigadier General George Lincoln testified that even if the British withdrew their last ten thousand combat troops from Greece, the British Military Mission would continue its task of training the Greek soldiers. But this was small consolation. Not only did the mission number a mere few hundred noncombatants, but its efforts had led to no noticeable improvement in Greek military performance. Writing to the president, Republican Representative Francis H. Case sounded an ominous warning even as he spoke in favor of the bill: "No country, ours or any other, is wise enough or rich enough, or just plain big enough to run the rest of the world."[40]

Congress approved the Greek-Turkish aid bill on May 22, 1947, but only after Vandenberg had attached an amendment reconciling the measure with the UN Charter. The vote was wide and bipartisan: 67 to 23 in the Senate, with 35 Republicans for the bill and 16 opposed, and 287 to 107 in the House, with 127 Republicans for and 93 against. In accordance with White House recommendations, the bill included $400 million in aid, with three-fourths of the allotment, the greater part of it military in nature, going to Greece. Under the Vandenberg amendment, U.S. assistance would terminate if either the Security Council or the General Assembly decided that "action taken or assistance furnished by the United Nations makes the continuance of such assistance unnecessary or undesirable." To strengthen the amendment, the United States agreed to forgo the "exercise" but not the "right" of veto in the Security Council. Thus U.S. aid would end if either of the recipient countries filed a request based upon majority popular support (which was unlikely in either Greece or Turkey) or if the president decided that the program had succeeded or, on the other hand, that it had no chance to escape failure. Barring such developments, the aid program would extend through June 30, 1948, with the option of renewal. Many congressional members tended to agree with Republican Senator Henry Cabot Lodge, Jr., who declared that "there is nothing whatever in this bill which involves the United States in combat operations in Greece." Moreover, Lodge believed the administration correct in arguing that U.S. strategy in Greece required both economic and military aid; each form of assistance complemented the other, so that they were inseparable. The new law proclaimed that the broad purpose of the assistance program in Greece and Turkey was to maintain "their national integrity and their survival as free nations."[41]

By the end of May U.S. aid efforts were under way in both countries, but the emergency in Greece continued to draw the most attention. Both missions reported to the coordinator of the program, George McGhee, who presided over a staff of seventy working in Washington and who was himself responsible to the undersecretary of state. The chief of the American Mission for Aid to Turkey was Edwin C. Wilson, also still ambassador to Turkey. The Greek arrangement was different, and as events would show, it provided its own problems. The chief of the American mission in Greece was not Ambassador MacVeagh but Dwight Griswold, a hard-nosed, often irascible Republican and former Nebraska governor who had fought alongside Truman during World War I and who, at the time of his appointment, was an official working with the U.S. military government in Germany. Griswold and MacVeagh would soon become a study in themselves of contrasting life-styles and approaches to the Greek problem: whereas the former was brash, blunt, and demanding, the latter was cultured, scholarly, and diplomatic. The military arm of the mission in Athens, the United States Army Group Greece (USAGG), consisted of fifty-four members, along with a small naval section of no more than thirty. U.S. military personnel would advise the Greeks on how to use the military and naval matériel as it arrived through assistance channels. They would cooperate with members of the British Military Mission, who retained their responsibilities for training the Greek army.[42]

The initial optimism that characterized the assistance program was soon dashed by the rapidly spreading war in Greece and by problems within the aid effort itself. The Greek army's first offensive against the guerrillas in April had ended in a failure that resulted primarily from its own ineptitude. Although government forces outnumbered their opponents 165,000 (including gendarmes) to 28,000, the guerrillas overcame their disadvantages in manpower and matériel by engaging in hit-and-run tactics and by receiving help from civilians whom the government found it nearly impossible to identify. The government's central objective, to encircle the enemy, entailed a quick pursuit operation and a rapid closing of the border, but the border was over six hundred miles long and wound treacherously through rugged mountains and dense forests. In addition, the day after passage of the Greek-Turkish aid bill, the UN investigating commission reported evidence of outside assistance to the guerrillas and other violations of the border by Yugoslavia, Albania, and Bulgaria. Rumors (never substantiated) were spreading in Greece (fostered by the Greek embassy in Washington) that the war was widening because of the imminent involvement on the guerrilla side of "international brigades" recruited from surrounding Eastern European states. Further, the director of USAGG, General William Livesay, encountered numerous problems in trying to mobilize the Greek military forces, and the personal and professional differences between Griswold and MacVeagh threatened to bring down the aid program from within.[43] In sum, the U.S. experience in Greece was beset with persistent and almost wholly unpredictable problems.

During the summer of 1947, however, the tensions associated with the perceived threat from the Soviet Union served to validate the United States' involvements in Greece and Turkey in the minds of many Americans. Marshall spoke at Harvard University in June about the enormous economic problems in Western Europe and urged support for a government program of assistance that would undercut the possibility of totalitarian exploitation. The following month, Congress passed the National Security Act, which replaced the amorphous National Military Establishment with the Department of Defense, provided legal sanction for the Joint Chiefs of Staff, established the National Security Council as an advisory body to the president, and founded the Central Intelligence Agency to collect and analyze intelligence information on a global scale. At the same time, Kennan (writing under the pseudonym "X") popularized his theories in an article entitled "The Sources of Soviet Conduct," which was published in the July issue of *Foreign Affairs*. The United States, according to Kennan, should react against the Soviets' indirect tactics with a "vigilant application of counter-force at a series of constantly shifting geographical and political points, corresponding to the shifts and maneuvers of Soviet policy." Although great confusion has erupted over whether Kennan took a universalist approach in foreign affairs, it seems clear that he still maintained that the United States had to seek to contain the spread of Communism in only those areas considered vital to U.S. interests.[44] But the number of areas thought vital was on the increase.

Even though Soviet involvement in these events was at the most indirect, the prevailing assumptions in Washington about the Kremlin's behavior had converted appearances into reality. Stalin doubtless favored the establishment of a Communist regime in Greece—*if* it came on its own and did not prompt U.S. intervention. But he would not risk a confrontation with the United States when he lacked atomic capacity and his Eastern European alliance system was not yet intact. Christopher M. Woodhouse, a British observer in Greece and author of numerous books on the subject, insisted that Stalin never seriously considered extending direct assistance to the guerrillas. But Washington could not be sure.[45] The Truman administration's overriding consideration was to halt what it perceived as Soviet aggression on a worldwide scale. Though the Kremlin had eased the pressure on Turkey, it had apparently increased the tempo in Greece and was threatening to do the same in Western Europe.

CHAPTER SIX

The Search for a Creative Peace Through the Marshall Plan

While the United States was implementing the Truman Doctrine in Greece and Turkey, the Cold War was intensifying in Western Europe. Many observers warned that postwar economic hardships on the Continent constituted threats to political stability, democratic institutions, and free enterprise. As Churchill declared, Europe was "a rubble heap, a charnel house, a breeding ground of pestilence and hate." Forrestal told Secretary of the Treasury John Snyder that "the world could only be brought back to order by a restoration of commerce, trade and business." The United States had contributed $9 billion in aid to Western Europe since V-E Day through organizations such as the United Nations Relief and Rehabilitation Administration (UNRRA), but by the middle of 1947 Europe lay vulnerable to totalitarianism because of the widespread hunger, destruction, and despair resulting from World War II. France and Italy seemed especially susceptible to revolution. Indigenous Communist parties were powerful in both countries and anticipated victories in approaching elections. UNRRA was fading as an economic force, particularly after the United States pulled out in 1946 amid charges that Communist regimes in Eastern Europe were distributing goods only to their political supporters. Acheson assured Europeans that the United States would continue assistance, but only "in accordance with our judgment and supervised with American personnel." Yet for the United States to discriminate among those countries seeking aid would widen the division between East and West. And European recovery seemed unlikely without the cooperation of Germany, whose participation was not acceptable to either France or the Soviet Union.[1]

The spring of 1947 brought more discouraging news: another meeting of the Council of Foreign Ministers had deadlocked in Moscow over the

German reparations issue, demonstrating the increasing differences among the Allies and adding urgency to the problems in Europe. By mid-April the French and Soviets had combined to block any progress toward drafting a peace treaty with their mutual enemy. Because French demands for security entailed territorial and economic encroachments on Germany, Stalin was encouraged to prolong the issue in hopes of seeing the members of the Western alliance drift farther apart. As the line hardened that separated the Eastern and Western zones of Germany, Marshall and Bevin advocated increased industrial production in their occupation zones as part of an effort to make them self-sufficient. Marshall insisted that "the vital center of Europe" was Germany and Austria because of their "large and skilled population" and "great resources and industrial plants." The Soviet Union, he urged, could not be allowed to win control of either state.[2]

Even Churchill's lurid descriptions had hardly done justice to the far-flung devastation on the Continent. Vast numbers of Europeans were unemployed and unable to purchase needed goods, the previous year's drought had nearly destroyed the crop yield, and the most severe winter in modern history—that of 1946–47—had brought blizzards followed by spring floods. Famine was a distinct possibility. In addition, ten million Germans had returned to their homeland from territories annexed by Poland, causing more drains on already scarce supplies. As prices soared and currency inflated, cigarettes became the chief medium of exchange in Germany. England could do little to help. The government in London had severely rationed the use of coal, an action that not only hurt people personally but further crippled an already staggering industrial complex by forcing over half of the country's factories to close. Financial assistance by itself was not enough. To meet present needs, the British were drawing heavily on the recent U.S. loan and, at the present rate, would exhaust that fund by late 1948. Should the Communist parties in France and Italy emerge triumphant, the British again (as in World War II) would be the sole democratic government in that part of the world.

Marshall's flight home from the Moscow Conference afforded him time for introspection. The problems he had encountered with the Soviets in the Moscow negotiations underlined his support for European assistance. "The patient is sinking while the doctors deliberate," he declared in a nationwide radio address on April 28, the day of his return to Washington. Immediate action was needed. The next day Marshall asked Kennan, then assigned as lecturer in the National War College, to establish a Policy Planning Staff in the State Department to determine how the United States might remedy the European situation. Marshall had only one directive: "Avoid trivia."[3]

The Clifford report of September 1946 had foreshadowed the European aid effort by calling on the United States to "support and assist all democratic countries which are in any way menaced or endangered by the U.S.S.R." In a statement that capsulized the central aim of the administration, the report had asserted that the United States "can do much to ensure that economic opportunities, personal freedom and social equality are made possible in countries outside the Soviet sphere by generous financial assistance."[4]

Another impetus to U.S. assistance came from a State-War-Navy Coordinating Committee (SWNCC) appointed by Acheson, which in late April 1947 submitted an interim report emphasizing that U.S. security rested on military and economic collaboration with friends abroad. Although the report contained no specific plan, it urged the United States to protect resources integral to "strategic objectives, or areas strategically located, which contain a substantial industrial potential, which possess manpower and organized military forces in important quantities, or which for political or psychological reasons enable the U.S. to exert a greater influence for world stability, security and peace." Because of the massive costs and destruction of World War II, the Europeans lacked the finances to underwrite the production of their own goods and thereby build a greater purchasing capacity. Unless economic conditions dramatically improved in Europe, the report warned, nations on the Continent could not continue buying U.S. goods. A marked fall in the United States' export surplus would hurt its economy. Thus a comprehensive program of foreign aid would serve U.S. interests, economically as well as strategically. SWNCC concluded that stabilization could come only through the economic integration of Europe and the reintegration of Germany into a long-sought system of multilateral world trade.[5]

In a broader sense, the bases for such an assistance effort lay in the Truman administration's move toward accepting responsibility for protecting and preserving the non-Communist world. The Truman Doctrine had been the first large step in that direction. Acheson recalled that during his talks with the president relating to the impending Greek-Turkish aid program, the point repeatedly arose that Greece and Turkey were "part of a much larger problem growing out of the change in Great Britain's strength and other circumstances." The undersecretary thought "it important and urgent that study be given by our most competent officers to situations elsewhere in the world which may require analogous financial, technical and military aid on our part." He immediately asked Assistant Secretary of State John Hilldring (who was also chairman of SWNCC) to initiate a study of the European problem. A few hours later Clayton sent a memorandum to Acheson, written after a trip to review conditions on the Continent, that recommended a $5 billion appropriation to help non-Communist nations suffering from the war. He also urged the United States to take over management of the Ruhr's coal production. To Clayton, a Houston businessman who owned the largest cotton-export firm in the world, the remedy was to reduce trade barriers and promote multilateralism: "The United States must take world leadership and quickly to avert world disaster." Later he was more emphatic: "*The United States must run the show.*"[6]

Thus the White House was ready to expand on the larger strategy underlying the Truman Doctrine. The guidelines for the extension of foreign aid were clear: the areas assisted had to be vital to U.S. interests and in danger of losing their freedom, and the United States had to have the capacity to help them. No one in the administration questioned the importance of Western Europe to the United States' security. Acheson referred to the region as the "Keystone in the arch which supports the kind of a world which we have to have in order to conduct our lives." In early May he had found a receptive audience in Cleveland, Mississippi, where he delivered an address arguing that Western Europe had to be free from Soviet control in order to save U.S. prosperity and halt the spread of Communism. Few could doubt that the Continent was in trouble or that the United States was able to provide assistance. The immediate problem, unlike that in Greece, was economic and not military. But unless the problem was soon alleviated, it could (as in Greece) assume serious political and military dimensions as well. Failure to take action could heighten the widespread sense of desperation until, in developments similar to those following World War I, its people would *choose* a totalitarian form of government. The equivalent response to the threat to stability posed by Europe's economic unrest was economic assistance.[7] The only question was whether the Truman administration could persuade Congress to support the remedy.

Less than a month later the Kennan committee presented a report that became the basis of the U.S. economic aid program for Europe. In a memorandum preceding the report, Kennan urged the government to use its assistance as leverage to encourage Western European nations to form a political organization. Such aid should be in the form of grants, not loans. To avoid further ideological division, the United States should permit Eastern European countries to participate. If the United States distinguished among recipients, it would not appear magnanimous before the world, and it would encourage the Communists in both France and Italy to obstruct their countries' participation in the aid program. The report of the Policy Planning Staff drew upon Kennan's ideas and on SWNCC's call for an integration of the economies of Europe and the establishment of a political federation that would include Germany. Kennan incorporated these ideas into a program that would implement both immediate and long-range aid. A substantial increase in coal output was vital to the Continent, and that depended on putting the mines of the Rhine Valley into operation. Indeed, the coal- and steel-producing Ruhr and Saar regions were vital to Europe's reconstruction. German rehabilitation had to take place in conjunction with that of the rest of Europe. Above all, Kennan wanted an aid program that would avert a confrontation with the Soviets. The United States should aim, said the report, "not to combat communism but the economic maladjustment which makes European society vulnerable to exploitation by any and all totalitarian movements and which Russian communism is now exploiting."[8]

The Kennan committee report concluded that the initiative for such a program must come from Europe: "The role of this country should consist of friendly aid in the drafting of a European program and of the later support of such a program, by financial and other means, at European request." But, the report warned, the application for assistance "must come as a joint request from a group of friendly nations, not as a series of isolated and individual appeals." Otherwise, the United States would have to choose which nation would receive what type of aid and how much, thereby subjecting the administration in Washington to blame for unpopular or unsuccessful parts of the program. Besides, Kennan later declared, the Europeans needed to resolve their economic problems by learning "to think like Europeans, and not like nationalists."[9]

The Truman administration hoped to entice Eastern Europe from its allegiance to the Kremlin and knew that this objective would be easier to achieve if the Soviet Union was not part of the assistance offer. When some advisers warned that Americans would oppose helping Communist nations, Kennan, Clayton, and Bohlen joined in insisting that the issue would not arise. During a meeting in Marshall's office, Kennan urged that the United States "play it straight" with the Soviets. "If they responded favorably," he argued, "we would test their good faith by insisting that they contribute constructively to the program as well as profiting from it. If they were unwilling to do this, we would simply let them exclude themselves. But we would not ourselves draw a line of division through Europe." Kennan emphasized that openly excluding the Soviets would cost the United States in world opinion by making it appear responsible for a divided Europe. Marshall agreed. The United States would have to extend the invitation and take the risk of incurring higher aid costs while having to overcome anti-Soviet feeling in Congress. On several occasions, Marshall and other spokesmen for the administration expressed hope that the Soviets and their allies would participate in the program. But Kennan was confident that two stipulations in the proposed bill—that recipients prove need by opening their files to inspection and that they allow Americans to participate in the process of economic reconstruction—would make it unacceptable to the Soviets. Clayton noted other safeguards. The Soviets would not be eligible for either short- or long-term aid because they were less devastated than Western Europe and had the basic requirements for survival, and their failure to join the World Bank had ruled out the possibility of their receiving loans from that institution.[10]

The White House realized that Soviet participation would undermine the aid program. If the Kremlin agreed to accept U.S. aid, the growing feelings of anti-Communism in Congress would receive great impetus and wreck passage of the bill. And even if Congress approved the proposal, the ensuing arguments over appropriations would obstruct hopes for success. In the worst-case scenario, the Soviets could compare their wartime damages to those in Europe and emerge with astronomical demands for aid that would be difficult to refute. Forrestal recorded in his diary that "the great objective that Marshall had was to ascertain whether cooperation with Russia was possible or not, and to show to both the world and our country that every effort had been made on our part to secure such cooperation so that we should have the support of public opinion in whatever policy we found it necessary to adopt thereafter."[11] The White House concluded that the problem of including the USSR would not arise.

Aid to Germany, which the Kennan committee's plan envisaged, was an anathema not only to the Soviet Union but also to France. Although Germany had recently been defeated and was now occupied by Britain, France, the Soviet Union, and the United States, it remained potentially powerful because of its manpower and vast deposits of coal and other industrial resources. The United States was caught in a dilemma. To stave off totalitarian exploitation of Western Europe, the nations of that region had to have an economic base that rested on German contributions. Without Germany's active participation in the economic rehabilitation of the Continent, the costs of U.S. assistance would rise in proportion to those amounts not furnished by the Germans. But political considerations were also important. To push for Germany's revival would alienate a French ally who had been victimized by German invasions in 1871, 1914, and 1940. Indeed, France called for reparations in the form of control over the coal-mining regions of the Saar and for the separation of the Ruhr and Rhineland from Germany. A restored Germany would likewise infuriate the Soviets, who themselves had undergone a number of German invasions, twice in the twentieth century. France, however, was the immediate obstacle to a successful aid program. The U.S. ambassador in Paris, Jefferson Caffery, reported Bidault's fear that the Ruhr, Rhineland, and Saar would "serve as a springboard for aggression against France: not German as such but from a Russian-dominated Germany."[12] The United States had to convince the French that the Communist danger to the Continent was greater than the threat of Germany.

■ ■ ■ At Harvard's commencement ceremonies in June the secretary of state outlined the essentials of what became known as the Marshall Plan. Before a large audience shaded by elm trees, Marshall depicted the "economic, social, and political deterioration" of Europe and argued that it was conducive to the triumph of totalitarianism. Although he did not suggest a way to accomplish the integration of the Continent, he urged the European governments to take the initiative in formulating an assistance plan that the United States would underwrite. Drawing heavily from the ideas in Kennan's report and in Clayton's memorandum of late May on the European crisis, Marshall warned that the administration should not distinguish between the types of governments receiving U.S. aid: "Any government that is willing to assist in the task of recovery will find full co-operation . . . on the part of the United States government. Any government which maneuvers to block the recovery of other countries cannot expect help from us." The United States' policy, he said, was "directed not against any country or doctrine but against hunger, poverty, desperation, and chaos."[13]

Marshall did not present a specific "plan" of reform but spoke in general terms of relieving Europe of the economic misery that Clayton had seen firsthand. Although it now appears that at the time of Marshall's speech, European production and trade were increasing and the only country with people starving was Germany, Clayton's observations led him to emphasize that "steadily deteriorating" economic, social, and political conditions were threatening to "overwhelm Europe." The division of labor had crumbled, according to his account, leaving millions of urban dwellers on the verge of starvation. The European capitalist system was in danger, and the United States had to take the lead in bringing about what Marshall termed a "cure rather than a mere palliative."[14]

In response to Marshall's invitation, Bevin and Bidault met in Paris in late June, and then asked Molotov to join them. Stalin was at first hesitant to comply with the request. He knew that his refusal to attend would strengthen ties among the Western countries and perhaps undercut the efforts of domestic Communist parties throughout Europe. He also realized that acceptance of the U.S. aid plan would entail Western involvement in Soviet affairs. Further, U.S. economic assistance might threaten Soviet security by stimulating a resurgent Germany and by enticing Eastern European nations to move closer to the West. After weighing the opposing factors, he sent Molotov to the meeting.[15]

The tripartite conference in Paris was characterized by invective and divisiveness. The U.S. stipulations of European integration and German reintegration caused heated and vituperative disagreements. Bevin was not enamored of the call for integration. What he envisioned was some kind of organizational network that would maintain his country's status as a major power—a customs union that would be free of either U.S. or Soviet control and that would consist of Western Europe and the British Commonwealth as separate entities connected by common interests. Bidault remained adamantly opposed to German involvement in any program, but because of the restraints forced upon him by the Communist party at home, he was willing to give Britain the lead in the negotiations. Molotov also rejected German participation until the four powers reached agreement on a treaty that would relegate Germany to a permanent secondary status. When he asked Bidault if the French would forgo reparations and approve increased German industrial production to promote Europe's recovery, the French foreign minister was evasive. Internationalization of the Ruhr soon became the French bargaining card for participation in the aid effort. The chances seemed bleak for an aid program that strictly followed U.S. lines.[16]

Molotov, however, drove the British and French together when he, with some justification, asked Bidault what he and Bevin "had done behind his back." Had they conspired with the Americans against his government? Molotov's suspicions were not entirely unfounded. Clayton had been in London between June 24 and 26 to, in his own words, "discuss Marshall's proposal with the heads of the principal governments concerned" (Britain, France, Italy, and the Benelux nations). Bevin and Bidault had already met in Paris before Clayton arrived in London. Whether or not Molotov knew about these prior meetings, he was expressing a long-standing Soviet fear that the Western governments were in collusion against the USSR.[17]

Molotov's reservations about the U.S. offer drove a wedge between the Soviet Union on the one side and France and Britain on the other. The Soviet foreign minister, joined by eighty-nine economic advisers and clerks, studied the aid proposal and eventually denounced it as another program in U.S. imperialism. The United States would exert too much control, said the Soviets. Rather than requiring recipients to make individual requests, it should permit each nation to prepare an inventory of its needs and should demand only a comprehensive list for all participants. In addition, Europeans should draw up needs and work out terms for U.S. assistance only after the United States had declared its conditions and assured congressional funds. Molotov, of course, was trying to mask deeper concerns. Though such an aid plan would be beneficial to all recipients, it would tie Eastern Europe with Western Europe and thereby undermine the Soviet sphere of influence. The Soviets did not want to become reliant on the West, and they refused to approve the establishment of a supranational organization that would determine individual aid allotments. Bevin understood Molotov's predicament and wryly remarked to the Soviet commissar: "Debtors do not lay down conditions when seeking credits from potential creditors." In a later exchange involving many of the same issues, Bevin smiled and commented: "If I were to go to Moscow with a blank check and ask you to sign it I wonder how far I would get at your end." Bidault agreed with Bevin that Molotov sought to subvert the conference, to stir up French opinion against the United States, and to block concessions that might encourage the Soviet Union's "hungry satellites" to participate. Both men consequently rejected Molotov's suggestions on the grounds that they amounted to a rejection of U.S. calls for a comprehensive plan, a joint recovery effort, and a sharing of resources. They would accept help from the United States, Bevin and Bidault announced, with or without Soviet participation. Molotov accused the United States of attempting to divide Europe by interfering in the internal affairs of other nations, and with that got up and left the conference.[18]

The Truman administration was relieved by Molotov's departure. W. Averell Harriman, secretary of commerce and former ambassador to the Soviet Union, later declared that "Bevin did a superb job of getting Molotov out of Paris—by careful maneuvering. Bidault claims to have had a part in it. But Bevin had the courage to invite Molotov and the bluntness to get rid of him. This confirmed my impression that Molotov is essentially a dull fellow. He could have killed the Marshall Plan by joining it." Kennan insisted years afterward that the Soviets would never have consented to "cooperation in overcoming real barriers in East-West trade." They could not have subjected themselves to the United States. "So, in a sense, we put Russia over the barrel. . . . When the full horror of [their] alternatives dawned on them, they left suddenly in the middle of the night."[19]

Molotov, however, had struck a tender nerve when he charged the Truman administration with attempting to intervene in other countries' domestic concerns. The notion had its supporters in the United States as well as the Soviet Union. Republican Senator Henry Cabot Lodge, Jr., declared during the hearings on the European aid bill that "this Marshall plan is going to be the biggest damned interference in internal affairs that there has ever been in history." He concluded that "it doesn't do any good to say we are not going to interfere when the people in power stay there because of us." To counter this and other forms of opposition, the administration at length decided to formally tie Marshall, a respected and trusted war hero, with the aid proposal. Clifford had recommended calling it the "Truman Plan," but the president refused. "Are you crazy?" he asked. "If we sent it up to that Republican Congress with my name on it, they'd tear it apart. We're going to call it the Marshall Plan."[20]

Lodge and other critics refused to acknowledge that there was no reasonable alternative to the type of involvement implied in the aid effort. Congress would reject an aid bill that contained no controls over the matériel once it arrived in foreign ports. Past experiences with UNRRA had shown that aid did not always reach those who needed it. The crucial point was that the administration was convinced that intervention was acceptable in this case because the United States' goals were laudable or at least rational. Certainly Americans preferred to assist only those governments willing to help their own people and to promote democratic philosophies. And it would be naive to suppose that matériel sent to leaders in power would not have a favorable impact on their tenure in power. A wise investor makes no investment without inserting safeguards over its use. The White House understandably wanted assurance that only those people in need received the goods, and it expected returns in the form of economic and political stability in Europe that would thwart totalitarianism and help guarantee U.S. security.

Bevin and Bidault had hoped that Molotov would not participate in the aid plan and, taking advantage of his departure, immediately invited twenty-two other European nations to Paris in July to consider Marshall's proposal. Indeed, Bevin told Acheson that "the withdrawal of the Russians made operations much more simple." But not all invited nations agreed to attend. Eight governments under Soviet influence—Albania, Bulgaria, Czechoslovakia, Finland, Hungary, Poland, Rumania, and Yugoslavia—either ignored the invitation or announced their refusal to attend because, as they said, they suspected an imperialist plot. Czechoslovakia and Poland at first seemed interested. While the Paris meeting was under way, however, a Czech delegation led by Foreign Minister Jan Masaryk was in Moscow attempting to negotiate a trade treaty. Stalin, in reply to a question about Czech participation in the U.S. aid program, bitterly denounced the effort as an attempt "to form a Western bloc and to isolate the Soviet Union." He coldly continued: "We look upon this matter as a question of principle, on which our friendship with Czechoslovakia depends. . . . All the Slavic states have refused. . . . That is why, in our opinion, you ought to reverse your decision." The alternative was ominous: "If you take part in the conference, you will prove by that act that you allow yourselves to be used as a tool against the Soviet Union." The Czech and Polish governments backed down under this pressure and decided not to send representatives to Paris.[21]

By autumn, sixteen Western European nations had established the interim Committee for European Economic Cooperation (CEEC) to prepare a report on the objectives and needs of a European recovery program. Indeed, the White House expected CEEC to constitute a crucial step toward the economic and political integration of the Continent. The result, however, was not what the United States wanted. The participants preferred autonomy to subordination of their sovereignty under a supranational organization, and they did not favor joint programs aimed at fitting each production effort to Europe's overall needs. The British, for example, did not approve the Americans' call for a united Europe as a prerequisite for aid, but they also recognized that Congress would be reluctant to pass a bill if the European countries did not take the initiative toward resolving their own problems. According to the British chargé in Washington, Jock Balfour, his country had to show itself to be a good investment area. It could not seem to be "a poor risk and in grave danger of becoming a permanent pensioner of Uncle Sam." At the same time, however, Balfour understood that Europe—and particularly England—had to have a strong economy as "essential for American security and prosperity."[22]

The CEEC proceedings demonstrated the widespread economic and political differences between the United States and Western Europe as well as those among the Western European nations themselves. According to some observers the European governments submitted veritable "shopping lists" to the United States. One representative later insisted that "everybody cheated like hell in Paris, everybody." After a summer of deliberation, CEEC agreed to Germany's involvement in the program and asked for $22.3 billion of aid to be distributed over a four-year period and aimed at achieving economic rehabilitation within that time.[23]

The Soviets moved quickly to ensure that U.S. aid did not weaken their control over Eastern Europe and to minimize its impact on Western Europe. They gradually eliminated political parties in Hungary, guaranteeing a Communist election victory that Truman called "an outrage." They entered defense agreements with Bulgaria, Finland, Hungary, and Rumania, which supplemented those pacts earlier arranged with Czechoslovakia, Poland, and Yugoslavia. In October they established the Cominform in Belgrade, composed of the Communist parties of nine countries: the Soviet Union, Bulgaria, Czechoslovakia, France, Hungary, Italy, Poland, Rumania, and Yugoslavia. A Cominform manifesto called the "Truman-Marshall Plan" a "farce, a European branch of the general world plan of political expansion" by the United States. The Soviets also announced their own economic aid program, the Molotov Plan, which consisted of a series of bilateral treaties aimed at helping Communist regimes in Europe but which in fact did little to meet their needs. Communist-led strikes erupted in France and Italy, and the resulting disorder and violence tended to undermine the people's confidence in their governments and their pro-U.S. policies.[24]

While the European nations were debating their approach to the U.S. offer of assistance, the Truman administration promoted the aid bill by working closely with Senator Vandenberg, the Republican chairman of the Foreign Relations Committee. Vandenberg supported the impending assistance program for Europe as a continuation of the policy exemplified by the Truman Doctrine. He expressed his fears: that "independent governments, whatever their character otherwise, will disappear from Western Europe; that aggressive communism will be spurred throughout the world; and that our concept of free men, free government and a relatively free international economy will come up against accumulated hazards which can put our own, precious 'American way of life' in the greatest, kindred hazards since Pearl Harbor." The White House had anticipated Vandenberg's support; with the senator on board, the administration felt secure enough to ask for $597 million of interim assistance for Austria, France, and Italy as a "vital prelude" to the aid program. Interim aid would be the first step in a broad recovery program that would help clear away congressional opposition to other calls for help. Vandenberg urged the president to appoint a bipartisan group to make a report on the aid plan, terming this step a prerequisite to his cooperation.[25]

The administration responded with several measures designed to build public support for the program. To study the impact of the Marshall Plan on business, the president established the Committee on Foreign Aid, which was chaired by Harriman and consisted of leaders of business, banking, labor, and education. The chairman of the newly created Council of Economic Advisers, Edwin Nourse, led an investigation of the impact of an aid bill on the nation's economy. Truman also appointed a committee under the leadership of Secretary of the Interior Julius Krug to analyze the effect of the program on the nation's reserve of natural resources. And Attorney General Tom Clark and director of the FBI J. Edgar Hoover headed a campaign to whip up patriotic sentiment across the country, the highlight of which was a Freedom Train that traveled from coast to coast displaying such famous American documents as the Declaration of Independence, the Constitution, and the Emancipation Proclamation.[26]

The White House received encouraging reports from all these groups. The Harriman committee concluded that an aid plan would benefit business and recommended that in view of the "open ideological war" against the Soviets, the United States should send $17.2 billion of assistance to Europe over the next four years to protect the United States' own "vital interest—humanitarian, economic, strategic, and political." Nourse and Krug were confident that the United States could withstand the cost; indeed, the Council of Economic Advisers reported that the nation could underwrite an aid effort of $22.3 billion over the same period. To mobilize support, former Secretaries of War Henry L. Stimson and Robert Patterson (both Republicans) joined Acheson (who had recently resigned as undersecretary of state) in establishing the Committee for the Marshall Plan to aid European Recovery. It cooperated with the State Department in lobbying for public favor through newspapers, petitions, a speaker's bureau, and letter-writing campaigns to members of Congress. Presidential assistant Richard E. Neustadt later called the committee "one of the most effective instruments for public information seen since the Second World War."[27]

Congress approved an interim aid program that was essentially what the administration had wanted, $522 million of assistance for Europe, along with what the Republicans demanded and Truman had not sought —$18 million for Chiang Kai-shek's Nationalist government in China. Although the administration had wanted to keep European and Asian aid programs distinct and had for weeks resisted an assistance bill for the Chinese, its need for support from the China bloc in Congress proved decisive. Marshall accepted the outcome. The goal of U.S. policy "from this point on," he told the cabinet in November, was "the restoration of [the] balance of power in both Europe and Asia."[28]

■ ■ ■ In the aftermath of another frustrating meeting of the Council of Foreign Ministers in London (the fifth), Truman touched off a nationwide debate over the assistance program when in December he made a special appearance before Congress and asked for an appropriation of $17 billion of aid over the next four and a quarter years. The United States, he declared, would "contribute to world peace and to its own security by assisting in the recovery of sixteen countries which . . . [were] devoted to the preservation of the free institutions and enduring peace among nations." Cooperation with Europe was "proof that free men can effectively join together to defend their free institutions against totalitarian pressures and to promote better standards of life for all their peoples." The return of European political and economic order would stimulate U.S. trade, he said, and stop the growth of Communism.[29]

Reaction was swift and heavy on both sides of the issue. On the right, isolationist Senator Robert Taft dismissed the Marshall Plan as a "European T.V.A." or an "international New Deal" and told an English dignitary that even though the Marshall Plan was "very good," he opposed "fix it" programs and preferred the "Key-nation approach" over the "global approach." Taft joined former President Herbert Hoover in warning that although they too wanted to halt Soviet aggression, a massive aid program would involve the United States abroad and necessitate higher taxes and stricter economic regulation at home. From the left, Henry Wallace argued that the "Martial Plan" was the work of U.S. monopolists and imperialists who were helping themselves at the expense of justice and peace. Other Americans insisted that the government had already permitted too much wealth to leave the country and warned that the program might further hurt East-West relations. *Newsweek*'s conservative economist and commentator Henry Hazlitt warned the House Committee on Foreign Affairs that greater centralized control in Europe would hurt production, cause more inflation, and enlarge Europe's dollar deficit. Recovery, he argued, had to come from free enterprise. The United States should make its aid conditional on European reforms that would discourage nationalization programs conducive to statist and socialist regimes. Defenders of the Marshall Plan included conservative business groups like the Chamber of Commerce and the National Association of Manufacturers. But most private support came from academics, journalists, agricultural groups, big trade unions, and various influential organizations such as the Council on Foreign Relations, the Business Advisory Council, the Committee for Economic Development, and the National Planning Association. They rejected the call for a free market as inefficient and costly, and they favored the administration's goals of economic planning, Keynesian fiscal policy, more collaboration between the public and private sectors, and multilateral trade relations on a worldwide scale.[30]

In the course of events, the heightening Cold War encouraged Congress to comply with the president's request. As Kennan had foreseen, the confrontation between East and West was proving to be a global affair. Palestine was a hot spot in the Middle East; in the Far East war threatened in Korea and Chiang's Nationalists in China seemed on the verge of collapsing before the repeated assaults of Mao Tse-tung's Communist forces. In Europe the Communists in Czechoslovakia seized control of the government in February, the Soviets were exerting pressure on Finland to sign a mutual defense pact, the Communist party was expected to win the mid-April elections in Italy, and the situation in Germany was becoming explosive. Bohlen predicted a political battle with the Soviet Union over Germany and saw little chance of settling other issues on the Continent "until that crisis comes to a head."[31]

Of all the problems, the fall of Czechoslovakia to the Communists was the one that sent what Truman called "a shock throughout the civilized world." On March 14, three days after the Senate approved the European aid bill by a wide margin, he went before Congress to exhort Americans to support efforts to counter the Soviet menace to freedom. Declaring the Czech crisis to be symptomatic of a global threat, Truman called for a revival of selective service and a program of universal military training that would entail a year-long period of basic training of civilians, designed to create an army of citizen reservists prepared for active duty in time of danger. There was a ray of hope in these dark times, he reported. That same day in Europe, five nations—Britain, France, Belgium, the Netherlands, and Luxembourg—signed the Brussels Pact (or Western Union), which established a fifty-year treaty of defense and might help to bring order to the Continent. But much remained to be done. The Soviets and their agents, the president insisted, had "destroyed the independence and democratic character of a whole series of nations in Eastern and Central Europe."[32]

The United States' long-standing ties to Czechoslovakia made the collapse of its government particularly unsettling. The Czech republic had been created following World War I, largely through the efforts of President Woodrow Wilson. Its first president was Thomas Masaryk, succeeded upon his death by Eduard Benes. Even though Benes was still in office in 1948, the Soviet Union had forced him to accept Communist party members into the government after World War II. Elections in 1946 had then produced a coalition regime in which the Communists were the largest single group. Prime Minister Klement Gottwald was a Communist, as was the minister of the interior, Vaclav Nosek. The foreign minister, however, was Jan Masaryk (the son of the first Czech president), a liberal who had been educated in the United States and who claimed no party affiliation. A stalemate prevailed until the nation prepared for elections in May 1948. The previous February, Nosek began replacing non-Communists in the police force with Communists, a move that led to the resignation of twelve non-Communists from the cabinet. Gottwald then instructed Benes to appoint a new cabinet containing no one who was anti-Communist. Benes stalled, but he was in failing health and he could not count on Western assistance against his enemies. As the Communists cracked down with mass arrests, the Soviet Union's deputy foreign minister, Valerian Zorin, arrived in Prague, allegedly to oversee the distribution of a recent arrival of Soviet wheat. The message of intimidation was clear. Though the Soviets were not directly involved in the events leading to the government's fall, the Red Army was encamped on the Czech border at the time.[33]

The Truman administration was hotly indignant but unable to do anything. Benes (who died less than a year later) gave in to Gottwald on February 25, and even though Masaryk remained as foreign minister, the Czech government was now Communist. News of the coup sent what Acheson called "a very considerable chill" through the United States' diplomatic representatives in Europe; a number expressed feelings of déjà vu as they compared 1948 with the 1938 crisis following the ill-fated Munich Conference. The day after this second fall of Czechoslovakia the U.S. ambassador in Prague, Laurence Steinhardt, wrote Marshall that the Czech Communists had "browbeaten and exercised a degree of duress on President Benes strikingly similar to methods employed by Hitler in dealing with heads of state." In Washington the president told his daughter that the United States faced "exactly the same situation with which Britain and France were faced in 1938–39 with Hitler." The National Security Council declared that "Stalin has come close to achieving what Hitler attempted in vain. The Soviet world extends from the Elbe River and the Adriatic on the west to Manchuria on the east, and embraces one fifth of the land surface of the world." Washington regarded the Czech coup as an ominous change in the status quo, but it felt powerless to do anything because Czechoslovakia lay within the Soviet sphere of influence.[34]

The threatening news continued to arrive in Washington as the president prepared to deliver a major campaign speech in New York on the night of March 17. In the speech Truman warned that the Soviet Union was plotting the Communization of Finland as a prelude to taking all of Scandinavia. "We cannot sit idly by," he announced, "and see totalitarianism spread to the whole of Europe. . . . We must meet the challenge if civilization is to survive." A week before the president's address, word reached Washington that Masaryk had been found dead in Prague, his body lying on the ground below his apartment in the foreign ministry. Truman and many others—including a number of knowledgeable people then in Prague—attributed the alleged suicide to foul play. Before a large crowd in New York the president attacked Henry Wallace, who had declared that the Communists had taken over Czechoslovakia to protect themselves from a right-wing coup that the United States had intended to engineer. "I do not want and I will not accept the political support of Henry Wallace and his Communists," Truman declared. The audience cheered. "If joining them or permitting them to join me is the price of victory, I recommend defeat. These are the days of high prices for everything, but any price for Wallace and his Communists is too much for me to pay. I'm not buying."[35]

Though some writers have claimed that the president exaggerated the dangers in Europe, in truth he was relating his understanding of these events to the American people as he and his advisers saw them. Firsthand observers in Europe and analysts in Washington believed that the Communist threat was real and insisted that the United States was the only nation with the means for taking remedial action. Truman admitted that the administration cultivated public support for its foreign policy by taking advantage of the Soviets' "crazy" actions. Without them, he added, "we never could have got a thing from Congress." But this admission does not provide grounds for implying that the danger was imagined. The historic vulnerability of the Soviet Union's western borders presented a convincing argument for its expansion into Eastern Europe, whether for security or aggression. Until the documents in the Kremlin become available to researchers, one cannot be sure that Stalin would have refrained from taking military measures in Czechoslovakia or other troubled areas located within the Soviets' sphere of interest. A military reaction by the United States was inconceivable—both because the areas were in the Soviet sphere and because the U.S. military establishment had been seriously weakened by postwar demobilization and disarmament. In addition, although the American people were repelled by recent events in Europe, they were unwilling to support a military response. Nonetheless, as leader of the non-Communist world, the United States bore the responsibility of protecting countries that were in danger of collapse and that were capable of being saved. The president had to mobilize his people behind a foreign aid program designed to unify Europe and restore economic stability.[36]

Congressional reaction to the president's speech and to the events in Europe was immediate: in April the legislature enacted the Economic Cooperation Act, or Marshall Plan, by a wide margin of 329 to 74 in the House and 69 to 17 in the Senate. The resulting European Recovery Program provided $5 billion of aid to participating countries for the first year, with an additional $2 billion in other assistance. As was the case with the Greek-Turkish aid bill, Republicans and conservative southern Democrats recognized the tight relationship between U.S. and European interests and accepted the administration's warnings of the danger emanating from Communism. Perhaps more important, however, a poll taken in April 1948 revealed that 56 percent of Americans favored the aid effort as a humanitarian act. Truman hailed the law as "a striking manifestation of the fact that a bipartisan foreign policy can lead to effective action." And House Speaker Joseph Martin, Jr., highlighted the country's acceptance of its new role in international affairs by later writing that "events of the previous decade had made the United States the leader of the non-Communist nations. The country could not, if it wished, isolate itself from a world suddenly drawn close together. We had to carry the burden of leadership, costly as it was."[37]

The European Recovery Program met most of the administration's expectations. In it, Congress listed four steps by which Europe was to become part of a multilateral world trade system by the close of 1951, the expiration year of the program: increased production, domestic financial stability, expanded foreign trade, and economic cooperation among the nations. The Economic Cooperation Administration (ECA) would be an independent agency but would function under the State Department's direction in matters of foreign policy. The ECA would deal with domestic and foreign operations (not policy) by working under an administrator in Washington, a special representative of ambassadorial rank in Europe, and recovery experts in each participating country. In accordance with bipartisan policy, a Republican, Paul G. Hoffman, was chosen to head the ECA. President of Studebaker Corporation, he had been one of industry's representatives on the Harriman committee and was an ardent believer in multilateral trade. U.S. aid would go to member nations of the Organization for European Economic Cooperation (OEEC), which was established in Paris that same April. OEEC was to recommend, according to U.S. guidelines, how to distribute American aid and how to promote European economic cooperation and production. To remove trade restrictions, a European Payments Union would be established in two years to facilitate intra-European payments and thus encourage OEEC nations to move toward economic integration on a permanent basis.[38]

OEEC was designed to be a supranational organization, but it never fully achieved that status. In the first place, France reneged on its earlier agreement to invite German representatives to OEEC meetings; the U.S. military governor in Germany, General Clay, and his British counterpart, General Sir Brian Robertson, protested vigorously, but the French told the Germans not to attend. Even though German advisers were gradually "infiltrated" into the meetings, hard feelings remained. In the second place, the establishment of ECA missions in countries receiving aid helped to prevent OEEC from becoming the locus of authority. Further, the organization failed to arrange systematic investments among the European nations, and it never got involved in the process of determining and evaluating the effectiveness of assistance distribution. Finally, an OEEC member put his finger on one of the biggest problems when he prophetically observed that for the organization to work, its members "had to demonstrate that they were not cheating in favor of their own countries or showing undue partiality." Despite these shortcomings, OEEC imposed some order by providing valuable economic information that the governments had previously refused to share. If OEEC did not bring centralized authority on a Continental level, it did so on a regional basis and thus kept the door open for the formation of a truly supranational organization in the future. Additionally, the U.S. Congress smoothed some of the tendencies toward national control by establishing the use of counterpart funds, or local currency amassed from the sale of goods furnished by Americans. Under this system, the recipient government would control the funds but with the stipulation that it must consult with the United States about allotting as much assistance for relief and rehabilitation as for other economic projects. Thus the United States would share in control over funds, but as in the past, the ultimate economic and political power in Europe remained in the individual nations.[39]

■ ■ ■ When Truman signed the Marshall Plan into law, he activated an economic aid program that, in the American view, combined the nation's idealistic and realistic goals and thus was capable of meeting the dangers stemming from the new kind of conflict facing the West. The National Security Council insisted that the United States was engaged in a "struggle for power, or 'cold war,' in which our national security is at stake and from which we cannot withdraw short of eventual national suicide." To face this global danger, the United States had to take "a worldwide counteroffensive against Soviet-directed world communism." In New York the Council on Foreign Relations reversed its position and insisted that making "concessions" to the Soviets would not reduce their suspicion of the West. "The emphasis," argued the council, "is now definitely on firmness." Congressman John Davis Lodge of Connecticut warned against trying to "put Humpty Dumpty together again," and John Foster Dulles insisted that the time was "ripe for a really creative act." The congressional hearings showed that the Truman administration intended to revive the European economy in an effort to build a balance of power on the Continent that would contain the Soviet Union. The Truman Doctrine and the Marshall Plan, the president once proclaimed, were "two halves of the same walnut." As the former authorized military assistance to two countries (Greece and Turkey) in danger of Communist takeover through force of arms, the latter provided economic aid to Western European nations suffering from economic hardships that made them vulnerable to appeals by domestic Communist parties. White House aide George M. Elsey described the Marshall Plan simply as the "Truman Doctrine in action."[40]

If the Marshall Plan was what some writers have called a revolutionary end to isolationism and the beginning of the "American Century," it was also an evolutionary outgrowth of vast changes in the corporate structure of the United States that had been in motion since the period following World War I. By the mid-1940s a move was under way to reduce the role of direct government administration of both domestic business concerns and foreign recovery programs by establishing independent agencies that were under the management of those from the private sector and that were tied to private groups by advisory committees. Just as a search for economic and political order was under way in the United States' domestic affairs, the same process was beginning to take hold in foreign policy. Formulators of the Marshall Plan argued that economic growth and the molding of a single market in Europe could come only through the development of a supranational institution built on the principle of federalism that would encourage economic planning and control, cooperation between public and private groups, elimination of trade barriers, and easy convertibility of currencies. The principles of corporate efficiency that had begun to permeate U.S. business during the 1920s became a model for the makers of the Marshall Plan as they attempted to bring technical and management skills to the nation's diplomacy.[41]

Internationally, the Marshall Plan had numerous attractions that were, it must be admitted, not totally compatible. European integration, of course, was not a guaranteed step toward a global multilateral commercial system. To many observers, the Marshall Plan's stimulus to increased production would weaken the appeal of totalitarianism in Western Europe, revive hopes for the multilateral world trading system envisioned in the Bretton Woods agreements of 1944, and promote the spread of democracy on a global scale. To a number of Republicans—including Vandenberg and Dulles—the reconstruction of Europe would bring about a self-sufficiency on the Continent that would allow eventual U.S. withdrawal and thus a return to isolationist principles. The potential for problems emanated from the contradictory, if not mutually exclusive, nature of multilateralism and self-sufficiency. If in theory U.S. economic planners intended the Marshall Plan to be multilateral because it promoted international economic interdependence, in reality the Soviets' refusal to participate in the assistance program assured the development of a closed trading bloc of Western countries. The Truman administration sought to link the United States' strategic and political-economic objectives and thereby promote world peace and national security. The outcome would constitute the elements of what one State Department officer called a "creative peace": restraints on German nationalism; the reconciliation of Germany's rehabilitation with the security and economic concerns of France; and a balance of power strong enough to thwart Soviet expansion.[42]

The Marshall Plan demonstrated the administration's growing recognition of the irreconcilable interests of East and West in the Cold War. Some of the president's policymakers had declared that the one-world concept of Woodrow Wilson and Wendell Willkie was moribund. Burton Berry of the Foreign Service insisted that the time had come to "drop the pretense of one world." Kennan likewise spoke of a "two-world situation" before a Policy Planning Staff meeting. In early 1945 he had written Bohlen that the United States and its allies were heading toward a "basic conflict" with the Soviet Union over a "political program" that was "so hostile to the interests of the Atlantic community as a whole, so dangerous to everything which we need to see preserved in Europe." In a recommendation that Bohlen found "utterly impossible" for a democracy to accept, Kennan called for an outright division of Europe into spheres of influence. Within two years, however, Bohlen underwent a dramatic shift in attitude and admitted to "complete disunity between the Soviet Union and the satellites on one side and the rest of the world on the other." The unavoidable outcome, he continued, would be for each side to tighten its political, economic, financial, and military bonds to enable it to deal better with the other. Marshall concurred in November, when he again called for a reestablishment of the balance of power in Europe and Asia.[43]

The Marshall Plan and the Truman Doctrine exemplified two aspects of the Truman administration's approach to foreign policy. The totalitarian threat to free institutions had taken the form of a new sort of war fought on all fronts—economic, political, and diplomatic, as well as military. In Greece and Turkey, the immediate threat was military, whereas in Western Europe and the Near East the problem had not yet moved beyond the need for economic correctives. In all cases, however, the common goal of U.S. assistance was the economic rehabilitation of all countries concerned. The means toward that objective were different because the believed degree of danger was not the same. The Truman Doctrine and the Marshall Plan, then, were natural outgrowths of the administration's emphasis on flexibility and restraint.

■ ■ ■ CHAPTER SEVEN

Emerging Crisis in Berlin

Before either the Truman Doctrine or the Marshall Plan had a chance to work, the world's attention turned to a crisis slowly but surely emerging in Berlin. Whereas the problems in the Near East and Western Europe drew U.S. responses equivalent to the dangers, it looked for a time as though the crisis that erupted in Germany during the summer of 1948 would elicit a U.S. reaction out of proportion to the threat posed to its interests. The most severe test of the Truman administration's restraint took place in Berlin, the crossroads of East and West. The basis of the problem was clear. The conquering powers of World War II had occupied the city and, in a move that now seems to have been inescapable, had not only divided Germany into occupation zones but separated Berlin into sectors as well. Moreover, Berlin was located over a hundred miles within the Soviet zone, and the West was left with no guaranteed access to the city. It was almost certain that the Communists would try to hold West Berlin hostage in an effort to win a favorable German settlement.

In the minds of Stalin and his associates the Marshall Plan constituted an immense threat to Soviet security because the economic restoration of the Continent entailed the unification of Western Europe and the restoration of Germany. Because the resolution of Europe's problems was inextricably intertwined with the resolution of the German question, Germany would remain a focal point of trouble for years. Indeed, the first direct confrontation of the Cold War between the USSR and the United States developed in 1948 when the Soviets imposed a blockade on Berlin that the Truman administration interpreted as an effort to force the Western powers out of the city, prevent the establishment of a West German government, and allow the reunification of Germany along Communist lines.

The Berlin blockade demonstrated again that Germany was crucial to the European and world balance of power and that that country's strategic location, vast manpower, and rich industrial resources made it an immensely attractive prize in the competition between East and West. The crisis tested Western unity and underlined the growing split between East and West. Most important, it showed that the antagonists' goals in Germany, as interpreted in the opposing capitals, were irreconcilable. The president declared that the conflict concerning access to Berlin involved "a struggle over Germany and, in a larger sense, over Europe." The Soviet Union was testing the United States' "capacity and will to resist." The blockade, he believed, was "part of a Russian plan to probe for soft spots in the Western Allies' positions all around their own perimeter." Stalin's objective was "to force us out of Berlin." Some writers insist, however, that the Kremlin's purpose was not necessarily to drive the West out of the city but to compel a reopening of four-power discussions in an effort to prevent a revived Germany that might, for a third time in the twentieth century, pose a military threat to the USSR. Whatever the Soviet intention, neither side could tolerate a unified and unfriendly Germany. As it had done with the Truman Doctrine and Marshall Plan, the Truman administration intended to counter what it regarded as Soviet aggression with a measured and flexible response designed to avoid confrontations conducive to war. The United States had to maintain credibility with its allies while sending a message to the Kremlin that democracy would triumph in this new kind of conflict that depended upon patience, endurance, and self-control. Both in a symbolic and in a strategic sense, Berlin became a critical battleground of the Cold War.[1]

The Truman administration's perception of Soviet intentions regarding Germany now seems to have been distorted. The specific issues that pitted East against West were reparations, occupation policies, currency reform, control over the Ruhr's economic resources, and the level of industrial development. But overshadowing these matters was the broader issue of whether the United States and Britain could succeed in restoring a German nation strong enough to halt Soviet expansion and vigorous enough to spur the rehabilitation of the Continent.[2] The United States was convinced that the blockade was part of a master plan designed to promote the collapse of Allied unity and implant Communism throughout Germany. In truth, however, the Soviets' policy regarding Germany was not consistent and underwent important changes from 1945 to 1949. Immediately after World War II the Soviets wanted a unified but demilitarized Germany under their control. Tito's emissary, Milovan Djilas, claims that in the spring of 1946 Stalin was exuberant with wartime victories when he declared that "all of Germany must be ours, that is, Soviet, Communist." Molotov told Byrnes in that same year that after the Soviets had extracted reparations from the defeated Reich, he preferred a united but neutralized Germany. This goal appears to have remained constant throughout the latter half of the decade, but the Kremlin was nonetheless realistic enough to know that the chances for achieving a unified and weak Germany were fading in proportion to the growing Western presence in Europe. Having failed to achieve German reunification by 1947, the Soviets were content to seek half a loaf: a territorial division that would leave a strong East Germany and a weak West Germany. Maxim Litvinov, wartime ambassador to the United States and by 1947 deputy foreign minister, expressed the Soviets' willingness to accept a partial victory when he told CBS correspondent Richard Hottelet that since "each side wants a unified Germany—under its control," the country "will obviously be broken into two parts." At a meeting with Yugoslav and Bulgarian delegates in early 1948, Stalin likewise revealed his inclination to accept two Germanies when he asserted, "The West will make Western Germany their own, and we shall turn Eastern Germany into our own state."[3]

If Stalin was sending signals of his interest in a two-Germanies solution, the Truman administration either ignored them or did not pick them up; wartime agreements and Washington's firm policy of resistance toward the Soviets dictated rigid opposition to any compromise built upon permanent East-West divisions of Germany and Berlin. The White House instead regarded such Soviet hints as a guise for leading the West to relax its vigilance in Germany and thereby permit the Soviets to engage in a quiet campaign of infiltration and intimidation that would gradually bring all Germany under their control. Once this goal was accomplished, the administration maintained, the Soviets intended to force the West out of Berlin and thus complete the closing of the iron curtain. Guided by that belief, the United States worked with the British and then the French to hold onto West Berlin while building a democratic West Germany that would counter the Soviet challenge. From Stalin's perspective, he could not allow the construction of such a state: it would serve as the nucleus of a resurrected and unified Germany that would become the linchpin of Europe's industrial revival under Western management and direction. There were other considerations. Stalin had to maintain an aggressive foreign policy because of domestic reasons. He faced grave internal political troubles that would soon lead to a broad reshuffling of government figures in Moscow and the removal of several formerly trusted allies who appeared to have been soiled by exposure to the West. Finally, several writers believe that Stalin was both paranoid and vindictive and that he considered almost every move taken by the West to be hostile.[4] An East-West collision seemed likely—as long as each side demanded preeminence in Germany. For the first time in the Cold War the major antagonists openly confronted one another. And for the first time since August 1945 the United States entertained the notion of using the atomic bomb.[5]

■ ■ ■ Paradoxically, perhaps, the roots of the Berlin crisis lay in the harmonious relationship among the Allies during World War II. No one in 1944–45 warned of any potential danger from Berlin's becoming an enclave inside the Soviet zone. The West did not anticipate problems in moving between zones and was pleased to gain a position in the city from which it could administer its occupation forces. In addition, before the United States participated in discussions regarding postwar Germany, the Soviets had approved a British proposal that placed Berlin within the Soviet zone but under joint occupation. Roosevelt was unhappy with these recommendations, however, because they did not assign any part of Berlin to the United States. On a National Geographic Society map he drew in rough zones that awarded the United States a disproportionately large part of Germany in the northwest, pushed the British to the south, granted the Soviets a small strip in the east, and appeared (owing to the lack of clarity in the sketch) to put Berlin either inside the U.S. zone or between the U.S. and Soviet zones. The Joint Chiefs of Staff presented a counterproposal in March 1944 that, probably because of Churchill's arguments at Teheran in November 1943 and later State Department studies, called for a tripartite division of Berlin while placing it inside the Soviet zone; but the boundaries contained in the proposal were so confusing and inequitable that the U.S. ambassador in London, John Winant, opposed submitting the document to the European Advisory Commission. Roosevelt finally relented and approved the British proposal.[6]

After the Red Army invaded Germany in January 1945, the West expressed no alarm when the Soviets unilaterally assumed control over territorial and governmental matters, permitted the installation of Communist organizations, allowed troops and industrial groups to appropriate matériel from Berlin that had been intended for the West, and, interestingly enough, set all clocks to Moscow time. Consequently, when the West assumed responsibility for its own zones in July, the Soviets and the German Communists were already in a dominant position. The main objective of the United States, Britain, and France in 1945 was to achieve a good working relationship with the Soviets. Colonel Frank Howley, chief of the military government in the American zone, described a meeting of U.S., British, and Soviet commanders in early July: "I think it was a good indication of the policy we were to follow in Berlin for many months, doing almost anything to win over the Russians, allay their suspicions, and convince them we were their friends." He later noted that the Soviets were "hard bargaining, hard playing, hard drinking, hard boiled, and hard headed." Regarding negotiations, he added, "If you are soft anywhere, you'd better stay away from them. If you are competent, informed, fair, and 'fearless,' you'll get along fine."[7]

Euphoria over the impending end of the war and the Western objective of maintaining Allied unity alleviated any apprehensions regarding Western access to Berlin. Neither the West's military commanders nor its representatives on the European Advisory Commission tried to secure either a corridor into Berlin through Soviet-occupied territory or a written assurance of access to the city.[8] The matter was not even discussed during the war because the United States intended to seek an agreement afterward within the context of general military settlements. Besides, the Soviet representative on the European Advisory Commission declared that "the presence of American and British forces in Berlin 'of course' carried with it all necessary facilities of access."[9]

The Potsdam Conference of July–August 1945 firmed up many of the wartime understandings and, for that reason, left the mistaken impression that the German problem was nearing resolution. In accordance with the Teheran and Yalta conferences, the Allies agreed to democratize Germany after cleansing it of Nazism, militarism, and industrialism. But the Soviets suffered a serious setback at Potsdam when the Allies failed to agree on the reparations issue—on either amount or type. Byrnes had opposed the Soviets' call at Yalta for $20 billion (with half to the Soviet Union) as a "basis for discussion" later in Moscow. Instead, he recommended that the occupying powers exact reparations from their own zones, as the Soviets were already doing. After the Yalta Conference, as noted previously, the United States received reports that the Soviets were dismantling German capital equipment in their zone and transporting it to the USSR. Growing distrust of Stalin encouraged the Truman administration to push for a reparations program that would meet the needs of Western Europe and Germany. With that goal in mind, the West secured a provision at Potsdam that reparations payments "should leave enough resources to enable the German people to subsist without external assistance." Stalin, perhaps surprisingly, was amenable to compromise. In return for 25 percent of the industrial plant dismantled in West Germany, he agreed to provide raw materials and manufactured items from East Germany and to meet Poland's allotment of reparations from the Soviets' own share. The Allies called for four-power divisions of both Germany and Berlin (the French share, Stalin stipulated, to be derived from the zones originally assigned to Britain and the United States) and the stationing of a garrison in each area. However, during the occupation period (whose duration was never defined) the powers would treat Germany as a single economic unit. To discuss issues arising from the war, the conferees established the Council of Foreign Ministers.[10]

Under the authority of an Allied Control Council in Berlin, Greater Berlin was divided into four sectors of occupation. To coordinate the city's administration, the commanders-in-chief appointed four city commandants who would constitute the Kommandatura, the Americanized version of a vaguely defined Russian word referring to a joint governing authority. The Soviets insisted that the principle of unanimity govern all decisions and that the United States and Britain furnish food and coal to the Western sectors of the city. The potential for trouble lay in the rule of unanimity, for under it the Soviets could veto any proposal considered dangerous to their interests. General Clay, then deputy U.S. military governor in Germany, was so intent on cooperating with the Soviets that he only later grasped the far-reaching implications of the unanimity rule. In reference to access rights, he declared: "I must admit that we did not then fully realize that the requirement of unanimous consent would enable a Soviet veto in the Allied Control Council to block all of our future efforts."[11]

The defeat of Germany had created a power vacuum in Europe that quickly exposed the differing motives of the Allies. As Western forces moved into Berlin, Soviet officials insisted on exclusive control over traffic and were hesitant to relinquish the U.S. zone. These actions conflicted with an agreement worked out with the Soviets in June. Clay and his British counterpart, General Sir Ronald Weeks, had made a verbal agreement—a "temporary arrangement"—with Soviet Marshal Georgi Zhukov that the Allies could use, as a privilege and not as a right, a highway, a railroad, and two air corridors into the city. When the Allies began to need these facilities, however, the Soviets stressed the temporary nature of the agreement and seemed ready to announce its revocation.[12]

Even though Soviet policies in Germany were becoming a concern of the West, France was the most immediate problem. Indeed, in late 1945 Clay returned to Washington to insist to the State Department that the French, not the Soviets, were upsetting four-power harmony in Berlin. The French had cause for discontent. According to arrangements made at Yalta they were to participate in the occupation of Germany, but they had not been invited to Potsdam. Between the conferences, they had gained a zone in West Germany that was derived from parts of the U.S. and British zones, but the Allies had not made a decision regarding Berlin until, at Potsdam, the British awarded two boroughs from their own sector to the French.

Leaders in Paris were resentful about being left out of the Potsdam Conference and did not feel bound by its agreements to allow the revival of political parties and to treat Germany as an economic unit. They wanted security, which, Paris insisted, could come only from major territorial and economic concessions from Germany that included huge reparations, separation of the Ruhr and Rhineland from Germany, a long occupation by the Allies, and French incorporation of the coal-bearing region of the Saar. The French staunchly opposed a centralized administration for Germany because it would undercut their demands pertaining to the Ruhr, Rhineland, and Saar. Bidault feared that under Soviet control these areas would pose as much of a threat to France as they did under the Germans.[13]

Relations between the Eastern and Western allies followed a shifting course. In November the Allied Control Council approved the establishment of three air corridors (each twenty miles in width) from West Germany into Berlin, which could be used on an unrestricted basis. The following month Stalin supported Byrnes's proposal to establish a four-power treaty to keep Germany disarmed for twenty-five years. And in early 1946 the four powers agreed to establish an Air Safety Center in Berlin. But in East Germany the Soviets steadily consolidated Communist control by placing German Communists in important positions and by incorporating the economy into their alliance system. The Soviets also began rebuilding parts of East Germany's industry to produce goods for reparation purposes.[14]

The United States suspected that the Soviets intended to Communize all Germany. In Kennan's Long Telegram of February 1946 he warned of Soviet expansionism, and in March he noted that the Potsdam provisions for centralized agencies would further the Soviets' aim by making it difficult to restrict the growth of their influence in the Western zones. The U.S. ambassador in Moscow, Walter Bedell Smith, argued that the Soviet goal was "to create in Eastern Germany an anti-fascist republic as a preliminary to a Soviet socialistic state, or at least a state oriented directly towards Moscow." Proof for these allegations seemed to be mounting. During an April meeting of the Council of Foreign Ministers in Paris, Molotov suddenly showed no interest in his long-standing call for a four-power treaty that would disarm Germany, leading Byrnes to believe that the Soviets had changed position and now wanted the United States off the Continent. In an analysis that suggested an imminent departure from previous U.S. policy, advisers in Washington concluded that Potsdam's call to punish Germany was ill advised because it encouraged the growth of Communism there. The only way to undercut the Communists was to rebuild the German economy.[15]

Further impetus for a change in the United States' German policy came from the troubles that erupted in Berlin when the Soviets tried to force the Social Democratic party (which was Socialist) to merge with the Communists. Even though most Social Democrats were hesitant, it appeared that such an alignment might actually take place: the chairman of the party was favorable, U.S. and British military figures were initially indifferent, nearly all Germans in Berlin were preoccupied with their own miseries, and many had become disenchanted with the West for its willingness to accommodate the Soviets. Of three non-Communist groups in the city, the Social Democrats were the most powerful; they had more than fifty thousand members and had been the principal political party in the country professing democracy before the Nazis came to power. Indeed, the Social Democrats believed that the Nazis could not have achieved prominence if the working-class parties had been united in opposition. They now agreed with the other non-Communist parties in Germany that cooperation was the only way to reunite the city.[16]

In a referendum held on March 31, 1946, those opposing a merger of the parties easily won, but the Communists nonetheless made political headway. The balloting took place only in West Berlin; the Soviets closed the polls in East Berlin soon after they opened, claiming that "voting irregularities" had occurred. Although most Social Democrats gathered a week later to assert their independence, others joined the Communists to form the Socialist Unity party, which won immediate recognition by the Soviet military government in the Eastern zone.[17]

Meanwhile, tensions grew between East and West over the unification of Germany. The West's first open break with the Soviets came in early May, when Clay halted a shipment of industrial machinery from dismantled plants in West Germany that was being taken to the Soviet zone. The Soviets, he argued, had not agreed on the common use of German goods in the four zones, and they had not furnished information on the reparations being taken from their zone. Such policies had placed the Americans "in the position not only of financing reparations to the Soviet Union but also of agreeing to strip our own zone . . . without getting the benefits which would come from the amalgamation of all zones." The West, he feared, would soon be "without plants and without an agreement." In a July meeting of the Council of Foreign Ministers in Paris, Byrnes invited Britain, France, and the Soviet Union to join the United States in establishing a unified economic administration of Germany. The British approved, the French did not, and Molotov repeated the demands he had made at Yalta for $10 billion in reparations to the USSR and four-power control over the Ruhr's industries.[18]

Even though the West appeared to regard Molotov's calls for reparations and shared control of the Ruhr as a monotonous refrain, the chances are that satisfaction on these two counts might have eased the growing problem in Germany. Byrnes later thought so. He declared that Molotov's twin demands were "the real desires of the Soviet high command." Indeed, one writer has insisted that the West might have squandered a chance to resolve the German problem by refusing these demands. Another writer believes that Stalin might have let go of East Germany if he had received reparations and assurances of a demilitarized Germany.[19] Whatever the truth, the West perceived these Soviet demands as mere building blocks toward the Kremlin's ultimate objective of achieving dominance over a unified Germany. To make any concessions would lead only to more demands until, finally, there was nothing more to give because the Soviets would have it all.

In September Byrnes's inspirational speech delivered in Stuttgart signaled an important and far-reaching change in U.S. policy toward Germany. The economic agreement hammered out at Potsdam was not working, he insisted. More direct U.S. help was necessary in bringing security to Europe and in assuring the economic rehabilitation of Germany and its move toward self-government. In short, the Truman administration had decided to move toward the partition of Germany between East and West by shelving the Potsdam agreements calling for economic unity of the country. The British ambassador in Washington grasped the ramifications of the speech. Lord Inverchapel noted that the White House had recognized that an East-West stalemate regarding Germany was more advantageous than continual wrangling over a peace treaty involving all the Allies. With the new objective in mind, Byrnes of course dropped the Morgenthau Plan's call for punitive measures, which had crept into the Potsdam terms. Some writers have called the speech a response to Molotov's announcement in Paris that his country opposed taking the Ruhr and Rhineland, whereas others have termed it the beginning of a U.S. offensive in the Cold War. The issue was more complicated. Byrnes was aware of French resistance to German unification, but he was under instructions to indict the Soviet Union for Potsdam's failures and to send a message of support both to Germany and to the United States' allies in Europe. He preferred to resolve the French problem in a private way because he realized that a public row with the government in Paris would work to the Soviets' advantage. In addition, he knew that taking the Ruhr and Rhineland from Germany would have worldwide economic and political impact because it would hurt the country's economy as well as violate the principle of self-determination. Byrnes pointed instead toward a merger of the U.S. and

British zones and, as shown earlier, a prolonged U.S. involvement on the Continent. "Security forces," he declared, "will probably have to remain in Germany for a long period." Lest there be a misunderstanding, Byrnes drove home his major point: "We will not shirk our duty. We are not withdrawing. We are staying here and will furnish our proportionate share of the security forces."[20]

The domestic political situation in Germany became heated in October as the Communists suffered a crushing defeat in the first postwar elections in Berlin and the Soviets switched to other tactics to win control. By autumn a provisional constitution was in effect, one that Colonel Howley in the U.S. military government's office called "a brief but good document, entirely democratic, and from the legal point of view full of flaws." But he thought it sufficient until the newly elected officials could write a new constitution. In the election campaign the Communist-led Socialist Unity party used the press and radio to win votes; it furnished food, drinks, and gifts to children; and it interfered with the non-Communist Social Democrats' efforts to meet and campaign in East Berlin. The strategy failed. The Social Democrats received nearly 49 percent of the entire city's vote; the Socialist Unity party got 20 percent in all Berlin and only 21 percent in the Soviet sector. The Soviets tried to counter the results by working with German Communists to build a power coalition in the city assembly that would operate under Communist direction. A long period of political unrest ensued, as democratic leaders in Berlin tried to gain control over most of the offices as well as a number of nongovernmental agencies.[21]

By the end of 1946 the German situation had deteriorated dangerously. In December the British and Americans merged their German zones into Bizonia. A Council of Foreign Ministers meeting in New York failed to resolve the growing German problem, although a committee was appointed to submit a report to the next meeting, scheduled for Moscow during the spring of 1947. "There's no way to argue with a river," Acheson later remarked about negotiating with the Soviets. "You can channel it; you can dam it up. But you can't argue with it." Before the Allied Control Council on February 26 the Soviet representative, Vasily Sokolovsky, accused the United States and Britain of attempting to separate their zones from the rest of the country and then demanded a plebiscite on the issue of unification. To generate popular support for a referendum, he appealed to German nationalism and lobbied the press and public officials in the Soviet zone. The Truman administration responded by barring the Soviets from the Ruhr while working furiously to restore Bizonia's economy and to establish a West German government that would align with the West.[22]

In the meantime, in response to reports from American observers that the Allies had as yet been unable to establish interzonal trade, control inflation, raise morale, and reverse economic stagnation, Truman asked the former chief executive Herbert Hoover to head a special mission to investigate the economic situation in Germany. Hoover returned with a discouraging report that the White House released in February 1947. "The housing situation in the two zones is the worst that modern civilization has ever seen," said the report. "The coal famine all over Western Europe and the unprecedented severity of the winter have produced everywhere the most acute suffering. As an example in Germany, no household coal has been issued in Hamburg since October. . . . Over half of the 6,595,000 children and adolescents, especially in the lower-income groups, are in a deplorable condition. . . . In some areas famine edema . . . is appearing in the children." Nearly 30 percent of German youths died before reaching their first birthday. "The increasing death toll among the aged is appalling." A summer drought in 1947 led to a crop yield of 20 percent less than that of the previous year. By January 1948 food stocks were at a bare minimum; Hamburg had less than three weeks' supply of grain and flour; strikes had spread throughout Germany, many of them fueled by bitterness toward the Allies. It appeared, then, that the problems the Marshall Plan was designed to remedy were about to engulf Germany.[23]

The Hoover report included several recommendations, all certain to cause difficulties with the Soviets. In the interests of Europe as well as Germany, the country's industry had to expand in a nonmilitary manner. Therefore, except for the confiscation of war plants, the removal of Germany's industries to satisfy reparations demands would have to stop. The report also called for German retention of the Ruhr and Rhineland (in accordance with Byrnes's Stuttgart speech) and for the U.S. and British zones to become self-sufficient. In essence, Germany's capital equipment was to be used for productive purposes, an approach that was vital to Europe's revival. The report received enthusiastic support from the War Department.[24]

The Russians staunchly opposed the West's first step toward economic recovery, a program of currency reform intended to control inflation. In a move that would actually guarantee more inflation, they rejected four-power control over the printing process and demanded their own set of plates. It was not the first time that the Soviets had tried this approach. They had adopted the same tactic with occupation currency in 1945, greatly inflating the supply and forcing the United States to honor demands with its own dollars. Although conventional wisdom in 1946–47 held that the 1945 Soviet-printed currency had been part of a Communist conspiracy, the United States honored the currency because of its desire to avoid any move that might alienate the Soviets. The Departments of State and Treasury (who were responsible for the plates) hesitated to deny the Soviets' request for their use because, as General John H. Hilldring explained, then "the first decision that the American government could not agree with its partners to get along in the solution of the problems of Germany would have been made by the United States." The Soviets now sought to delay the West's currency measures by arguing about details in meetings of the Allied Control Council and the Council of Foreign Ministers. They also used propaganda in the press, made appeals to German nationalism, encouraged protests from Eastern European allies, and exerted pressure on German officials in West Berlin.[25]

In early 1947 the Soviets and Americans in Germany attempted to intimidate each other with a mutual show of force. Soviet fighters flew over Berlin, a move that led Clay to respond by sending an American fighting group over the city in a formation that spelled out "U.S." On July 2 several B-29 bombers flew over Berlin. When the Soviets protested, Clay blandly explained that the United States was demonstrating its determination to take part in the city's security. A U.S. officer who was in the headquarters of the Soviet military government at the time declared that Soviet officers ran to the window and shook their fists at the planes.[26]

The Moscow meeting of the Council of Foreign Ministers in March underlined the growing intransigence of the two sides. Secretary of State Marshall realized that he had no leverage with which to force a favorable settlement of the German problem. He also knew that the United States seemed to have drawn the battle lines in the Cold War by proclaiming the Truman Doctrine two days after the conference began. Molotov again demanded $10 billion in reparations and four-power supervision of the Ruhr. He also wanted each commander empowered to overrule any German efforts to take actions affecting his zone. These demands convinced Marshall that the Soviets favored economic disruption as a means of spreading Communism in Germany. There seemed to be no alternative to the firm course plotted out by Byrnes at Stuttgart. Marshall sought to strengthen the Western zones in Germany as a single economic and political unit that entailed French involvement along with Germany's alignment with the West. Such a division of Germany, of course, necessitated the indefinite commitment of U.S. troops. In line with a memorandum prepared by John Foster Dulles, Marshall supported a general European settlement aimed at rehabilitating Western Germany and integrating it into the Continental economy. En route home from Moscow, Marshall stopped in Berlin and exhorted Clay to push hard for a stronger Bizonia.[27]

Even though France had been a major barrier to the establishment of centralized agencies for Germany, the United States remained suspicious about Soviet motives and assigned primary blame to the Kremlin. Marshall insisted that the Soviets' "refusal to carry out [the Potsdam] agreement was the sole cause of the merger." One writer has argued, however, that the United States unfairly accused the Soviets of wrecking a German settlement. Indeed, both Clay and his political adviser, Robert Murphy, insisted that the Soviets had not violated the Potsdam accords. Clay wrote Army Chief of Staff Eisenhower in July 1946 that "it is difficult to find major instances of Soviet failure to carry out agreements reached in [the] quadripartite government of Germany." The problem lay in "failure to agree on interpretations" of those agreements. "In most instances," Clay declared, "French unwillingness to enter into agreements relative to governing Germany as a whole makes it difficult to place blame on [the] Soviets." Murphy had earlier offered the same assessment. In an argument that was partly a response to Kennan's Long Telegram warning of Soviet aggressive behavior, Murphy wrote Washington that the Soviets had been "meticulous in their observance of the several principles of the Potsdam Agreement." He added that "the fact of the matter is that there is foundation for the Soviet suspicion and distrust [of the British and French] in this particular instance."[28] Despite these firsthand accounts, Washington held to its belief that the French problem was secondary to the primary goal of stopping the spread of Communism in Germany.

The Truman administration certainly regarded the French as a major obstacle to a resolution of the German question, though it was convinced that the Soviets were more dangerous and would therefore be more difficult to convert than the French. Technically, of course, the United States did break the Potsdam agreements by working toward a separate West Germany, but the White House was convinced that the Kremlin's demands for respecting the terms of the treaty were a mere sham. Hence, according to the American argument, the Soviets had violated the spirit of the agreements, and thereby released the United States from its obligations, by engaging in a deceptive and nefarious campaign intended to push the West out of Germany. And as one might also argue, no nation is bound to a pact injurious to that nation's own vital interests. By March 1947 U.S. advisers were deeply concerned about Soviet threats in Europe and the Near East that, in turn, endangered the United States' own safety. John Hickerson of the State Department's Office of European Affairs declared that "there can be no question of 'deals or arrangements' with the Soviet Union. That method was tried once with Hitler and the lessons of that effort are fresh in our minds. One cannot appease a powerful country intent on aggression. If the lessons we learnt from dealing with Hitler mean anything, concessions to the Soviet Union would only whet their appetite for more." The United States intended to persuade France that Soviet expansion was more dangerous to peace than a German resurgence. If that quiet approach did not work, the Americans would join the British in exerting economic and political pressure on the French to force them to support the establishment of a strong West Germany.[29]

In an effort to promote Western unity, Marshall and Bevin directed their military governors in Germany to prepare a governing system for Bizonia that would include French participation. But the government in Paris was reluctant to become part of what it regarded (correctly) as an anti-Soviet policy. In addition, the French wanted to use their participation in Bizonia as leverage for keeping Germany weak by separating the Rhineland and the Ruhr. Finally, the French repeated their opposition to increasing the volume of industrial production in the Western zones. Marshall continued to exert pressure on Bidault to take part in the talks regarding Germany. At one point the White House threatened to cut off potential Marshall Plan funds if he refused. That threat, combined with Molotov's obstreperous behavior, drove the French into a merger with the U.S. and British zones and thereby encouraged the move toward establishing a government of West Germany.[30]

By November both Smith in Moscow and Clay, then in Washington for consultations, considered the division in Germany unavoidable and warned that the Soviets might close off Berlin to force out the West. Marshall would not be deterred. He declared in a speech in Chicago, the "restoration of Europe involves the restoration of Germany. Without [a] revival of Germany's economy there can be no revival of Europe's economy."[31]

Another meeting of the Council of Foreign Ministers, this one in London during November and December 1947, heightened the fear that the USSR might use access to Berlin as leverage to force the West to accept a unified, demilitarized Germany subject to Kremlin exploitation. At that gathering Marshall rejected Molotov's demands for reparations, four-power supervision of the Ruhr, and the establishment of a government for all Germany capable of negotiating a treaty with the four powers. The United States, Marshall complained, could not be expected to send economic aid into West Germany while the Soviets were removing goods from East Germany. When Marshall pressed for East-West cooperation in the rehabilitation of Germany, Molotov adamantly refused to divulge information about economic problems within the Soviet zone. Bevin sarcastically asserted, "Every time we ask [Molotov] for information we get insults, insinuations, or accusations." After one bitter assault on the West,

Molotov was visibly stunned when Marshall remarked that the foreign secretary's outrageous behavior made it "rather difficult to inspire respect for the dignity of the Soviet government." The conference adjourned on Marshall's motion, but only after Molotov, according to Clay, made "almost every conceivable charge" against the West. The United States and the Soviet Union, Clay continued, were now locked in a new type of conflict, "a competitive struggle, not with arms but with economic resources, with ideas and with ideals." The director of the CIA warned the president that the failure of the London meeting might "cause the USSR to undertake a program of intensified obstructionism and calculated insult in an effort to force the U.S. and the other Western powers to withdraw from Berlin."[32]

■ ■ ■ In early 1948 an Army General Staff study prophetically warned that in an attempt to force the West out of Berlin, the Soviets would generate "administrative difficulties" in the city. The first sign of such a policy came in February, when Soviet officials barred British representatives from political meetings in East Berlin. When the Western delegates complained at the Allied Control Council, Sokolovsky dryly declared the city part of the Soviet zone and accused the Allies of using "their position to prejudice their right to remain in Berlin." The following day, at a meeting of the Kommandatura, General Alexander Kotikov twice mentioned that Berlin was part of the Soviet zone. These assertions appeared to be part of a larger scheme; the Soviets had also for weeks disrupted the West's military rail service to Berlin. Murphy warned the State Department that the Soviets intended to end four-power rule in Germany and could take a step in that direction by ignoring the verbal agreements regarding the West's surface access to Berlin. On March 5 Clay had these matters in mind, along with recent events in Czechoslovakia and the need to secure more congressional appropriations for the U.S. Army, when he cabled a top-secret warning of Soviet intentions to the U.S. Army director of intelligence: "For many months, based on logical analysis, I have felt and held that war was unlikely for at least ten years. Within the last few weeks, I have felt a subtle change in Soviet attitude which I cannot define but which now gives me a feeling that it may come with dramatic suddenness." Two days later Truman wrote on a memorandum from Marshall: "Will Russia move first? Who pulls the trigger?"[33]

In response to growing Soviet threats in Germany, the ambassadors of the United States, Britain, France, and the Benelux nations had gathered in London in February to work toward the establishment of a West German state. The atmosphere was taut. Two days after the conference opened,

Czechoslovakia fell to the Communists in a Soviet action that Kennan attributed to the imminent passage of the Marshall Plan as well as to Western efforts to establish a West German government.[34] Not without justification, the Soviets complained that the meeting in London constituted a violation of the Potsdam agreement establishing four-power control over Germany. Indeed, in Moscow Stalin told Yugoslav and Bulgarian delegates that there would be no German reunification.[35] The conferees nonetheless continued their discussions and released a public communiqué on March 6 that called for the economic integration of the three Western zones of Germany into Trizonia and for control of the Ruhr by the three Western countries. The communiqué also urged the participation of West Germany in the Marshall Plan. Further, it recommended that the three Western zones combine to form the independent country of West Germany, which would have a "federal form of government." French concern with Germany was now "outmoded and unrealistic," Marshall triumphantly wrote the U.S. embassy in Paris. Not only was the Soviet Union the real threat, but French security itself depended on the "integration of Western Europe including [the] western German economy." The incorporation of all Germany into the "eastern orbit" would have "dire consequences for all of us."[36] The delegates went on public record in expressing hope for an agreement with the Soviet Union on Germany, but declared that they would go ahead with their plans regardless. Such a resolution of Germany's political and economic problems was necessary, they explained, because the situation was having "increasingly unfortunate consequences for Western Europe."[37]

The Soviets voiced their disapproval of Western plans at an explosive meeting of the Allied Control Council in Berlin on March 20. Near the end of the session, Sokolovsky demanded information on German agreements concluded at the recent conference in London. The Western delegates coolly responded that matters discussed in London had been in the form of recommendations only, and that their military governors had not received official information on the proceedings. Sokolovsky denounced the recommendations as illegal and read a long, caustic indictment of Western behavior. When the British representative prepared to answer the charges, the Soviet commander, who was acting as chair, interrupted: "I see no sense in continuing this meeting, and I declare it adjourned." In a move that was obviously orchestrated, all Soviet representatives stood as one and walked out. Murphy told Marshall that the walkout was part of the effort to drive the West out of Berlin and thus "liquidate this remaining 'center of reaction' east of [the] Iron Curtain." Truman asserted that the collapse of the Allied Control Council (Sokolovsky never convened it again) "merely formalized what had been an obvious fact for some time, namely, that the four power control machinery had become unworkable." For Berlin, he declared in his memoirs, "this was the curtain-raiser for a major crisis."[38]

In Washington on March 22 the president, Marshall, and the new secretary of the army, Kenneth Royall, made the decision that the U.S. Army—not the State Department—would control the nonmilitary aspects of the U.S. occupation program. Clay, they said, should cancel his plans to retire at the end of 1948 and remain indefinitely as military governor in Germany and commander of U.S. forces in Europe. Four days later the cabinet authorized a counterblockade—an embargo on selected goods considered important to Soviet or allied production.[39] Even if the Kremlin did not have a coordinated strategy, the White House believed it did—and acted accordingly.

Lieutenant General Curtis LeMay, commander of the U.S. Air Force in Europe (USAFE), warned of the limitations on U.S. military power in Europe but nonetheless moved ahead with contingency plans for war with the Soviets. He had been disgruntled for some time by the administration's apparent inability to recognize the emerging threat from the East. He admitted, however, that in view of the disparity in conventional forces between the Eastern bloc and the Western allies, "USAFE would be stupid to get mixed up in anything bigger than a cat fight at a pet show." The United States had only a single fighter squadron and a few transports and radar operators in Germany, and the Soviets could easily cut the United States' supply lines to Frankfurt, where most of its troops in Germany were quartered. This dire situation, LeMay sarcastically complained, was attributable to "a logical outgrowth of the God-bless-our-buddy-buddy-Russians-we-sure-can-trust-them-forever-and-ever philosophy which flowered away back in the Roosevelt Administration." To reduce the danger, LeMay characteristically acted on his own. He privately worked with the French and Belgian air forces in establishing strategic bases behind U.S. forces and behind the Rhine River. There USAFE cached supplies in case hostilities should erupt. Since foreign troops were not allowed in French and Belgian territory, Americans were sent there secretly in civilian clothing and by trains. LeMay told Clay of these preparations, but the latter apparently said nothing to the Department of the Army.[40]

On April 1 the Soviets escalated tensions by imposing a partial blockade on Berlin. The day before, Soviet officials in the city informed Clay that guards would begin inspecting U.S. military and civilian personnel and the baggage of the civilians when they entered the Soviet zone of Germany by either railroad or highway. The new regulations, a Soviet general explained, were intended to safeguard the Soviet zone against "subversive and terrorist elements." Another Soviet official declared that the new procedures were part of an effort to stop black-marketing. The only baggage exempt from inspection would be that of U.S. military personnel or civilians working for their government. Soviet officials would also have to approve passage of the military's freight trains. One explanation emphasized the prevention of looting; another tied the action to "technical reasons" that included improper freight labels, passes to Germans that were not in accordance with regulations, and accusations against Germans engaged in what was vaguely referred to as "speculation."[41]

Clay was irate and sought White House approval for the use of force. Although admitting that an examination of the identification papers of passengers entering the Soviet zone by motor vehicles seemed appropriate, he insisted that an inspection of either their baggage or anything on military passenger or freight trains was not. U.S. commandants might provide passenger lists and manifests, but they "cannot permit our military trains to be entered by the representatives of other powers." Acting on his own, Clay made preparations to stop this intrusion and informed Washington that "our train commandants have been instructed accordingly." Clay warned that the Soviets eventually intended to push the United States out of Europe. "Evacuation in [the] face of the Italian elections and European situation is to me almost unthinkable." The Soviets, he continued, would surely not cut off Berlin's food because such an act would alienate the people. "We have lost Czechoslovakia. . . . We retreat from Berlin. When Berlin falls, Western Germany will be next. If we mean to hold Europe against Communism, we must not budge. . . . I believe the future of democracy requires us to stay."[42]

In a series of transatlantic teleconferences, Washington rejected Clay's recommendations for the use of force but agreed with him that no Soviet officers were to board U.S. military trains. The president, the State Department, the Department of the Army, and the Joint Chiefs of Staff concurred that Clay should order the U.S. trains through the Soviet checkpoints and refuse to permit the entrance of Soviet guards. But, Royall warned Clay, there was to be no shooting except in self-defense. Clay was not pleased: "Any weakness on our part will lose us prestige important now. If [the] Soviets mean war, we will only defer the next provocation for a few days. . . . I do not believe this means war but any failure to meet this squarely will cause great trouble." The army chief of staff, General Omar Bradley, emphasized to Clay that Truman's decision was firm. "If our action now should provoke war," Bradley warned, "we must be sure that the fault is not ours." Clay was to reject the Soviet demands for inspection and order the trains to begin moving. But he was not to increase the number of guards on the trains, and he was not to provide them with additional weapons. "Furthermore," Bradley insisted, "it is important that our guards not fire unless fired upon." Clay tried to ease the anxiety in Washington: "Please understand that we are not carrying a chip on our shoulder and will shoot only for self-protection."[43]

At midnight on April 1, three U.S. trains entering the Soviet zone of Germany were ordered to stop. One of the U.S. commandants backed down under pressure and allowed Soviet guards on board. After the inspection, the train was permitted to resume passage. But when the Soviets tried to board the other trains, the two U.S. commandants refused permission. The guards did not try to force their way onto the trains. They were in charge of traffic control, however, and they switched the two trains off the main lines, where they could not move without the use of force. The trains stayed on the siding until morning and then pulled back under Clay's orders. The "Russians meant business," he insisted. In a meeting of the three Western military governors that same morning, British General Robertson warned that "if we keep on talking indefinitely we might wake up some fine morning to find the Hammer and Sickle already on the Rhine."[44]

Clay believed that the Soviets would back down before a show of force and argued for sending an armed truck convoy through their checkpoints. His suggestion garnered little support among either his superiors in Washington or his British colleagues in Berlin. The day after Clay presented his proposal, the CIA and the intelligence groups of the State Department, army, navy, and air force submitted a report emphasizing the Soviet Union's military advantages on the ground in Western Europe. As Bradley further realized, the Soviets could stop the trucks' passage without the use of force: they could close the roads for repairs, or "a bridge could go out just ahead of you and then another bridge behind, and you'd be in a hell of a fix." Robertson likewise was skeptical. The Soviets could stop the convoy by merely lining tanks across the road; in battle they might win. He admitted that the Soviets were on legal ground in seeking documents for personnel and goods passing into their sector. And, Robertson noted, the Soviets carefully stayed within the rules by approving entry when they found the papers to be valid.[45]

Clay again took action. First he pulled the U.S. trains from the Soviet zone and canceled schedules. Then he implemented a small airlift from Wiesbaden to Tempelhof Airport, carrying up to a hundred tons of goods daily, to supply U.S. personnel in Berlin.[46]

Within a week the threat of a confrontation loomed again as the Soviets began to interfere with air traffic into West Berlin. Soviet fighter planes had been "buzzing" Allied transports within the authorized air lanes since late 1946. Now the Soviets proposed a ban on the use of flight instruments that would, because of Germany's notorious flying weather, hurt the airlift and put an end to nighttime entry. Further, the Allies would have to secure Soviet clearance for all flights, and the only ones approved would be those intended to fill the needs of occupation forces. On April 5 a Soviet fighter plane harassing a British transport over Berlin collided with it over Gatow Airport in the British sector, sending both planes down in a fiery crash. All died, including the Soviet pilot and two Americans who were among the fourteen on board the transport. Churchill called for some form of measured retaliation, including inspection of Soviet crews entering Western ports or the obstruction of their ships' passage through the Suez and Panama canals. But U.S. and British officials simply ordered their fighters to begin escorting unarmed aircraft. Sokolovsky initially issued a statement of regret for the incident, along with an assurance that his government had no intention of harassing the West. But the remarkable tameness of the West's reaction was perhaps responsible for a change in Soviet demeanor. The following day, Sokolovsky wrote Robertson, accusing the British pilot of causing the incident and concluding with a threat: "I hope you will issue the necessary orders to British planes for the strict following of air safety directives outlined by the Allied Control Council. This will forestall me from the necessity of taking measures for the protection and security of traffic over the Soviet occupation zone of Germany."[47]

The British were infuriated yet cautious, and soon the cooler heads among them prevailed. The Americans wanted to send a joint note of complaint to the Kremlin, but the British warned that such a note could be interpreted as an ultimatum should the Soviets counter with a refusal to recognize the West's rights in the city. Marshall wanted the Kremlin to know that the United States intended to stay in Berlin and would "resist force with force." The British, however, would not give in, and no note was sent. In the meantime a British inquiry into the crash held the Russian pilot responsible but could not prove anything more than an accident; the Soviets accused the British of distorting the facts and called for more restrictions on flights through the corridors (including the right to approve all flights twenty-four hours in advance). The Soviets also lamented "the absence . . . of precise rules approved by the Control Council for air traffic along routes over the Soviet zone." Since the West had no written guarantee of access to air corridors, their use had been "designated by the Soviet authorities" and could therefore be withdrawn. The Soviets complained that Western pilots were "highly inexperienced and badly need[ed] stricter control." These charges were surprising because about a year earlier, the USSR had asked Americans to help train Soviet air force personnel in air safety.[48]

Even though Stalin had indicated his willingness to negotiate the establishment of two Germanies, Americans continued to attribute the Soviets' behavior to their intention to remove the West from Berlin and seize control of the entire country. Western perceptions of Stalin's objectives, however, were radically different from what the reality now seems to have been. The CIA warned that withdrawal in the face of Soviet pressure would "constitute a political defeat of the first magnitude." The State Department affirmed that Berlin had become "an important symbol of the determination of the US and the other western powers to contest the Soviet claim to mastery of Germany and of Europe; withdrawal would be a great blow to western prestige in Europe and to the strategic position of the US and its associates vis-à-vis the USSR." Clay stressed the humiliation that would result from a U.S. withdrawal and tied the problems in Berlin to Soviet anxiety over the currency reform program. He told Bradley: "You will understand, of course, that our separate currency reform in near future followed by partial German government in Frankfurt will develop the real crisis. Present show probably designed by Soviets to scare us away from these moves." Berlin, Clay believed, was "the most vulnerable and difficult spot for us to defend."[49]

The White House remained in a precarious position—but only in part because the West lacked written assurance of surface access to Berlin. Although Clay held himself responsible for the problem, Truman dismissed that argument and was probably justified in claiming that "it would have made very little difference to the Russians whether or not there was an agreement in writing."[50] Indeed, Clay originally had not wanted a written agreement because he hoped to gain full access to the city. He later admitted that he should have demanded total access as a condition for Western withdrawal into its own occupation zones. But he, like Truman, believed that the Soviets would have ignored written guarantees. Even had they done so, one writer suggests, the United States and its allies would at least have been on safe legal ground in challenging Soviet violations if they had been able to cite some form of written agreement. Clay also was sure, however, that the United States' "large and combat-experienced army in Germany" could have overcome access problems by forcing its way into Berlin. The president preferred a less provocative course. Two weeks after Truman's June 1945 claim to Stalin regarding access, Marshall (who was then army chief of staff) instructed Eisenhower to work out terms with Soviet commanders. But the talks resulted only in verbal assurances from the Soviets.[51] A State Department legal adviser was perhaps correct in arguing that despite the lack of a written agreement, the United States had the right to send passenger and freight trains to and from Berlin because the Soviet Union had set a precedent by long permitting these actions. But the Soviets held the military advantage in the city, and the Western argument carried no weight in Moscow.[52]

If the United States and Britain should have foreseen trouble with the USSR over Berlin, they could not have avoided that trouble short of withdrawing from the city. Even on the specious assumption that the Soviets would have consented to the formal establishment of Western corridors into Berlin, neither the Americans nor the British seem to have recognized the broad implications of the access question, and therefore they made no such proposal during the discussions over the postwar division and occupation. Further, Truman had not pushed for a written agreement from the Soviet Union in June 1945 or during the Potsdam Conference of the next month. Had either the British or the Americans made the attempt at Potsdam or earlier, the West would have been on sounder legal ground in seeking access later on. Even then, however, they surely realized that international law was merely a language through which nations spoke to one another; it was no substitute for power mobilized in behalf of national self-interest. Nor should one forget that during the halcyon days of spring 1945, the administration's concern was to win Soviet trust; by the middle of the year attention had turned to defeating Japan. Given the competing interests of East and West in postwar Germany, the problem was inescapable.

The crisis over Berlin meanwhile served as an impetus to the formation of a North Atlantic military alliance that might bring the long-desired postwar order to Europe. The British and French had been urging such a move, and the National Security Council lent its support by warning that the Marshall Plan was not enough to safeguard Europe. The United States, according to the council, had to deter the Soviet Union from "further aggression" by demonstrating the West's "determination to resist" with "organized force." The United States should talk with Brussels Pact members about negotiating a collective security agreement for "the North Atlantic area." It should then approach Denmark, Iceland, Norway, Sweden, and Italy—if the Communists did not win in Italy's approaching elections. At the appropriate time the alliance members should invite Austria, Spain, West Germany, and others to participate in a mutual defense pact. The Senate, urged the council, could encourage bipartisan support by passing a resolution stating that the United States supported the Brussels Pact and the establishment of other regional and collective defense pacts in accordance with article 51 of the UN Charter. In response to the council's recommendations, the "Vandenberg Resolution" was drafted by the Michigan senator and Undersecretary of State Robert Lovett to encourage U.S. participation in such pacts, and the Senate soon approved by the wide margin of sixty-four to four.[53]

The instability in the German situation had combined with the growing tension over Palestine to make a showdown between East and West seem imminent, either in Germany or in the Middle East or in both.[54]

■ ■ ■ CHAPTER EIGHT

Equivalent Response

Berlin Blockade and Airlift

During the summer of 1948 the Soviets revamped their strategy for achieving a favorable German settlement. The Communists had lost political ground in Berlin, the three non-Communist political parties in West Berlin were acting independently, a vigorous trade union movement had sprung up, and the establishment of a free university seemed imminent. To undercut German morale, the Soviets openly claimed Berlin as part of their sector and predicted a Western withdrawal, obstructed the movement of people and goods between West Germany and Berlin, and publicly criticized the city's mayor and department heads, collectively known as the magistrat. The West repeatedly denied plans for a military withdrawal, but the German people remained skeptical and worried about Soviet reprisals after a departure.[1]

The Soviet Union engaged in a variety of tactics intended to create uncertainty about the West's commitment to Germany. To heighten the West Berliners' sense of insecurity, Soviet army officers drove slowly through Allied residential areas in West Berlin, leaving the impression that they were selecting future living quarters. Communists published claims that Berlin's food supply was dangerously low and that city officials had appealed in vain to the West for help. The director of the city's Food Office denied the assertions and drew a wry remark from the pro-West *Tagesspiegel:* "The communist central organ, which wants to make Berliners worry about their food supply by citing statements which never have been made, thereby distinguishes itself by the fact that its lack of love for the truth is exceeded by its lack of conscience." But the Communists' spokesman, *Neues Deutschland,* countered with a disturbing story beneath the headline "General Clay Says Berlin Cannot Be Supplied by Air." The food supply in the U.S. sector, according to the account, could not last more than a few days. The USSR had meanwhile announced a reform proposal for Berlin that, according to a British military official, was an effort to show that occupation was a failure, that the city belonged to the Soviets, and that they alone cared about the German people. In an attempt to undermine the credibility of the magistrat, the Soviets first offered firewood to West Berlin but then interfered with the efforts of city truck drivers to enter the Soviet sector.[2]

During June signs of cooperation among the Western powers only served to alienate the Soviet Union even more. The London Conference on Germany reconvened and on June 7 announced the London Recommendations for the establishment of a West German government. In addition to the integration of Germany into the larger European economy, the program proposed placing the Ruhr under control of the six countries at the conference and Germany and, in a move that received France's reluctant support and thereby marked a sharp reversal of its policy, urged German leaders to draft a constitution for a German federal government. Later that month the delegates in London took advantage of the adjourned Allied Control Council in Berlin to announce currency measures designed to halt inflation and black-marketing in Germany. On June 16 the Soviets walked out of the Kommandatura. The move had been preceded by over twelve hours of arguing, followed by Howley's request near 11 P.M. to retire for the evening while leaving his deputy in charge. Regarding Howley's suggestion as an insult, the Soviet delegate stood and called it a "hooligan action" and, over the chair's protest, dramatically led his companions out of the meeting.[3]

Clay was convinced that the West's plans for currency reform in Germany were primarily responsible for tightened Soviet controls over Berlin. The introduction of such a reform would have political as well as economic ramifications that would jeopardize Soviet interests. Not only would the new currency measures provide the financial foundation of a separate political and economic system, but they would enable the nation distributing the banknotes to exert considerable influence over the German economy and thus over the government. Moscow had wanted a weak Central Europe free of Western involvement. But currency reform, combined with the Marshall Plan, would promote the rehabilitation of Germany and thereby encourage the political and economic revival of the Continent. The Soviets had to control the currency in Germany if they were to establish political hegemony.[4]

It was the currency issue, in fact, that was both the short-term cause of and the pretext for the Berlin blockade. After West German banks closed for the weekend on Friday, June 18, the Western allies informed the press that on Monday in their German zones, save for Berlin, a new currency would replace the reichsmark. Sokolovsky protested the move as a violation of the Potsdam agreements and warned that it would permanently divide Germany. In a public statement to the German people, he claimed Soviet control over Berlin in declaring: "Bank notes issued in the western occupation zones of Germany are not being admitted for circulation in the Soviet occupation zone of Germany and in Berlin, which is part of the Soviet occupation zone." If this program went into effect, he warned, he would likewise introduce new currency in the Soviet zone and expand it into all Berlin. In the magistrat a Communist member boasted to his colleagues that the Soviets had "taken Berlin under their protection" and that four-power administration had "gone to the devil." On June 19 the Soviets implemented new travel restrictions, allegedly to prevent devalued currency from flooding East Germany. All movement of people, vehicles, and passenger trains was to stop, although freight and canal traffic from West Germany to Berlin could continue—after inspection. That same day Soviet officials barred the entry of several freight cars on the ground that they were old and hazardous. The United States responded the following day by suspending rail deliveries into East Berlin and by instituting another small airlift for its personnel.[5]

Meanwhile, the currency dispute forced West Berliners to take sides between East and West. On June 23 the Soviets distributed their currency in Berlin, and Clay (without consulting the White House) joined Robertson in announcing that the West would introduce its new deutschemark into the Western sectors of the city the following day. To accept the Soviet currency as the only medium of exchange, Clay disgustedly declared, would have made Westerners mere "guests in Berlin." Certain confusion lay ahead: the city would have two currencies, each competing against the other and with no exchange rate established between them. As the municipal assembly prepared to discuss the matter in the late afternoon of June 23, demonstrators forced their way into city hall and nearly filled the gallery in the chamber while a mob led by Communists carrying red banners and signs gathered outside the building. Amid the turmoil the speaker announced his refusal to convene the meeting until the gallery was emptied. Pandemonium ensued. Shouting and shoving took place inside the building; outside, a loudspeaker mounted on a truck blared speeches by Communists. When a call for the police brought no response, suspicions of complicity between police and protesters were aroused. The chaos came to an end only when the Communist assembly members signaled the demonstrators to leave.[6]

The meeting began around 6:00 P.M., two hours later than scheduled.

After much deliberation the magistrat announced its decision: the Soviet currency order would apply only in the Eastern sector of the city, whereas the Western sectors would use the Western-issued currency. For the problem of interzonal trade, the magistrat had no solution except to say that the Germans in Berlin would have to make the adjustment to a dual currency system. The Communist members loudly protested the decision as a capitulation to Western colonialists. Despite threats from both inside and outside the building, the assembly approved the magistrat's decision. The excitement, however, was not over. Adjournment of the meeting was followed by a battle in the streets. Some assembly members were beaten as they came out of the building. One of those assaulted and seriously hurt was a woman from the Social Democratic party who had been a prisoner in a Nazi concentration camp during the war; some pro-Western Berliners quickly drew comparisons between the Communists and the Nazis. *Neues Deutschland* defended the demonstrators as democratic workers and ran its story under a lengthy headline: "The Workers, Furious at Those Who Are Trying to Split Berlin, Demand Stormily: Only East Currency for Greater Berlin—Majority of the Magistrat, Against All Reason, for Double Currency and Customs Barriers in Berlin—For Chaos, Hunger and Unemployment." A Soviet army publication claimed that the workers' actions were the results of frustration caused by the assembly's cowardice in facing the people.[7]

On June 24 Soviet authorities fomented an international crisis by imposing a total surface blockade (rail, highway, and water) of West Berlin. In addition, they froze bank deposits in the city's central bank, which was located in the Soviet sector, and they sharply reduced the flow of electricity from power stations in the Eastern sector into the Western parts of the city. They attributed the blockade to problems beyond their control, explaining that "technical difficulties" on the railroad had forced a suspension of freight and passenger traffic. A Soviet army publication tied the cutback in electric power to a "technical difficulty" in the power plant that necessitated limiting daily voltage to the Western sectors to the hours between 11 P.M. and 1:00 A.M. The measure threatened to halt the pumps in the sewage disposal system and to reduce the water supply to a dangerous level. Although the Soviets publicly expressed concern over the food shortages in the West (particularly in the French sector, where there were no stocks), they nonetheless emphasized that food entering Berlin would be allowed only in the Eastern sector. This decree was especially provocative because it canceled a special arrangement that had permitted the entry of milk and vegetables for babies in West Berlin.[8]

The Soviet Union appeared to be in a no-lose situation. Even though the West's air access remained, Stalin apparently thought a surface blockade sufficient to cut the West's connection with the 2.4 million inhabitants of West Berlin. No formal agreement assured such passage, he declared, and he likewise dismissed the claim that the West's occupation of Berlin and three years of use had established a legal right to surface contact. Not only did Stalin consider himself legally justified in taking such blunt action, but he thought it strategically sound. The Western allies, he doubtless believed, were so divided over the German question that they could not put up effective resistance. The blockade seemed certain either to force the West out of the city and allow Moscow complete control over East Germany or to secure the long-sought four-power agreement on all of Germany that would assure the Soviets a pivotal governing position (even in West Germany) because of the principle of unanimity. The West would have to decide whether to stay in Berlin and agree to the Soviets' demands for Germany or to pull out and concede the city to the Soviets. Either result would enhance the Kremlin's prestige and strategic position in Europe.[9]

The same day the Soviets imposed the blockade on Berlin, they issued the Warsaw Declaration, announcing their aims regarding Germany. At a two-day conference of Soviet and allied foreign ministers in the capital of Poland, the Soviets attacked the London Recommendations as violations of the Potsdam agreements and countered with the following demands: German demilitarization; German fulfillment of reparations requirements; four-power control over the Ruhr's industry; four-power agreement on the establishment of a provisional democratic government for all Germany; and a peace treaty with Germany that met the Potsdam agreements and that allowed the occupation powers to withdraw within a year of the treaty.[10] With an eye to world opinion, the Communist foreign ministers couched their demands in terms of restoring those wartime agreements that had aimed at preventing the reconstruction of an aggressive Germany.

The West regarded the Warsaw Declaration as an effort to install a Communist regime in Germany and to block the economic rehabilitation of the Continent. The Soviets would make political gains because of the program's heralded support for a government composed of "representatives of democratic parties and organizations of Germany." Since Communist-front organizations called themselves the "democratic" groups, they would acquire a disproportionate share of power. In addition, the satisfaction of Molotov's long-standing demands regarding the Ruhr and reparations would hamper Western Europe's economic restoration by requiring a large-scale diversion of West Germany's industrial production from the

Marshall Plan. And, curiously enough, Molotov's reparations figure remained in stone at $10 billion, despite untold amounts of East German goods that the Soviets had already carted away.[11]

If the purpose of the Warsaw Declaration was to establish a basis for four-power negotiations, the Truman administration stood in opposition to this goal: any such attempt would reopen the entire German question for discussion and obstruct the creation of a government in West Germany. Mutual distrust between East and West had led to steadily escalating moves and countermoves in Berlin that now focused the conflict on the opposing objectives contained in the London program and the Warsaw Declaration. The issues were not new, but the situation had become more volatile because of the blockade and the need for counteraction by the West. The CIA director in Washington advised the president that the USSR's sole objective in any negotiations regarding Germany was to block the consolidation of the West. The White House concluded that the blockade and the Warsaw Declaration had a common Soviet aim, that of undermining the establishment of a West German government. The Soviets' proposal of an all-German government would further spread Communism, for such a government would have as its capital Berlin—which was located in East Germany and which would thereby be susceptible to Soviet and Communist pressures. Not surprisingly, the Americans believed, the Soviet Union preferred to settle the Berlin issue within the context of a broad German agreement.[12]

The blockade jolted the White House into a search for an equivalent reaction that would maintain Western credibility without leading to war. The West had wrongfully assumed that the Soviets would not take any action that risked alienating West Berliners; now, with the blockade, the West suddenly had to come to grips with its own uncertainty about whether the city could be held. If any hope had remained for rapprochement with the Soviets, the blockade obliterated that illusion. Howley perhaps best expressed the West's change in attitude toward the Soviets. "We went to Berlin in 1945," he declared, "thinking only of the Russians as big, jolly, balalaika-playing fellows, who drank prodigious quantities of vodka and liked to wrestle in the drawing room. We now know—or should know–that we were hopelessly naive. You can't do business with the Russians," he insisted. "They can't be trusted." Ignoring the reality that it was the United States that first publicly discarded the Potsdam agreements regarding Germany, Howley complained that the Soviets "will promise anything, sign anything, provided it benefits them, and will scrap the pledge the moment it doesn't. . . . The Russians are the world's most colossal liars, swindlers, and cutthroats, and there is no reason to think they will change." The Truman administration was convinced that the Soviet Union had initially violated the spirit of Potsdam by seeking all of Germany. Further proof of its expansionist intentions came from its broken Yalta pledge of self-determination in Eastern Europe and from its instigation of troubles in Iran, Turkey, and Greece. The White House had to take action in Germany. To leave West Berliners dependent upon the USSR for food and supplies would be to abandon them. Further, the credibility of the United States was at stake: ten thousand Americans were in the city, the movement toward a North Atlantic military alliance was well under way, and West Berliners were already angry with their allies for failing to make a stand against the Soviets. A city official complained to an American: "We don't mind fighting with our backs to the wall, but you are no wall against which we can place ourselves."[13]

The West first had to reassure the people of West Berlin that they would not be stranded. Rumors were rampant: water was running out; sewage problems would lead to epidemics; the West was ready to withdraw; Soviet troops were coming in. Western spokesmen repeatedly assured the Germans that withdrawal was out of the question. In a move that demonstrated the Western powers' will to resist and that had substantial effect, the British suspended regular coal and steel shipments to the Soviet zone—not as a reprisal, they insisted, but because the Soviets had failed to return sixteen thousand freight cars used earlier. This order cut off monthly deliveries of a million tons of coal and thirty thousand tons of steel from the Ruhr. Howley meanwhile spoke to the German people over radio in an effort to quell the rumors and to assure them that enough food was available for thirty days. "We are not getting out of Berlin. We are going to stay. I don't know the answer to the present problem—not yet—but this much I do know. The American people will not stand by and allow the German people to starve." In a highly effective move he promised mothers that powdered milk would be delivered and explained how to prepare it. Then, to the Soviets, he issued a warning that had not been cleared first with Washington: "We have heard a lot about your military intentions. Well, this is all I have to say on the subject. If you do try to come into our sector, you better be well prepared. We are ready for you."[14]

On June 25 Clay likewise acted on his own and, following a British suggestion, authorized an expanded airlift to furnish provisions for the German people as well as for Allied personnel. In trying to work out a long-range strategy with Washington, Clay again broached his proposal, first made during the train episode, of sending an armed convoy. He wanted Brigadier General Arthur H. Trudeau to head a convoy out of the U.S. zone that would include two hundred trucks escorted by U.S. troops armed with recoilless rifles, a battalion of engineers equipped to repair and clear roads, a British infantry battalion, and French tank destroyers and armored cars. Trudeau announced that his men were anxious to force their entrance into Berlin. LeMay, at U.S. Air Force headquarters in Wiesbaden, was ready to provide air support by ordering an attack upon airfields in East Germany. The excitement of the moment threatened to override the shortcomings in Clay's convoy plan. In addition to the problems mentioned earlier, Trudeau did not have enough pontoon bridges to cross the waterways without having to lay them down and pick them up for use again as the convoy made its arduous way toward Berlin. "I am still convinced," Clay wrote his superiors in Washington, "that a determined movement of convoys with troop protection would reach Berlin and that such a showing might well prevent rather than build up Soviet pressures which could lead to war." He admitted to "the inherent dangers in this proposal since once committed we could not withdraw." But Clay warned that the West had to supply the Berliners because withdrawal would have a devastating political impact worldwide.[15]

But, despite his reservations, Clay's call for supply by air became the West's answer to the Berlin blockade. Robertson had earlier recommended an airlift. Indeed, he already had approval from the Royal Air Force to supply British military personnel beginning June 25, and the British cabinet was discussing the possibility of sending supplies to civilians as well. But, Clay wondered, was an airlift capable of supplying over two million people on an ongoing basis? The United States had more than a hundred transport and troop carrier planes, but they were twin-engine C-47s having a maximum cargo capacity of only two and a half tons. The British had considerably less to offer, the French no transports at all. Clay needed to know the Germans' feelings on the sacrifices that lay ahead. He asked Ernst Reuter, a Social Democrat and mayor-elect of Berlin, if his people were supportive and if they were willing to undergo a rough winter. Reuter had been a Communist until the early 1920s and was now bitterly opposed by the Soviets. He had been elected lord mayor by the city assembly shortly after the forced resignation of Otto Ostrowski in 1946. The Soviets, however, used the veto in the Kommandatura to bar him from office. When the city assembly refused to accept the Soviet decision, Reuter served as mayor in name only, his office remaining empty for eighteen months. Now he told Clay that the USSR was bluffing and assured him that Berliners would stand with the West.[16]

Clay attached great political importance to an airlift, even though few at the time (including the U.S. Air Force) thought it could be effective over an extended period. Howley was dubious: "I couldn't quite visualize how planes could supply 920,000 German families." Clay initially encountered the same skepticism when he sought assistance from LeMay:

"Curt," Clay asked over the phone, "do you have any planes there that can carry coal?"

"Carry what?" LeMay at first replied.

"Coal," Clay repeated.

"We must have a bad connection," LeMay remarked. "It sounds as if you're asking if we have planes for carrying coal."

"Yes, that's what I said . . . coal."

After a moment of stunned silence, LeMay declared: "Sure. The Air Force can deliver anything! How much do you want?"

"All you can haul," Clay asserted.[17]

LeMay was concerned that the diversion of planes would endanger the strike capability of the United States in the event of war, and he frankly doubted that the operation could work; the situation seemed comparable, he declared, to that in England in 1942 "when we were holding on by our fingernails." But LeMay did everything possible to shift pilots from desk and other duties so that the airlift could begin at the same time as the British program—the next day, June 25. Clay regarded the airlift as a crucial affirmation of the United States' commitment to the Germans in the face of "one of the most ruthless efforts in modern times to use mass starvation for political coercion." And he was determined to make it work. Years afterward he said he had acted on his own initiative because of the uncertainty in the White House. "I didn't ask Washington. I acted first. I began the airlift with what I had, because I had to first prove to Washington that it was possible. Once I'd proved it, it was no longer hard to get help."[18]

The decision for an airlift offered an attractive but apparently only temporary response to the crisis. Clay had presented a third option for the White House, one that lay between the use of force and a withdrawal from Berlin. An airlift would avert a direct confrontation with the Soviets and force them to make the decision for or against the use of violence. The administration in Washington regarded the airlift not as a solution to the Berlin problems but as a stopgap measure intended to buy time for deciding what further steps to take.[19] In the meantime, the White House had adhered to its policy of acting with restraint while avoiding a stand that had the potential of escalating the situation beyond control.

Clay continued to urge direct action against the Soviets, for despite their military superiority in the region, he did not agree with those around him who feared that the USSR would go to war. Howley had doubts about the Soviets' reluctance to fight. They could send up to three dozen divisions to any area, whereas the West's occupation force totaled a mere twenty thousand—and even that figure was misleading because it included civilians and dependents. Howley later declared that the Red Army would have defeated the United States' two battalions "before you could say 'Politburo'!" Clay insisted, however, that there was no danger of open hostilities. In a teletyped conversation with his superiors in Washington, he was emphatic: "I do not expect armed conflict. Principal danger is from Russian-planned German Communist groups." The people of Berlin were supportive of the West, he declared. "We should not destroy their confidence by any show of departure." The real issue was "western Germany and its part in European recovery." If the Soviets want war, he said, "it will not be because of [the] Berlin currency issue but only because they believe this the right time."[20]

Meanwhile, East and West traded charges in a bitter public exchange. On June 26 the Communists opened an attack on the West in the press, on radio, and in the streets. They blamed the British for the blockade, warned that coal stocks would run out in ten days and food in thirty, and insisted that four-power occupation was over and that Germany would soon be reunited under one government. On street corners and in pamphlets, Communist spokesmen declared that the Berlin crisis would end only after the West pulled out of the city. The French had now publicly adopted their Western allies' hard-line stand and insisted that they would stay "at all costs." In the London newspapers the Foreign Office reaffirmed its position: "The statement that we intend to stay in Berlin holds good. The opinion of the whole world will condemn the ruthless attempt by the Soviet Government to create a state of siege in Berlin and so, by starving the helpless civilian population, to secure political advantages at the expense of the other Allied Powers." Churchill, who was leader of His Majesty's Loyal Opposition, proclaimed his support for the Labour ministry and warned at a public rally that "the Communist Government of Russia has made up its mind to drive us and France and all the other Allies out and turn the Russian zone in Germany into one of its satellite states." In the House of Commons Bevin drew cheers from all sides when he promised that his government would not withdraw from Berlin. From the opposition Sir Anthony Eden warned: "If ever there was a time to stand firm, it is now: if ever there was a cause in which to stand firm it is this." Harold Macmillan likewise announced his support, though solemnly warning that the West had to "face the risk of war."[21]

To ward off the enormous pressure to take more stringent action against the Soviet Union, the Truman administration approved the airlift begun by Clay. Admiral Leahy, the president's chief of staff, had no faith in the airlift and feared that a Soviet attack might lead to a "dangerous incident." Robert Murphy in Berlin expressed his misgivings by alluding to the recent Communist coup in Czechoslovakia. He urged Marshall to avoid "the Munich of 1948" by refusing to appease the Soviets; in his judgment, the Western powers should forcibly reopen the surface routes and end the blockade. Clay also wanted to do more. He recommended that the White House close U.S. ports and the Panama Canal to Soviet vessels. Truman, however, believed that Murphy's suggestion could lead to war and that Clay's would inflict economic damage only on the United States. Clay's call for an armed convoy came up for consideration again, but it still aroused no support. The blunt fact was that Allied soldiers totaled sixty-five hundred, whereas the Soviets had eighteen thousand. General Albert C. Wedemeyer, director of Army Plans and Operations, later observed that the Soviets had an overwhelming military superiority: "Our forces would have been annihilated." Howley years afterward agreed: "We would have got our *derrières* shot off." The president, Howley explained, put the "improvised 'air lift' " on a "full-scale organized basis" so that the West "might be able to feed Berlin until the diplomatic deadlock could be broken."[22]

But the president also relented to advisers in Washington who insisted upon a stronger response to the blockade. In emergency discussions held in Secretary of the Army Royall's Pentagon office on Sunday afternoon, June 27, Forrestal, Lovett, Bradley, Navy Secretary John L. Sullivan, and Air Force General Lauris Norstad explored the options. They admitted that to stay in Berlin would risk embarrassment and war, but they noted that to leave would undermine U.S. policy in Europe and stimulate the spread of Communism. The only choice was to continue the airlift while making a show of strength. The administration, they decided, should ask how Clay felt about the dispatch of two more B-29 squadrons (twenty planes of the kind that had dropped the atomic bombs over Japan) to join the single squadron already in Germany, and should ask Ambassador Lewis Douglas in London about the wisdom of likewise sending B-29s to England.[23]

Truman was amenable to the scaled-up reaction and insisted that the United States would not pull out of Berlin. He grasped the symbolic importance of the city and its connection with the rest of the German question. Bolstered by the recent pronouncements of support from France and Britain, the president insisted on a policy of firmness. Despite the seeming finality of this statement, Royall claimed that Truman later gave only "tentative approval" to remaining in Berlin while saying that he wanted to study the options. If so, his behavior was probably prudent rather than indecisive: he was keeping his options open while waiting to see whether the airlift would succeed and what the next Soviet move would be. Truman recognized the Soviets' military advantages in Central Europe and was not going to lock the United States into a position where the only choice was between a humiliating withdrawal and a war that would devastate both antagonists as well as the German people. For the moment, however, the president's position was firm. As Lovett reviewed the Pentagon discussions with him the next day, Truman interrupted to declare that there were no alternatives. Regardless of the chances for conflict, "we were in Berlin by terms of an agreement" and "the Russians had no right to get us out by either direct or indirect pressure." Lest there be doubt, he declared: "We're staying. Period."[24]

On June 28 Marshall informed the embassy in London that rather than follow Murphy's proposed use of force in Berlin, the United States would "supply the city by air as a beleaguered garrison." But he added that the White House was taking an additional step: "Subject to final checking by the Secretary and the President we will further increase US air strength in Europe." Not surprisingly, Clay supported the idea of sending additional transports (fifty more B-29s) to Germany as a demonstration of "Allied firmness," and the president immediately approved. Although the planes were not fitted for atomic bombs, they were capable of hitting Moscow. Their dispatch was intended to send a message to the Soviet Union.[25]

■ ■ ■ The crisis in Berlin was complicated further by its being only one of several issues commanding the attention of the United States during the summer of 1948. Events in Germany could not be separated from the ongoing problems in Greece and Turkey and from the early implementation of the Marshall Plan. In June, however, a new situation arose that threatened to destabilize all Central Europe: the growing rift between Yugoslavia and the Soviet Union. The administration in Washington became convinced that Tito's challenge to Stalin required the Kremlin to make its authority felt both inside and outside its spheres of control.[26] Yugoslavia was not as vulnerable to pressure as Czechoslovakia had been, however, because it was not contiguous with the Soviet border and could depend on the Mediterranean for contact with the non-Communist world. Tito had backed the Cominform, but his nationalism often interfered with Stalin's demand for total compliance with all pacts made by Communist nations. The Soviet premier once stormed: "I will shake my little finger—and there will be no more Tito." But all his efforts to get rid of Tito, including an attempted coup, had failed. Stalin then called a meeting of the Cominform in June 1948 to expel Tito for "taking the route of nationalism." In the meantime, as U.S. aid teams supplied the Greek army in its guerrilla war, as U.S. economic assistance became a reality in Western Europe, and as the verbal battle raged between Tito and Stalin, the Western allies attempted to meet the Soviet challenge in Germany while continuing work on a North Atlantic military alliance that might bring order out of the growing chaos. In response, the Soviets initiated a series of purges in Central Europe that within two years led to the collapse of nearly 25 percent of the Communist regimes in the region. And, of course, the Kremlin continued the Berlin blockade.[27]

The heightening Cold War in Europe had direct impact on the CIA. In December 1947 the White House had greatly escalated the nation's potential involvement in other countries' internal affairs by approving CIA participation in covert psychological operations. By June of the following year the organization's activities had expanded to include those of a covert political nature. Kennan, as director of the State Department's Policy Planning Staff, had argued for assigning political activities to the CIA, a step that he knew could lead to involvement in other countries' elections. The Special Studies Group he advocated, however, would be under careful State Department direction, though not on a formal basis. Years afterward Kennan explained that "we were alarmed by the inroads of the Russian influence in Western Europe beyond the point where Russian troops had reached." In France and Italy, for example, the Soviets had installed "front organizations" for the Communists. But the National Security Council went beyond Kennan's recommendation. On June 18 it established the Office of Special Projects, which later became known as the Office of Policy Coordination. Rather than being a distinct group under State Department auspices, it was established within the CIA and soon engaged in subversive activities designed to bring down Eastern European regimes friendly to the Soviet Union.[28]

Both the blockade and the airlift meanwhile took their toll on the West. To save on coal and power, the West cut back on electricity and transportation. The USSR exerted more pressure by instructing the treasury in Berlin (which was in the Soviet zone) to discontinue payments for the West's occupation expenses. Despite protests, the draws came to a stop; the Western powers were forced to appropriate money from their own budgets to meet the ballooning costs in Berlin. In addition, the Soviets enhanced frustration by causing complications and delays in German efforts to meet the city's weekly payrolls. U.S. and British pilots all the while followed a grueling schedule that consisted of nine hours in the air and eighteen of ground duties, followed by eight hours of sleep. Most of the flights were by instruments, a difficulty that added to the strain. West Berlin had two airports, Tempelhof and Gatow, only two minutes apart by air. That neither airport had ground radar units added further complications to habitually foul weather and heavy air traffic. In early July the first crash of a plane involved in the airlift occurred, killing four Americans.[29]

While the crisis worsened, the administration in Washington remained undecided about a long-term solution. Soviet representatives removed files from the offices of the Kommandatura and took down the Soviet flag in front of the building. Within a week Soviet fighters appeared to be interfering with the airlift; U.S. and British commanders, in response, ordered their pilots to fly above five thousand feet and well within the air lanes. The Soviets dismissed the West's complaints by declaring that U.S. officials had earlier violated the air regulations "unilaterally and arbitrarily." According to Kennan, who headed an almost continuous series of Policy Planning Staff meetings on the blockade, "No one was sure, as yet, how the Russian move could be countered or whether it could be successfully countered at all. The situation was dark, and full of danger."[30]

On Saturday, July 3, the three Western military governors met at Sokolovsky's headquarters near Potsdam in an effort to resolve the currency issue and the blockade. According to Clay, "Sokolovsky interrupted to state blandly that the technical difficulties would continue until we had abandoned our plans for [a] West German government." For the first time, Clay noted, the Soviets had attributed the blockade to the London Recommendations and put the West on notice that they would not discuss the blockade except in relation to the full German matter. Marshall, however, was opposed to a meeting of the Council of Foreign Ministers because the Soviet Union would use the blockade as leverage for discussing the whole German issue—including the London Recommendations. To approve such a four-power meeting would endanger the establishment of a West German government; to reject it would suggest that the West was unwilling to negotiate. The United States did not want the blockade to lead to a renunciation of the London program.[31]

An exchange of notes between East and West exacerbated the situation. In early July the American, British, and French ambassadors delivered identical notes of protest against the blockade to the Soviet ambassadors in Washington, London, and Paris. The West, said the notes, would agree to four-power talks regarding Berlin only after the USSR lifted the blockade. Eight days later, on July 14, the Soviets replied to the protest with a bitter denunciation of the West's policies. They refused to lift the blockade as a condition for talks and blamed the West for causing the crisis by pursuing "a separate currency reform," introducing "a special currency for the western sectors of Berlin," and seeking "the dismemberment of

Germany." Since Berlin was in the Soviet zone, and since the West had violated the wartime agreements regarding administration of the city, the West had lost its "right to participate in the occupation of Berlin."[32]

The Soviet reply was particularly alarming to the president. He disconsolately told Bohlen that the note constituted a "total rejection of everything we had asked for." That night, while Truman waited under the podium in Philadelphia to accept the presidential nomination, he told his daughter that war seemed likely.[33]

The White House continued to search for a safe position. On one side of the issue, columnist Walter Lippmann and former State Department official Sumner Welles urged the administration to grant concessions. Lippmann insisted that war should not begin on the counsel of "exasperated men in Berlin, nor decided on the frivolous speculation that the Russians will not fight if we act violently." On the other side, Clay yet again proposed sending an armed convoy to call the Soviets' bluff. Most Americans seemed to agree that some form of pressure was needed. William Donovan, the former head of the wartime Office of Strategic Services, delivered a radio address that was broadcast into the U.S. and British sectors in Berlin and that called for imposing worldwide economic sanctions, "even if it means war." Polled about whether the Allies should supply Berlin by force, 86 percent of the American respondents said yes and only 8 percent no.[34]

The National Security Council convinced the president to make a major show of force by sending sixty B-29 Superfortresses to the British Isles. In a *New York Times* story dated July 16, the White House announced that the B-29s would leave for England the following day to engage in a routine mission, but added ominously that the planes were "atomic-capable" and hinted that they carried nuclear warheads. Widespread speculation resulted, for it was not known until the 1970s that the planes had not yet been adapted to carry such a cargo. Intimidation of the Soviets had a good chance for success—as long as they did not regard the Truman administration's actions as bluffs. If Stalin was unsure about what the United States might do in the immediate sense, he was perhaps well informed about the United States' nuclear capacity. One of his agents, Donald Maclean, was in Washington from 1946 to 1948 as Britain's joint secretary of the Combined Policy Committee on Atomic Energy, and therefore had access to information on atomic stockpiles.[35]

The practical obstacles to using the bomb seemed almost insurmountable. Since the war the unassembled parts of the nation's atomic weaponry had at first been stored in a basement in Los Alamos before being transferred to an air force base near Albuquerque and then (in an effort to thwart sabotage) being moved temporarily to a spot close to the country's gold supply at Fort Knox. The U.S. nuclear arsenal in mid-1948 was small and not ready for deployment; it consisted of fewer than fifty bombs (not all of which were usable) and only thirty B-29s capable of delivering them. Further, there was a lack of both trained crews and facilities for loading. A specialized crew would need a minimum of two days to assemble the bombs and move them to B-29s equipped to drop them in combat. And even if this process went smoothly, the need for administrative approval would extend the preparation period. U.S. scientists had recently developed a better bomb design assuring easier construction and a burst of greater energy; the potential of doubling the atomic stockpile by the end of the year was thereby offered. But problems that remained in assembly and delivery made the nation's atomic shield almost illusory at the height of the Berlin crisis.[36]

The presence of the planes nonetheless proved the United States' commitment to Europe and enhanced the retaliatory capabilities of the West by reversing the military withdrawal from the Continent that had been under way since 1945. Indeed, their arrival placed them within striking distance of the Soviet Union and probably suggested to America's allies and to the USSR that the United States was prepared to bomb Moscow if war developed. When a Soviet spokesman sarcastically remarked that "the British Isles had now become an aircraft carrier," Churchill exploited that statement publicly and repeatedly as he affirmed Britain's new position as leader in defending the West. The dispatch of B-29s to Britain, of course, ran the risk of stampeding the Soviet Union into war. Numerous U.S. military advisers warned that use of the bomb would cause Stalin to order an invasion of France and send troops to the English Channel. The Soviets were undoubtedly aware of the small number of atomic bombs the United States possessed, but nevertheless the dispatch of the bombers to Britain probably acted as a restraint on the Kremlin's response to the airlift—or so it appeared to U.S. policymakers.[37] The danger was ongoing, however. Neither side could be sure of what the other would do, and thus an outcome that no one wanted remained a possibility.

The decision to send the B-29s to Europe had the indirect effect of resurrecting the debate over control of atomic weapons. Harriman, the secretary of commerce, wanted the bomb to become part of the United States' military repertoire. He urged Undersecretary of the Army William Draper to emphasize to the president that if war erupted, the United States would have to work with Britain and France in using "all of the weapons at our disposal." According to the president's daughter, Truman "had to fend off demands from Secretary of Defense Forrestal to authorize the use of the atomic bomb." The possible deployment of the bomb led some advisers to propose transferring its control to the military. On the day when Harriman made his recommendation, Royall sent a memo to Forrestal that set out "tentative ideas" about a series of escalating steps that might resolve the Berlin crisis. In addition to an expanded airlift, a note to Stalin claiming Western rights in the city, presentation of the blockade issue to the UN, and resort to an armed convoy if the Soviets ignored the UN's recommendations, Royall included a far-reaching proposal: if a convoy were required, the United States should "make preparations for fighter and bomber support, and at the same time have A-bombs available (in England or elsewhere) for immediate use, and . . . such use [should] be left entirely to the military."[38]

During the tense summer of 1948 the Department of Defense sought to acquire control over the bomb. Forrestal presented a formal request in late July for an executive order moving its custody from the Atomic Energy Commission to the military. The transfer, he argued, would unify the military command as well as assign responsibility for the bomb to those most familiar with it. The chairman of the AEC, David E. Lilienthal, strenuously objected. He insisted that the bomb was more than a means of military destruction: it had diplomatic and international ramifications that went far beyond the issue in Germany. In accordance with the Constitution, Lilienthal added, civilians had to maintain control over the military. The president agreed with Lilienthal that the bomb was not a purely "military weapon" and that its use would inflict countless civilian casualties. Royall impatiently rejoined that once committed to war, the nation must have victory as its sole concern. Besides, if 98 percent of the financing for atomic energy was allotted for weapons, such weapons ought to be used when necessary. Refusal to use them, he argued, "doesn't make any sense." Truman was perturbed with this narrow view and adamantly refused to give in to the pressure: "You have got to understand that this isn't a military weapon," he told Royall. "It is used to wipe out women and children and unarmed people. . . . You have got to understand that I have got to think about the effect of such a thing on international relations. This is no time to be juggling an atom bomb around." He promised to make a careful study of the matter before rendering a decision.[39]

Two days later the president announced to his cabinet that he had rejected the military's request for transferring custody of the bomb from the AEC. He could not relinquish a constitutional power vested in him as commander-in-chief, he said, and he strongly opposed having "some dashing lieutenant colonel decide when would be the proper time to drop one." Moreover, he wanted to maintain control and hence flexibility in responding to the Soviet threat. Truman, Lilienthal later insisted, assured Clark Clifford that custody of the bomb would always remain in the hands of the presidency. According to Forrestal, however, the president privately told him that political considerations had affected his decision and that he would examine the matter again after the presidential election in the fall. Whatever Truman believed about the question, he recognized that custody of the bomb was not the crucial point: the decision to use it was far more important, and that power remained with him as commander-in-chief.[40]

Throughout the Berlin crisis the president labored to maintain bipartisan support for his foreign policy. He brought Republicans into decision making, won Vandenberg's support in the Senate Foreign Relations Committee, and used Marshall and Lovett (himself a Republican) in an attempt to persuade the opposition party's candidate for the presidency, Governor Thomas Dewey of New York, to avoid Berlin as a political issue in the campaign. On July 19 Marshall and Lovett met in the State Department with Dewey's foreign affairs spokesman, John Foster Dulles, to find out the candidate's views before the administration talked with the British and French. Dulles then joined a meeting of the "Berlin Group," a special task force of State Department officials, headed by Bohlen, who had been assigned to the crisis. Dulles assured the advisers that the Soviets did not want war; he advocated a flexible policy that would permit them a way out of the perilous confrontation without damage to their prestige. He recommended that the White House privately inform Stalin (not Molotov, because he tended to act hastily) that it was willing to negotiate about Berlin and other parts of the German issue, but that it was also prepared to dispatch supplies to Berlin in trucks that could be stopped only by force. This procedure, Dulles wryly added, would give the Soviets time to repair the roads. Not everyone agreed with him, although most recognized the importance of taking into consideration the USSR's sensitive position.[41]

Again to win time and as a temporary alternative to more serious measures, Truman approved an expanded airlift. He presided over a July 22 meeting of the National Security Council during which Marshall and Clay (who had arrived from Berlin for consultations) warned once more that withdrawal would have a negative impact on European morale.[42] Clay had long argued against negotiations because the only terms acceptable to the Soviet Union were four-power control over the Ruhr and renunciation of the attempt to establish a government for West Germany. To Draper, Clay declared that Germany would remain a problem until the Marshall Plan had "invigorated western Europe so that it [might] develop a military strength which [would make] Soviet domination of Europe impossible."[43] Clay reported that the airlift was succeeding and insisted that its enlargement was the most feasible way to buy time for the Marshall Plan. At present, fifty-two C-54s and eighty C-47s were making two round trips a day with more than 250 landings. At least seventy-five more C-47s were needed to fill expected needs for coal in the winter. After the meeting the president talked with Clay about the Berlin problem in detail, and Clay later declared: "I left his office inspired by the understanding and confidence I received from him." But Air Force Chief of Staff General Hoyt Vandenberg warned that the proposal to relocate more transports would hurt the United States' strategic position worldwide. Such a program would interfere with contingency war plans because the planes were necessary to carry both atomic weaponry and its assembly experts to overseas targets. Truman, however, insisted that an airlift "involved less risks than armed convoys" and ordered Vandenberg to provide the planes.[44]

The National Security Council subsequently approved directives that made possible an expansion of the airlift, including the construction of a new airfield in Berlin and the dispatch of the planes necessary to enlarge the airlift. It also accepted Clay's recommendation to reduce U.S. dependents in Berlin to a thousand by the end of August. Finally, it opted for a strong verbal protest to Stalin. Murphy, who was at the council meeting, was unhappy with the decision not to challenge the blockade with anything more than the airlift. He should have resigned, he later said: "I still deeply regret that I was associated with an action which caused Soviet leaders to downgrade United States determination and capability." Acheson dismissed Murphy's criticism of the airlift as "silly."[45] The indecisiveness that had characterized the administration during the early days of the crisis had given way to a firm but short-of-war policy largely (and perhaps paradoxically) structured by on-site military advisers.

The president remained anxious to avoid actions that could demand a counteraction conducive to war. He was, moreover, forced to work within the rigid constraints of his nation's military weaknesses in conventional forces and the monumental implications of an atomic strike. On the one side, he could rely on a scant two divisions of ground forces, only one of which could be readied quickly. On the other, he could not authorize use of the bomb (assuming it was available for deployment) unless there was an unmistakable and direct threat to national security. Even its use as an instrument of diplomatic pressure was open to question. Forrestal recalled discussing the dilemma at a luncheon with government officials in late July. "I said in view of the tensions in the European situation that I felt it was difficult for me to carry out my responsibilities without resolution of the question whether or not we are to use the A-bomb in war. I observed also that it seemed to me that the Secretary of State had a deep interest in this, because, if there were any questions as to the use of this weapon, he was automatically denied one of the most potent cards in his pack in negotiation."[46] Most advisers, however, favored the airlift as the best way to demonstrate the United States' endurance without going to war. Acheson later insisted that the airlift did not constitute the West's capitulation in Berlin: "One can as well say that to put one's hands up at the command of an armed bandit is to surrender one's hard-won right to keep them down."[47]

The airlift was critical in raising the morale of West Berliners and in easing the crisis. Until the end of July most of the city's residents had not decided whether to resist the Soviet Union. Although they either opposed Communism or were not Communists, their feelings were not sufficiently strong to manifest themselves in action. Moreover, they were not fully confident of the West's resolve to protect Berlin. The airlift, however, demonstrated that the West intended to stay, that it would furnish food, and that a policy of nonviolence reduced the likelihood of war. With this encouragement, German animosity toward the Soviets grew apace. In a well-publicized episode Berliners demonstrated their support for the West by rejecting a food offer from the USSR. One city resident remarked that "no one wanted to have anything to do with Russians; the days when they entered Berlin were still too fresh in our memories for that."[48] After the airlift became the chief U.S. response to the blockade, a test of patience ensued between East and West that allowed the focus of activity to return to diplomacy. Tension in Berlin persisted, but the fear of war began to recede. Clay, now back in Berlin, assured journalists that the airlift would succeed and declared that he saw "an excellent chance" for a peaceful resolution of the crisis. At a press conference in Washington, the president responded to a question about the chances for peace: "I think they are good. In fact, I think they are excellent."[49]

There was a further ameliorative factor at this point. Even though the Western powers remained cut off from surface access to West Berlin, they speeded up work on the establishment of a North Atlantic military alliance.

■ ■ ■ CHAPTER NINE

From Berlin to NATO

The Establishment of Order in Western Europe

By mid-summer of 1948 the Russians began to regard the crisis precipitated by the Berlin blockade as counterproductive to their goals and injurious to their interests. If the intent of the interdiction was to force the West into negotiations over Germany, the blockade was not working. Rather, by making Berlin a symbol of the East-West conflict, the blockade had evoked an equivalent response from the United States that was winning worldwide support.[1] The Soviets nonetheless maintained the blockade, probably still hoping that it would promote negotiations and knowing that they could lift it immediately if war threatened. In addition, as Stalin's biographer believes, the premier's growing megalomania, combined with his belief that the United States was preoccupied with the approaching presidential election, pushed him to continue his dangerous policy in hope that it would wear down the West. Finally, the Soviets thought that the maintenance of tension over Berlin might keep the focus on the West and away from their domestic and alliance troubles.

In the meantime the National Security Council meeting of July 22 had clarified the administration's policy: the United States would stay in Berlin while using the airlift to help the besieged city and seeking a peaceful resolution of the problem. Thus the effect of the blockade was the opposite of what the Soviets had intended. The West was more firmly entrenched in the city than before, and Washington's measured yet resolute reaction maintained credibility with allies and refurbished its image as defender of the right of self-determination. Indeed, the Anglo-American airlift had turned into a great human interest story that cast the onus onto the Soviets. Further, and more ominous from the Soviet perspective, the blockade had tightened Western unity, stimulated the establishment of a West German government that would be linked with the West, and provided greater impetus for a North Atlantic defense treaty that might combine with the Truman Doctrine and Marshall Plan in finally bringing postwar order to Europe.

Despite these gains for the West, the White House realized the need to find a way out of the confrontation in Berlin that would avoid humiliation for either party. War remained possible if the alternative was a serious blow to the prestige of either side.[2]

■ ■ ■ To present the Soviets with a firm and undivided front at home, Washington had to ensure the continuation of a bipartisan foreign policy. It was particularly important, the administration believed, to keep the Berlin issue out of what promised to be one of the hottest presidential campaigns in the nation's history. Toward those ends, Lovett sought Dulles's support by keeping him informed of developments regarding Germany. The strategy worked. On July 25 Dewey announced through the *New York Times* that he agreed with the administration's decision to hold onto Berlin. The Republicans instead focused on China and called for a military buildup in the United States, while the Democrats condemned Communism both inside and outside the country and promised strict enforcement of laws against subversion. The timing of Dewey's decision was important to the administration; on July 30, during the shock of the Czech coup and the Berlin blockade, the House Un-American Activities Committee heard claims that Communists had infiltrated the Department of State. The most sensational case involved Alger Hiss, who was accused by Whittaker Chambers of being a party agent during the 1930s. Hiss, a Harvard Law School graduate, had been associated with several executive departments, and while in the State Department had worked as an adviser at the Yalta Conference, which was already coming under fire for Roosevelt's alleged "giveaways" in Eastern Europe and the Far East. With Dewey's campaign under control, Truman was able to ward off potentially dangerous attacks on his containment policy while adhering to a tough but short-of-war stance against the Soviets.[3]

The White House did not share its Western allies' hopes about resolving the Berlin crisis through negotiations with the Soviet Union, but it agreed to make another effort. France appeared to favor pulling out of Berlin if a suitable arrangement could be found. Britain seemed to vacillate between getting out and staying. The United States defended the West's right to be there and was not willing to negotiate a departure. Although few Allied leaders considered the airlift capable of supplying the city on a long-term basis, they preferred its continuance along with attempted negotiations to the alternative of more stringent action. Talks would also buy time for the airlift to have greater effect, for the Allies to resolve their differences, and for the West to build its air and ground power in Europe.[4]

In late July the president sent Bohlen to Europe to arrange a tripartite appeal that might persuade Stalin to lift the blockade. Bohlen arrived first in Berlin, where he was joined by Ambassadors Smith from Moscow and Douglas from London. After conferring with Clay, the three diplomats departed for London to talk with British and French representatives. The atmosphere was strained, in part because Bevin seemed convinced that his U.S. allies had accepted the likelihood of war. At one point in the discussions he remarked only half-jokingly: "I know all of you Americans want a war, but I'm not going to let you 'ave it."[5] The Allied representatives approved expanded military preparations (largely owing to Bevin's urging), but they also agreed to instruct their ambassadors in Moscow—Frank Roberts from Britain (Bevin's assistant standing in for Ambassador Sir Maurice Peterson, who was ill) and Yves Jean Joseph Chataigneau from France, in addition to Smith—to submit simultaneous protests to the Soviet government and ask Stalin to meet with them.[6]

The Western delegates at first had difficulty arranging four-power talks in Moscow. They were told that Molotov was on vacation and that his assistant, Deputy Foreign Minister Andrei Vyshinsky, was also away from the office; but the ambassadors finally received permission to meet on an individual basis with the junior deputy, Valerian Zorin. On July 30 they gave Zorin an aide-mémoire asking for a meeting with Stalin and Molotov to discuss Berlin and "its wider implications." From the Soviet perspective, the prospects of an advantageous settlement must have seemed good. Even though the West maintained its legal claim regarding Berlin, it had apparently authorized its emissaries in Moscow to accept what the Kremlin had wanted all along: four-power discussions aimed at a general resolution of the whole German problem. Doubtless believing that the West was finally ready to negotiate within Soviet guidelines, Zorin at first placidly observed that the Western note contained nothing to encourage such a meeting but then agreed to forward the request to his superiors. The impact of the West's proposal was immediate. The next day the three representatives were informed that Molotov had returned to Moscow and, in a stipulation that Smith thought was a shrewd effort to maneuver one of the delegates into revealing exactly what the West wanted, would meet with them individually that evening. Sensing that he had the upper hand, the Soviet foreign minister cavalierly attributed all problems to the London program and called for discussions on Berlin within the context of broad negotiations about Germany. Molotov added that he "hoped Generalissimo Stalin would agree to meet the representatives of the three governments."[7]

On the evening of August 2 the three Westerners met once more with Molotov, but this time Stalin chose to join them. The aging premier's presence signified the importance of the meeting, for it was well known that he did not participate in negotiations unless a settlement seemed certain. Smith was senior among his colleagues and acted as spokesman. The session was a "poker game," he recalled, during which Stalin appeared in great humor. The premier gruffly and almost glibly insisted that the Soviet goal was not to force the West out of Berlin: "After all, we are still Allies." But he quickly dropped this tack and admonished his visitors that the West had given up occupation rights by attempting to establish a West German government. Indeed, according to Smith's account, Stalin regarded this as "the only real issue." If the West succeeded in such a venture, Stalin warned, "there would be nothing to discuss." Four-power occupation of Berlin was workable only with a unified Germany, but the London Conference had made that unity impossible. In exchange for lifting the blockade, Stalin demanded that the West forgo the London program temporarily, until four-power discussions could take place on Germany. The Western representatives rejected this demand and insisted on shared occupation of the city. In truth, the Soviet position was consistent with earlier statements and was not entirely unreasonable. But Smith suspected that Stalin's call for a return to wartime agreements was a subterfuge designed to buy time for a deeper Soviet entrenchment in Berlin and ultimate control over all Germany. He later observed that Stalin seemed to have "confronted us with the flat alternative of getting out of Berlin in ignominious defeat or of staying on under sufferance and abandoning our announced plan of setting up a separate government for Western Germany."[8]

After two hours of disagreement, the possibility of a breakthrough suddenly appeared. Shortly before midnight Stalin sat back in his chair, lit a cigarette, and smiled as he asked Smith: "Would you like to settle the matter tonight?" Nothing would suit him more, Smith replied. Stalin then indicated that he would end the blockade if the West would withdraw the deutsche mark in Berlin in favor of the Soviet mark, and agree to four-power talks. In return, the Soviets would no longer seek a postponement of the London program as a condition for settlement but would merely record their "insistent wish" that it be dropped.[9]

Smith and his companions were encouraged by the change in Stalin's demeanor and agreed to pass on his proposals to their governments with recommendations for approval. In the privacy of Smith's office afterward, the three Western diplomats congratulated themselves while remaining wary of hidden meanings behind Stalin's apparent concessions. They had secured the simultaneous resolution of the blockade and currency issues (with implied four-power supervision over the Soviet mark) and had committed the West only to discussing the larger German question. If the discussions failed, work toward putting the London program in place could be resumed. The details of the arrangement, however, remained to be settled. Smith was still suspicious even as he wrote Marshall with some optimism: "Doubt if I have ever seen Molotov so cordial and if one did not know real Soviet objectives in Germany would have been completely deceived by their attitude as both literally dripping with sweet reasonableness and desire not to embarrass."[10]

But despite Smith's recommendation, the administration in Washington opposed Stalin's terms because it still believed that his underlying intention was aggressive. Clay and Bohlen convinced Marshall that nothing had changed: the Soviet premier still called for the West to abandon plans for a West German government in exchange for an end to the blockade. Progress toward implementing the London program had to continue, they insisted. Clay also complained that the Soviets had not specifically guaranteed four-power control over the currency; without that, he emphasized, they could gradually push the West out of Berlin. Less than a week before, the USSR had caused widespread disorder by freezing the magistrat's accounts in the city's central bank. Soviet economic controls, Clay warned, would lead to Soviet political controls that would undermine Germany's faith in the West. Marshall agreed. The United States could not allow Soviet currency to become the sole medium of exchange in Berlin without four-power supervision. He instructed Smith to express satisfaction with Stalin's decision to forgo his demand for an end to the West German government and, without stating so, made clear that Smith was to ignore the premier's desire to record his "insistent wish" against the idea.[11]

Attempts to draft a final settlement in long, gloomy meetings on August 6, 9, 12, and 16 convinced the Western negotiators that Stalin's amiability and openness had been a facade. Both he and Molotov seemed unfriendly and recalcitrant while discussing details. When Smith presented the Western draft calling for an end to "all restrictions" on transportation and communication, setting out conditions regarding the use of the Soviet mark in Berlin, and assuring four-power talks on Germany, Molotov rejected the entire document. It contained nothing about Stalin's "insistent wish" regarding the London program, Molotov emphasized repeatedly in the three-hour meeting on August 6. Smith pointed out that in practical terms there was no problem because the Germans were not scheduled to meet on the matter until September 1 and their study would extend well beyond a meeting of the Council of Foreign Ministers on Germany. Molotov simply moved to another item and refused to approve four-power control over the Soviet mark. The Soviets claimed to feel betrayed. As Molotov saw it, the Western allies four days previously had been so eager to end the blockade that they would permit Soviet control over the currency and postpone the London program; now they had suddenly reversed themselves by demanding four-power control and refusing to make any promises regarding Germany.[12]

At their meeting on August 9 Molotov moved matters back to square one by coupling the end of the blockade with an agreement to defer the establishment of a West German government. The foreign minister repeated that the West had no legal right to be in Berlin and that Stalin's reference to the removal of "all transport restrictions" included only those enacted after June 18—when the West implemented currency reform in the city. Smith realized that these terms would award the Soviets control over Berlin. Although he and his colleagues thought that Molotov and Stalin were guilty of bad faith, the truth was that the hardened Soviet position was attributable to a misreading of the West's intentions. Marshall had never altered his insistence on protecting the London program and on sharing control over the currency. But the Kremlin had derived the mistaken notion that the Western powers were willing to compromise, and now, angry with what they saw as an abrupt and unjust change of heart, they escalated their demands. Molotov's draft proposal denied the West's occupation rights in Berlin, did not mention currency control, and agreed to lift only those restrictions imposed after June 18. Western access rights to the city would then come from "the present agreement," which was a tacit cancellation of all earlier arrangements. Indeed, the proposed rights were not explained. Molotov also wanted the West to abandon the London program by approving the statement that the West "did not propose for the time being to deal with the question of the formation of a government for Western Germany." Finally, he accused the West of breaking four-power control by means of the London Conference. If the West agreed to restore four-power control to Germany, Molotov remarked, "then it might also be restored in Berlin."[13]

Not surprisingly, Marshall rejected Molotov's draft. Though willing to allow some restrictions on passage into Berlin, Marshall was convinced that approval of the June 18 date would suggest that the blockade had been a defensive measure implemented in response to Western provocations. Besides, many of the restrictions imposed before June 18 were unsatisfactory. He concluded that the differences dividing East and West were unresolvable and that the West might well have to force open the city. Indeed, Clay later declared that he received a directive to develop an armed convoy plan without telling either the British or the French. From the Kremlin's perspective, the heart of the problem was the London program, which, if successful, would establish a West German government capable of endangering Soviet interests in Central Europe. The currency issue was also not susceptible to compromise, because of its far-reaching economic and political ramifications. Further, the West discerned few advantages in restoring quadripartite control over Germany, especially since the Soviets showed no inclination to retreat from their insistence on the ruling principle of unanimity. Smith sensed that the Soviets were losing interest in the talks and warned that they would continue to seek concessions by shifting the focus to events in Berlin. Two more meetings failed to break the deadlock.[14]

Marshall recommended that Smith appeal for another round of direct talks with Stalin, and on August 23 the premier complied by joining Molotov in a meeting with the Western representatives. As in their first gathering, Stalin appeared conciliatory, in stark contrast to the sour demeanor of his companion. Each side seemed for a time to move closer to the other—but this was an illusion. Stalin agreed to lift all transport restrictions, including those imposed before June 18, and to accept the establishment of a financial commission that would control Berlin's currency but operate under supervision of the four military commanders. Indeed, Smith declared that Stalin was "quite categorical that this commission would be the controlling body and said he did not mind using the word control." As to a West German government, Stalin approved the issuance of a public communiqué declaring that the London program was discussed in "an atmosphere of mutual understanding" and that a decision was "deferred until the next meeting of the Council of Foreign Ministers." But Roberts immediately objected, fearing that acceptance of any reference to congeniality would imply that the Soviets had forced the West to abandon the London program in exchange for an end to the blockade. Smith emphasized that the United States could not approve the proposals without the inclusion of a specific statement that "no agreement had been reached" on this subject. After two hours of talks, Stalin provided an appropriate requiem for the all but defunct settlement by announcing his departure for a vacation. Molotov remained for three hours with the Western delegates in a vain attempt to work out the terms of a joint communiqué and a directive to the four military governors in Berlin.[15]

Follow-up meetings with Molotov took place in an atmosphere heavy with tension. On August 27 the foreign minister made no attempt to conceal his dissatisfaction with the West for rejecting the Moscow draft. After considerable wrangling, the delegations agreed to meet again three days later and coldly adjourned. At the next meeting Molotov insisted that all discussions be confidential and, on that basis, rejected a communiqué. The representatives approved the issuance of a directive to the military governors in Berlin that offered little hope for a resolution of the problem. The four governors were to lift the restrictions that had "recently been imposed"; declare the Soviet mark the sole currency in Berlin; assign currency regulation to the German Bank of Emission located in the Soviet zone; and establish a financial commission to "control the practical implementation of the financial arrangements indicated above." The directive seemed to follow Stalin's assurances by assigning control over the bank to the commission, but when Smith called for more specific wording, Molotov cut him off by declaring that the directive was clear as it stood.[16]

The Moscow agreement contained contradictory assumptions and loose provisions that were susceptible to varying interpretations. The West thought the Soviets had agreed to lift all restrictions levied since March and that a four-power financial commission would control bank operations, but the agreement did not specifically affirm either of these points. The draft said that the restrictions "recently" imposed would be ended—although, when questioned, Molotov testily replied that this of course included those put in place before June 18. Currency circulation would be the responsibility of the Soviet bank, which was to be, as Stalin had agreed, under commission control—or so it seemed from the Western perspective. The West considered the settlement a package, that is, that it encompassed not only the specifics in the directive but the verbal assurances given by Stalin and Molotov as well. The Soviets, however, intended to adhere only to the written directive. If Stalin's purpose was to block a settlement by making ambiguous proposals that would be subject to endless argument, that strategy had enormous potential. It would shift the blame for failed negotiations onto the West if the delegates rejected his proposals. In addition, while the West was preoccupied in Moscow, the Communists in Berlin could attempt to broaden their base by exerting more pressure on city officials. That same August, heightened propaganda called for a new "democratic and progressive" city administration.[17]

The Moscow talks left the appearance of a settlement, but in reality they had resulted in a diplomatic stalemate that, because of the importance of Germany to both sides, could only be a harbinger of future troubles. Clay warned Washington that the Moscow agreement contained no specific guarantee of the West's right to take part in quadripartite supervision of Berlin. Indeed, his drumlike assurances of more problems caused Lovett to remark that the general was "now drawn as tight as a steel spring." The impasse seemed indissoluble. The Soviets demanded negotiations on the whole German question as a condition for lifting the blockade; the Western allies continued to believe that the USSR's objective was to force them out of Berlin and, in any case, refused to enter four-power talks under duress. Indeed, the West offered no assurances of discussions even if the Soviets lifted the blockade.[18] The two sides were as far apart after the Moscow discussions as before.

Soon afterward, on August 31, the four military governors met in Berlin in the first of a series of meetings that succeeded only in confirming the rocklike divisions that separated East and West. Despite Clay's thinly veiled animosity, he worked with the others to put the Moscow directive into effect. On September 1, in the midst of the four-power sessions, the German Constituent Assembly met in Bonn under the chairmanship of Konrad Adenauer to begin planning the establishment of a government of West Germany. Follow-up meetings of the military governors stretched into early September, the atmosphere becoming increasingly testy as Sokolovsky coldly refused to lift any transportation restrictions and rejected four-power control over currency. Further, he claimed the right of the Soviets to conduct maneuvers in the air corridors used by the West. That statement drew an immediate rejoinder from Clay. Nonmilitary planes were involved in the airlift, he indignantly declared, and safety regulations prohibited such maneuvers. Sokolovsky denied the existence of such regulations and, although he never followed through on his threats, continued to assert the right to use the lanes. In the seventh and final meeting, on September 7, the military governors again failed to agree on the responsibilities of the financial commission. Sokolovsky meanwhile kept the atmosphere tense by demanding Soviet control over the city's trade and threatening to introduce restrictions on air transportation.[19]

■ ■ ■ Perhaps, in a paradoxical sense, the chance for a Berlin settlement lay in clarifying the division between East and West rather than in searching for an agreement over specific, stormy, and, in actuality, nonnegotiable issues. The British ambassador to the United States, Lord Inverchapel, thought so as early as February 1948. Both U.S. officials and private persons, he wrote the Foreign Office, believed that "the division of Germany and absorption of the two parts into rival Eastern and Western spheres [was] preferable to the creation of a no-man's land on the border of an expanding Soviet hegemony."[20] The tragedy is that Stalin, it now seems clear, had been pushing in this direction since at least early 1948. For this reason, then, the United States deserves part of the blame for the crisis. As has been pointed out, the American government was convinced, however erroneously, that Stalin's major objective was to drive the West out of Berlin as the first step in securing control over all Germany. The West therefore countered with a move toward the establishment of a West German state that, to the Kremlin, must have looked like a hostile effort to resurrect Russia's longtime enemy. The saving factor amid the heightening frustration and deepening distrust was that neither East nor West wanted war, a shared goal which suggested that the avenue of escape might be to focus the differences between the antagonists by arranging a permanent partition of Germany. The establishment of two Germanies did not offer the optimum solution for either Cold War adversary, but the mutual and public acknowledgment of a stalemate was preferable to a continued escalation of demands that could lead to war.

Smith had been correct in warning that the storm center would shift to Berlin: the USSR stepped up the pressure in an attempt to secure its objectives. In the Pentagon on Labor Day, Lovett talked at length with Bradley and Forrestal about the Soviets' willingness to twist the truth in Germany. The three men agreed that the Kremlin did not want an agreement and preferred acting on its own. It was difficult, Lovett dourly remarked, to negotiate with someone "whose head is full of bubbles." The following day, September 7, the president called a special meeting of the National Security Council to discuss Berlin (the first meeting solely on that subject since July 22). After a review of the situation, Marshall warned that the Soviet Union would engage in other obstructionist tactics, such as inciting civil violence in West Berlin. The council approved his suggestion to take the matter before the UN Security Council if the diplomats failed to reach agreement in Moscow. The National Security Council also approved an increase in the number of C-54s for the airlift from 125 to 200. Just before Marshall's meeting with the joint chiefs on the next day, Clay warned from Berlin that U.S. discussions with Moscow were "too much of a plea and not enough of a demand." If Moscow was not amenable, he noted, the matter must go to the UN—even if the only result was increased public awareness of the West's desire for peace.[21]

In the face of deadlocked negotiations, the hostilities threatened to spiral beyond control when the Truman administration again discussed using the atomic bomb in the event of war. The National Security Council had organized a study involving the State Department, the army, the navy, the air force, the CIA, and the National Security Resources Board, and on September 10 the group completed its work. NSC-30, its report, warned that refusal to use the bomb would encourage Soviet aggression and unsettle the United States' allies in Europe, who counted on the bomb to offset Soviet military strength on the Continent. If war broke out, said the report, the United States must be prepared to use "all appropriate means available, including atomic weapons." In a September 13 meeting in the White House, administration officials discussed approaching the British about building huts on their airfields to hold the bomb's component parts for rapid assembly. If London approved, the United States would gain ten days of preparation time during an emergency. At this point Forrestal inquired about the president's willingness to use the bomb. Truman replied, according to Forrestal's diary, that "he prayed that he would never have to make such a decision, but that if it became necessary, no one need have a misgiving but what he would do so."[22] On the question of whether the military should take jurisdiction over the bomb, as Forrestal had urged, the report took the position that custody should remain with the president. Truman himself still wanted to wait until after the election to give full consideration to the issue. That same day he recorded privately: "I have a terrible feeling afterwards that we are very close to war."[23]

Three days later the National Security Council approved the report: the president would continue to be the final voice in deciding whether to use the bomb if U.S. security was in danger.[24]

Public sentiment both inside and outside the country favored use of the bomb, and not only in the event of a previous outbreak of war. In the house of the *Washington Post*'s publisher, Philip L. Graham, a large group of influential newspaper editors and publishers had met with Marshall, Lovett, and Bohlen and expressed confidence that the American people would expect the United States to use the bomb if war erupted over Berlin. Two months later Attlee told Forrestal of Britain's widespread support for that firm stand. But some observers wanted to go farther. Indeed, even the normally hawkish Forrestal expressed concern about the numerous Americans who were calling for the administration to wage a preventive war against the Soviets while it still had an atomic monopoly. And as one writer has shown, those Americans advocating such strategy were not confined to what has been called the "lunatic fringe." Among those who referred to the United States' atomic monopoly as a "wasting asset" and showed interest in preventive war were General Leslie Groves of the Manhattan Project; William L. Lawrence, a *New York Times* science correspondent and the nation's most influential writer on nuclear matters; physicist Leo Szilard; the U.S. Navy; and the U.S. Air Force, which was the most supportive of the idea. Though the U.S. government never seriously considered adopting a preventive war strategy, Bohlen and Kennan pondered the question in the State Department, and Churchill in England argued for a nuclear showdown in 1948.[25]

Although the White House continued to believe that the Soviets did not want war, it still feared that war could occur if either side misinterpreted the other's intentions. A Policy Planning Staff paper bolstered that conception by concluding that the Soviet Union was not planning to instigate a war but was nonetheless seeking its ends by "political means, accompanied—of course—by the factor of military intimidation." These dangerous tactics, obviously, could bring war by miscalculation. In mid-September Smith assured Marshall that war seemed unlikely but underlined the importance of perceptions in international relations. The Soviets, he wrote, "discounted completely the possibility that we might actually force the issue to [the] point of hostilities, just as we estimated no similar intention on their part." He added that "their belief has been reinforced during [the] protracted course of [the] Moscow talks."[26]

The specter of a war brought on by misunderstanding stiffened the West's resolve to keep communication lines open. The Western allies accordingly tried the diplomatic approach again. Marshall had arrived in Paris to attend the UN General Assembly proceedings opening on September 20, but his presence allowed the allies to discuss the Berlin issue on a face-to-face basis. The secretary of state brought Dulles with him and arranged for the three Western representatives involved in the Moscow talks to gather in the French capital as well. For the next two months Marshall and his advisers met with the British and French delegations led by Bevin and French Foreign Secretary Robert Schuman. Even if nothing specific resulted, Marshall must have believed that the impression of Western unity would send an unmistakable message to the Kremlin.[27]

Smith was convinced that the UN option was the only way out of a problem that the United States had helped to create by attaching excessive symbolic importance to Berlin. When the White House called him home from Moscow for consultations, he repeated this argument at a Policy Planning Staff meeting on September 28. "We should never have let ourselves get into an exposed salient like Berlin under such conditions," Smith declared. "From the military point of view, it makes no sense whatever to have U.S. forces in an enclave that could be chopped off with ease. From the political point of view, Berlin has become the important symbol it is largely because we ourselves have made it so. However," he regretfully added, "that is all water over the dam; my hope for the future is that the U.N. will offer a chance for us to get out of Berlin." Smith doubted that the USSR would provoke a conflict. If the United States intended to remain, it could do so "at great cost, at some hazard, and with diminishing effectiveness except for the business of supplying ourselves, mainly to maintain our symbolic presence there."[28]

While Western diplomats worked out a scenario in which they would draft a note to the Kremlin and then take the issue before the Security Council if rebuffed, the governments of the United States, Britain, and France unanimously agreed to remain in Berlin and to expand the airlift. Bevin's suggestion that the three allies seek renewed negotiations with the Soviets in Moscow was overruled. Marshall sensed that his colleagues were wavering and tried to instill confidence in the West's ability to emerge triumphant. "In every field," he declared, "the Russians are retreating. From now on, Berlin is the only foothold which they have against us; everywhere else, and particularly in Germany, they are losing ground. We have put Western Germany on its feet and we are engaged in bringing about its recovery in such a way that we can really say that we are on the road to victory."[29]

On September 22 the Western allies sent identical notes to the Soviet embassies in Washington, London, and Paris, seeking a lifting of the blockade as a modus vivendi for general negotiations. If the Soviet response was not satisfactory, the three had already decided, they would take the Berlin question to the UN. Less than a week later, as the gathering in Bonn moved toward the establishment of a West German government, the Soviets declared their refusal to lift the blockade and then broke the four-power pledge of secrecy by announcing through Tass that the West was responsible for the breakdown in negotiations. These Soviet actions confirmed the three Western powers in their decision against attempting to reopen the talks in Moscow. They formally agreed to take the Berlin issue before the Security Council, to send a final note to the Kremlin, and to counter the Tass story by releasing a communiqué informing the world that the blockade was illegal and that the Soviet Union was purposefully endangering peace by obstructing negotiations. In early October the Soviets argued that in accordance with the Potsdam agreements and the military directive of late August, the Council of Foreign Ministers, not the Security Council, should deal with Berlin and Germany. Marshall and Bevin insisted that the blockade must be lifted before they would consent to a meeting of the foreign ministers. On October 5, over Soviet protests, the Berlin issue was put on the Security Council agenda.[30]

On that same day Marshall suddenly had to turn his attention from Paris in an effort to prevent domestic politics in the United States from intruding on the Berlin crisis, with possibly disastrous results. The president's foreign policy had come under bitter attack during the political campaign from the Progressive party's candidate, Henry Wallace, and in response Truman had decided to send his friend Chief Justice Fred Vinson as a personal representative to talk with the Soviet premier. The president later explained that he had wanted Stalin "to unburden himself to someone on our side he felt he could trust fully." He added, however, that "if the Russians were hell-bent for communizing and dominating the world on a rule-or-ruin basis, there was little we could do by the negotiation route. Even then we had . . . to keep trying." Truman insisted that his only objective was to see if Vinson "could not get Stalin to open up." Although the president also thought the special mission might yield political gains in the coming election, as well as undercut those Americans advocating preventive war, Marshall (who had returned to Washington at Truman's request) vigorously protested that the effort would undermine the UN strategy and alienate the United States' allies by seeking a German settlement through unilateral talks. In the meantime someone leaked the Vinson story to the press, and the result was a public outcry against appeasement. Despite the counsel of several White House advisers, the president sided with his secretary of state. "I have heard enough. We won't do it."[31]

No sooner had the State Department quashed the Vinson mission than it had to face a rebellion among the military. The Joint Chiefs of Staff submitted a report warning the administration that its policies could lead an unprepared American nation into war. The joint chiefs declared that the country's "present military power" could not "effectively support the supply of Berlin by air lift on an indefinite basis" without "a diversion of military effort" that would "continue progressively to affect seriously and adversely" the country's ability "to meet its primary national security responsibilities." Insistence on staying in Berlin "in any event" implied the White House's willingness to go to war in an effort to hold onto the city. The joint chiefs warned that the administration's foreign policy reach exceeded the nation's military grasp. A war "in our present state of readiness and for the Berlin issue" was "neither militarily prudent nor strategically sound." When the National Security Council met to consider the report, Lovett wryly remarked that the joint chiefs had a "case of the jitters" and emphasized that the decision to stay in Berlin "in any event" had taken place with total awareness of the United States' military strength. Under pressure from Lovett and other defenders of the administration, the joint chiefs agreed to revise their study. On October 21 they submitted a new report that contained no expression of doubt about White House policy, but warned that the airlift could not go on indefinitely and declared that if it ceased to be effective the administration would have to make the hard decision whether Berlin was worth a war. They also recommended approval of Clay's request for adding sixty-six C-54s to the airlift.[32]

As the White House continued to deal with unforeseen problems erupting from the crisis in Germany, Truman sought to assure the American public that he could handle the USSR and that he would neither back down nor resort to war. Before the American Legion Convention on October 18 he declared that the United States would maintain a firm posture without going to war. The world knew that "weakness and appeasement" encouraged aggression. The United States wanted "mutual conciliation," he assured the audience, but that should not be mistaken for appeasement. "We will never be a party," he added, "to the kind of compromise which the world sums up in the disgraced name of Munich."[33]

In the meantime the Security Council had failed to resolve the Berlin crisis. Its six neutral members had recommended a total lifting of the blockade, new four-power discussions on the currency issue, and a meeting of the Council of Foreign Ministers to deal with the whole German matter. But on October 25 the Soviet delegate vetoed the resolution, and the UN proceedings on Berlin came to a standstill.[34]

If the administration had doubts about the popularity of its Berlin policy, those doubts were removed by the president's victory in the November election. According to one writer, Dewey's decision to forgo the foreign policy issue in the campaign probably turned out to be the crucial factor in his defeat. By the fall of 1948 much of the animosity toward Truman's Cold War policies had dissipated, largely because of his handling of the Berlin crisis. Regardless of whether the short-of-war stance was a major factor in the outcome, the White House believed it was. The Democrats won control over both Houses of Congress, and criticism of the administration eased markedly. The election confirmed the determination of the United States and its allies to maintain the airlift while tightening the counterblockade against East Berlin and to refuse to consider either the resumption of negotiations in Moscow or the convening of the Council of Foreign Ministers. When Kennan urged the administration to seek a negotiated settlement of the entire German problem, he found little support for any program built on compromise.[35]

As U.S. observers had feared, violence erupted in Berlin when the Soviets tried to consolidate Communist control. Communist demonstrators in Berlin repeatedly broke up attempts by the city assembly to meet until, in early September, the assembly members abandoned the Berlin City Hall in the Soviet sector and voted to meet permanently in West Berlin. By early October the Communists had begun a purge of Socialist Unity party members and of public officeholders that, combined with the suppression of other political groups and tighter supervision over the Eastern zone, drove a large number of East Germans into West Berlin and West Germany. According to some estimates, an average of fifty refugees a day escaped into the Western sectors of the city. Resistance to the Communists' measures grew in West Berlin, leading increasingly to the separation of the city into two disparate units. In Washington Kennan warned the secretary of state that even though a "military danger" was growing from each adversary's desire to protect prestige, the Soviets would continue to emphasize political methods while using "military force . . . only as a means of intimidation." The danger stemming from "political conquest" was greater than the military threat. "The political war . . . is now in progress; and, if there should not be a shooting war, it is this political war which will be decisive." Marshall agreed.[36]

By the end of November the political divisions had hardened in both East and West Berlin almost in conjunction with those divisions on the international level. Fritz Ebert, the Soviet-supported son of the Weimar Republic's first president, became head of the newly elected magistrat in East Berlin, which claimed provisional authority over the entire city. But in the elections of December 5 in West Berlin, the non-Communist Social Democratic party won over 64 percent of the vote and elected Ernst Reuter lord mayor of Berlin. Five days later the CIA advised Truman that Soviet recognition of the new governing body in East Berlin signaled the Kremlin's willingness to accept a partition of the city. In late December the Truman administration publicly acknowledged that unification of Berlin was not possible because recent political developments had irrevocably divided the city in its economics, its politics, and its administration. The establishment of two Berlins was nearly an accomplished fact.[37]

■ ■ ■ The threatened confrontations in Berlin demonstrated that even though neither East nor West wanted war, neither side was willing to retreat and thereby suffer a loss of prestige. Each antagonist had pushed the other to the limit, but both shrank from the precipice. In this new type of international conflict, the primary aim of each adversary was to secure maximum benefits without forcing a confrontation that would put national honor on the line and in the process make a graceful retreat impossible. By the beginning of 1949 each side had achieved all it could short of armed conflict. The task ahead was for the concerned parties to acknowledge the new realities.

The West received mixed signals regarding Soviet policy in Germany during the early part of 1949. On the one hand, the USSR seemed interested in easing international tensions. The Kremlin suppressed an anti-West speech delivered in East Berlin by a high Soviet official, and in late January Walter Ulbricht, a leading member of the Socialist Unity party, declared in a speech: "We do not consider Berlin a Soviet zone city, but the German capital." On the other hand, the Communists continued their efforts to establish control over East Berlin and to gain leverage in the Western part of the city. Communist propaganda intensified, East Berlin police engaged in arbitrary arrests, and the Communists reinstituted the use of "house wardens," a system by which the Nazis during the war had maintained close surveillance in individual sectors of the city. Now, under Soviet auspices, minor officials distributed ration cards and handled welfare tasks, turning in anyone not loyal to leaders. The Soviets also tightened the blockade. They built new barriers along the borders, reduced the number of checkpoints, assigned more policemen along the boundaries, and confiscated Western marks from West Berliners entering the Eastern sector.[38] Over Soviet-sponsored Radio Berlin in late April, the Communists stepped up their attacks on the West: "What has American imperialism to offer us in the way of culture? Is it the boogie-woogie culture and the sensational and immoral films which appeal to the lowest instincts? Is it poisoning of our youth by the dirty fantasy of a Henry Miller and the dirty hands of a Jean Paul Sartre! Is it the shameless exploitation of the poverty of our young women which makes them into soldiers' prostitutes and infects our girls with American syphilis at the price of a bar of chocolate and a few Camels!"[39]

West Berlin nonetheless seemed beyond the Soviets' reach. The airlift was succeeding far beyond any expectations, the city's government was operating smoothly under Reuter's leadership, and trade was growing as the Western zones became an economic unit. The West's counterblockade was also becoming effective. According to the West Berlin press, several factories in the Eastern sector of the city laid off workers or cut their hours. The biggest economic boon, however, was the law that established the Western mark as the only medium of exchange in West Berlin. Before this move the currency system was in chaos, largely because the Eastern mark was worth no more than 30 percent of the Western. The results were predictable: West Berliners wanted their pay in Western marks but wanted to spend Eastern marks; business people and industrialists complained that their income was in Eastern marks though they were expected to meet expenses with Western marks. Finally, on March 20, the dual currency system was dropped. Reuter called this decision the most clear-cut evidence of the Allies' intention to stay. The West was now tied economically as well as politically to its sector of Berlin.[40]

Meanwhile, the first sign of a break in the Berlin crisis appeared. On January 21 Ambassador Smith was in Paris, where he met with Kingsbury Smith, an influential American journalist who was the European manager of the International News Service. Over drinks the ambassador remarked that the Soviets "wanted to get off the hook in Berlin but did not know how to." Kingsbury Smith cabled Stalin a few days later for a reaction to the ambassador's claim. Would the USSR end the blockade if the West postponed the establishment of a West German state until the Council of Foreign Ministers could meet and work toward a German settlement? Stalin replied that he would lift the blockade under one condition: the West must simultaneously lift its counterblockade. The Soviet advantage was clear. As Drew Middleton later reported in the *New York Times,* the reestablishment of interzonal commerce would enable the Soviets to save face by lifting the blockade "in the interests of the Germans." Acheson, who had returned to the administration in January as secretary of state, agreed with the president that Stalin was signaling an interest in negotiations that the United States ought to heed. Bohlen immediately notified Acheson that the most noteworthy feature of the offer was Stalin's lack of reference to the currency issue.[41] Under instructions from Washington, the deputy chief of the U.S. delegation to the UN, Philip Jessup, informally asked the Soviets' UN representative, Jacob Malik, if the omission was intentional, and a month later, in the privacy of his office on Park Avenue, Malik replied that it was "not accidental." If the two sides could agree upon a date for the council meeting, he assured Jessup, the blockade could end immediately.[42]

The Truman administration was convinced that its policies had pushed Stalin into winding down the Berlin crisis as part of a worldwide Soviet peace offensive that began in early 1949.[43] It did not seem coincidental that Stalin's appeal for a Berlin settlement came at the very time when the Truman Doctrine forced the Communists in the Greek civil war to publish their terms for peace, when the movement toward a separate West German government was about to bear fruition, when the Marshall Plan was becoming increasingly successful, when the airlift was a triumph in every way possible, and when the West was about to institute its most stunning achievement, the North Atlantic defense treaty. The only expedient left for the Soviets was to call for negotiations over Berlin that made no reference to the issue that had sparked the blockade—currency reform. Whether Soviet expansionist policies in Europe had brought the Kremlin closer to war than it deemed safe, or whether Stalin wanted to pause and revamp controls both at home and within the Soviet alliance system, the Kremlin was ready to end the crisis.

Doubtless the chief factor in finally defusing the Berlin situation was the signing of the North Atlantic Treaty in Washington on April 4. For the first time in its history, the United States—joining with Canada and ten European nations, Belgium, Britain, Denmark, France, Iceland, Italy,

Luxembourg, the Netherlands, Norway, and Portugal—became a member of a permanent peacetime military alliance. In accordance with article 5 of the charter, the twelve nations declared that an armed attack on one was an armed attack on all, and promised "to unite their efforts for collective defense." The treaty reduced France's reluctance to accept the London Recommendations for Germany and brought real unity to the West. Three days later Truman received notification that Acheson had reached agreement with Bevin and Schuman on all points pertaining to the establishment of a West German government. And on May 8, the fourth anniversary of the Nazi surrender, the Parliamentary Council in Bonn approved a constitution in preparation for the establishment of the Federal Republic of Germany. According to Acheson, "The success of these negotiations on German affairs had been greatly facilitated by the conclusion of the North Atlantic Treaty. Without it, I doubt that we could have come to a successful conclusion of the agreements at this time."[44]

The military alliance of 1949 was the central ingredient in the Truman administration's ongoing effort to bring order to postwar Europe. The formation of the UN four years earlier had been a major stride in this direction. The Rio Pact of September 2, 1947—or the Inter-American Treaty of Reciprocal Assistance—was in accordance with article 51 of the UN Charter, which approved individual and collective self-defense until the Security Council could act. The essential purpose of the Marshall Plan, as the secretary of state had privately emphasized, was to restore the European balance of power by working within UN guidelines.[45] During the signing ceremonies of the North Atlantic Treaty, Acheson asserted that the United States had taken the first two steps toward safeguarding Europe when it enacted the Truman Doctrine and the Marshall Plan. The third and climactic step was the new treaty. Bevin insisted that military defense was necessary because "progress in the economic field [would] not in itself suffice to call a halt to the Russian threat."[46] The North Atlantic Treaty was another aspect of the Truman administration's multifaceted foreign policy, which, again, was designed to provide responses commensurate to provocations.

This is not to say, however, that the Truman presidency had drafted and implemented a blueprint for the restoration of Continental order; as the British had taken the lead in the process that culminated in the Truman Doctrine, so had the impetus for a military alliance come from London. In late 1947 Bevin told Marshall, "We must devise some western democratic system comprising the Americans, ourselves, France, Italy etc., and of course the Dominions." The goal should be to "create confidence in western Europe that further Communist inroads would be stopped." In mid-January of the following year, Marshall learned that Bevin had won French support in proposing that the Benelux nations ally with London and Paris in a treaty of mutual defense. Bevin explained to the secretary of state that the objective was a "Western democratic system" composed of the Americas, the Dominions, Scandinavia, the Low Countries, France, Italy, Greece, and perhaps Portugal. "As soon as circumstances permit," Bevin continued, Spain and Germany should also be included. Marshall assured him of U.S. support.[47]

Events on the Continent in early 1948 had prodded the architects of a military alliance to move quickly. The Czech coup of February was pivotal in increasing interest on both sides of the Atlantic. The French were so alarmed by the outcome in Czechoslovakia that their foreign secretary, Georges Bidault, called on the United States to join a military pact against the Soviet Union. Two days later, when Stalin asked Finland to enter a mutual assistance agreement, anxiety spiraled upward throughout the West. Marshall wrote the U.S. embassy in Rome that the United States must decide how "to assist in checking further Communist expansion in Europe through steps designed to strengthen [the] confidence of non-Communist elements and deter Soviets from further fifth-column action along [the] Czech model." The collapse of Czechoslovakia, he emphasized, had convinced Americans to "support strong measures." That same day the British notified Marshall that Norway feared an invitation from Stalin to join a defense pact and wanted to know what help the West might provide if the Soviets attacked. Within twenty-four hours Marshall informed the British ambassador in Washington that the United States was "prepared to proceed at once in the joint discussions on the establishment of an Atlantic security system." The result was the Brussels Pact, which Marshall called "an essential prerequisite to any wider arrangement in which other countries including the United States might play a part."[48]

The events of this critical last half of the decade were so tightly intertwined that it is difficult to determine exact cause and effect. Clay thought the revival of West Germany through the airlift was the key to success, whereas Smith in Moscow attributed the triumph to the counterblockade. Both the airlift and the counterblockade were essential to the outcome, of course, but it seems that in an ironic twist Stalin's German policies were both the chief cause of and the chief remedy for the crisis. Although he had wanted to drive the Western allies farther apart, he had succeeded in welding them together. His decision to hold West Berlin hostage was ill-advised—predictably destined to unite the West and turn world opinion against the Soviet Union. Further, the blockade led to an explosive situation in which Stalin's only choice was to grope for a graceful but transparently ignominious retreat or to engage in a war with a unified and atomic-equipped West while himself burdened with debilitating troubles both at home and within the Eastern European alliance system. Fear of Soviet aggression had driven the European nations into a defensive alliance; Soviet policies in Berlin were no small part of that fear and were therefore an important stimulus to Stalin's greatest concern, the North Atlantic Treaty. Then, as Truman believed, the formation of NATO contributed to the resolution of the Berlin crisis. "Russia's toughness and truculence in the Berlin matter," he later wrote, caused "many Europeans to realize the need for closer military assistance ties among the western nations, and this led to discussions which eventually resulted in the establishment of N.A.T.O."[49]

The blockade finally came to an end on May 12. On that day the four powers issued a communiqué announcing that both sides would immediately lift all restrictions imposed on Berlin since March 1, 1948, and that the Council of Foreign Ministers would convene eleven days afterward in Paris to "consider questions relating to Germany and problems arising out of the situation in Berlin, including also the question of currency in Berlin."[50]

The West was convinced that the Soviets had agreed to lift the blockade only when its continuation threatened to undermine their position in Europe. If Stalin thought he had achieved his objective of four-power talks on the entire German question, he also must have agreed with Western diplomats who believed that the blockade had hurt the Soviet Union by stimulating the establishment of a West German govenment along with a North Atlantic defense treaty.[51] Further, Soviet prestige was reeling from the combined effect of the airlift and the counterblockade. The airlift lasted 324 days and brought in thirteen thousand tons of goods a day. It had not come without staggering costs, both in a material sense and in lives. By the time the airlift ended, seven British and seventeen U.S. planes had had accidents that killed forty-eight. Although the counterblockade did not take major effect until the spring of 1949, it led to a huge cut in trade between East Germany and Western Europe, and it denied entry into East Germany of many important industrial resources from West Germany, including chemicals, steel, and manufactured materials. To apply more pressure, the United States also persuaded its allies to follow its example of halting reparations payments to Eastern European governments. While exports to Eastern Europe dropped by 45 percent in 1948, the Soviets' own economic problems prevented them from helping their allies.[52] If the Soviet purpose had been to rearrange the European balance of power in its favor, the result had been precisely the opposite: Soviet policies had pushed the Western alliance together while in turn tying it closely to the West Germans. Had the West refused to intervene in the Berlin crisis, the Soviets most likely would have incorporated the Western part of the city into their zone of occupation and at least delayed the recovery of West Germany and the establishment of an autonomous government in Bonn.[53]

West Germans regarded the airlift as the crucial factor in liberating them from what they called a Soviet war against humanity. Many compared the Soviets with the Nazis, charging both with war crimes. One German official publicly declared in July 1948: "I think that these days there is probably no German whose thoughts do not turn to the Nurnberg court which again and again, as a foundation for a new international law, raised the accusation of crimes against humanity." And in December another official insisted: "It is all the same, ladies and gentlemen, under which symbol or under which political ideology misery appears. Fear is fear, terror is terror, hunger is hunger, concentration camp is concentration camp, whether it appears under this or that political label." During an interview three years after the end of the blockade, a German political leader emphasized that the airlift had been of "tremendous psychological importance" in convincing the German people that the West would not withdraw from Berlin. Throughout the crisis, they did everything possible to hold onto American protection.[54]

The Truman administration's objective in the ensuing Paris discussions was consistent with that of the Marshall Plan: to establish a balance of power on the Continent by integrating a sound West Germany into an economically and politically rehabilitated Western Europe. "Our major premise," Acheson wrote the embassy in London, "is that our concern is with the future of Europe and not with Germany as a problem by itself." Germany had to be part of Europe's recovery along democratic lines. The Marshall Plan provided the economic ties, NATO the military. The guideline for Germany, Acheson said, was "whether the unification can be achieved under conditions which help and do not retard the unification of free Europe." A few days later Acheson repeated the same idea in an off-the-record remark to journalists. The administration's "fundamental policy," he declared, was "to go full steam with a West German government." This necessitated the incorporation of West Germany into a strong Western Europe as part of an anti-Soviet effort. In a statement suggesting either a change in administration policy or a bit of wishful thinking,

Acheson alluded to the possibility of rolling back the iron curtain: "Our basic policy and aim at Paris is to push freedom as far east as possible. If a united Germany contributes to that aim, fine; if not, to hell with it."[55]

Since the establishment of a West German government would of necessity lead to the creation of an East German government (the Communist-controlled and Soviet-supported German Democratic Republic was established in October 1949), a permanent partition seemed the inevitable result of Western policy. From Washington's perspective there was no choice. The United States had abandoned its efforts to unify Germany because the maintenance of international tension would hurt the rehabilitation of Europe and, in turn, encourage the spread of Communism. The Soviet Union had likewise realized the impracticality of securing a one-Germany solution and realistically accepted the likelihood of two. Indeed, since Stalin had probably been pursuing this same objective since early 1948, the ensuing crisis over Berlin takes on the image of a dark Shakespearean tragedy in that the threats and counterthreats were so purposeless. Mutual suspicions, however, blocked any chance of compromise through reasoned negotiations and instead assured emotional exchanges that needlessly raised the specter of war.[56]

Amid continued unrest in Berlin, the Council of Foreign Ministers convened in Paris as scheduled, on May 23. Three days earlier disgruntled West Berlin railroad workers went on strike and forced the Soviet-controlled company to shut down. Since the West had declared the Soviet mark invalid, the railway owners had refused to meet the payroll of those living in West Berlin with the Western mark, a refusal that translated into a huge cut in pay for the workers. Although the West favored the strikers—particularly after they fought with Soviet police—the closing of the railroad meant that, as Acheson declared, "we were engaged in blockading ourselves."[57] The Soviets in Paris meanwhile resumed their efforts to turn back the clock to pre-blockade days. Deputy Foreign Minister Vyshinsky sought to revive the Potsdam terms by demanding the reestablishment of both the Allied Control Council and four-power supervision of the Ruhr, along with the installation of an all-German administrative and economic council created out of the economic agencies already in the zones. In reality, however, the Soviets had grudgingly accepted a lengthy occupation that, with the West entrenched on the other side of the city's dividing line, assured lasting acrimony and mercurial outbreaks of trouble. As Kennan remarked incisively, the Soviets realized that "without unreasonable advantages they cannot hope to maintain any influence at all." Their trumpeted call for an all-German council had built-in safeguards that assured Soviet predominance. Such a council required the concurrence of the Allied Control Council itself, and Soviet approval would be necessary before the latter could act.[58] A monumental problem thus remained: since all parties possessed the right of veto, the outcome would be a stalemate on substantive issues that had the potential to heighten frustration and, in turn, breed new troubles.

On May 28 Bevin presented the Western plan, which likewise had no chance for passage because it rested on the London program and the Bonn constitution. Enactment of these measures, Acheson argued, would prove the West's commitment to the West Germans and to the North Atlantic Treaty. The outcome would also undermine the Soviet aims of blocking a West German government and manipulating the country's economic agencies in such a way as to hamper the Marshall Plan.[59] The West called for nationwide implementation of the Bonn constitution, four-power supervision of elections in the Eastern sector after Soviet withdrawal, German control over industries, and majority-vote decisions by the four powers during the occupation. Not surprisingly, Vyshinsky rejected these proposals, complaining that they "aimed to impose [Western] rule on Eastern Germany without [the] participation of Eastern Germans and [the] USSR."[60]

The Paris meeting was deadlocked, and seemingly permanent division of Germany a fait accompli. Acheson and Bohlen believed that in light of the West's recent successes in Europe, the Kremlin's central concern was to hold onto what it had. Even if the Soviets alienated the German populace by their iron-fisted policies, they had no choice but to exert tighter controls and risk placing themselves in an increasingly tenuous position.[61] On June 20 the two sides recognized that joint measures were not possible and reached a basic understanding that seemed to stamp finality on a partitioned Germany. The Soviet emphasis on unanimity had encouraged this outcome. Vyshinsky's proclamation that the Soviet Union "would never subordinate itself to the rule of the majority" drew from Acheson the wry remark that the "four powers can do what they like in Berlin so long as it is what the USSR wants."[62] Recognition of this stalemate was the only feasible solution. Although the United States would have access to Berlin and there would be discussions and trade across city and national lines, two Berlins and two Germanies had come into being.[63]

The partition of Germany was a product of *realpolitik*. While the Paris proceedings continued, Acheson told the press on June 23 that the modus vivendi was "a very modest document" that offered assurances against a new blockade and that encouraged four-power talks on Germany. "Here again, that is not much. It is simply a way of dealing sensibly with . . .

established fact." Obstructions and limits remained on the West's passage into Berlin; a week after the lifting of the blockade one American observed that the city was still "in a state of semi-blockade." But tension had dropped remarkably, to the comforting status of an uneasy calm. Mutual recognition of the necessity of German partition eased fears that the opposition would try to seize everything; for the moment, Germany ceased to be the front line of the Cold War.[64]

■ ■ ■ The Berlin crisis had constituted a new and unique chapter in the Cold War. The Soviets stirred up mob behavior in the streets, attacked the West through propaganda, and obstructed the legislative process in representative assemblies. They appealed to wartime agreements that, on the face of it, kept them within the letter of the law and thereby gave rise to lasting questions about the purity of Western motives. All these tactics had been used before. Holding an entire city hostage, however, was a new and ominous stratagem. To wear down resistance to negotiations over the entire German question, the Soviets resorted to intimidation, extreme demands, and drawn-out discussions over any number of issues. The White House resisted because it was convinced of the Kremlin's aggressive goals in Germany. The Soviets meanwhile regarded the West's attempt to construct a West German state as a hostile attack on their nation's security that they had to checkmate with the establishment of a Communist East German government. That neither side wanted war is shown by U.S. documents and by the Soviets' repeated willingness to retreat before pressure. But the mutual misperceptions of the antagonists were complicated by pressure tactics that could have induced war by either miscalculation or frustration.

The West, faced with what it perceived as a new kind of Soviet strategy, at first reacted with a policy that was uncertain, indecisive, and unplanned. Few of the Allies grasped the complexity of the situation until months into the blockade. Eventually, however, the West organized its forces and made quick decisions that proved successful in matching means with ends. It implemented the airlift, an improvised response that proved appropriate to the danger. It sent B-29s as a show of force and as an effort to raise European morale and encourage Western unity. It kept open the avenue of negotiations while discussing the possibility of using atomic weaponry in the event of war. Most of all, the West won German cooperation, which was the key to success. In addition to furnishing supplies, the airlift demonstrated to the Germans (and to the Soviet Union) that the democracies were determined to hold onto West Berlin. The West's ground and air forces in Europe might not have had much military effect, but their presence perhaps helped to deter the USSR from military actions that might have caused war. On the basis of what the West thought was the Soviets' objective in Berlin, its policy was effective.[65]

But the time of vigilance had not passed, according to Acheson. During the elation over the lifting of the blockade, he somberly warned the British that the Soviets had changed only their strategy and not their goals.[66]

■ ■ ■ CHAPTER TEN

Toward New Directions in the Cold War

If the Truman administration was correct in its assessment of Soviet behavior, the West's successes in Europe would cause the Kremlin to focus its aggression elsewhere. From 1946 to 1949 the White House developed responses that were equivalent to challenges; in a pattern that was both frustrating and alarming, however, each success seemed to lead to—indeed, to provoke—a more dangerous situation. By 1950 the Truman Doctrine, the Marshall Plan, the Berlin airlift, and NATO had brought economic, political, and military order to the Continent, making it predictable that Soviet expansion would take new directions in the world. Many within the U.S. foreign policy community feared that as the USSR recovered from World War II, it might resort to direct military aggression.

■ ■ ■ The Truman Doctrine had not achieved immediate success in Greece; in fact, the civil war there intensified as U.S. aid began arriving. Pressure increased on the United States to send combat troops, but the White House adhered to the advice of the Joint Chiefs of Staff, who warned in late 1947 that the United States was "not now capable of deploying sufficient armed forces in Greece to defeat an attack into Greece by the combined forces of Albania, Yugoslavia and Bulgaria; most emphatically not if these countries receive either covert or active Soviet support."[1] The administration instead authorized U.S. military officials to extend operational advice to Greek soldiers in the field.[2] In the meantime the British government, under intense pressure from Washington, postponed the withdrawal of its final five thousand troops and continued its training program for Greek soldiers. The results were evident: the Greek military establishment gradually improved in leadership, morale, and performance.[3] But even these developments seemed insufficient to reverse the negative flow of the war. On Christmas Eve of 1947 the rebels' leader, General Markos Vafiadis, announced the establishment of the Provisional Greek Government in the north, in preparation for securing outside recognition and assistance from neighboring Communist regimes.[4] As the war threatened to become international in scope, it also seemed to reach a new level of atrocity: the guerrillas began transferring thousands of children from Greece into neighboring Communist countries. Though the guerrillas defended this move as a humanitarian effort to safeguard the youths from the war, the government in Athens hotly accused its enemy of kidnapping and genocide, and exerted pressure on the Truman administration to take decisive action.[5]

The Soviets' role in the Greek war remains problematic, although the preponderance of evidence reinforces the conviction that if there was an involvement, it was not more than indirect until the Truman Doctrine began taking effect by early 1948. The arrival of U.S. military aid and operational advisers in Greece caused Stalin to order an end to the struggle. One writer believes that Stalin's effort to defuse the Greek conflict was a sign of his refusal to accept the existence of a Cold War—even after the Truman Doctrine had gone into effect. This argument challenges both the traditional historians, who have argued that the Soviet Union began the Cold War earlier, and the revisionists, who have called the Truman Doctrine speech the United States' declaration of Cold War on the Soviets. Whatever the long-range implications of Stalin's decision, it seems certain that he had come to regard the Greek war as a losing proposition. Years afterward two of Tito's cohorts, Milovan Djilas and Vladimir Dedijer, insisted that the Soviet premier directed Bulgaria and Yugoslavia to wind down the conflict in Greece. At a Moscow meeting in February 1948 Stalin lashed out at Bulgarian and Yugoslav representatives for encouraging the war and thereby bringing about a deeper involvement of the United States in the region. "We do not agree with the Yugoslav comrades that they should help further the Greek partisans," Stalin rigidly declared. "The uprising in Greece has to fold up." When Yugoslav Vice-Premier Edvard Kardelj insisted that the Greek guerrillas could win "if foreign intervention does not grow and if serious political and military errors are not made," Stalin shot back: "If, if! No, they have no prospect of success at all. What do you think, that Great Britain and the United States—the United States, the most powerful state in the world—will permit you to break their line of communication in the Mediterranean Sea! Nonsense. And we have no navy. The uprising in Greece must be stopped, and as quickly as possible."[6]

Stalin's sole objective, of course, was his country's best interests. In

October 1944 he had agreed to the percentages arrangement that conceded British hegemony in Greece in return for Soviet control over other Eastern European countries. Later that same year he had not intervened in the December Revolution when British forces put down the Communists in Athens. And yet, according to a recent account by Dedijer, the Soviets sent thirty antiaircraft guns to the Greek guerrillas. Dedijer, who was involved in Yugoslavia's aid program, claimed that over the course of the war his own government sent the guerrillas rifles, machine guns, antitank weapons, land mines, clothing, and food. They also received weapons and food from Albania and Bulgaria, as well as various nonmilitary items from Hungary, Rumania, and Czechoslovakia. Although Stalin would have welcomed a Communist government in Greece during the early months of the war, his wait-and-see attitude changed suddenly when the United States proclaimed the Truman Doctrine and began sending aid and advisers. U.S. intervention in Greece, Dedijer later explained, would "endanger [Stalin's] already-won positions" and cause "possible international complications" that would threaten Soviet vital interests.[7]

Despite its continued belief in Soviet involvement in Greece, the Truman administration held to its policy of restraint. The Athens government finally emerged with a victory in October 1949, for several reasons, U.S. military assistance only one among them. In addition to the matériel earlier mentioned, the United States supported the use of napalm in the Greeks' air operations, replaced General William Livesay with a hardened combat leader of World War II, General James A. Van Fleet, and sent about fifty navy Helldivers to be used in strafing and bombing during the climactic government offensive of August against the guerrillas' mountain fortress in the north at Grammos.[8] Stalin's reluctance to help the guerrillas was another factor, as was Yugoslavia's rift with the Soviet Union. Fear of Soviet reprisals forced Tito to close the border, denying the guerrillas their major refuge and most important source of outside assistance. The guerrillas' defeat was also attributable to the division within their command over leadership and strategy that led to the removal of Markos in early 1949 and to the final and fatal shift to conventional tactics.[9] Still another ingredient—one often overlooked—was the Truman administration's foreign policy. Under its guidelines, the United States maintained the support of the Greek people, pursued a multifaceted response that permitted advisers to adjust to ever-changing circumstances in the war, exerted at least indirect pressure on Stalin to terminate the war before a growing U.S. military presence proved injurious to Soviet interests in Eastern Europe, and kept a tight restraint on escalated involvement. Although the United States was powerless to do anything about the twenty-eight thousand children removed from Greece during the war, the Truman Doctrine was vital in restoring order to the country and saving it from the Communist-led insurgency.[10]

The Truman Doctrine was also successful in Turkey. To help the Turkish government ward off a feared Soviet military invasion, the United States provided supplies and training to the military establishment. As of June 1950 over nineteen thousand Turkish officers and enlisted personnel had graduated from American-style courses established by U.S. advisers. Of these graduates, nearly eighteen thousand were trained in Turkey; the rest attended U.S. military schools or institutions in the United States or Germany. The Americans reorganized the entire Turkish military establishment, creating what a U.S. assessment termed the potential for a "much more effective resistance" against any Soviet invasion until outside help arrived.[11]

The United States likewise achieved most of the goals associated with the Marshall Plan. Though Truman and Harriman had expressed hopes that the European aid effort would force open the iron curtain by attracting the populace to better ways of living, the outcome was considerably different. Like the Truman Doctrine, the Marshall Plan became military in character. By the time it came to a close on December 30, 1951, 80 percent of its assistance was military. The Berlin crisis had stimulated more interest in developing the United States' military strength and had encouraged its membership in NATO. The outbreak of the Korean War in June 1950 aroused fear that similar troubles could erupt in Europe, and led to a drive to build the West's defensive system—a step that further emphasized the necessity of integrating West Germany into the European strategic network. The following year the administration combined the Economic Cooperation Administration with the Military Defense Aid Program to form the Mutual Security Program, which sought "the economic unification and political federation of Europe." And as the Truman Doctrine sharpened the line between East and West in the Near East, the Marshall Plan did the same thing in the heart of the Continent by helping to rebuild Western Europe and prompting the Soviet Union to exercise greater controls over Eastern Europe.[12] The important observation, however, is that even though the Marshall Plan and Soviet countermeasures further divided Europe, the stalemated outcome was, perhaps paradoxically, more conducive to easing the Cold War than to intensifying it.

Given the Truman administration's assumptions regarding Soviet behavior, it saw no alternative to a foreign aid program that entailed active intervention in the domestic affairs of recipient countries. To ignore the problems in Europe was impossible, for both humanitarian and security reasons. To take military action was equally out of the question; even if the enemy had been clearly identifiable, the United States lacked the means and probably the will to fight. A U.S.-supervised program of economic assistance was the only viable choice.

An irony soon became apparent: although the American emphasis on integrating the Continent ultimately blocked Soviet and Eastern European participation in the program, that strategy likewise helped to obstruct the European unity that was essential to the development of an inter-European trading system. British opposition to European integration was clear from the outset. In March 1948 the cabinet in London rejected total European cooperation under supranational control in favor of a plan assigning final authority to individual national delegations working on a project-by-project basis. Britain must not become "just another European country," Bevin declared. It intended to continue exercising its international role through the Commonwealth. Thus, under an arrangement that the Scandinavian countries supported, the Organization of European Economic Cooperation would be controlled by member nations rather than by a centralized governing authority. Without Germany's involvement as yet assured, the White House asked the French to define the conditions by which they would accept German membership.[13]

The response came in May 1950, when French Foreign Minister Robert Schuman presented a plan designed to advance the two major objectives of the Marshall Plan—European integration and German reintegration. The Schuman Plan aimed at reconciling the recovery of Germany with French security and economic concerns by putting the Continent's coal and steel production under a supranational authority that included France as a member, that participated in the development of German industry, and that, by integrating the West Germans into Western Europe's economic and political system, obviated their need to rearm. The plan was based on French calls for a customs union, a stronger OEEC, European political and military institutions, and international supervision of the Ruhr. It was, Schuman declared, "the first step in the federation of Europe." The Schuman Plan went into effect in 1951 when the European Coal and Steel Community was formed with six OEEC countries as members: France, West Germany, Italy, and the three Benelux nations. The French realized that in view of Britain's refusal to join, West Germany was needed to counter the Soviets' military strength on the Continent. The United States was supportive because the Schuman Plan encouraged the economic integration of Europe through the liberalization of trade, the development of supranational institutions and political federations, and the reconciliation of France and Germany. Indeed, the Truman administration had hopes that the plan would eventually permit the rearmament of Germany and hence greatly promote the chances of Western security.[14]

The Marshall Plan remains the subject of controversy, but it seems clear that it was essential to the ongoing process of economic recovery in Europe. One writer declares that the longtime disintegration of the European commercial system necessitated U.S. control over assistance in order to ease the continued insistence on national authority and achieve the integration vital to rehabilitation. Another writer sharply disagrees. Europe's collapse was not impending, he insists; the revival of the Continent had begun in 1945—before the Marshall Plan allegedly came to the rescue. Indeed, he concludes, the outcome in Europe would have been the same without the Marshall Plan.[15]

Although the evidence suggests that recovery was under way before the injection of U.S. aid, the Marshall Plan was an important catalyst to that development. It helped to liberalize trade barriers, brought commercial efficiency by using U.S. management ideas, encouraged coordination and centralized control, and boosted economic reconstruction. The results were evident: the rate of inflation stabilized; production and trade levels increased; extremist groups lost headway in their attempts to unseat government leaders; and plans for military integration proceeded apace. Admittedly, the European Payments Union was only a partial success, because of the lack of a balance of payments and of a sufficient foreign exchange. But the growth in the economic order encouraged Europeans to do more on their own, thereby helping to achieve the United States' strategic and political goals by fostering the establishment of a multilateral world. By the time the assistance program ended, ECA grants totaled $12.4 billion, and Western Europe's industrial output had grown 40 percent above its prewar level. Moreover, the program was probably instrumental in undercutting the Communist party in France and in bringing about the defeat of the Communists in Italy's elections.[16]

The Truman Doctrine, the Marshall Plan, the Berlin airlift, and NATO were inseparable parts of the administration's effort to counter the multitude of threats to order posed by the Communists in postwar Europe. In the immediate sense of raising morale and implanting a sense of security, the programs were a reasonable success; in terms of stimulating long-range economic and military growth, they were enormously effective. If the Cold War can be likened to a game of chess, the United States and its Western allies had checkmated the Soviet Union in Europe.

■ ■ ■ The Cold War, however, had already taken a new and more dangerous turn during the autumn of 1949. On September 3, U.S. Air

Force detectors in Alaska picked up signs of radioactivity in the hemisphere which suggested that the USSR had detonated a nuclear device. Two days later the radioactive count was so high that there could be no mistake: its source lay somewhere between Guam and the North Pole and between Japan and the British Isles. It quickly became clear that the radioactivity was due to nuclear fission resulting from either the test of an atomic weapon or an accident involving a reactor. The rush of air carrying the radioactivity had already crossed North America and was moving toward the British Isles. The U.S. Air Force asked Vannevar Bush, who was president of the Carnegie Institution, to head a panel of scientists to investigate. On September 19 the panel informed Truman that the reports were "consistent with the view that the origin of the fission products was the explosion of an atomic bomb whose nuclear composition was similar to the Alamogordo bomb and that the explosion occurred between the 26th and 29th of August at some point between the east 35th meridian and the 170th meridian over the Asiatic land mass." Four days later the president made a grave public announcement: "We have evidence that within recent weeks an atomic explosion occurred in the U.S.S.R." [17]

The United States' atomic monopoly, which had compensated for the nation's conventional weaknesses, had abruptly come to an end. Although Truman doubted that the Soviets had developed an actual bomb and therefore did not appear unduly alarmed by the revelation, the news caused intense anxiety in other circles, both inside and outside the government. Some advisers believed that the military balance was shifting in the Soviets' favor and that the explosion in Siberia had opened "windows of vulnerability" to the United States. Acheson told journalists at the UN that U.S. security was endangered and that the administration would seek a massive program of military expansion. Indeed, the explosion encouraged congressional approval of the Mutual Defense Assistance Act, which provided military support for the North Atlantic Treaty. The House, in fact, approved a larger appropriation than it had been willing to grant before the president's announcement. Senator Tom Connally grimly warned his colleagues in a Senate-House conference committee proceeding: "Russia has shown her teeth." Perhaps Senator Vandenberg said it best: "This is now a different world." [18]

The Soviet blast led immediately to an effort by the United States to expand its atomic research. The president approved the building of new plants under AEC auspices to produce more bombs. The joint chiefs assured him that increased production would lead to "significant gains from the military standpoint in terms of lower unit cost of weapons, probable shortening of a war, increased military effectiveness, decreased logistical and manpower requirements for the prosecution of certain tasks in war, and increasing flexibility in the conduct of the war." But pressure grew for more than a mere addition to the number of bombs in the U.S. arsenal. Admiral Lewis Strauss of the AEC sent a memorandum to his colleagues on October 5, warning that "the time has now come for a quantum jump in our planning. . . . [W]e should now make an intensive effort to get ahead with the super [hydrogen bomb]." The thermonuclear or fusion bomb would have much greater destructive potential than the two atomic bombs exploded over Japan. In 1942 a team of scientists led by J. Robert Oppenheimer (who had directed the Los Alamos project during World War II) had noted that creation of such a bomb was possible. But he did not regard it as the means by which "to save the country and the peace." He joined Lilienthal, the chairman of the AEC, in calling the hydrogen bomb "a weapon of genocide" and therefore "evil." Less than a week after Strauss's recommendation, however, a special National Security Council committee made up of Acheson, Lilienthal, and Secretary of Defense Louis A. Johnson recommended that the president promote an "acceleration of the atomic energy program . . . in the interests of national security." On October 19 Truman approved.[19]

Both foreign and domestic events put pressure on the Truman administration to make this show of strength. On October 1 the leader of the Communists in China, Mao Tse-tung, triumphantly announced the establishment of the People's Democratic Republic, marking the end of the long civil war against Chiang Kai-shek's Nationalist forces and leaving him no choice but to flee the mainland to Formosa. In the United States an angry debate broke out among Americans regarding their nation's responsibility for the fall of China, and anxiety over the suspected spread of Communism increased as the second trial of the accused Communist agent Alger Hiss (the first trial had ended with a hung jury) got under way.[20] The White House was under siege from all sides and could not appear soft on Communism. With the Soviet Union apparently approaching nuclear equality with the United States, the president had to support the new research efforts.

But Truman encountered considerable opposition within his administration to the development of a hydrogen bomb. He again called together Acheson, Lilienthal, and Johnson to study the question and submit a proposal. On January 31, 1950, the committee recommended that he authorize a study of the technical prospects of building such a weapon, and that he also instruct the secretaries of state and defense "to undertake a reexamination of our objectives in peace and war and of the effect of these objectives on our strategic plans, in light of the probable fission [atomic] bomb capability and possible thermonuclear bomb capability of the Soviet Union." Lilienthal objected that a larger bomb would be an obstacle to peace: "We keep saying, 'We have no other course'; what we should say is 'We are not bright enough to see any other course.'" The president nonetheless declared that in view of public pressure brought by Communist advances in Asia and by the spread of anti-Communist feeling in the United States, he had to go ahead with the program. "Can the Russians do it?" he asked the committee. The three men replied affirmatively. "In that case," Truman said, "we have no choice. We'll go ahead." That same day the White House released a public announcement that the president had directed the AEC "to continue its work on all forms of atomic weapons, including the so-called hydrogen or superbomb."[21]

In early 1950 a growing wave of anti-Communist feeling inside the United States provided added impetus to the movement to beef up the nation's arsenal. Klaus Fuchs, who had helped to build the atomic bomb in New Mexico and who was now head theoretical physicist of the British Atomic Energy Research Establishment, was arrested in London and charged with being an atomic spy for the Soviet Union. A few days later Senator Joseph McCarthy heightened the nationwide fear already stemming from the Hiss case by declaring that Communists had infiltrated the State Department. In this climate all hesitation about building the hydrogen bomb disappeared. At the same time, however, the president told his staff that no one wanted to use the hydrogen bomb and that it was to exist for "bargaining purposes" with the USSR. Johnson agreed with the joint chiefs that the United States must "proceed forthwith on an all-out program of hydrogen-bomb development." The Soviets had already taken the initiative the previous November in building a hydrogen bomb of their own. On March 10, 1950, Truman approved a crash program aimed at producing the new weapon.[22]

The second recommendation of the special committee, a total reexamination of the nation's military needs, led to a top-secret document known as NSC-68 that the president received on April 7, 1950. Although nominally prepared by the State and Defense departments, the brunt of the work fell on Acheson and Paul Nitze, the latter of whom had recently succeeded Kennan as head of the State Department's Policy Planning Staff. The study warned that the United States' military strength was "becoming dangerously inadequate" and that the Soviet Union was "developing the military capacity to support its design for world domination." Then, in an argument that Kennan and Bohlen opposed because it credited the Kremlin with too much method, NSC-68 declared that the "fundamental design of those who control the Soviet Union and the international communist movement [was] to retain and solidify their absolute power, first in the Soviet Union and second in the areas now under their control." What made this objective especially dangerous, the study continued, was that the Soviet Union was "animated by a new fanatic faith, antithetical to our own." The United States' strategy was faulty because of the vast difference between the nation's military strength and its commitments. Major changes were necessary. Failure to make them "would result in a serious decline in the strength of the free world relative to the Soviet Union and its satellites. . . . It [was] imperative that this trend be reversed by a much more rapid and concerted build-up of the actual strength of both the United States and . . . the free world." The job required much sacrifice and would therefore necessitate "significant domestic financial and economic adjustments." But the United States had no choice. The "absence of order among nations [was] becoming less and less tolerable."[23]

Thus did the Soviet Union's development of the atomic bomb cause the Truman administration to expand its definition of the nation's vital interests and call for a dramatic increase in the degree of force needed to maintain them. Whereas Kennan had argued for defending only carefully selected strategic areas, particularly military-industrial centers, NSC-68 broadened the areas of concern to include everything along the Soviet perimeter. That is, the study meshed vital with peripheral interests, instead of following Kennan's admonition to maintain a distinction between them. NSC-68 warned that without a huge military buildup (perhaps a tripled budget), the United States would confront a "dangerous situation" by 1954; by that time the Soviets would possess the atomic power needed to devastate the United States. In the meantime they would continue to rely on proxies to carry out objectives through "piecemeal aggression." To contain the USSR, NSC-68 emphasized this weapons buildup as an essential part of a broad program of national security that offered choices other than capitulation or war. The administration still regarded negotiation as a means of achieving the ultimate objective of world stability. But the "whole success of the proposed program," according to the study, depended "ultimately on recognition by this Government, the American people, and all peoples, that the cold war [was] in fact a real war in which the survival of the free world [was] at stake." Failure to deal with this new kind of warfare would lead to "gradual withdrawals under pressure" until the United States discovered one day that it had "sacrificed positions of vital interest."[24]

The president did not question the assumptions underlying NSC-68 but simply forwarded the study to the National Security Council with a request that it analyze the implications and costs of the recommended increase in military strength. The biggest problem was evident: how to persuade the American people to support such a program.

The White House was convinced that the Soviet threat to national security had reached a new level of intensity that had become global and, as a matter of course, necessitated an equivalent response. "Our aim in applying force," NSC-68 declared, "must be to compel the acceptance of our terms consistent with our objectives, and our capabilities for the application of force should, therefore, within the limits of what we can sustain over the long pull, be congruent to the range of tasks which we may encounter." In the meantime the United States had to use "the current Soviet cold war technique" against the Soviets themselves. NSC-68 called for "dynamic steps to reduce the power and influence of the Kremlin inside the Soviet Union and other areas under its control," steps that included covert actions aimed at "fomenting and supporting unrest and revolt in selected strategic satellite countries." On the basis of the Soviets' assumed interest in world domination and their startling growth in military strength, NSC-68 warned of "an indefinite period of tension and danger" for the West, "a period that should be defined less as a short-term crisis than as a permanent and fundamental alteration in the shape of international relations." The United States had to "strike out on a bold and massive program of rebuilding the West's defensive potential to surpass that of the Soviet world, and of meeting each fresh challenge promptly and unequivocally." NSC-68 concluded that this policy meant "virtual abandonment by the United States of trying to distinguish between national and global security."[25]

Looked at dispassionately, NSC-68 put forward a strategy that was both questionable and highly dangerous, because it advocated an aggressive policy intended to reestablish a military balance with the Soviet Union. Acheson and Nitze believed that the Soviets' development of nuclear power in 1949 had upset the post–World War II standoff between the United States' atomic monopoly and the Soviet army. Indeed, recent events had presented the ominous prospect of the Soviets' precipitating a war. The United States therefore had to seek what Acheson called a "retraction of Soviet power"—a "rollback"—by a military buildup that would permit the development of "situations of strength" sufficient to discourage the USSR from risking a confrontation. The chief peril was that even though NSC-68 specifically ruled out a surprise attack on the Soviet Union, its logic held open the possibility of a preventive war resulting from ultimatums and tests of credibility. Thus could threats and counterthreats bring conflict by escalation. Other pitfalls became clear. While advocating a military program intended to protect the nation's interests, the document greatly expanded the definition of those interests. Further, its decision to regard all Communists as threats to the United States encouraged the fear of a Communist monolith that many Americans had already conjured into existence. Moreover, a refusal to negotiate meaningfully until the Soviets were converted from their way of life was tantamount to the unrealistic strategy of seeking total victory. NSC-68 promoted means and objectives that were not in harmony and in this sense helped to lay the groundwork for Korea and Vietnam.[26]

The long-range implications of the study, however, became lost in the immediacy of the moment. From the White House perspective, evidence in support of NSC-68's assessment of Soviet expansionist intentions came on June 25, 1950, when war broke out in Korea. Until then, the administration was having trouble convincing the American people to support military expansion. "Korea came along and saved us," Acheson later observed.[27]

■ ■ ■ The dire situation in Europe following World War I had demonstrated that economic and political instability was conducive to totalitarianism and that the remedies were to restore order and security inside threatened nations and to reestablish a balance of power on the Continent. To prevent similar problems in the post–World War II era, the Truman administration reacted with a controlled policy of firmness and vigilance. The Truman Doctrine, the Marshall Plan, the Berlin airlift, NATO—all four programs brought about the economic and political rehabilitation of Europe and the establishment of a defensive network strong enough to resist the Communist threat. According to the Truman administration, Greece and Turkey symbolized the non-Communist world's capacity for holding the line against Soviet expansion into the eastern Mediterranean and the Middle East. Once the United States had moved to safeguard Greece, Turkey, and Iran, the Communists switched their attention to Berlin, which also came to symbolize the West's ongoing struggle with the East. In the meantime the White House instituted the Marshall Plan to promote the economic integration of Western Europe and the reintegration of Germany into that system. From the prolonged totalitarian threat came the steady development of North Atlantic unity that culminated in postwar order with the organization of NATO and the passage of the Mutual Defense Assistance Program. Despite the administration's early efforts to avoid sharpening the differences between East and West, the outcome was a polarization of interests rather than a balance of power on the Continent. Although such polarization can be dangerous to peace, the result in this instance was an uneasy calm in Europe by 1950 that was largely attributable to the realistic delineation of two spheres of influence and mutual recognition of the sanctity of each.

According to the logic of containment, the West's success in stabilizing Europe would force the Soviet Union to turn the focus of the Cold War into other areas—most immediately the Far East. Like the Near East and Western Europe, postwar Korea was economically and politically unstable and thus susceptible to Communist influence. Korea would become the new front line of the global conflict between the non-Communist world and the forces of totalitarianism.

The Truman administration's foreign policy in Europe rested on the principles of flexibility and restraint. The White House reacted to each challenge with a response that it considered equal to the degree of danger. In Greece and Turkey, where the problem was initially military security and in the long range economics, the Truman Doctrine proved adjustable to ever-changing circumstances. In Western Europe, where the totalitarian threat had not progressed beyond the economic level, the Marshall Plan was sufficient to meet the challenge. And in Berlin the airlift averted a dangerous escalation of the situation until the West's counterblockade could take effect and the diplomats could secure a face-saving settlement. Because in Greece, Turkey, Germany, and the Balkans the Communist danger threatened to produce war, the North Atlantic governments saw the need for a climate of security that would be conducive to economic recovery; thus did they seek a military arrangement that would eventually include German participation in NATO along with other mutual defense guarantees. Then, in late 1949, the Soviets achieved a world balance of terror by developing their own atomic device. Though the Truman administration at first believed that Soviet internal and external problems made an invasion of Western Europe unlikely for at least another five years, the North Korean attack caused policymakers to rethink this timetable. Kennan was not an alarmist, but even he warned against "armed action by German units, along the Korean pattern." The CIA now believed that the Soviets might "deliberately provoke . . . a general war" before 1954.[28]

As the Cold War shifted to the Far East, the White House prepared to confront greater dangers that would again call for the establishment of clearly defined spheres of control and for equivalent responses to new challenges.

■ ■ ■ **NOTES**

ONE ■ THE GRAND ALLIANCE AND THE ROAD TO VICTORY

1. For a discussion of the forces, events, and circumstances leading to the formation of the Grand Alliance, see David Reynolds, *The Creation of the Anglo-American Alliance, 1937–1941: A Study in Competitive Cooperation* (Chapel Hill, 1981); Arnold A. Offner, *The Origins of the Second World War: American Foreign Policy and World Politics, 1917–1941* (N.Y., 1975); Robert Dallek, *Franklin D. Roosevelt and American Foreign Policy, 1932–1945* (N.Y., 1979); Robert A. Divine, *The Reluctant Belligerent: American Entry into World War II* (N.Y., 1979); Warren F. Kimball, *The Most Unsordid Act: Lend-Lease, 1939–1941* (Baltimore, 1969); and Stephen E. Ambrose, *Rise to Globalism: American Foreign Policy Since 1938* (N.Y., 1988).
2. *Churchill and Roosevelt: The Complete Correspondence,* ed. Warren F. Kimball (Princeton, 1984), contains the most complete description, in documents with commentary, of Churchill's world view. See also John Colville, *The Fringes of Power: Downing Street Diaries, 1939–1955* (London, 1985).
3. See Vojtech Mastny, *Russia's Road to the Cold War: Diplomacy, Warfare, and the Politics of Communism, 1941–1945* (N.Y., 1979). Other useful works on Stalin's foreign policy are Adam B. Ulam's *Expansion and Coexistence: Soviet Foreign Policy, 1917–1973* (N.Y., 1974), and Robert C. Tucker's *The Soviet Political Mind: Stalinism and Post-Stalin Change* (N.Y., 1971), the latter of which examines Stalin's psychological makeup and its impact on his domestic and foreign policies.
4. See *Churchill and Roosevelt* and Dallek, *Roosevelt and American Foreign Policy.* Robert A. Divine provides an excellent overview of Roosevelt's wartime diplomacy in *Roosevelt and World War II* (Baltimore, 1969). A fine recent study is Eric Larrabee's *Commander in Chief: Franklin Delano Roosevelt, His Lieutenants, and Their War* (N.Y., 1987).
5. For an excellent discussion of the Roosevelt administration's policies toward the Soviet Union and the diplomacy of the loan, see George C. Herring, Jr., *Aid to Russia, 1941–1946: Strategy, Diplomacy, the Origins of the Cold War* (N.Y., 1973).
6. Martin Gilbert, *Winston S. Churchill,* vol. 3, *Road to Victory, 1941–1945* (Boston, 1986), 126–208. See also Gaddis Smith, *American Diplomacy During the Second World War, 1941–1945* (N.Y., 1985), and Kent R. Greenfield, *American Strategy in World War II: A Reconsideration* (Baltimore, 1963).

7. Christopher Thorne, *Allies of a Kind: The United States, Britain and the War Against Japan, 1941–1945* (N.Y., 1978), 91–130, 131–53, 273–87. See also Mark A. Stoler, *The Politics of the Second Front: American Military Planning and Coalition Warfare, 1941–1943* (Westport, Conn., 1977).
8. See William Roger Louis, *Imperialism at Bay: The United States and the Decolonization of the British Empire, 1941–1945* (N.Y., 1978), and Theodore A. Wilson, *The First Summit: Roosevelt and Churchill at Placentia Bay, 1941* (Boston, 1969).
9. Warren F. Kimball, "Lend-Lease and the Open Door: The Temptation of British Opulence, 1937–1942," *Political Science Quarterly* 86 (June 1971): 232–57.
10. Quoted in Milovan Djilas, *Conversations with Stalin* (N.Y., 1962), 81.
11. For a concise account of Soviet-American relations during World War II as well as a classic postrevisionist interpretation of the origins of the Cold War, see John L. Gaddis, *The United States and the Origins of the Cold War, 1941–1947* (N.Y., 1972).
12. The most comprehensive as well as the most recent account of wartime diplomacy is Dallek's *Roosevelt and American Foreign Policy.* The standard revisionist accounts are Lloyd C. Gardner, *Architects of Illusion: Men and Ideas in American Foreign Policy, 1941–1949* (Chicago, 1970), and Gabriel Kolko, *The Politics of War: The World and United States Foreign Policy, 1943–1945* (N.Y., 1968). For balanced accounts of the conflicting war aims of the major powers and of wartime planning for the peace, see William L. Neumann, *After Victory: Churchill, Roosevelt, Stalin and the Making of the Peace* (N.Y., 1967), and Sir John Wheeler-Bennett and Anthony Nicholls, *The Semblance of Peace: The Political Settlement After the Second World War* (London, 1972).
13. For the Anglo-American wartime dialogue, see, in addition to Thorne's *Allies of a Kind* and Louis's *Imperialism at Bay,* Robert Beitzell, *An Uneasy Alliance: America, Britain, and Russia, 1941–1943* (N.Y., 1972), Henry Butterfield Ryan, *The Vision of Anglo-America: The U.S.-U.K. Alliance and the Emerging Cold War, 1943–1946* (Cambridge, 1987), and Randall Bennett Woods, *A Changing of the Guard: Anglo-American Relations, 1941–1947* (Chapel Hill, 1990).
14. Diary of Henry A. Wallace, May 22, 1943, N.B. 21, box 7, Papers of Henry A. Wallace, U. of Iowa, Iowa City.
15. Cherwell to Churchill, Apr. 22, 1942, PREM 4/17/3, Records of Prime Minister, Public Record Office, Kew.
16. Eden memo on Anglo-Soviet relations, June 14, 1944, W.P. (44)323, CAB 66, Records of British War Cabinet, PRO.
17. Quoted in Felix Gilbert, *The End of the European Era: 1890 to the Present* (N.Y., 1970), 332–33.
18. Eden memo, June 14, 1944, W.P. (44)323, CAB 66, PRO.
19. Diary of Hugh Dalton, Feb. 1, 1944, 1:30, London School of Economics, London.

20. J. F. Carter to Edward Stettinius, July 25, 1944, 841.0017-2544, RG 59, Records of Department of State (hereafter cited as DS), National Archives, Washington, D.C.
21. See, for example, Files of Edward R. Stettinius, Dec. 7–23, 1944, vol. 12, RG 59, DS.
22. Thorne, *Allies of a Kind,* 138.
23. Mastny, *Russia's Road to Cold War,* 71–72, 110, 181–82.
24. Thomas Jones, *A Diary with Letters, 1931–1950* (N.Y., 1954), 507–8.
25. William O. McCagg, Jr., *Stalin Embattled, 1943–1948* (Detroit, 1978), 75–96.
26. Ibid., 99, 131.
27. Ibid., 48.
28. Ibid., 42–47.
29. Ibid., 163.
30. Grigg to Montgomery, July 25, 1944, 9/8/18, Papers of Sir Percy Grigg, Churchill College, Cambridge U., Cambridge.
31. For a discussion of isolationism and nationalism in the United States during World War II, see Richard E. Darilek, *A Loyal Opposition in Time of War: The Republican Party and the Politics of Foreign Policy from Pearl Harbor to Yalta* (Westport, Conn., 1986); Wayne S. Cole, *Roosevelt and the Isolationists, 1932–1945* (Lincoln, 1983); Justus D. Doenecke, *Not to the Swift: The Old Isolationists in the Cold War Era* (Lewisburg, Pa., 1979); and Ralph B. Levering, *American Opinion and the Russian Alliance, 1939–1945* (Chapel Hill, 1976).
32. The best treatment of the internationalist revival in the United States is Robert A. Divine's *Second Chance: The Triumph of Internationalism in America During World War II* (N.Y., 1967).
33. Claire Booth Luce et al. to Hull, Mar. 15, 1944, box 10, Papers of Charles P. Taft, Library of Congress, Washington, D.C.
34. "British Policy Towards Nations of Western Europe: The American Position," Apr. 13, 1944, box 10, Files of John D. Hickerson, RG 59, DS.
35. "Principal Problems in Europe," Sept. 26, 1944, roll 5, Papers of Adolf Berle, Franklin D. Roosevelt Library, Hyde Park, N.Y.
36. Gaddis Smith, *Dean Acheson* (N.Y., 1972), 1–25.
37. Acheson to Stettinius and Hull, Jan. 28, 1944, box 27, Papers of Dean Acheson, Harry S. Truman Library, Independence, Mo.
38. Quoted in James F. Schnabel, "The History of the Joint Chiefs of Staff and National Policy, Vol. I: 1945–1947," Feb. 1979, MS in Modern Military Division, NA, 14–15.
39. *Churchill and Roosevelt,* 3:709.
40. Ibid., 767.
41. W. Averell Harriman and Elie Abel, *Special Envoy to Churchill and Stalin, 1941–1946* (N.Y., 1975), 227.
42. See Warren F. Kimball, *Swords or Ploughshares? The Morgenthau Plan for Defeated Nazi Germany, 1943–1946* (N.Y., 1976). Other useful works on the

"German question" are John H. Backer, *The Decision to Divide Germany: American Foreign Policy in Transition* (Durham, 1978), and Tony Sharp, *The Wartime Alliance and the Zonal Division of Germany* (Oxford, 1975).

43. Smith, *American Diplomacy,* 142–43. Albert Resis argues that the percentages deal was only part of a much larger arrangement, in which the United Kingdom tacitly recognized Soviet control in Eastern Europe and Moscow agreed to the resurrection of the British Empire in the Far East. Resis, "The Churchill-Stalin Secret 'Percentages' Agreement on the Balkans, Moscow, October 1944," *American Historical Review* 83 (Apr. 1978): 368–87. See also Joseph M. Siracusa, "The Meaning of Tolstoy: Churchill, Stalin, and the Balkans: Moscow, October 1944," *Diplomatic History* 3 (Summer 1979): 443–63.
44. Philip Earl Green, "Conflict over Trade Ideologies During the Early Cold War: A Study of Foreign Economic Policy" (Ph.D. diss., Duke U., 1978), 61–65 (quotations from 64–65).
45. William Taubman, *Stalin's American Policy: From Entente to Detente to Cold War* (N.Y., 1982), 10.
46. Quoted in Djilas, *Conversations with Stalin,* 73.
47. Quoted in Gaddis, *U.S. and Origins of Cold War,* 144.
48. Ryan, *Vision of Anglo-America,* 81–82; McCagg, *Stalin Embattled,* 54–55. For a detailed description of Anglo-American diplomacy in regard to Poland during the close of World War II and the beginning of the Cold War, see Ryan, *Vision of Anglo-America,* 73–119.
49. See Richard C. Lukas, "The Big Three and the Warsaw Uprising," *Military Affairs* 39 (Oct. 1975): 129–34, and Harriette L. Chandler, "The Transition to Cold Warrior: The Evolution of W. Averell Harriman's Assessment of the U.S.S.R.'s Polish Policy, October 1943–Warsaw Uprising," *East European Quarterly* 10 (Spring 1976): 229–45.
50. Harriman to Hopkins, Sept. 10, 1944, box 157, Papers of Harry Hopkins, Roosevelt Lib.
51. Quoted in Michael S. Sherry, *Preparing for the Next War: American Plans for Postwar Defense, 1941–1945* (New Haven, 1977), 169. For a discussion of Kennan's Long Telegram of Feb. 1946, see below, chap. 4.
52. Conversation among Hull, Beaverbrook, and Berle, July 24, 1944, roll 5, Berle Papers, Roosevelt Lib.
53. Gaddis, *U.S. and Origins of Cold War,* 126, 155.
54. Charles E. Bohlen, *Witness to History, 1929–1969* (N.Y., 1973), 338–39.
55. In *Shattered Peace: The Origins of the Cold War and the National Security State* (Boston, 1977), Daniel H. Yergin argues that during the closing stages of World War II the U.S. foreign policy establishment divided into two camps. One followed the "Yalta axioms," which called for peaceful coexistence with the Soviet Union. The other responded to the "Riga axioms," which saw the Soviet Union as bent on world domination through revolution and advocated a policy of confrontation. According to Yergin's thesis, this division first became apparent with the State Department reorganization of late 1944.

56. In addition to Herring, *Aid to Russia,* see Thomas G. Paterson, "The Abortive Loan to Russia and the Origins of the Cold War, 1943–1946," *Journal of American History* 56 (June 1969): 70–92.
57. Quoted in Leon Martel, *Lend-Lease, Loans, and the Coming of the Cold War: A Study of the Implementation of Foreign Policy* (Boulder, 1979), 69.
58. Quoted in Green, "Conflict over Trade Ideologies," 125.
59. Ibid.
60. See Harriman to Hopkins, Jan. 15, 1944, box 157, Hopkins Papers, Roosevelt Lib.
61. White to Morgenthau, Mar. 7, 1944, box 7, Papers of Harry Dexter White, Princeton U., Princeton.
62. Morgenthau to FDR, May 16, 1944, book 732, diaries of Henry Morgenthau, Jr., Roosevelt Lib.
63. Ibid.
64. *From the Morgenthau Diaries,* vol. 3, *Years of War, 1941–1945,* ed. John Morton Blum (Boston, 1959), 305–6.
65. See Green, "Conflict over Trade Ideologies," 138–39.
66. McCagg, *Stalin Embattled,* 53–54.
67. Taubman, *Stalin's American Policy,* 74–75.
68. The Yalta Conference was the subject of intense debate by journalists, politicians, and academics during the 1950s and 1960s. Defenders of the Roosevelt administration contended that U.S. policy constituted a pragmatic effort to save as much of Europe as possible from Communist domination while still preserving the peace. Critics charged the administration with selling out Eastern Europe and the Far East to the Kremlin. See John L. Snell et al., *The Meaning of Yalta: Big Three Diplomacy and the Balance of Power* (Baton Rouge, 1956), and Athan G. Theoharis, *The Yalta Myths: An Issue in U.S. Politics, 1945–1955* (Columbia, Mo., 1970). Diane Shaver Clemens's *Yalta* (N.Y., 1970) views the conference as characterized by compromise on all sides rather than as a victory for either East or West. See, finally, Russell D. Buhite, *Decisions at Yalta: An Appraisal of Summit Diplomacy* (Wilmington, Del., 1986).
69. Quoted in Gaddis, *U.S. and Origins of Cold War,* 164.

TWO ■ HARRY S. TRUMAN AND THE POLICY OF MEDIATION

1. See, for example, Melvyn P. Leffler, "Strategy, Diplomacy, and the Cold War: The United States, Turkey, and NATO, 1945–1952," *Journal of American History,* 71 (Mar. 1985): 807–25.
2. An excellent survey of Truman's foreign policy during his first year in office is Lisle A. Rose's *After Yalta* (N.Y., 1973).
3. Bohlen, *Witness to History,* 212.

4. Robert J. Donovan, *Conflict and Crisis: The Presidency of Harry S Truman, 1945–1948* (N.Y., 1977), xiv–xvii. See also Alonzo L. Hamby, *Beyond the New Deal: Harry S. Truman and American Liberalism* (N.Y., 1973).
5. In his recently published study of Truman's prepresidential years, Richard Lawrence Miller contends that Truman was the ultimate machine politician and remained so even after his election to the Senate. Miller, *Truman: The Rise to Power* (N.Y., 1986).
6. See Harry S. Truman, *Off the Record: The Private Papers of Harry S. Truman*, ed. Robert H. Ferrell (N.Y., 1980).
7. Arthur Krock, *Memoirs: Sixty Years on the Firing Line* (N.Y., 1968), 221.
8. Gaddis, *U.S. and Origins of Cold War*, 198–99.
9. For a detailed study of Britain's efforts to mold the United States' postwar policy, see Richard A. Best, *"Co-operation with Like-minded Peoples": British Influences on American Security Policy, 1945–1949* (Westport, Conn., 1986). Another useful recent study is Robin Edmonds's *Setting the Mould: The United States and Britain, 1945–1950* (N.Y., 1986).
10. McCagg, *Stalin Embattled*, 168.
11. Ulam, *Expansion and Coexistence*, 401.
12. Ibid., 401–2.
13. *Parliamentary Debates* (Commons), 5th ser., vol. 508, 1671–3.
14. *Harold Nicolson, Diaries and Letters*, vol. 2, *The War Years, 1939–1945*, ed. Nigel Nicolson (N.Y., 1967), 455.
15. *The Diaries of Sir Alexander Cadogan, 1938–1945*, ed. David Dilks (N.Y., 1972), 739.
16. Roberts to C. F. A. Warner, Apr. 30, 1945, FO 371/47854, Records of British Foreign Office, PRO.
17. Sargent memo with Warner minute, Apr. 2, 1945, FO 371/47881, PRO.
18. Roberts to C. F. A. Warner, Apr. 25, 1945, FO 371/47882, PRO. For a detailed discussion of British perceptions of the Soviet threat to Europe, see Victor Rothwell, *Britain and the Cold War, 1941–1947* (London, 1982).
19. War cabinet conclusions, Apr. 3, 1945, W.M. (45)39, CAB 65, PRO.
20. Files of Edward R. Stettinius, Mar. 18, 1945–Apr. 7, 1945, vol. 5, RG 59, DS.
21. See Gaddis, *U.S. and Origins of Cold War*, 201–2, and Harriman and Abel, *Special Envoy*, 447–49.
22. Quoted in Sherry, *Preparing for Next War*, 181.
23. "Russia's Postwar Foreign Policy," Feb. 8, 1945, vol. 2, Papers of James V. Forrestal, Princeton U., Princeton.
24. Quoted in Donovan, *Conflict and Crisis*, 43.
25. Gaddis, *U.S. and Origins of Cold War*, 204.
26. Grew to Truman, May 1, 1945, box 172, President's Secretary's File, Papers of Harry S. Truman, Truman Lib.
27. Will Williams to Tom Beck (*Collier's*), May 2, 1945, N.B. 34, box 12, Wallace Papers, U. of Iowa.

28. Taubman, *Stalin's American Policy,* 88–89.
29. Gaddis, *U.S. and Origins of Cold War,* 224–25.
30. Vandenberg to Taft, May 2, 1945, box 613, Papers of Robert A. Taft, LC.
31. Files of Stettinius, Mar. 18, 1945–Apr. 7, 1945, vol. 5, RG 59, DS.
32. Ibid.
33. Harriman to Stettinius, Apr. 11, 1945, vol. 2, Forrestal Papers, Princeton U.; Williams to Beck, May 2, 1945, N.B. 34, box 12, Wallace Papers, U. of Iowa; Gaddis, *U.S. and Origins of Cold War,* 215–16.
34. Green, "Conflict over Trade Ideologies," 153–54.
35. Quoted in ibid., 188. For an in-depth analysis of this incident, see George C. Herring, Jr., "Lend-Lease to Russia and the Origins of the Cold War, 1944–1945," *Journal of American History* 56 (June 1969): 93–114.
36. For a thorough discussion and analysis of the reparations issue, see Bruce Kuklick, *American Policy and the Division of Germany: The Clash with Russia over Reparations* (Ithaca, N.Y., 1972).
37. See Stephen E. Ambrose, *Eisenhower and Berlin, 1945: The Decision to Halt at the Elbe* (N.Y., 1967).
38. Quoted in Gaddis, *U.S. and Origins of Cold War,* 208.
39. In *Churchill's German Army: Wartime Strategy and Cold War Politics, 1943–1947* (Beverly Hills, 1977), Arthur L. Smith, Jr., argues that Churchill allowed German army units that should have surrendered to the Soviets to surrender to the British instead. Moreover, in anticipation of an East-West conflict, the United Kingdom kept these units intact long after the war was over, thus helping to precipitate the Cold War.
40. Grew to Truman, May 4, 1945, box 175, President's Secretary's File, Truman Papers, Truman Lib. In fact, Grew and a number of his advisers believed that Anglo-American troops ought to be used to force observance of the Yalta accords. By late Apr. 1945 the Yugoslav partisan forces of Josef Broz Tito had not only seized control of their native land from the Germans but also occupied Trieste and Venzia Giulia at the head of the Adriatic, a region that both Italy and Yugoslavia had claimed since World War I. The State Dept., which was convinced that Tito was a tool of the Kremlin, urged the White House and the Joint Chiefs of Staff to authorize Eisenhower and Alexander to clear Yugoslav troops out of the disputed area. Memorandum on Yugoslavia, Apr. 15, 1945, White House Central Files, Permanent File, Truman Papers, Truman Lib.; Grew to Truman, n.d. and May 8, 1945, box 175, President's Secretary's File, ibid.
41. See Sherry, *Preparing for Next War,* 182.
42. Diaries of Henry L. Stimson, Apr. 23, 1945, roll 9, Center for Research Libraries, Chicago.
43. See Schnabel, "History of Joint Chiefs," NA, 13–17.
44. Hurley to Truman, May 21, 1945, box 3, Map Room Files, Truman Papers, Truman Lib.

45. Halifax to F.O., May 5, 1945, FO 371/44536, PRO.
46. Unknown correspondent to Wallace, May 2, 1945, N.B. 34, box 12, Wallace Papers, U. of Iowa.
47. Wallace diary, May 22, 1945, ibid.
48. See Alfred Schindler to George F. Tilton, May 14, 1945, Papers of Alfred Schindler, Truman Lib.
49. Davies to Byrnes, May 10, 1945, box 191, Papers of James F. Byrnes, Clemson U., Clemson, S.C.
50. Cox to Hopkins, Feb. 3, 1943, box 7, Hopkins Papers, Roosevelt Lib.
51. Lippmann to Byrnes, May 10, 1945, folder 199, Byrnes Papers, Clemson U.
52. Quoted in Robert M. Hathaway, *Ambiguous Partnership: Britain and America, 1944–1947* (N.Y., 1981), 36–37.
53. Truman to Eleanor Roosevelt, May 10, 1945, in Truman, *Off the Record,* 21–22.
54. "Latest Opinion Trends," May 24, 1945, box 175, President's Secretary's File, Truman Papers, Truman Lib.
55. Truman diary, June 7, 1945, in Truman, *Off the Record,* 44.
56. Quoted in Wayne Stone Knight, "The Nonfraternal Association: Anglo-American Relations and the Breakdown of the Grand Alliance, 1945–1947" (Ph.D. diss., American U., 1979), 15–18.
57. Ibid.
58. Quoted in Terry H. Anderson, *The United States, Great Britain, and the Cold War, 1944–1947* (Columbia, Mo., 1981), 63.
59. Herbert Feis, *From Trust to Terror: The Onset of the Cold War, 1945–1950* (N.Y., 1970), 17–18.
60. George T. McJimsey's new biography of Harry Hopkins, *Harry Hopkins: Ally of the Poor and Defender of Democracy* (Cambridge, Mass., 1987), is especially good on Hopkins's role in wartime and postwar diplomacy.
61. Bohlen, *Witness to History,* 222.
62. Hopkins to Truman, May 29 and 31, 1945, box 7, Naval Aide File, Truman Papers, Truman Lib.
63. Ulam, *Expansion and Coexistence,* 403–4.
64. Hopkins to Truman, May 29–31, 1945, and Truman to Hopkins, June 5, 1945, box 7, Naval Aide File, Truman Papers, Truman Lib.; Gaddis, *U. S. and Origins of Cold War,* 234–35.
65. See Anderson, *U.S., G.B., and Cold War,* 63–67.
66. Churchill to Truman, June 4, 1945, box 7, Naval Aide File, Truman Papers, Truman Lib.
67. Bohlen, *Witness to History,* 223.
68. Churchill to Truman, June 4, 1945, box 7, Naval Aide File, Truman Papers, Truman Lib.
69. Balfour to Halifax, May 21, 1945, FO 371/44536, PRO.
70. Donnelley and Warner minutes, June 2, 1945, ibid.
71. Orme Sargent minute, May 31, 1945, FO 371/47882, PRO.

72. Warner minute, June 2, 1945, FO 371/44836, PRO.
73. G. M. Wilson minute, May 30, 1945, FO 371/47882, PRO.
74. Quoted in Ambrose, *Rise to Globalism,* 109.
75. Quoted in Anderson, *U.S., G.B., and Cold War,* 88.
76. Quoted in James MacGregor Burns, *Roosevelt: The Soldier of Freedom, 1940–1945* (N.Y., 1970), 262.
77. Quoted in Hathaway, *Ambiguous Partnership,* 149.
78. Truman diary, July 7, 1945, in Truman, *Off the Record,* 48.
79. Quoted in Green, "Conflict over Trade Ideologies," 156. See also Gaddis, *U.S. and Origins of Cold War,* 222–23.
80. Green, "Conflict over Trade Ideologies," 157.
81. See Charles L. Mee, Jr., *Meeting at Potsdam* (N.Y., 1975).
82. Green, "Conflict over Trade Ideologies," 152–56.
83. Margaret Dewar quoted ibid., 87–90.
84. The two most recent and comprehensive accounts of the Truman administration's decision to use the atomic bomb against Japan and, subsequently, to employ it as a bargaining device in negotiations with the Soviet Union are Martin J. Sherwin's *A World Destroyed: The Atomic Bomb and the Grand Alliance* (N.Y., 1975) and Gregg Herken's *The Winning Weapon: The Atomic Bomb in the Cold War, 1945–1950* (N.Y., 1980). See also Barton J. Bernstein, "Roosevelt, Truman and the Atomic Bomb, 1941–1945: A Reinterpretation," *Political Science Quarterly* 90 (Spring 1975): 23–69. In part these analyses attempt to balance earlier works by Gar Alperovitz, who argued that the real motive behind the decision to drop the bomb was intimidation of the Soviet Union, and Herbert Feis, who saw the weapon as a justifiable response to a treacherous enemy: Alperovitz, *Atomic Diplomacy: Hiroshima and Potsdam* (N.Y., 1965); Feis, *The Atomic Bomb and the End of World War II* (Princeton, 1966).
85. Quoted in Sherwin, *A World Destroyed,* 209.
86. Halifax to F.O., Aug. 13, 1945, FO 371/4437, PRO.
87. Byrnes to Truman, Nov. 5, 1945, and J. E. Doyle to Byrnes, Nov. 5, 1945, box 172, President's Secretary's File, Truman Papers, Truman Lib.
88. Dalton diary, July 12, 1945, 1:33, LSE.
89. Quoted in Hathaway, *Ambiguous Partnership,* 213. See also *Roosevelt and Frankfurter: Their Correspondence, 1928–1945,* ed. Max Freedman (Boston, 1968), 726, and Sherwin, *A World Destroyed,* 85–88, 109–11.
90. Sherwin, *A World Destroyed,* 85–88, 109–11.
91. Ibid., 194.
92. Quoted ibid., 227.
93. For a day-by-day account of the events leading up to the bombing of Hiroshima and Nagasaki, see Dan Kurzman, *Day of the Bomb: Countdown to Hiroshima* (N.Y., 1986). See also Richard Rhodes, *The Making of the Atomic Bomb* (N.Y., 1986).
94. Herken, *Winning Weapon,* 20.

95. For a detailed account of the background of JCS 1067, see Walter L. Dorn, "The Debate over American Occupation Policy in Germany in 1944–45," *Political Science Quarterly* 72 (Dec. 1957): 481–501.
96. "Internationalization of Ruhr and Saar," JCS recommendation, June 26, 1945, box 2, Naval Aide File, Truman Papers, Truman Lib.
97. Gaddis, *U.S. and Origins of Cold War,* 238.
98. Grew to Byrnes, July 9, 1945, box 3, Naval Aide File, Truman Papers, Truman Lib.
99. Donnelley minute, June 17, 1945, FO 371/44536, PRO.
100. Churchill to Truman, May 12, 1945, box 4, Map Room Files, Truman Papers, Truman Lib. See Roberto Rubel, "Prologue to Containment: The Truman Administration's Response to the Trieste Crisis of May 1945," *Diplomatic History* 10 (Spring 1986): 141–60.
101. Minutes of the third meeting, June 19, 1945, box 2, Naval Aide File, Truman Papers, Truman Lib.
102. Harriman to Byrnes, June 17, 1945, box 189, President's Secretary's File, ibid.
103. Donnelley minute, July 1, 1945, FO 371/44537, PRO.
104. Taubman, *Stalin's American Policy,* 112.
105. "Italy: Territorial Problems: Libya," June 30, 1945, box 2, Naval Aide File, Truman Papers, Truman Lib.; Grew to Byrnes, July 16, 1945, ibid.; minutes of first session, July 17, 1945, ibid.; "Memo for President: British Plans for Italy," May 11, 1945, box 175, President's Secretary's File, ibid.
106. McCloy memo for State, War, Navy Committee, July 19, 1945, box 4, Naval Aide File, ibid.
107. Cadogan, *Diaries,* 765.
108. For a detailed account of the Potsdam Conference, see Mee, *Meeting at Potsdam.*
109. Taubman, *Stalin's American Policy,* 112.
110. Quoted in Donovan, *Conflict and Crisis,* 84, and in Gaddis, *U.S. and Origins of Cold War,* 243.
111. Walter Brown notes on Potsdam Conference, July 24, 1945, folder 54, Byrnes Papers, Clemson U.
112. Quoted in Gaddis, *U.S. and Origins of Cold War,* 243.

THREE ■ WALKING THE TIGHTROPE: JAMES F. BYRNES AND THE DIPLOMACY OF THE MIDDLE WAY

1. Quoted in Hathaway, *Ambiguous Partnership,* 179, 180.
2. Quoted in Henry Pelling, "The 1945 General Election Reconsidered," *Historical Journal* 23 (June 1980): 400.
3. See ibid., 399–414.
4. Quoted in Nicolson, *Diaries and Letters,* 2:470. See also Winant to Byrnes,

June 13, July 2, and July 7, 1945, 5841.00/6–1345, 841.00/7–245, and 841.00/7–745, DS.

5. Michael Foot, *Aneurin Bevan: A Biography* (London, 1962), 25.
6. See Donald Cameron Watt, *Personalities and Policies: Studies in the Formulation of British Foreign Policy in the Twentieth Century* (Notre Dame, 1965), 57–78.
7. Dalton diary, July 12, 1945, 1:33, LSE.
8. Cadogan, *Diaries,* 776.
9. Dalton diary, Feb. 25, 1946, 1:34, LSE.
10. Quoted in Knight, "Nonfraternal Association," 30.
11. Alan Bullock, *The Life and Times of Ernest Bevin* (London, 1960), 1:98–99.
12. Quoted in Trevor D. Burridge, *British Labour and Hitler's War* (London, 1976), 158.
13. Dalton diary, Oct. 16, 1945, 1:32, LSE.
14. For Bevin's efforts to harness U.S. power to British interests, see Ritchie Ovendale, *The English-Speaking Alliance: Britain and the United States, the Dominions and the Cold War, 1945–1951* (Boston, 1985), and Alan Bullock, *Ernest Bevin: Foreign Secretary, 1945–1951* (N.Y., 1983).
15. See, for example, Halifax to F.O., Aug. 11, 1945, FO 371/4437, PRO.
16. See Hathaway, *Ambiguous Partnership,* 254, and M. A. Fitzsimmons, *The Foreign Policy of the British Labour Government* (Notre Dame, 1953), 34.
17. Dalton diary, July 12, 1945, 1:33, LSE.
18. See Gaddis, *U.S. and Origins of Cold War,* 247–48.
19. Ibid., 250–52.
20. Herken, *Winning Weapon,* 36.
21. Gaddis, *U.S. and Origins of Cold War,* 250–52.
22. Henry A. Wallace, *The Price of Vision: The Diary of Henry A. Wallace, 1942–1946,* ed. John Morton Blum (Boston, 1973), 508.
23. Diaries of James V. Forrestal, Aug. 21, 1945, Cabinet Meeting—Atomic Bomb, Sept. 21, 1945, vol. 2, Princeton U.
24. Herken, *Winning Weapon,* 32.
25. Halifax to F.O., Aug. 13, 1945, FO 371/4437, PRO.
26. Dalton diary, July 12, 1945, 1:33. LSE.
27. *Parliamentary Debates* (Commons), 5th ser., vol. 413.
28. Quoted in "British See Bomb as Key to Cooperation," *New York Times,* Nov. 5, 1950.
29. Attlee to Truman, Aug. 16, 1945, box 6, Naval Aide File, Truman Papers, Truman Lib.
30. Attlee to Truman, Sept. 25, 1945, ibid.
31. Attlee to Truman, Oct. 12, 1945, ibid.
32. Dalton diary, Oct. 17, 1945, vol. 1, LSE.
33. Quoted in Hathaway, *Ambiguous Partnership,* 215–16.
34. Quoted in Green, "Conflict over Trade Ideologies," 162–63.
35. For a discussion of congressional isolationists and their role in the Cold War,

see Doenecke, *Not to the Swift,* 73–130. See also John T. Rourke, "Congress and the Cold War," *World Affairs* 139 (Spring 1977): 259–77.

36. Quoted in Sherry, *Preparing for Next War,* 199.
37. In his *"Lessons" of the Past: The Use and Misuse of History in American Foreign Policy* (N.Y., 1973), Ernest R. May comments on the pervasiveness and impact of the "Munich Analogy."
38. See Sherry, *Preparing for Next War,* 198–99, 218; and JCS to Stimson and Forrestal, Sept. 19, 1945, SWNCC no. 282, State-War-Navy Coordinating Committee Case Files, Center for Research Libraries, Chicago.
39. Quoted in Anderson, *U.S., G.B., and Cold War,* 89–90.
40. Clements, *Byrnes and Origins of Cold War,* 3–7.
41. For a detailed discussion of U.S. relations with Eastern Europe during the breakup of the Grand Alliance, see Geir Lundestad, *The American Non-Policy Towards Eastern Europe, 1943–1947: Universalism in an Area Not of Essential Interest to the United States* (N.Y., 1975).
42. Walter Brown chronicle of London Foreign Ministers' Conference, Aug. 11–Sept. 20, 1945, box 629, Byrnes Papers, Clemson U.
43. Dalton diary, Oct. 5, 1945, 1:34, LSE.
44. Johnathan Knight, "Russia's Search for Peace: The London Council of Foreign Ministers, 1945," *Journal of Contemporary History* 13 (Jan. 1978), 137–63.
45. Djilas, *Conversations with Stalin,* 70.
46. Mee, *Meeting at Potsdam,* 59.
47. Dalton diary, Sept. 10, 1946, 1:34, LSE.
48. CFM-London, Sept. 16, 1945, box 619, Byrnes Papers, Clemson U.
49. Brown chronicle, Sept. 20, 1945, box 629, ibid.; memo of conversation by Bohlen, Sept. 16, 1945, 740.0019, RG 59, DS; Gaddis, *U.S. and Origins of Cold War,* 265–66.
50. Taubman, *Stalin's American Policy,* 120–21.
51. Brown chronicle, Sept. 20, 1945, box 629, Byrnes Papers, Clemson U.
52. Wallace, *Price of Vision,* 490.
53. Davies to Byrnes, Oct. 5, 1945, box 191, Byrnes Papers, Clemson U.
54. Gaddis, *U.S. and Origins of Cold War,* 275.
55. *New York Times,* Oct. 10, 1945.
56. Ethridge to Byrnes, Dec. 8, 1945, box 172, President's Secretary's File, Truman Papers, Truman Lib.
57. Weekly Political Summary, Nov. 28, 1945, FO 371/44574, PRO.
58. Halifax to Bevin, Dec. 21, 1945, ibid.
59. *Parliamentary Debates* (Commons), 5th ser., vol. 14/4, 38.
60. Halifax to Bevin, Dec. 21, 1945, FO 371/44574, PRO.
61. Dalton diary, Oct. 5, 1945, 1:33, LSE.
62. Quoted in Knight, "Nonfraternal Association," 66–67.
63. Halifax to Bevin, Dec. 21, 1945, FO 371/44574, PRO.
64. Quoted in Knight, "Nonfraternal Association," 67.
65. Anderson, *U.S., G.B., and Cold War,* 100–102.

66. Bruce R. Kuniholm, *The Origins of the Cold War in the Near East: Great Power Conflict and Diplomacy in Iran, Turkey, and Greece* (Princeton, 1980), 151.
67. See Anderson, *U.S., G.B., and Cold War,* 100–102.
68. Herken, *Winning Weapon,* 69, 81.
69. Ibid., 83–85.
70. Patricia Dawson Ward, *The Threat of Peace: James F. Byrnes and the Council of Foreign Ministers, 1945–1946* (Kent, Ohio, 1979), 63–66.

FOUR ■ CONFRONTATION AND CONTAINMENT: FROM THE IRON CURTAIN SPEECH TO THE PARIS PEACE CONFERENCE

1. The standard orthodox history of the Cold War in Europe is Feis, *From Trust to Terror.* See also Norman A. Graebner, ed., *The Cold War: A Conflict of Ideology and Power* (Lexington, Mass., 1976). In addition to Gardner's *Architects of Illusion,* the most important revisionist analysis is Joyce and Gabriel Kolko's *The Limits of Power: The World and United States Foreign Policy, 1945–1954* (N.Y., 1972). For a postrevisionist synthesis see, in addition to Gaddis's *U.S. and Origins of Cold War,* Thomas G. Paterson, *On Every Front: The Making of the Cold War* (N.Y., 1979).
2. James P. Warburg to Dean Acheson, Oct. 31, 1945, box 27, Acheson Papers, Truman Lib.
3. Dulles to Charles Halleck, Nov. 19, 1945, Papers of John Foster Dulles, Princeton U.
4. Mundt and Bolton to Truman, Oct. 25, 1945, box 186, President's Secretary's File, Truman Papers, Truman Lib.
5. Chairman's letter—Republican National Committee, Oct. 15, 1945, box 175, ibid.
6. "Stop World War III," Jan. 11, 1946, box 613, Robert Taft Papers, LC.
7. Weekly Political Summary, Nov. 3, 1945, FO 371/44539, PRO.
8. Gaddis, *U.S. and Origins of Cold War,* 293; Knight, "Nonfraternal Association," 87–88.
9. Donnelley minute on Balfour to Gage, Sept. 12, 1945, FO 371/445741, PRO.
10. Balfour to Mason, Jan. 11, 1946, FO 371/51627, PRO.
11. Halifax to F.O., Sept. 2, 1945, FO 371/44538, PRO.
12. Brogan minute on political situation in United States, Jan. 1, 1946, FO 371/51606, PRO.
13. Donnelley minute on Weekly Summary, Mar. 27, 1946, FO 371/51607, PRO.
14. Michael Butler to Orme Sargent, Jan. 10, 1946, FO 371/56763, PRO.
15. Balfour to Mason, Jan. 11, 1946, FO 371/51627, PRO.
16. Donnelley minute on Weekly Political Summary, Jan. 8, 1946, FO 371/51606, PRO.

17. Donnelley and Gage minutes on Weekly Political Summary, Jan. 24, 1946, ibid.
18. Taubman, *Stalin's American Policy,* 128–29.
19. Halifax to F.O., Feb. 17, 1946, FO 371/51606, PRO.
20. Donnelley minute, Feb. 17, 1946, ibid.
21. Matthews to Acheson and Byrnes, Feb. 11, 1946, box 10, Files of John D. Hickerson, RG 59, DS.
22. For a discussion of the context in which the Long Telegram was written and accepted, see Robert L. Messer, "Paths Not Taken: The United States Department of State and Alternatives to Containment, 1945–1946," *Diplomatic History* 1 (Fall 1977): 297–319.
23. Quoted in Bohlen, *Witness to History,* 175.
24. See Knight, "Nonfraternal Association," 85–86.
25. Halifax to F.O., Feb. 17, 1946, FO 371/51606, PRO.
26. Donnelley minute, Jan. 4, 1946, FO 371/44574, PRO.
27. Roberts to F.O., Mar. 2, 1946, FO 371/568140, PRO. See also Donnelley minute, Feb. 22, 1946, FO 371/51606, PRO.
28. Anderson, *U.S., G.B., and Cold War,* 100–101.
29. See Donovan, *Conflict and Crisis,* xiv–xvii.
30. See Gaddis, *U.S. and Origins of Cold War,* 287–89.
31. Anderson, *U.S., G.B., and Cold War,* 107.
32. Donnelley minute, Jan. 17, 1946, FO 371/51606, PRO.
33. Gaddis, *U.S. and Origins of Cold War,* 296.
34. Quoted in Knight, "Nonfraternal Association," 86.
35. Ibid., 87.
36. Brant to Truman, Jan. 14, 1946, box 186, President's Secretary's File, Truman Papers, Truman Lib.
37. Grew to Truman, July 3, 1945, box 175, ibid.
38. Quoted in Gaddis, *U.S. and Origins of Cold War,* 289.
39. Weekly Political Summary, Jan. 18, 1946, FO 371/51606, PRO.
40. Donovan, *Conflict and Crisis,* 194–95.
41. Gaddis, *U.S. and Origins of Cold War,* 310–11.
42. Taubman, *Stalin's American Policy,* 149.
43. Kuniholm, *Origins of Cold War in Near East,* 326–40.
44. Donovan, *Conflict and Crisis,* 194–95.
45. J. Philip Rosenberg, "The Cheshire Ultimatum: Truman's Message to Stalin in the 1946 Azerbaijan Crisis," *Journal of Politics* 41 (Aug. 1979), 933–40. See also Gary R. Hess, "The Iranian Crisis of 1945–46 and the Cold War," *Political Science Quarterly* 89 (Mar. 1974): 117–46; and Kuniholm, *Origins of Cold War in Near East,* 304–37.
46. For an in-depth analysis of Churchill's views on the Soviet Union, the United States' role in European affairs, and the genesis of the Fulton speech, see Fraser J. Harbutt, *The Iron Curtain: Churchill, America, and the Origins of the Cold War* (N.Y., 1986), 159–216.

47. Quoted in Donovan, *Conflict and Crisis,* 190.
48. Churchill to Truman, Nov. 8, 1945, box 115, President's Secretary's File, Truman Papers, Truman Lib.
49. Quoted in Donovan, *Conflict and Crisis,* 190–91.
50. Quoted in Fraser J. Harbutt, "American Challenge, Soviet Response: The Beginning of the Cold War, February–May, 1946," *Political Science Quarterly* 96 (Winter 1981–82): 632.
51. Quoted in Knight, "Nonfraternal Association," 94.
52. Ibid.
53. "Sinews of Peace"—British Information Service Advance Release, Mar. 5, 1946, box 115, President's Secretary's File, Truman Papers, Truman Lib.
54. Fred Arkin to Truman, May 5, 1946, box 771, Official File, ibid.
55. Sidney Kaufman to Truman, Mar. 5, 1946, box 237, ibid.
56. Shirley McDevitt to Truman, Mar. 6, 1946, ibid.
57. See Norman Ober to Truman, Mar. 7, 1946; Lyn Westen to Truman, Mar. 19, 1946; Louis Coffin to Truman, Mar. 18, 1946; and Paul Gibson to Truman, May 6, 1946, ibid.
58. Halifax to Bevin, Mar. 9, 1946, FO 371/51624, PRO.
59. Taubman, *Stalin's American Policy,* 144.
60. *Parliamentary Debates* (Commons), 5th ser., vol. 416, Nov. 23, 1945, 1162–1348.
61. Quoted in Knight, "Nonfraternal Association," 102.
62. Vaughn to Kenneth Marshall, Apr. 19, 1946, box 16, President's Personal File, Truman Lib.
63. Butler to Wincour, Mar. 18, 1946, FO 371/51624, PRO.
64. Donnelley and Mason minutes on U.S. reaction to Churchill speech, Mar. 3, 1946, ibid.
65. Wallace, *Price of Vision,* 556.
66. Quoted in Ward, *Threat of Peace,* 78.
67. Quoted ibid., 81.
68. Union of Soviet Socialist Republics: State Dept. policy statement, May 14, 1946, box 196, Byrnes Papers, Clemson U.
69. The first week in April, Vandenberg had written Dulles reproaching him for mincing words in an article on Soviet-American relations. The future secretary of state, he argued, should come down from his ivory tower, denounce Communist totalitarianism for the evil that it was, and call upon the Russians to repent. Vandenberg to Dulles, Apr. 7, 1946, Dulles Papers, Princeton U.
70. Ward, *Threat of Peace,* 88–89.
71. See memo of conversation among Georges Bidault, Byrnes, and Matthews, May 1, 1946, and extracts from informal meeting held in Paris, May 2, 1946, box 627, Byrnes Papers, Clemson U.
72. See Ward, *Threat of Peace,* 93–96, and Anderson, *U.S., G.B., and Cold War,* 120–21.
73. Wallace diary, Feb. 20, 1946, N.B. 13, box 38, U. of Iowa.

74. Herken, *Winning Weapon*, 163–71.
75. Ibid., 190–91.
76. Patterson to Douglas S. Freeman, Mar. 26, 1946, box 19, Freeman folder, Papers of Robert Patterson, LC.
77. See George C. Herring, Jr., "The United States and British Bankruptcy, 1944–1945: Responsibilities Deferred," *Political Science Quarterly* 86 (June 1971): 260–80.
78. Richard P. Hedlund, "Congress and the British Loan of 1946" (Ph.D. diss., U. of Kentucky, 1978), 153.
79. Perry L. Withers to Jesse H. Jones, Apr. 17, 1946, box 189, Papers of Jesse H. Jones, LC.
80. Weekly Political Summary, July 1946, FO 371/51607, PRO.
81. Ibid.
82. Senate, *Anglo-American Financial Agreement: Hearings Before the Committee on Banking and Currency*, 79th Cong., 2d sess. (Washington, D.C., 1946), 391–92.
83. Quoted in Knight, "Nonfraternal Association," 110.
84. *Wall Street Journal*, Mar. 8, 1946.
85. Quoted in Hedlund, "Congress and British Loan," 141.
86. "Relations with Russia," July 22, 1946, box 27, Acheson Papers, Truman Lib.
87. See Ward, *Threat of Peace*, 121–22. Still the standard work on U.S. occupation policy in Germany is John Gimbel, *The American Occupation of Germany: Politics and the Military, 1945–1949* (Stanford, 1968). See also Edward N. Peterson, *The American Occupation of Germany: Retreat to Victory* (Detroit, 1977).
88. Vandenberg to Dulles, May 13, 1946, Dulles Papers, Princeton U.
89. Roberts to Warner, June 18, 1946, FO 371/56763, PRO.
90. Ward, *Threat of Peace*, 140.
91. Wallace, *Price of Vision*, 616.
92. Russell to Byrnes, Sept. 16, 1946, box 619, Byrnes Papers, Clemson U.
93. Clayton to Byrnes, Sept. 17, 1946, and Truman to Byrnes, June 19, 1946, ibid.
94. Ward, *Threat of Peace*, 152–167.
95. Ibid., 176.
96. Ibid., 172–80.
97. Gage minute, Mar. 5, 1946, FO 371/51606, PRO.

FIVE ■ A POLICY OF FIRMNESS: THE TRUMAN DOCTRINE AND GLOBAL STRATEGY

1. Vojtech Mastny argues that the Soviet Union sought "power and influence far in excess of its reasonable security requirements." Stalin's actions, Mastny later adds, were determined by "the Soviet system which had bred him and

which he felt compelled to perpetuate by his execrable methods; that system was the true cause of the Cold War." Mastny, *Russia's Road to Cold War,* 283, 306; see also 312–13. William Taubman attributes many of the Cold War's origins to "mutual misperception." Taubman, *Stalin's American Policy,* 8–9. Robert C. Tucker insists that the years after World War II "marked not only the high tide of Stalin's autocracy, but also the climax of his personality disorder." Tucker, *Soviet Political Mind,* 220; see also 229–30. For accounts of Stalin's paranoia and vindictive nature, see Nikita Khrushchev, *Khrushchev Remembers,* trans. and ed. Strobe Talbott (Boston, 1970), 246–58.

2. The *New York Times* correspondent was Anne O'Hare McCormick. See her article in the edition of Feb. 5, 1949, enclosed in Francis F. Lincoln Papers, Truman Lib. The "Northern Tier" consisted of Greece, Turkey, and Iran.
3. Kuniholm, *Origins of Cold War in Near East,* 59, 356, 379–80; Joseph M. Jones, *The Fifteen Weeks (February 21–June 5, 1947)* (N.Y., 1955), 60; Dean Acheson, *Present at the Creation: My Years in the State Department* (N.Y., 1969), 199–200; Theodore A. Couloumbis, *The United States, Greece, and Turkey: The Troubled Triangle* (N.Y., 1983), 11–12. Signatories to the Montreux Treaty were Bulgaria, France, Great Britain, Greece, Japan, Rumania, Turkey, the Soviet Union, and Yugoslavia. See Harry N. Howard, *The Problem of the Turkish Straits* (Washington, D.C., 1947), 2, 36–37; "Turkey: Political Background," Feb. 4, 1948, folder in Acheson Papers, Truman Lib.; and Leffler, "Strategy, Diplomacy, and Cold War," 807–25. The Pact of Friendship had been in existence since 1925.
4. Jones, *Fifteen Weeks,* 59, 61; Leffler, "Strategy, Diplomacy, and Cold War," 813; Gaddis, *U.S. and Origins of Cold War,* 336; Robert L. Messer, *The End of an Alliance: James F. Byrnes, Roosevelt, Truman, and the Origins of the Cold War* (Chapel Hill, 1982), 192; "State Dept. Briefing Book," July 1, 1946, p. 8, Byrnes Papers, Clemson U.; NEFIS Intelligence no. 141: "The Aims, Methods and Means of Soviet Russia in Asia and the Middle East," May 16, 1946, pp. 8, 11, 24, William D. Leahy Files, Records of JCS, NA (quoting Dutch intelligence report); Howard, *Problem of Turkish Straits,* 39; Elbridge Durbrow (chargé in Moscow) to Byrnes, Aug. 5, 1946, U.S.-Greek Internal Political Affairs, RG 59, DS.
5. Donovan, *Conflict and Crisis,* 251; Stephen G. Xydis, "The Truman Doctrine in Perspective," *Balkan Studies* 8 (1967): 248–49; Acheson, *Present at Creation,* 195–96; Jones, *Fifteen Weeks,* 62–65; Couloumbis, *U.S., Greece, and Turkey,* 11–12; Kuniholm, *Origins of Cold War in Near East,* 373, 373 n. 193; Gaddis, *U.S. and Origins of Cold War,* 336–37; Harry S. Truman, *Memoirs: Years of Trial and Hope, 1946–1952* (Garden City, N.Y., 1956), 97–98; Howard, *Problem of Turkish Straits,* 39–43.
6. Clifford, "American Relations with the Soviet Union," Sept. 24, 1946, pp. 1, 3–4, 12–14, 60–62, 68, 71, 73–74, 78–79, President's Secretary's File, Truman Papers, Truman Lib.; Oral History Interview with George M. Elsey (White

House adviser) (Apr. 9, 1970), 261–66, Truman Lib.; Donovan, *Conflict and Crisis,* 221–22; Gaddis, *U.S. and Origins of Cold War,* 321–22, 322 n. 7. Elsey wrote much of the Clifford report.

7. Clifford, "American Relations with Soviet Union," 75, President's Secretary's File, Truman Papers, Truman Lib.; George F. Kennan, *Memoirs, 1925–1950* (Boston, 1967), 247–51, 301–4; "Soviet Military Intentions," Sept. 18, 1946, CIG [Central Intelligence Group] Special Study No. 4, pp. i–ii, 2, President's Secretary's File, Truman Papers, Truman Lib.; memo for Leahy from Hoyt S. Vandenberg, director of Central Intelligence, Sept. 25, 1946, enclosure: "Strategic Services Unit, War Dept., Subject of Soviet Activity in Shanghai, from Source 'Z'—Field Evaluation C-3," July 7, 1946, Leahy Files, Records of JCS, NA; "Revised Soviet Tactics in International Affairs," Jan. 6, 1947, CIG, ORE 1/1, pp. 1–5, President's Secretary's File, Truman Papers, Truman Lib.; Oral History Interview with Clark Clifford (Mar. 1971–Feb. 1973), 89–90, Truman Lib.

8. "The Greek Situation," Feb. 7, 1947, CIG, ORE 6/1, pp. 1–2, 12, President's Secretary's File, Truman Papers, Truman Lib.; Jones, *Fifteen Weeks,* 11.

9. "State Dept. Briefing Book," 14, Byrnes Papers, Clemson U.; State-War-Navy Coordinating Subcommittee for Near and Middle East—"U.S. Security Interests in Greece," Sept. 7, 1946, p. 1, and encl.: memo for sec. of state, ABC-400.336 Greece, sec. I-A, pp. 1, 3, RG 107, Records of War Dept., NA; Lincoln MacVeagh to George C. Marshall, Feb. 7, 1947, Dept. of State, *Foreign Relations of the United States* (hereafter cited as *FRUS*), *1947,* vol. 5, *The Near East and Africa* (Washington, D.C., 1971), 16; Howard Jones, *"A New Kind of War": America's Global Strategy and the Truman Doctrine in Greece* (N.Y., 1989), 14.

10. John O. Iatrides, *Revolt in Athens: The Greek Communist "Second Round," 1944–1945* (Princeton, 1972), 221–24, 279; Christopher M. Woodhouse, *The Struggle for Greece, 1941–1949* (Brooklyn Heights, N.Y., 1976), chap. 5; Dimitrios G. Kousoulas, *The Price of Freedom: Greece in World Affairs, 1939–1953* (Syracuse, N.Y., 1953), 151; Kousoulas, *Revolution and Defeat: The Story of the Greek Communist Party* (London, 1965), 232; Lawrence S. Wittner, *American Intervention in Greece, 1943–1949* (N.Y., 1982), 37; Mastny, *Russia's Road to Cold War,* 204–5, 207–12, 230–31; Resis, "Churchill-Stalin Secret 'Percentages' Agreement," 368–87; Stephen G. Xydis, "The Secret Anglo-Soviet Agreement on the Balkans of October 9, 1944," *Journal of Central European Affairs* 15 (Oct. 1955): 248–71; Winston Churchill, *Triumph and Tragedy* (Boston, 1953), 226–35.

11. William H. McNeill, *The Greek Dilemma: War and Aftermath* (Philadelphia, 1947), 231, 233–35; Frank Smothers, William H. McNeill, and Elizabeth D. McNeill, *Report on the Greeks: Findings of a Twentieth Century Fund Team Which Surveyed Conditions in Greece in 1947* (N.Y., 1948), 29; John O. Iatrides, "American Attitudes Toward the Political System of Postwar Greece," in Theodore A. Couloumbis and John O. Iatrides, eds., *Greek-American Rela-*

tions: A Critical Review (N.Y., 1980), 60–61; Heinz Richter, *British Intervention in Greece: From Varkiza to Civil War, February 1945 to August 1946* (London, 1985), 442–43; Bickham Sweet-Escott, *Greece: A Political and Economic Survey, 1939–1953* (London, 1954), 50–52.

12. Richter, *British Intervention in Greece,* 507–8; Kuniholm, *Origins of Cold War in Near East,* 399; Evangelos Averoff-Tossizza, *By Fire and Axe: The Communist Party and the Civil War in Greece, 1944–1949* (New Rochelle, N.Y., 1978), 172–73; Ole L. Smith, "Self-Defence and Communist Policy, 1945–1947," in Lars Baerentzen, John O. Iatrides, and Ole L. Smith, eds., *Studies in the History of the Greek Civil War, 1945–1949* (Copenhagen, 1987), 159, 168–70.

13. "The Greek Situation," Feb. 7, 1947, CIG, ORE 6/1, pp. 11–12, President's Secretary's File, Truman Papers, Truman Lib.; Christopher M. Woodhouse, *Apple of Discord: A Survey of Recent Greek Politics in Their International Setting* (London, 1948), 267; Geoffrey Chandler, *The Divided Land: An Anglo-Greek Tragedy* (London, 1959), 152–53; Stephen G. Xydis, *Greece and the Great Powers, 1944–1947: Prelude to the "Truman Doctrine"* (Thessaloniki, 1963), 195, 229, 617 n. 16; Cyrus L. Sulzberger, *A Long Row of Candles: Memoirs and Diaries [1934–1954]* (N.Y., 1969), 324, 335; Dominique Eudes, *The Kapetanios: Partisans and the Civil War in Greece, 1943–1949* (N.Y., 1972), 284; Woodhouse, *Struggle for Greece,* 179–80, 184, 193–94; Averoff-Tossizza, *By Fire and Axe,* 177; Jones, "*New Kind of War,*" 19–21. For aid to the guerrillas, see Elisabeth Barker, "The Yugoslavs and the Greek Civil War of 1946–1949," in Baerentzen, Iatrides, and Smith, eds., *Studies in History of Greek Civil War,* 303. She cites figures from a book published by Vladimir Dedijer, who was a cohort of Yugoslavia's leader, Josef Broz Tito.

14. See Walter Lippmann, *The Cold War* (N.Y., 1947). The first government document to use the term "cold war" was NSC-7, "The Position of the United States with Respect to Soviet-Directed World Communism" (Mar. 30, 1948). Herken, *Winning Weapon,* 249–50.

15. Jones, "*New Kind of War,*" 7 (quoting Byrnes); "State Dept. Briefing Book," 14, Byrnes Papers, Clemson U.; State-War-Navy Coordinating Subcommittee for Near and Middle East—"U.S. Security Interests in Greece," Sept. 7, 1946, encl.: memo for sec. of state, ABC-400.336 Greece, sec. I-A, pp. 1, 2, RG 107, War Dept.; Joseph M. Jones, "Background Memorandum on Greece," Mar. 3, 1947, Papers of Joseph M. Jones, Truman Lib.; "Public Information Program on U.S. Aid to Greece: FPI 30, append. A: General Survey of Greek Situation," Mar. 3, 1947, pp. 4–5, U.S.-Greek Internal Political Affairs, RG 59, DS; Taubman, *Stalin's American Policy,* 133–34. See also Werner G. Hahn, *Postwar Soviet Politics: The Fall of Zhdanov and the Defeat of Moderation, 1946–1953* (Ithaca, N.Y., 1982), 22–23.

16. The British Military Mission in Greece also retained 1,380 officers and enlisted men. George M. Alexander, *The Prelude to the Truman Doctrine: British Policy in Greece, 1944–1947* (Oxford, 1982), 214, 225–27, 234.

17. Ibid.; Jones, "*New Kind of War,*" 22.
18. "Report of UNSCOB [UN Special Committee on the Balkans]," Dec. 19, 1946, supp. 8, UN General Assembly, *Official Records,* 3d sess., 1948, p. 1; Mark Ethridge (head of UN commission) to Marshall, Feb. 17 and Feb. 21, 1947, *FRUS, 1947,* 5:24, 38–39; Kenneth Matthews, *Memories of a Mountain War, Greece: 1944–1949* (London, 1972), 14, 136–51; Jones, "*New Kind of War,*" 25–26; Alexander, *Prelude to Truman Doctrine,* 214, 225–27, 234.
19. Jones, "*New Kind of War,*" 24.
20. Ibid., 29–31; Porter testimony, Apr. 1, 1947, Senate, *Legislative Origins of the Truman Doctrine: Hearings Held in Executive Session Before the Committee on Foreign Relations on S. 938: A Bill to Provide for Assistance to Greece and Turkey,* 80th Cong., 1st sess. (Washington, D.C., 1973), 70, 99; Porter to Undersec. of State for Economic Affairs William L. Clayton, Feb. 17, 1947, pp. 2–5, and Porter to Truman, Mar. 3, 1947, Papers of Paul A. Porter, Truman Lib.
21. MacVeagh to Marshall, Feb. 11, 1947, *FRUS, 1947,* 5:17; Porter to Marshall, Feb. 19 and Feb. 22, 1947, ibid., 26, 40; Porter to Acheson, Apr. 25, 1947, encl.: tentative report of American economic mission to Greece, "Summary and Recommendations of the Report," RG 59, DS; Report of the American economic mission to Greece, Apr. 30, 1947, pp. 2, 5, Porter Papers, Truman Lib.; Porter diary, Jan. 20 and 22 and Feb. 1 and 6, 1947, box 1, ibid.; *Time,* Feb. 24, 1947, p. 35; Francis F. Lincoln, *United States' Aid to Greece, 1947–1962* (Germantown, Tenn., 1975), 7. Lincoln was a State Dept. adviser on economic affairs.
22. Anderson, *U.S., G.B., and Cold War,* 173–75; Hathaway, *Ambiguous Partnership,* 300–301; author's interview with Loy Henderson (May 24, 1979); MacVeagh to Marshall, Feb. 24, 1947, U.S.-Greek Internal Political Affairs, RG 59, DS; aide-mémoire from British embassy to State Dept., Feb. 21, 1947, *FRUS, 1947,* 5:32–37; Truman, *Memoirs,* 99; Acheson, *Present at Creation,* 217; Donovan, *Conflict and Crisis,* 278; Jones, *Fifteen Weeks,* 3–8.
23. Acheson, *Present at Creation,* 217–19; author's interview with Henderson (May 24, 1979); Oral History Interview with Loy Henderson (June 14 and July 5, 1973), 87–88, Truman Lib.; Acheson to Marshall, Feb. 21, 1947, *FRUS, 1947,* 5:29–31; Marshall to Sen. William F. Knowland, Mar. 25, 1948, U.S.-Greek Internal Political Affairs, RG 59, DS; Kuniholm, *Origins of Cold War in Near East,* 409 n. 80; James V. Forrestal, *The Forrestal Diaries,* ed. Walter Millis (N.Y., 1951), 245; interview with Acheson (Feb. 18, 1955), 36, "Memoirs File," box 1, Post-Presidential Files, Truman Papers, Truman Lib.; Leahy diaries, Feb. 27, 1947, p. 17, Papers of William D. Leahy, LC. On the domestic importance of a convincing program, see Gaddis, *U.S. and Origins of Cold War,* 337–46.
24. Oral History Interview with Henderson (June 14 and July 5, 1973), 21, Truman Lib.; minutes of Special Committee to Study Assistance to Greece and Turkey, Feb. 24, 1947, *FRUS, 1947,* 5:45–47; memo from chairman of special com-

mittee (Henderson) to Acheson, ca. Feb. 24, 1947, ibid., 47–48; "Analysis of the Proposals," ibid., 51–53; Marshall to Truman, Feb. 26, 1947, ibid., 58; minutes of meetings of secs. of state, war, and navy, Feb. 26, 1947, U.S.-Greek Internal Political Affairs, RG 59, DS (text underlined in the original).

25. Melvyn P. Leffler, "From the Truman Doctrine to the Carter Doctrine: Lessons and Dilemmas of the Cold War," *Diplomatic History* 7 (Fall 1983): 245–66; "Analysis of Proposals," *FRUS, 1947,* 5:54–55.

26. FPI 30, Mar. 3, 1947, pp. 3–5, U.S.-Greek Internal Political Affairs, RG 59, DS.

27. Notes on meeting between Truman and congressional leaders, Mar. 10, 1947, Leahy diaries, 1947, p. 21, Leahy Papers, LC; Acheson, *Present at Creation,* 219; David S. McLellan, *Dean Acheson: The State Department Years* (N.Y., 1976), 115; Jones, *Fifteen Weeks,* 139–41, 143; Jones, "*New Kind of War,*" 42; Truman, *Memoirs,* 103–4; Arthur H. Vandenberg, *The Private Papers of Senator Vandenberg,* ed. Arthur H. Vandenberg, Jr. (Boston, 1952), 340.

28. Cabinet meeting notes, Mar. 7, 1947, President's Secretary's File, Truman Papers, Truman Lib.; cabinet meeting notes, Mar. 7, 1947, General Correspondence, box 19, Patterson Papers, LC; Susan M. Hartmann, *Truman and the 80th Congress* (Columbia, Mo., 1971); Jones, *Fifteen Weeks,* 90–91, 117–25; Clayton memo, Mar. 5, 1947, folder entitled "Confidential Marshall Plan Memoirs," box 42, Papers of William L. Clayton, Truman Lib.; Joseph M. Jones, "Background Memorandum on Greece," Mar. 3, 1947, Jones Papers, ibid.; Truman, *Memoirs,* 101; Oral History Interview with Henderson (June 14 and July 5, 1973), 86–87, Truman Lib.; author's interview with Henderson; "The Drafting of the President's Message of March 12, 1947," chronology, ca. Mar. 13, 1947, Joseph M. Jones Papers, Truman Lib.; John L. Gaddis, *The Long Peace: Inquiries into the History of the Cold War* (N.Y., 1987), 56.

29. Quoted in Jones, "*New Kind of War,*" vii, 43. For a good account of the president's speech, see Jones, *Fifteen Weeks,* 17–23.

30. Quoted in Jones, "*New Kind of War,*" vii–viii. Critics of the Truman Doctrine include William A. Williams, *The Tragedy of American Diplomacy* (N.Y., 1959); J. William Fulbright, *The Arrogance of Power* (N.Y., 1966); Richard M. Freeland, *The Truman Doctrine and the Origins of McCarthyism* (N.Y., 1970); Andreas Papandreou, *Democracy at Gunpoint: The Greek Front* (Garden City, N.Y., 1970); Kolko and Kolko, *Limits of Power;* Thomas G. Paterson, *Soviet-American Confrontation: Postwar Reconstruction and the Origins of the Cold War* (Baltimore, 1973); Paterson, *On Every Front;* Yergin, *Shattered Peace;* and Wittner, *American Intervention in Greece.* Among those defending the Truman Doctrine are Robert H. Ferrell, *George Marshall* (N.Y., 1966); Ferrell, *Harry S. Truman and the Modern American Presidency* (Boston, 1983); Cabell Phillips, *The Truman Presidency: The History of a Triumphant Succession* (N.Y., 1966); Feis, *From Trust to Terror;* Smith, *Acheson;* John L. Gaddis, *Strategies of Containment: A Critical Appraisal of Postwar American National Security Policy* (N.Y., 1982); Gaddis, *Long Peace;* Richard F. Haynes, *The Awesome Power: Harry S. Truman as Commander*

in Chief (Baton Rouge, 1973); McLellan, *Acheson;* Donovan, *Conflict and Crisis;* Kuniholm, *Origins of Cold War in Near East;* Donald R. McCoy, *The Presidency of Harry S. Truman* (Lawrence, Kans., 1984); and Walter Isaacson and Evan Thomas, *The Wise Men: Six Friends and the World They Made* (N.Y., 1986).

31. As readers will recall, during the Revolutionary War the Americans signed a military and economic alliance with the French against the British.

32. All citations in Jones, "*New Kind of War,*" 43–45. In Sept. 1946 Wallace delivered a speech in Madison Square Garden in New York, attacking the administration's domestic and foreign policy.

33. Kennan, *Memoirs,* 315; author's interview with Dean Rusk (then political adviser to UN, Nov. 3, 1978); Gaddis, *U.S. and Origins of Cold War,* 261–63, 282–84, 312–18, 337–46; T. Michael Ruddy, *The Cautious Diplomat: Charles E. Bohlen and the Soviet Union, 1929–1969* (Kent, Ohio, 1986), 72; Forrest C. Pogue, *George C. Marshall: Statesman, 1945–1949* (N.Y., 1987), 172–73.

34. Kennan to Henderson, Mar. 27, 1947, U.S.-Greek Internal Political Affairs, RG 59, DS; Kennan, "Comments on the National Security Problem [in Europe and Asia]," 1–4, 9–12, 15–17, encl. ibid.; Jones, "*New Kind of War,*" 46. For Kennan's views, see his Long Telegram to Byrnes of Feb. 24, 1946, in *FRUS, 1946,* vol. 6, *The Near East and Africa* (Washington, D.C., 1970), 696–709; his article signed "X," "The Sources of Soviet Conduct," *Foreign Affairs* 25 (July 1947): 566–82; Kennan, *Memoirs,* 354–57; and Kennan, "Containment Then and Now," *Foreign Affairs* 65 (Spring 1987): 885–90.

35. Gaddis, *Strategies of Containment,* 22–24, 58–65, 101; Kennan, "Containment Then and Now," 886.

36. Congressional hearings in Senate, *Legislative Origins of Truman Doctrine,* and House of Representatives, *Military Assistance Programs, Part 2: Assistance to Greece and Turkey,* vol. 6 (Washington, D.C., 1976). See also Acheson's written replies to Senate questions, encl. in Acheson to Vandenberg, Mar. 24, 1947, U.S.-Greek Internal Political Affairs, RG 59, DS; Interim Greece-Turkey Assistance Committee summarizing testimony, Apr. 24, 1947, ibid.; "Statement by Acting Secretary of State Dean Acheson Before the House Foreign Affairs Committee," Mar. 20, 1947, no. 6 (Greece and Turkey), Papers of Clark Clifford, Truman Lib.; and notes on Acheson's testimony before House Foreign Affairs Committee, Mar. 21, 1947, Papers of Frank McNaughton, ibid. For summation of congressional hearings, see Jones, "*New Kind of War,*" 47–61.

37. Acheson to Sen. Theodore Green (R.I.), Apr. 18, 1947, U.S.-Greek Internal Political Affairs, RG 59, DS; Jones, "*New Kind of War,*" 57–60; Michael B. Stoff, *Oil, War, and American Security: The Search for a National Policy on Foreign Oil, 1941–1947* (New Haven, 1980), 178, 206–8, 212–14; Stephen J. Randall, *United States Foreign Oil Policy, 1919–1948: For Profits and Security* (Montreal, 1985), 237, 241; Michael J. Hogan, "The Search for a 'Creative Peace': The United States, European Unity, and the Origins of the Marshall

Plan," *Diplomatic History* 6 (Summer 1982): 267–85; McLellan, *Acheson,* 112, 115; Kuniholm, *Origins of Cold War in Near East,* 301 n. 247, 427–28, 431. By the end of the war, five of the nation's largest oil companies had huge holdings in the Middle East—Standard Oil of New Jersey, Standard Oil of California, the Texas Company, Socony-Vacuum, and Gulf Oil. See Wittner, *American Intervention in Greece,* 17–22, 60, 232; Paterson, *Soviet-American Confrontation,* chap. 9; Forrestal diaries, May 2, 1947, 7:1610–11, Operational Archives, Naval History Division, Washington Navy Yard, Washington, D.C. (photocopies of originals at Princeton U.); and Arnold A. Rogow, *James Forrestal: A Study of Personality, Politics, and Policy* (N.Y., 1963), 180.

38. Acheson's written replies to Senate questions, 26, 51, 77, 92, encl. in Acheson to Vandenberg, Mar. 24, 1947, U.S.-Greek Internal Political Affairs, RG 59, DS; Acheson's testimony before House hearings on aid bill, Mar. 20, 1947, summary in McNaughton Papers, Truman Lib.; *PM,* Mar. 21, 1947, Democrat Clipping File, ibid.

39. Acheson's written replies to Senate questions, 10, 22, 49, 58, encl. in Acheson to Vandenberg, Mar. 24, 1947, U.S.-Greek Internal Political Affairs, RG 59, DS; Acheson testimony before House hearings on aid bill, Mar. 20, 1947, summary in McNaughton Papers, Truman Lib.; Acheson to Green, Apr. 18, 1947, U.S.-Greek Internal Political Affairs, RG 59, DS; Acheson, *Present at Creation,* 225; Acheson's testimony of Mar. 13, 1947, Senate, *Legislative Origins of Truman Doctrine,* 17; Jones, *Fifteen Weeks,* 193, 196, 262; *Time,* June 9, 1947, p. 27.

40. Anderson, *U.S., G.B., and Cold War,* 152; Yergin, *Shattered Peace,* 270–71; Paterson, *On Every Front,* 155–56; Senate, *Legislative Origins of Truman Doctrine,* 160, 162–64; House of Representatives, *Military Assistance Programs, Part 2,* vol. 6, app. 4, 454; Interim Greece-Turkey Assistance Committee summarizing testimony, Apr. 24, 1947, U.S.-Greek Internal Political Affairs, RG 59, DS; Case to Truman, May 10, 1947, Official File, Truman Papers, Truman Lib.

41. Jones, *Fifteen Weeks,* 184, 197–98; Acheson, *Present at Creation,* 224; Smith, *Acheson,* 48; hearings of Apr. 3, 1947, Senate, *Legislative Origins of Truman Doctrine,* 182; Vandenberg, *Private Papers,* 341–42, 344–49; "Analysis of Comment upon the Proposals by Senator Vandenberg Concerning Aid to Greece and Turkey," ca. Apr. 5, 1947, Joseph M. Jones Papers, Truman Lib. On Lodge, see his testimony of Apr. 2, 1947, Senate, *Legislative Origins of Truman Doctrine,* 141; *Congressional Record,* 80th Cong., 1st sess., Apr. 11, 1947, pt. 3, 93:3335–36; and William J. Miller, *Henry Cabot Lodge: A Biography* (N.Y., 1967), 190. Quotation from Public Law 75 in Jones, "*New Kind of War,*" 243. Congress passed the appropriations bill in July. A Korean aid bill and a push for more aid to China did not fare as well as the Greek-Turkish aid bill. According to Arthur Krock of the *New York Times,* the chairman of the House Appropriations Committee, Republican John Taber of New York, was like "a Pilgrim Father in the savage wilderness . . . [striving] to check and

reduce the ever-growing cost of government." Quoted in William Stueck, *The Wedemeyer Mission: American Politics and Foreign Policy During the Cold War* (Athens, Ga., 1984), 9; see also 25, 93–94.

42. George M. McGhee, "The Impact of Foreign Commitments upon the Coordinative Responsibilities of the Department of State," in *International Commitments and National Administration* (Charlottesville, 1949), 46–48; Truman to Griswold, June 3, 1947, and Griswold to Truman, June 5, 1947, Confidential File, Truman Papers, Truman Lib.; Lincoln, *U.S. Aid to Greece,* 40; Wittner, *American Intervention in Greece,* 101–2. USAGG had been sent to Greece before the aid bill was passed and was activated on the day of the bill's passage. Jones, "*New Kind of War,*" 61. Poor health forced Wilson's retirement in Oct. 1948. His replacement was the ambassador to Iraq, George Wadsworth, who likewise served as both ambassador and chief of mission. See Air Force, "Joint Military Mission for Aid to Turkey, History 1947–June 1950," pp. 7, 10–11, Public Relations Office, 570.9542-1, 1947–50, Simpson Lib., Maxwell Air Force Base, Montgomery, Ala.

43. Edgar O'Ballance, *The Greek Civil War, 1944–1949* (N.Y., 1966), 140, 142, 147–48; C. A. Munkman, *American Aid to Greece: A Report on the First Ten Years* (N.Y., 1958), 35–39; Jones, "*New Kind of War,*" 63–65, 74; copy of UN border commission report of May 23, 1947, box 6, file on Marshall Plan —reports, Greece and Turkey, Acheson Papers, Truman Lib. For Livesay's problems, see Jones, "*New Kind of War,*" 71–72. On the Griswold-MacVeagh difficulties, see ibid., 72–73, 88, 100, 103, 111–14, 131, 161, 163, 168, 277 n. 25. For a critical analysis of the Truman Doctrine in Greece, see Lawrence S. Wittner, "The Truman Doctrine and the Defense of Freedom," *Diplomatic History* 4 (Spring 1980): 161–87. Maj. Gen. Horace L. McBride was chief of the U.S. Army Group, American Mission for Aid to Turkey. He also became chief of the Joint Military Mission for Aid to Turkey in Nov. 1949. See Air Force, "Joint Military Mission for Aid to Turkey," 13; and JCS memo to McBride, Jan. 16, 1948, ABC-400.336 Turkey, RG 107, War Dept.

44. Ambrose, *Rise to Globalism,* 92; Gaddis, *Strategies of Containment,* 26; [Kennan], "Sources of Soviet Conduct." See also Kennan, *Memoirs,* 315. Kennan's identity became known shortly after publication of the article.

45. Jones, "*New Kind of War,*" 84–85, 224; Taubman, *Stalin's American Policy,* 149; Woodhouse, *Struggle for Greece,* 288–89. See also Wittner, *American Intervention in Greece,* 254–55.

SIX ■ THE SEARCH FOR A CREATIVE PEACE THROUGH THE MARSHALL PLAN

1. Paterson, *On Every Front,* 59; John L. Gaddis, *Russia, the Soviet Union, and the United States: An Interpretive History* (N.Y., 1990), 186–87; Ferrell, *Truman and Modern American Presidency,* 72; Forrestal, *Diaries,* 248; Hadley

Arkes, *Bureaucracy, the Marshall Plan, and the National Interest* (Princeton, 1972), 99, 350; Alan S. Milward, *The Reconstruction of Western Europe, 1945–51* (London, 1984), esp. xv, 2, 54; William Diebold, Jr., "The Marshall Plan in Retrospect: A Review of Recent Scholarship," *Journal of International Affairs* 41 (Summer 1988): 421–35. For a firsthand account of Europe's immediate postwar problems, see Thomas A. Bailey, *The Marshall Plan Summer: An Eyewitness Report on Europe and the Russians in 1947* (Stanford, 1977). The theme for this chapter largely derives from Hogan, "Search for a 'Creative Peace,'" 267–85.

2. Pogue, *Marshall,* 168–96; John Gimbel, *The Origins of the Marshall Plan* (Stanford, 1976), 15–16, 126, 130, 138–39; Jones, *Fifteen Weeks,* 221–22.
3. Acheson, *Present at Creation,* 228; Kennan, *Memoirs,* 325–26; Donovan, *Conflict and Crisis,* 288; Jones, *Fifteen Weeks,* 223–24, 240; Gimbel, *Origins of Marshall Plan,* 15–16. For the official history of the Marshall Plan, see Harry B. Price, *The Marshall Plan and Its Meaning* (Ithaca, N.Y., 1955).
4. Clifford, "American Relations with Soviet Union," Sept. 24, 1946, p. 75, President's Secretary's File, Truman Papers, Truman Lib.
5. Report of Special Ad Hoc Committee of State-War-Navy Coordinating Committee, Apr. 21, 1947, *FRUS, 1947,* vol. 3, *The British Commonwealth; Europe* (Washington, D.C., 1972), 204–19; Michael J. Hogan, *The Marshall Plan: America, Britain, and the Reconstruction of Western Europe, 1947–1952* (Cambridge, 1987), 40; Jones, *Fifteen Weeks,* 199. Gimbel argues that no plan existed. The SWNCC report, he insists, was "a hodgepodge of observations, recommendations, suggestions, and conclusions that the committee itself considered to be lacking in thorough analysis." Gimbel, *Origins of Marshall Plan,* 10. See also Melvyn P. Leffler, "The United States and the Strategic Dimensions of the Marshall Plan," *Diplomatic History* 12 (Summer 1988): 277–306; and Armin Rappaport, "The United States and European Integration: The First Phase," *Diplomatic History* 5 (Spring 1981): 121–49. For background, see Randall B. Woods, *A Changing of the Guard: Anglo-America, 1941–1946* (Chapel Hill, 1990).
6. Acheson to Robert Patterson, Mar. 5, 1947, *FRUS, 1947,* 5:94–95; Gimbel, *Origins of Marshall Plan,* 14; Clayton memo of Mar. 5, 1947, cited in Donovan, *Conflict and Crisis,* 283; Clayton memo of May 27, 1947, *FRUS, 1947,* 3:232. Marshall was not willing to go as far as Clayton in advocating central control by the United States. Pogue, *Marshall,* 207. For the Marshall Plan's emphasis on reestablishing the European balance of power and providing a better basis for the worldwide security of the United States, see Leffler, "Strategic Dimensions of Marshall Plan." See also Leffler, "The American Conception of National Security and the Beginnings of the Cold War, 1945–1948," *American Historical Review* 89 (Apr. 1984): 346–81. Charles L. Mee, Jr., regards the Marshall Plan as an effort to bring balance to a foreign policy that had gone too far in a military direction with the Truman Doctrine. Mee, *The Marshall Plan: The Launching of the Pax Americana* (N.Y., 1984), 75–76, 94–95. For

an excellent account of the complex, varied, and shifting motives behind the move toward the Marshall Plan, see Scott Jackson, "Prologue to the Marshall Plan: The Origins of the American Commitment for a European Recovery Program," *Journal of American History* 65 (Mar. 1979): 1043–68.

7. House of Representatives, Committee on International Relations, *Foreign Economic Assistance Programs, Part 2: Extension of the European Recovery Program* (Washington, D.C., 1976), 4:38; Imannuel Wexler, *The Marshall Plan Revisited: The European Recovery Program in Economic Perspective* (Westport, Conn., 1983), 4–5; Acheson, *Present at Creation,* 227–30; Donovan, *Conflict and Crisis,* 279–80. Paterson calls Western Europe "part of the American sphere of influence." Paterson, *On Every Front,* 59.
8. Donovan, *Conflict and Crisis,* 288; Kennan memo of May 16, 1947, *FRUS, 1947,* 3:220–23; Kennan to Acheson, May 23, 1947, ibid., 223; Kennan, *Memoirs,* 335–37; Gimbel, *Origins of Marshall Plan,* 11, 248–49; Jones, *Fifteen Weeks,* 249–52. Mee argues that Kennan and the Policy Planning Staff had compiled a "superb report" in that it combined "all of the worries and expectations, assumptions and aspirations that had been tossed about in the State Department during the past months: the fear of communism, the need for an anti-Communist program, the political usefulness of exploiting anti-Communist sentiments, the electoral requirements of the President, the economic fears of Will Clayton and others who thought as he did, the dreams of the Anglophiles such as Acheson and balance-of-power theorists such as Kennan himself, the greedy and the power-seekers, the altruists and humanitarians, those who wished to rebuild Germany and those who feared Germany, those who wished to help Britain and those who wished to take over Britain's sterling bloc. And what was most wonderful of all was that the new policy could be summed up in a single word: containment." Mee, *Marshall Plan,* 91–92.
9. Kennan, *Memoirs,* 335–37.
10. Ibid., 342; Milward, *Reconstruction of Western Europe,* 64 n. 18; Hogan, *Marshall Plan,* 52; Leffler, "Strategic Dimensions of Marshall Plan," 283; Jones, *Fifteen Weeks,* 253; Donovan, *Conflict and Crisis,* 289–90.
11. Forrestal, *Diaries,* 288.
12. Milward, *Reconstruction of Western Europe,* 54; Gimbel, *Origins of Marshall Plan,* 5, 38, 89 (quoting Caffery), 179, 188.
13. Gimbel, *Origins of Marshall Plan,* 6–7, 289 (quoting Marshall); Hogan, *Marshall Plan,* 43, 54; Jones, *Fifteen Weeks,* 31–36; Donovan, *Conflict and Crisis,* 289. The principal author of the secretary's speech was Bohlen. Hogan, *Marshall Plan,* 43; Pogue, *Marshall,* 210.
14. Clayton memo, May 27, 1947, *FRUS, 1947,* 3:230–31; Milward, *Reconstruction of Western Europe,* 2 n. 2, 3, 61, and esp. chap. 1; Arkes, *Bureaucracy, Marshall Plan, and National Interest,* 367 (quoting Marshall).
15. Donovan, *Conflict and Crisis,* 290; Paterson, *On Every Front,* 61; Walter LaFeber, *America, Russia, and the Cold War, 1945–1984* (N.Y., 1985), 60.

16. Hogan, *Marshall Plan,* 51–52, 109; Milward, *Reconstruction of Western Europe,* 142. Wexler concludes that "it is not *un*reasonable to suggest that, given the nature of the 'approach' outlined in the memorandum and the likely Soviet reaction to it, the Paris conference was probably doomed to failure before it even started." Wexler, *Marshall Plan Revisited,* 11. Hogan asserts that the British wanted to combine Western Europe with the British Commonwealth in a "middle kingdom" free of either U.S. or Soviet control. Hogan, *Marshall Plan,* 88.
17. Mee, *Marshall Plan,* 130 (quoting Molotov); Wexler, *Marshall Plan Revisited,* 10 (quoting Clayton).
18. Mee, *Marshall Plan,* 131, 134; Hogan, *Marshall Plan,* 51–52, 88; Donovan, *Conflict and Crisis,* 290; Paterson, *On Every Front,* 61.
19. For a good account of the Paris meeting, see Mee, *Marshall Plan,* 130–36. Harriman and Kennan quoted ibid., 136.
20. Paterson, *On Every Front,* 61 (quoting Lodge); Wexler, *Marshall Plan Revisited,* 9; Margaret Truman, *Harry S. Truman* (N.Y., 1973), 353 (quoting Clifford and Truman).
21. Hogan, *Marshall Plan,* 52, 60; Acheson, *Present at Creation,* 234–35; Wexler, *Marshall Plan Revisited,* 12; Kolko and Kolko, *Limits of Power,* 386 (quoting Stalin). See also Yergin, *Shattered Peace,* 316–17.
22. Wexler, *Marshall Plan Revisited,* 12; Milward, *Reconstruction of Western Europe,* 70–71, 87–89; Donovan, *Conflict and Crisis,* 290; Hogan, *Marshall Plan,* 87; Balfour to Michael Wright, Aug. 1, 1947, FO 371/61031, PRO; F. B. A. Rundall minute, Aug. 8, 1947, North American Department, ibid. (quoting Balfour to Hall-Patch, July 11, 1948). The sixteen participating nations were Britain, France, Austria, Belgium, Denmark, Greece, Iceland, Ireland, Italy, Luxembourg, the Netherlands, Norway, Portugal, Sweden, Switzerland, and Turkey.
23. Representative quoted in Theodore A. Wilson, *The Marshall Plan* (N.Y., 1977), 23.
24. Ulam, *Expansion and Coexistence,* 436; Gaddis, *Russia, Soviet Union, and U.S.,* 190 (quoting Truman press conference); Donovan, *Conflict and Crisis,* 311 (quoting Cominform); LaFeber, *America, Russia, and Cold War,* 60, 69–70; McCoy, *Presidency of Truman,* 126.
25. Donovan, *Conflict and Crisis,* 340–41; Hogan, *Marshall Plan,* 84; Vandenberg, *Private Papers,* 376, 382.
26. Mee, *Marshall Plan,* 217, 219–20; Wexler, *Marshall Plan Revisited,* 26–27; Donovan, *Conflict and Crisis,* 341; Milward, *Reconstruction of Western Europe,* 51, 82–83.
27. Donovan, *Conflict and Crisis,* 341; Paterson, *On Every Front,* 123; Wexler, *Marshall Plan Revisited,* 31; Michael Wala, "Selling the Marshall Plan at Home: The Committee for the Marshall Plan to Aid European Recovery," *Diplomatic History* 10 (Summer 1986): 247–65; Richard E. Neustadt, *Presidential Power: The Politics of Leadership* (N.Y., 1960), 49.

28. Donovan, *Conflict and Crisis,* 341; Forrestal, *Diaries,* 341; Stueck, *Wedemeyer Mission,* 103. See also Stueck, *The Road to Confrontation: American Policy Toward China and Korea, 1947–1950* (Chapel Hill, 1981), 58–59.
29. Wexler, *Marshall Plan Revisited,* 25; Donovan, *Conflict and Crisis,* 341–42; *Public Papers of the Presidents of the United States: Harry S. Truman, 1947* (Washington, D.C., 1963), 515; J. H. Dickinson minute, Dec. 24, 1947, FO 371/61035, PRO.
30. Maj. C. B. Ormerod to W. P. N. Edwards, Sept. 8, 1947, FO 371/61035, PRO (quoting Taft); LaFeber, *America, Russia, and Cold War,* 71; Hogan, *Marshall Plan,* 94–98 (quoting Hazlitt on 96), 101.
31. Bohlen memo of conversation, Aug. 30, 1947, *FRUS, 1947,* vol. 1, *General; The United Nations* (Washington, D.C., 1973), 762–65.
32. *Public Papers of the Presidents of the United States: Harry S. Truman, 1948* (Washington, D.C., 1964), 182, 360; Donovan, *Conflict and Crisis,* 136–37.
33. Donovan, *Conflict and Crisis,* 357–58; LaFeber, *America, Russia, and Cold War,* 72.
34. Paterson, *On Every Front,* 63 (quoting Acheson); Steinhardt to Marshall, Feb. 26, 1948, *FRUS, 1948,* vol. 4, *Eastern Europe; The Soviet Union* (Washington, D.C., 1974), 738–41; M. Truman, *Truman,* 359; Donovan, *Conflict and Crisis,* 358 (quoting NSC-7, Mar. 30, 1948).
35. Donovan, *Conflict and Crisis,* 358 and 360 (quoting Truman); LaFeber, *America, Russia, and Cold War,* 72; *Public Papers of Presidents: Truman, 1948,* 186.
36. Neustadt, *Presidential Power,* 50 (quoting Truman). See also Hogan, *Marshall Plan,* 52, 429–30; and McCoy, *Presidency of Truman,* 128.
37. McCoy, *Presidency of Truman,* 127–28 (quoting Truman); Joseph W. Martin, Jr., *My First Fifty Years in Politics* (N.Y., 1960), 193.
38. Hogan, *Marshall Plan,* 89, 101–3, 105, 108, 155; Donovan, *Conflict and Crisis,* 361; Mee, *Marshall Plan,* 248; Arkes, *Bureaucracy, Marshall Plan, and National Interest,* 100–101, 135–36, 147, 150, 211–12; Wexler, *Marshall Plan Revisited,* 5, 54, 59, 155, 198, 208, 210. Wexler shows that the European Payments Union served as a "clearing and settlement mechanism." Ibid., 200–201.
39. Wexler, *Marshall Plan Revisited,* 158; Arkes, *Bureaucracy, Marshall Plan, and National Interest,* 151–52, 156–58; Milward, *Reconstruction of Western Europe,* 179; Hogan, *Marshall Plan,* 85; Price, *Marshall Plan and Its Meaning,* 294 (quoting OEEC member).
40. Paterson, *On Every Front,* 62 (quoting NSC-7), 64 (quoting Council on Foreign Relations); Hogan, *Marshall Plan,* 89, 90 (quoting Lodge and Dulles); Paterson, *Soviet-American Confrontation,* 207 (quoting Elsey). See also Milward, *Reconstruction of Western Europe,* 53–54, 56–57.
41. Hogan, *Marshall Plan,* xii, 1–3, 19, 21–23, 26–27, 35, 37; Wexler, *Marshall Plan Revisited,* 144, 157; Gimbel, *Origins of Marshall Plan,* 258. See also Michael J. Hogan, "Revival and Reform: America's Twentieth-Century

Search for a New Economic Order Abroad," *Diplomatic History* 8 (Fall 1984): 287–310. This argument has become known as the "corporatist synthesis," with Hogan being a chief advocate. The so-called New School of thought has sparked a controversy among diplomatic historians. For the arguments, see John L. Gaddis, "The Corporate Synthesis: A Skeptical View," ibid. 10 (Fall 1986): 357–62, and Michael J. Hogan, "Corporatism: A Positive Appraisal," ibid., 363–72.

42. Milward, *Reconstruction of Western Europe,* 43, 57, 59, 221. The State Dept. officer quoted was Paul R. Porter (not to be confused with Paul A. Porter, who headed the economic mission to Greece in 1946). Gimbel argues that acceptance of multilateral trade theory did not mean acceptance of the open-door theory denounced by revisionist historians such as William Appleman Williams. Gimbel, *Origins of Marshall Plan,* 269. Multilateral trade was intended to establish harmonious economic and political relations that would be conducive to world peace. The open-door policy, Williams declares, rests on the argument that capitalism's welfare at home depends on economic expansion abroad, a reliance that places limitations on legitimate revolutionary changes in other countries. See Williams, *Tragedy of American Diplomacy.* For the argument that the Truman administration used chiefly economic means to promote U.S. security from 1945 until the outbreak of the Korean War in 1950, see Robert A. Pollard, "Economic Security and the Origins of the Cold War: Bretton Woods, the Marshall Plan, and American Rearmament, 1944–50," *Diplomatic History* 9 (Summer 1985): 271–89.

43. Gaddis, *Long Peace,* 57 (quoting Berry to Kennan, July 31, 1947), 48 and 57n (quoting Kennan); Bohlen, *Witness to History,* 174–77; Bohlen memo, Aug. 30, 1947, *FRUS,* 1947, 1:763–64; Forrestal, *Diaries,* 341 (citing Marshall). See also ibid., 307. For an excellent analysis of how the United States moved toward the spheres-of-influence idea in postwar Europe, see Gaddis, *Long Peace,* chap. 3. On the one-world argument, see Wendell Willkie, *One World* (N.Y., 1943), and Sumner Welles, *The Time for Decision* (N.Y., 1944). For the argument that the Marshall Plan further solidified the growing East-West division in Europe and helped to promote a stability conducive to peace, see A. W. DePorte, *Europe Between the Superpowers: The Enduring Balance* (New Haven, 1979), ix, 134.

SEVEN ■ EMERGING CRISIS IN BERLIN

1. Avi Shlaim, *The United States and the Berlin Blockade, 1948–1949: A Study in Decision-Making* (Berkeley, 1983), 12, 16, 18, 139; Truman, *Memoirs,* 123, 131; LaFeber, *America, Russia, and Cold War,* 75; Paterson, *On Every Front,* 64. William Taubman argues that the Soviets' chief concern was to keep Germany weak, whether or not that aim entailed Western departure from Berlin. See his *Stalin's American Policy,* 182. Adam B. Ulam says it "was not excus-

able" for the Western powers to believe that the USSR's purpose was to force them out of Berlin. The Soviets' central objective, he argues, was to prevent the establishment of a strong West Germany. Ulam, *The Rivals: America and Russia Since World War II* (N.Y., 1971), 148–49. See also Ulam's *Stalin: The Man and His Era* (N.Y., 1973), 686–88. Ulam believes that Stalin feared a rearmed West German state more than the United States' atomic monopoly. See his *Expansion and Coexistence,* 504.

2. Donovan, *Conflict and Crisis,* 363.
3. Shlaim, *U.S. and Berlin Blockade,* 19–20; Gimbel, *American Occupation of Germany,* 202–3; Manuel Gottlieb, *The German Peace Settlement and the Berlin Crisis* (N.Y., 1960), 15–16, 38–39; Djilas, *Conversations with Stalin,* 153–54 (quoting Stalin); Taubman, *Stalin's American Policy,* 153–54. See also DePorte, *Europe Between Superpowers,* 153. Revisionist historians have argued that the United States pursued economic expansion and the spread of capitalism in Germany. See Kuklick, *American Policy and Division of Germany,* esp. 2. For a convincing refutation, see Backer, *Decision to Divide Germany,* ix, 175–76. Jean Edward Smith argues that the Soviets "blundered into the blockade in response to a particular set of circumstances, and not, as the traditional mythology tells us, as part of a global conspiracy or master plan laid carefully in advance." Smith, "General Clay and the Russians: A Continuation of the Wartime Alliance in Germany, 1945–1948," *Virginia Quarterly Review* 64 (Winter 1988): 36.
4. Smith calls the Soviet blockade a defensive move against the Marshall Plan and the possible establishment of a West German government. Smith, "Clay and Russians," 35. See also LaFeber, *America, Russia, and Cold War,* 75. For Stalin's domestic difficulties, see Ulam, *Rivals,* 113; Ulam, *Stalin,* 643; Taubman, *Stalin's American Policy,* 139–40; and Hahn, *Postwar Soviet Politics.* For Stalin's personal characteristics, see Ulam, *Stalin;* Tucker, *Soviet Political Mind,* 220, 229–30; and *Khrushchev Remembers,* 246.
5. W. Phillips Davison, *The Berlin Blockade: A Study in Cold War Politics* (Princeton, 1958), xi; DePorte, *Europe Between Superpowers,* 154. Shlaim argues that use of the bomb was a serious option because the Berlin crisis was the "first open and direct confrontation between the principal Cold War antagonists themselves." Shlaim, *U.S. and Berlin Blockade,* 38.
6. Daniel J. Nelson, *Wartime Origins of the Berlin Dilemma* (University, Ala., 1978), 29–33, 57, 142, 144–45, 150. Roosevelt also opposed the British proposal because it made the United States responsible for postwar France, and it did not include occupation zones that corresponded with his interest in dismembering Germany. Ibid., 31. Jean Edward Smith chastises the State Department and the U.S. representatives on the European Advisory Commission for failing to secure agreements that would have prevented Berlin's isolation inside the Soviet zone. Smith, *The Defense of Berlin* (Baltimore, 1963), 23–24, 32–33.
7. Davison, *Berlin Blockade,* 4, 27–31; Frank Howley, *Berlin Command* (N.Y.,

of the United States Government which on the eve of a hazardous invasion would have been willing to shoulder the responsibility for a refusal" (Backer's italics). Ibid., 130.

26. Davison, *Berlin Blockade,* 47–72; Clay, *Decision in Germany,* 159.
27. Davison, *Berlin Blockade,* 15–16; Clay, *Decision in Germany,* 174; Shlaim, *U.S. and Berlin Blockade,* 27–29; Backer, *Decision to Divide Germany,* 170. Clay had been so upset with the Truman Doctrine and the United States' hard-line attitude toward the Soviet Union that he returned from Moscow to Berlin at the end of the second week of the conference, ready to resign. The United States was moving too close to the French, he insisted. But his friend General Eisenhower pointed out his duty as a soldier and convinced him to stay. Smith, "Clay and Russians," 31–32.
28. Gimbel, *American Occupation of Germany,* 121–23; Gimbel, *Origins of Marshall Plan,* 121 (quoting Marshall), 126, 188; Smith, "Clay and Russians," 21–22, 25. Gimbel argues that the State Dept.'s accusations against the Soviets regarding the reparations issue were a "deliberate and calculated distortion of the historical record." Gimbel, *Origins of Marshall Plan,* 138. Smith has remarked that it "may appear odd" that Murphy's letter (which arrived shortly after Kennan's Long Telegram of Feb. 1946) is not in the State Dept.'s *Foreign Relations* volume for this period. Smith, "Clay and Russians," 22.
29. Yergin, *Shattered Peace,* 171–72.
30. DePorte, *Europe Between Superpowers,* 151; Shlaim, *U.S. and Berlin Blockade,* 33.
31. Lucius D. Clay, *Germany and the Fight for Freedom* (Cambridge, Mass., 1950), 36; Harrington, "American Policy in Berlin Crisis," 41; Davison, *Berlin Blockade,* 18; Shlaim, *U.S. and Berlin Blockade,* 30 (quoting Marshall).
32. Shlaim, *U.S. and Berlin Blockade,* 31; Harrington, "American Policy in Berlin Crisis," 27–28, 110 (quoting CIA memo of Dec. 22, 1947); Clay, *Decision in Germany,* 348; Ferrell, *Marshall,* 140; Forrestal, *Diaries,* 353–54. Regarding Marshall's remark, Clay later declared: "This was the only time I ever saw Molotov wince perceptibly." Clay, *Decision in Germany,* 348. The CIA director was Adm. Roscoe H. Hillenkoetter.
33. Shlaim, *U.S. and Berlin Blockade,* 111 (quoting Army General Staff study); Clay, *Decision in Germany,* 351, 354; Davison, *Berlin Blockade,* 63, 73; Smith, *Defense of Berlin,* 100; Robert Murphy, *Diplomat Among Warriors* (Garden City, N.Y., 1964), 311–12; Murphy to Marshall, Mar. 3, 1948, *FRUS, 1948,* vol. 2, *Germany and Austria* (Washington, D.C., 1973), 878–79; Clay to Lt. Gen. Stephen J. Chamberlin, Mar. 5, 1948, *The Papers of General Lucius D. Clay, 1945–1949,* ed. Jean Edward Smith (Bloomington, 1974), 2:568; Forrestal, *Diaries,* 387; Donovan, *Conflict and Crisis,* 359 (quoting Truman). The editor of Clay's papers argues that Clay had been asked by Army Intelligence to write something intended to stir Congress to approve more military aid for Germany. The cable, Smith insists, "was not, in Clay's opinion, related to any change in Soviet strategy." Clay, *Papers,* 2:568. See also Smith, "Clay and

Russians," 33–34. Shlaim calls the cable a "cynical ploy." Shlaim, *U.S. and Berlin Blockade,* 107.

34. DePorte, *Europe Between Superpowers,* 152; Taubman, *Stalin's American Policy,* 182; Kennan, *Memoirs,* 401–2. The death of Jan Masaryk in March greatly intensified the atmosphere of the conference.

35. Donovan, *Conflict and Crisis,* 359; Djilas, *Conversations with Stalin,* 119.

36. Shlaim, *U.S. and Berlin Blockade,* 34; LaFeber, *America, Russia, and Cold War,* 75; communiqué of London Conference on Germany, Mar. 6, 1948, *FRUS, 1948,* 2:141–43; Marshall to U.S. embassy in France, Feb. 19, 1948, ibid., 71.

37. Davison, *Berlin Blockade,* 18; London communiqué of Mar. 6, 1948, *FRUS, 1948,* 2:142.

38. Murphy to Marshall, Mar. 20 and Apr. 1, 1948, *FRUS, 1948,* 2:883–84, 885; Clay, *Decision in Germany,* 355–57; Shlaim, *U.S. and Berlin Blockade,* 113–14; Gimbel, *American Occupation of Germany,* 204–5, 254; Davison, *Berlin Blockade,* 19–20; LaFeber, *America, Russia, and Cold War,* 75; Truman, *Memoirs,* 122.

39. Kennan, *Memoirs,* 401; Shlaim, *U.S. and Berlin Blockade,* 44, 117–18. Clay had wanted an unlimited embargo because he believed it virtually impossible to determine which goods were important to Soviet production. Ibid., 118–19.

40. Curtis E. LeMay, *Mission with LeMay: My Story* (N.Y., 1965), 411–13; Shlaim, *U.S. and Berlin Blockade,* 120–21. U.S. goods entered at Bremerhaven, located at the mouth of the Weser River in the northwest and 250 miles from Frankfurt.

41. Donovan, *Conflict and Crisis,* 363–64; Howley, *Berlin Command,* 192–93; Davison, *Berlin Blockade,* 65, 73.

42. Forrestal, *Diaries,* 408; Shlaim, *U.S. and Berlin Blockade,* 122; Donovan, *Conflict and Crisis,* 364; Clay, *Decision in Germany,* 360–61.

43. Shlaim, *U.S. and Berlin Blockade,* 44, 127; Forrestal, *Diaries,* 408; teleconferences between Clay and Royall and between Clay and Bradley, Mar. 31, 1948, Clay, *Papers,* 2:602–4, 605–6.

44. Clay to Bradley, Apr. 1, 1948, Clay, *Papers,* 2:607; Clay, *Decision in Germany,* 359; Smith, *Defense of Berlin,* 104; Donovan, *Conflict and Crisis,* 364; Shlaim, *U.S. and Berlin Blockade,* 129, 142 (quoting Robertson). British trains received the same treatment.

45. Smith, "Clay and Russians," 36; Shlaim, *U.S. and Berlin Blockade,* 130–31 (citing intelligence report and quoting Bradley).

46. Donovan, *Conflict and Crisis,* 364–65; Smith, *Defense of Berlin,* 105; Clay to Bradley, Apr. 1, 1948, Clay, *Papers,* 2:607; Clay, *Decision in Germany,* 358–59; Davison, *Berlin Blockade,* 64.

47. Lewis Douglas (U.S. ambassador in London), to Undersec. of State Robert Lovett, Apr. 17, 1948, *FRUS, 1948,* 2:895–96; Alexander L. George and Richard Smoke, *Deterrence in American Foreign Policy: Theory and Prac-*

tice (N.Y., 1974), 123; Donovan, *Conflict and Crisis,* 365; Davison, *Berlin Blockade,* 65–66 (quoting Sokolovsky on 66).

48. Marshall to Douglas, Apr. 30, 1948, *FRUS, 1948,* 2:900 n. 2; Shlaim, *U.S. and Berlin Blockade,* 141; Davison, *Berlin Blockade,* 66–67 (quoting Soviets on 67).
49. Djilas, *Conversations with Stalin,* 153; Taubman, *Stalin's American Policy,* 182; Shlaim, *U.S. and Berlin Blockade,* 12 (quoting CIA); State Dept. policy statement on Germany, Aug. 26, 1948, *FRUS, 1948,* 2:1314–15; Clay, *Decision in Germany,* 361; teleconference between Clay and Bradley, Apr. 10, 1948, Clay, *Papers,* 2:623; Lucius D. Clay, "Berlin," *Foreign Affairs* 41 (Oct. 1962): 47–58.
50. Truman, *Memoirs,* 122–23; teleconference between Clay and Royall, Mar. 31, 1948, Clay, *Papers,* 2:602–3; Clay, *Decision in Germany,* 25–26; Shlaim, *U.S. and Berlin Blockade,* 15; Nelson, *Wartime Origins of Berlin Dilemma,* 132–35.
51. Nelson, *Wartime Origins of Berlin Dilemma,* 132–34.
52. Ibid., 134, 142; Shlaim, *U.S. and Berlin Blockade,* 123–24; Donovan, *Conflict and Crisis,* 365.
53. Arkes, *Bureaucracy, Marshall Plan, and National Interest,* 112; Donovan, *Conflict and Crisis,* 365–66 (quoting NSC-9 on 366); Lawrence S. Kaplan, *The United States and NATO: The Formative Years* (Lexington, Ky., 1984), 42, 70.
54. LaFeber, *America, Russia, and Cold War,* 77–78; Paterson, *On Every Front,* 107.

EIGHT ■ EQUIVALENT RESPONSE: BERLIN BLOCKADE AND AIRLIFT

1. Davison, *Berlin Blockade,* 62–64.
2. Ibid., 62–64, 68–69.
3. Communiqué of London Conference on Germany, released to press on June 7, 1948, *FRUS, 1948,* 2:313–17; report of London Conference, June 1, 1948, ibid., 309–12; Murphy to Marshall, June 17, 1948, ibid., 908–9. See Howley's account in Howley, *Berlin Command,* 180–84. See also Taubman, *Stalin's American Policy,* 187; Davison, *Berlin Blockade,* 18, 20, 70; and Shlaim, *U.S. and Berlin Blockade,* 149–50, 154–55. On June 17, at 4:30 in the morning, the French National Assembly voted 297–189 for the London Recommendations but urged the government in Paris to make new arrangements on control of the Ruhr, to demand decentralized administration of Germany, and to push for four-power control. See Harrington, "American Policy in Berlin Crisis," 56, 68.

4. Shlaim, *U.S. and Berlin Blockade,* 158; LaFeber, *America, Russia, and Cold War,* 75–76; Donovan, *Conflict and Crisis,* 359; Gottlieb, *German Peace Settlement and Berlin Crisis,* 194. The French acquiesced in currency reform only after putting in writing a denial of responsibility for the decision. Clay, *Decision in Germany,* 364.
5. Davison, *Berlin Blockade,* 77, 89, 91–92; Clay, *Decision in Germany,* 364; Shlaim, *U.S. and Berlin Blockade,* 156–57; Smith, *Defense of Berlin,* 106; Donovan, *Conflict and Crisis,* 367. The legislation authorized the replacement of ten reichsmarks by one new deutsche mark. Davison, *Berlin Blockade,* 20. The French agreed to go along with the West but thought that their Anglo-American allies had exaggerated Berlin's importance and had therefore tied prestige to an area that was militarily vulnerable. Harrington, "American Policy in Berlin Crisis," 89.
6. Smith, *Defense of Berlin,* 106; Donovan, *Conflict and Crisis,* 367; Shlaim, *U.S. and Berlin Blockade,* 44, 158–59; Davison, *Berlin Blockade,* 90, 95–96. The Western banknotes were stamped "B" for Berlin. Shlaim, *U.S. and Berlin Blockade,* 161.
7. Davison, *Berlin Blockade,* 96–98; Smith, *Defense of Berlin,* 115. The assemblywoman was Jeanette Wolff. Ibid.
8. Davison, *Berlin Blockade,* 90, 98–99; Shlaim, *U.S. and Berlin Blockade,* 162; Smith, *Defense of Berlin,* 106; Howley, *Berlin Command,* 196–97.
9. Gimbel, *American Occupation of Germany,* 205–6, 254–55; Ulam, *Stalin,* 686–88; LaFeber, *America, Russia, and Cold War,* 76–77; Gaddis, *Russia, Soviet Union, and U.S.,* 191–93; Paterson, *On Every Front,* 65; Harrington, "American Policy in Berlin Crisis," 89; Davison, *Berlin Blockade,* 26.
10. Shlaim, *U.S. and Berlin Blockade,* 196–97; Davison, *Berlin Blockade,* 22–23.
11. Davison, *Berlin Blockade,* 23–25.
12. Ibid., 152; Shlaim, *U.S. and Berlin Blockade,* 196 (citing memo by director of the CIA Roscoe H. Hillenkoetter), 197.
13. Howley, *Berlin Command,* 11–12; Davison, *Berlin Blockade,* 77, 83, 84 (quoting city official), 93.
14. Davison, *Berlin Blockade,* 99–100; Howley, *Berlin Command,* 200.
15. Shlaim, *U.S. and Berlin Blockade,* 172, 202–3; Davison, *Berlin Blockade,* 104–5. For Clay's proposals, see Harrington, "American Policy in Berlin Crisis," 123–24.
16. Clay to Dept. of Army, June 25, 1948, *FRUS, 1948,* 2:918; Smith, *Defense of Berlin,* 97–98, 107.
17. Howley, *Berlin Command,* 204; Shlaim, *U.S. and Berlin Blockade,* 243; Davison, *Berlin Blockade,* 105; Murphy, *Diplomat Among Warriors,* 318; LeMay, *Mission with LeMay,* 415; Clay, *Decision in Berlin,* 365; Harrington, "American Policy in Berlin Crisis," 119–21 (quoted).
18. Davison, *Berlin Blockade,* 110; Shlaim, *U.S. and Berlin Blockade,* 206. For an absorbing account, see Ann and John Tusa, *The Berlin Airlift* (N.Y., 1988).
19. Shlaim, *U.S. and Berlin Blockade,* 206, 210.

20. Howley, *Berlin Command,* 10; teleconference between Clay and Royall, June 25, 1948, Clay, *Papers,* 2:700, 702–3; teleconference between Clay and Maj. Gen. Daniel Noce, June 26, 1948, ibid., 706; Clay, *Decision in Berlin,* 366; Smith, "Clay and Russians," 20–36.
21. Davison, *Berlin Blockade,* 107–8, 116; Harrington, "American Policy in Berlin Crisis," 93 (quoting French); Smith, *Defense of Berlin,* 109–10; *Parliamentary Debates* (Commons), vol. 452 (June 30, 1948), 2213–18, 2221–34.
22. Murphy to Marshall, June 26, 1948, and Lewis Douglas (U.S. ambassador in London) to Marshall, June 26, 1948, *FRUS, 1948,* 2:919–21, 921–26; Jacob Beam memo, June 28, 1948, ibid., 928–29; Davison, *Berlin Blockade,* 108; Truman, *Memoirs,* 123; Shlaim, *U.S. and Berlin Blockade,* 214; Howley, *Berlin Command,* 236. To the words quoted in the text Howley added: "except that I have never been known to use the word *derrière*." Ibid.
23. Forrestal, *Diaries,* 452–54; Marshall to Douglas, June 27, 1948, *FRUS, 1948,* 2:926–28; Shlaim, *U.S. and Berlin Blockade,* 219; Davison, *Berlin Blockade,* 109–10.
24. Forrestal, *Diaries,* 454–55; Marshall to Douglas, June 27 and 28, 1948, *FRUS, 1948,* 2:926, 930–31; Harrington, "American Policy in Berlin Crisis," 91–92.
25. Marshall to Douglas, June 28, 1948, *FRUS, 1948,* 2:931; Donovan, *Conflict and Crisis,* 367–68; Davison, *Berlin Blockade,* 110; Herken, *Winning Weapon,* 258–59; Harrington, "American Policy in Berlin Crisis," 110; Clay to Draper, June 27, 1948, Clay, *Papers,* 2:708; Davison, *Berlin Blockade,* 117; Forrestal, *Diaries,* 456.
26. Paterson, *On Every Front,* 65. For a criticism of U.S. intelligence regarding its failure to foresee the split nearly six months earlier, see Robert M. Blum, "Surprised by Tito: The Anatomy of an Intelligence Failure," *Diplomatic History* 12 (Winter 1988): 39–57. Blum admits, however, that the failure did not affect U.S. policy, because the Truman administration did not consider it wise to become involved. The White House did nonetheless try to encourage the rift by sending aid to Yugoslavia. See Lorraine M. Lees, "The American Decision to Assist Tito, 1948–1949," *Diplomatic History* 2 (Fall 1978): 407–22. Among studies of the schism, see Hamilton Fish Armstrong, *Tito and Goliath* (N.Y., 1951); Adam B. Ulam, *Titoism and the Cominform* (Cambridge, Mass., 1952); and Vladimir Dedijer, *The Battle Stalin Lost: Memoirs of Yugoslavia, 1948–1953* (N.Y., 1971).
27. LaFeber, *America, Russia, and Cold War,* 76.
28. Donovan, *Conflict and Crisis,* 366–67; Ambrose, *Rise to Globalism,* 95–96. From 1949 to 1953, for example, the United States cooperated with Britain in unsuccessfully trying to depose Albania's Enver Hoxha. See Nicholas Bethell, *The Great Betrayal: The Untold Story of Kim Philby's Biggest Coup* (London, 1984), 1–6, 36–39, 51–52, 94, 100–101, 105–6, 113–14; Bruce Page, David Leitch, and Phillip Knightley, *The Philby Conspiracy* (Garden City, N.Y., 1968), 197–202; Jones, "*New Kind of War,*" 304–5 n. 41, 307 n. 6, 313 n. 6; and Gaddis, *Long Peace,* 160.

29. Davison, *Berlin Blockade,* 125–26, 129; Harrington, "American Policy in Berlin Crisis," 117, 119.
30. Davison, *Berlin Blockade,* 118, 124; Kennan, *Memoirs,* 421.
31. Davison, *Berlin Blockade,* 122–23; Smith, *Defense of Berlin,* 116–17; Clay, *Papers,* 2:722–24; Clay, *Decision in Germany,* 367; Marshall to Douglas, July 3 and 9, 1948, *FRUS, 1948,* 2:946–48, 954–56; Harrington, "American Policy in Berlin Crisis," 102.
32. Davison, *Berlin Blockade,* 128; Shlaim, *U.S. and Berlin Blockade,* 231, 233 (quoting Soviets).
33. Harrington, "American Policy in Berlin Crisis," 102–3; Bohlen to Marshall, July 14, 1948, *FRUS, 1948,* 2:966; M. Truman, *Truman,* 12.
34. Shlaim, *U.S. and Berlin Blockade,* 241–42 (quoting Lippmann); Clay to Bradley, July 10, 1948, Clay, *Papers,* 2:734–35; Clay, *Decision in Germany,* 374; teleconference between Col. R. W. Mayo in Washington and Brig. Gen. V. E. Pritchard in Berlin, July 13, 1948, Clay, *Papers,* 2:736–38; Davison, *Berlin Blockade,* 126, 153; Forrestal, *Diaries,* 459–60; Truman, *Memoirs,* 124; Shlaim, *U.S. and Berlin Blockade,* 240–41.
35. Davison, *Berlin Blockade,* 129–30; Herken, *Winning Weapon,* 259 (quoting *N.Y. Times*); Gaddis, *Long Peace,* 109; Shlaim, *U.S. and Berlin Blockade,* 239. The first plane capable of delivering atomic bombs went to England during the summer of 1949. The planes that arrived in England in July 1948 became the basis of the first U.S. Strategic Air Command base in that area. In August the United States sent thirty more. Ibid., 236–38; Davison, *Berlin Blockade,* 155. Whether Stalin would have heeded such information on the United States' atomic capacity is problematic; in 1941 he failed to listen to Soviet intelligence warnings of a Nazi invasion. Taubman, *Stalin's American Policy,* 194, 275 n. 3.
36. Herken, *Winning Weapon,* 241, 263; David A. Rosenberg, "American Atomic Strategy and the Hydrogen Bomb Decision," *Journal of American History* 66 (May 1979): 62–87. See also Harry R. Borowski, *A Hollow Threat: Strategic Air Power and Containment Before Korea* (Westport, Conn., 1982).
37. Shlaim, *U.S. and Berlin Blockade,* 237, 240; Davison, *Berlin Blockade,* 156–57; Gaddis, *Long Peace,* 110; Herken, *Winning Weapon,* 259–60. Herken points out that "only the shadow of deterrence had crossed the Atlantic. The substance . . . remained behind." Ibid., 262.
38. Herken, *Winning Weapon,* 280; M. Truman, *Truman,* 34–35; Forrestal, *Diaries,* 538; Shlaim, *U.S. and Berlin Blockade,* 236, 245 (quoting Royall), 246.
39. Shlaim, *U.S. and Berlin Blockade,* 254–56. Lilienthal also insisted that the AEC was more efficient than the military. *The Journals of David E. Lilienthal* (N.Y., 1964–83), vol. 2, *The Atomic Energy Years, 1945–1950,* 388–91; Forrestal, *Diaries,* 460–61. The Dept. of Defense had recently replaced the National Military Establishment, which had consisted of the three services and department heads.

40. Forrestal, *Diaries,* 459 (quoting Truman). See also ibid., 461; Herken, *Winning Weapon,* 263; and Shlaim, *U.S. and Berlin Blockade,* 256–57.
41. Shlaim, *U.S. and Berlin Blockade,* 246–49. The Berlin Group was made up of Kennan, Charles Saltzman, Samuel Reber, Dean Rusk, and Jacob Beam.
42. Davison, *Berlin Blockade,* 153–54; Forrestal, *Diaries,* 459; Clay, *Decision in Germany,* 368; Truman, *Memoirs,* 124.
43. Clay to Draper, July 19, 1948, Clay, *Papers,* 2:743–46.
44. Shlaim, *U.S. and Berlin Blockade,* 244, 260–63; Truman, *Memoirs,* 125–26; Bohlen, *Witness to History,* 277–78; Clay, *Decision in Germany,* 368.
45. Shlaim, *U.S. and Berlin Blockade,* 263; Murphy, *Diplomat Among Warriors,* 317; Acheson, *Present at Creation,* 263. Clay refused to order out all U.S. dependents because he did not see the possibility of war. Smith, "Clay and Russians," 36.
46. Davison, *Berlin Blockade,* 155–56; Forrestal, *Diaries,* 459, 461–62.
47. Shlaim, *U.S. and Berlin Blockade,* 265; Acheson, *Present at Creation,* 263.
48. Davison, *Berlin Blockade,* 130–31, 133, 139; Smith, *Defense of Berlin,* 118–19.
49. Quoted in Shlaim, *U.S. and Berlin Blockade,* 269.

NINE ■ FROM BERLIN TO NATO: THE ESTABLISHMENT OF ORDER IN WESTERN EUROPE

1. Shlaim, *U.S. and Berlin Blockade,* 270, 305; Taubman, *Stalin's American Policy,* 139; Ulam, *Stalin,* 687. See also Ulam, *Rivals,* 150, and Ulam, *Expansion and Coexistence,* 454.
2. Truman, *Memoirs,* 123–31. The crisis was not without its light moments. During one long night's strategy session, the question of Berlin's sewers came up for discussion. Lovett smiled and remarked: "I wish General Clay would realize that our policy is open sewers, openly arrived at." Bohlen, *Witness to History,* 280.
3. Shlaim, *U.S. and Berlin Blockade,* 305–6; LaFeber, *America, Russia, and Cold War,* 78; Robert A. Divine, "The Cold War and the Election of 1948," *Journal of American History* 59 (June 1972): 90–110. Hiss filed suit against Chambers, who then produced microfilms of State Dept. documents that Hiss had allegedly pilfered. That Acheson refused to break with Hiss raised suspicions about the secretary's loyalties as well as those of the State Dept. The statute of limitations protected Hiss from the charges, but Richard M. Nixon, then a new California congressman, was instrumental in securing a conviction for perjury in Jan. 1950.
4. Davison, *Berlin Blockade,* 152; Drew Middleton, *The Struggle for Germany* (London, 1950), 158; Clay, *Decision in Germany,* 368.
5. Shlaim, *U.S. and Berlin Blockade,* 310; Bohlen, *Witness to History,* 279.
6. Douglas to Marshall, July 26, 1948, *FRUS, 1948,* 2: 986–88; teletype conference between State Dept. and U.S. embassy in London, July 26, 1948, ibid.,

989–93; Harrington, "American Policy in Berlin Crisis," 141.

7. Harrington, "American Policy in Berlin Crisis," 142–43; Smith to Marshall, July 30 and 31, 1948, *FRUS, 1948,* 2: 995–96, 996–98; Walter Bedell Smith, *My Three Years in Moscow* (Philadelphia, 1950), 239, 253.
8. Smith, *Three Years in Moscow,* 233, 242, 244; Smith to Marshall, Aug. 3, 1948, *FRUS, 1948,* 2: 999–1007; Shlaim, *U.S. and Berlin Blockade,* 313; Harrington, "American Policy in Berlin Crisis," 145.
9. Smith to Marshall, Aug. 3, 1948, *FRUS, 1948,* 2:1005; Smith, *Three Years in Moscow,* 245; Forrestal, *Diaries,* 469; Shlaim, *U.S. and Berlin Blockade,* 313–14.
10. Harrington, "American Policy in Berlin Crisis," 146; Smith to Marshall, Aug. 3, 1948, *FRUS, 1948,* 2:999–1007; Smith, *Three Years in Moscow,* 245–46; Shlaim, *U.S. and Berlin Blockade,* 313–14.
11. Teleconference between Clay (and Murphy) and Royall (and Bohlen), Aug. 3, 1948, Clay, *Papers,* 2:749–51; Clay to Bradley and Royall, Aug. 4, 1948, ibid., 752–53; teleconference between Draper and Clay, Aug. 7, 1948, ibid., 760; Bohlen, *Witness to History,* 280–81; memo by Bohlen, Aug. 4, 1948, *FRUS, 1948,* 2:1013–14; Marshall to Smith, Aug. 3, 1948, ibid., 1008–9; Harrington, "American Policy in Berlin Crisis," 147.
12. Harrington, "American Policy in Berlin Crisis," 147–48.
13. Ibid., 148–49; Smith to Marshall, Aug. 9, 1948, *FRUS, 1948,* 2:1024–27; Davison, *Berlin Blockade,* 159; Smith, *Three Years in Moscow,* 246–48; Shlaim, *U.S. and Berlin Blockade,* 317–18.
14. Marshall to Smith, Aug. 10, 1948, and Smith to Marshall, Aug. 12 and 17, 1948, *FRUS, 1948,* 2:1028–31, 1035–38, 1042–48; Harrington, "American Policy in Berlin Crisis," 149–50; Washington's instructions to Clay, Aug. 9, 1948, Clay, *Papers,* 2:763.
15. Marshall to Smith, Aug. 17, 1948, and Smith to Marshall, Aug. 24, 1948, *FRUS, 1948,* 2:1053–58, 1065–69; Smith, *Three Years in Moscow,* 248–51; Davison, *Berlin Blockade,* 159–60; Harrington, "American Policy in Berlin Crisis," 151–55.
16. Smith to Marshall, Aug. 27 and 30, 1948, *FRUS, 1948,* 2:1086–90, 1092–97; Smith, *Three Years in Moscow,* 251–52; Davison, *Berlin Blockade,* 160–61; Harrington, "American Policy in Berlin Crisis," 156.
17. Harrington, "American Policy in Berlin Crisis," 151–52, 155–58.
18. Shlaim, *U.S. and Berlin Blockade,* 198; Smith to Marshall, Aug. 25, 1948, *FRUS, 1948,* 2:1078–83; Marshall to Smith, Aug. 24, 1948, ibid., 1072–74, 1077; Marshall to Smith, Aug. 26, 1948, ibid., 1083–84; Smith, *Three Years in Moscow,* 252–53; teleconference between Clay and Col. H. A. Byroade, Aug. 24, 1948, Clay, *Papers,* 2:781–84; Forrestal, *Diaries,* 480 (quoting Lovett).
19. Murphy to Marshall, Aug. 31, 1948, *FRUS, 1948,* 2:1099–1100; Shlaim, *U.S. and Berlin Blockade,* 332–33, 344; Clay to Draper, Sept. 4, 1948, Clay, *Papers,* 2:816–26; Forrestal, *Diaries,* 480–81.
20. Inverchapel to F.O., Feb. 16, 1948, FO 371/68103B, PRO.

21. Forrestal, *Diaries,* 483–85 (quoting Lovett on 483); Truman, *Memoirs,* 135; Shlaim, *U.S. and Berlin Blockade,* 331–32; teleconference between Clay and Royall et al., Sept. 8, 1948, Clay, *Papers,* 2:846.
22. NSC-30, *FRUS, 1948,* vol. 1, *General; The United Nations* (pt. 2) (Washington, D.C., 1976), 624–28; Shlaim, *U.S. and Berlin Blockade,* 339–40; Forrestal, *Diaries,* 487.
23. Shlaim, *U.S. and Berlin Blockade,* 340; Truman, *Off the Record,* 148–49.
24. NSC decision, Sept. 16, 1948, *FRUS, 1948,* 1:630–31.
25. Forrestal, *Diaries,* 487–91; Shlaim, *U.S. and Berlin Blockade,* 341; Marc Trachtenberg (writer referred to in text), "A 'Wasting Asset': American Strategy and the Shifting Nuclear Balance, 1949–1954," *International Security* 13 (Winter 1988–89): 5–49, esp. 5–10.
26. NSC-20/2, Aug. 25, 1948, *FRUS, 1948,* 1:619; Shlaim, *U.S. and Berlin Blockade,* 309; Smith to Marshall, Sept. 16, 1948, *FRUS, 1948,* 2:1160–62.
27. Teleconference between Clay and Royall (and Draper), Sept. 19, 1948, Clay, *Papers,* 2:877. Although the president was involved in the election campaign, he maintained close contact with his emissaries through Lovett, who became acting secretary of state while Marshall was abroad.
28. Minutes of Policy Planning Staff meeting, Sept. 28, 1948, *FRUS, 1948,* 2:1194–97. Smith was a general during World War II.
29. Clay, *Decision in Germany,* 376–77; Clay to Bradley, Sept. 23, 1948, Clay, *Papers,* 2:878; minutes of meeting of Marshall, Bevin, and Schuman in Paris, Sept. 21, 1948, *FRUS, 1948,* 2:1177–80.
30. Lovett to Soviet Ambassador Alexander Panyushkin, Sept. 22, 1948, and Panyushkin to Lovett, Sept. 25, 1948, *FRUS, 1948,* 2:1180–81, 1181–84; record of meeting of sec. of state with British and French foreign ministers, Sept. 26, 1948, ibid., 1184–86; Shlaim, *U.S. and Berlin Blockade,* 286, 345–46, 350–52, 354–55, 366. Bevin and Schuman had agreed with Marshall's recommendation to take the issue before the Security Council in view of the emotions then characterizing the Palestinian discussions in the General Assembly. As Marshall noted, the chances for a favorable vote seemed good. Ibid., 351–52. He might have added that even a strong vote in the West's favor in the assembly would not necessarily have forced the Soviet Union to change policy. Putting the question on the agenda was a procedural matter that was not subject to veto; the results were 9–2 in favor of doing so. Ibid., 355. Neither the Soviet nor the Ukrainian representatives participated in the discussion. Editorial note, *FRUS, 1948,* 2:1213.
31. Shlaim, *U.S. and Berlin Blockade,* 356–57; Taubman, *Stalin's American Policy,* 186–87. See the account by Albert Z. Carr, a speechwriter who favored the Vinson mission, in his *Truman, Stalin and Peace* (Garden City, N.Y., 1950), 111–20. See also Truman, *Memoirs,* 212.
32. Kenneth W. Condit, *The History of the Joint Chiefs of Staff* (Washington, D.C., 1976), vol. 2, *1947–1949,* 151–55 (quoting Lovett on 154–55); Shlaim, *U.S. and Berlin Blockade,* 363–64.

33. *Public Papers of Presidents: Truman, 1948,* 815–18.
34. Shlaim, *U.S. and Berlin Blockade,* 367; Smith, *Defense of Berlin,* 123–24.
35. Divine, "Cold War and Election of 1948," 109; Shlaim, *U.S. and Berlin Blockade,* 369–71; Daniel F. Harrington, "Kennan, Bohlen and the Riga Axioms," *Diplomatic History* 2 (Fall 1978): 430–33.
36. Howley, *Berlin Command,* 214–17; Smith, *Defense of Berlin,* 121–23; memo by Kennan, Nov. 24, 1948, *FRUS, 1948,* vol. 3, *Western Europe* (Washington, D.C., 1974), 283–89; ibid., 284 n. 2; Davison, *Berlin Blockade,* 201–2.
37. Harrington, "American Policy in Berlin Crisis," 207; Shlaim, *U.S. and Berlin Blockade,* 372–73, 375–77; Davison, *Berlin Blockade,* 248; Smith, *Defense of Berlin,* 125–27.
38. Davison, *Berlin Blockade,* 255–58.
39. Quoted ibid., 259.
40. Ibid., 260–65.
41. Ibid., 254; Robert J. Donovan, *Tumultuous Years: The Presidency of Harry S Truman, 1949–1953* (N.Y., 1982), 40; editorial note, *FRUS, 1949,* vol. 3, *Council of Foreign Ministers; Germany and Austria* (Washington, D.C., 1974), 666–67; Bohlen, *Witness to History,* 283–84; Davison, *Berlin Blockade,* 268 (quoting Middleton's editorial dated Mar. 24, 1949); Acheson, *Present at Creation,* 267–70; Truman, *Memoirs,* 130–31.
42. Memos by Jessup of conversations with Malik, Feb. 15, Mar. 15, and Mar. 21, 1949, *FRUS, 1949,* 3:694–95, 695–96 (quoted), 701; Harrington, "American Policy in Berlin Crisis," 226–27; Truman, *Memoirs,* 130; Shlaim, *U.S. and Berlin Blockade,* 381–82; Smith, *Defense of Berlin,* 128–29; Davison, *Berlin Blockade,* 255, 270; Acheson, *Present at Creation,* 269–70; Bohlen, *Witness to History,* 284–85; Philip C. Jessup, "Park Avenue Diplomacy—Ending the Berlin Blockade," *Political Science Quarterly* 87 (Sept. 1972): 377–400.
43. Historians disagree over whether the Truman administration's perception of a Soviet peace offensive was correct. Among those who agree with this perception, see Marshall D. Shulman, *Stalin's Foreign Policy Reappraised* (N.Y., 1969), 1, and Taubman, *Stalin's American Policy,* 206. Taubman declares that Stalin's peace offensive in 1949 was brief and aimed specifically at delaying the signing of the North Atlantic Treaty. When the offensive failed, Stalin dropped it. Ibid., 197, 206. On the other side of the issue, see Tucker, *Soviet Political Mind,* 98–101.
44. Memo by Acheson of conversation, Mar. 31, 1949, *FRUS, 1949,* 3:156; Acheson memo for Truman, Apr. 8, 1949, ibid., 176; Acheson, *Present at Creation,* 286–90; Donovan, *Tumultuous Years,* 44, 50–51; Smith, *Defense of Berlin,* 133; Timothy P. Ireland, *Creating the Entangling Alliance: The Origins of the North Atlantic Treaty Organization* (Westport, Conn., 1981), 138; DePorte, *Europe Between Superpowers,* 154. The Senate approved the treaty 82–13, and the president ratified it on July 25.
45. Forrestal, *Diaries,* 341; Robert E. Osgood, *Alliances and American Foreign*

Policy (Baltimore, 1968), chap. 3; Donovan, *Tumultuous Years,* 45.

46. Donovan, *Tumultuous Years,* 45; Ireland, *Creating Entangling Alliance,* 37–41.

47. Waldemar Gallman (chargé in London) to Marshall, Dec. 22, 1947, *FRUS, 1948,* 3:1–2; summary of memo representing Bevin's views on formation of a Western Union, encl. in Inverchapel to Marshall, Jan. 13, 1948, ibid., 5; Martin H. Folly, "Breaking the Vicious Circle: Britain, the United States, and the Genesis of the North Atlantic Treaty," *Diplomatic History* 12 (Winter 1988): 59–77; Donovan, *Tumultuous Years,* 46.

48. Jefferson Caffery (U.S. ambassador in Paris) to Marshall, Mar. 2, 1948, *FRUS, 1948,* 3:34–35; Marshall to embassy in Rome, Mar. 11, 1948, ibid., 45–46; British embassy in Washington to State Dept., Mar. 11, 1948, ibid., 46–48; Marshall to British ambassador in Washington, Mar. 12, 1948, ibid., 48; Marshall to embassy in Paris, Mar. 12, 1948, ibid., 50; Kaplan, *U.S. and NATO,* 40–41, 61–63; Ireland, *Creating Entangling Alliance,* 68–69, 73–74; Harrington, "American Policy in Berlin Crisis," 259. See also Lawrence S. Kaplan, *NATO and the United States: The Enduring Alliance* (Boston, 1988).

49. Clay, *Decision in Germany,* 389; Smith, *Three Years in Moscow,* 257; Truman, *Memoirs,* 130–31.

50. Shlaim, *U.S. and Berlin Blockade,* 387; Smith, *Defense of Berlin,* 129–30; Davison, *Berlin Blockade,* 271; Harrington, "American Policy in Berlin Crisis," 227.

51. Davison, *Berlin Blockade,* xi; Harrington, "American Policy in Berlin Crisis," 227.

52. Davison, *Berlin Blockade,* 273, 275–77; Lafeber, *America, Russia, and Cold War,* 77; Shlaim, *U.S. and Berlin Blockade,* 378, 378 n. 192.

53. Davison, *Berlin Blockade,* 275–76, 280.

54. Ibid., 284, 286–87; Alfred Grosser, *Germany in Our Time: A Political History of the Postwar Years* (N.Y., 1971), 71.

55. Acheson to embassy in London, May 10, 1949, *FRUS, 1949,* 3:872–74; Harrington, "American Policy in Berlin Crisis," 238; Kaplan, *U.S. and NATO,* 5–6; Ireland, *Creating Entangling Alliance,* 4; Acheson, *Present at Creation,* 291.

56. Donovan, *Tumultuous Years,* 42, 51.

57. Howley, *Berlin Command,* 265; acting U.S. political adviser for Germany (James Riddleberger) to Acheson, May 20, 1949, *FRUS, 1949,* 3:840–42; Harrington, "American Policy in Berlin Crisis," 245–46 (quoting Acheson on 246).

58. Harrington, "American Policy in Berlin Crisis," 235–37. For the background of the foreign ministers' meeting, see *FRUS, 1949,* 3:856. See U.S. delegation at Council of Foreign Ministers' meeting to Truman and Acheson, May 24, 1949, ibid., 918; and proposal of Soviet delegation to council meeting, May 25, 1949, ibid., 1040–41.

59. Davison, *Berlin Blockade,* 238; paper prepared by Office of German and Austrian Affairs on U.S. position at council meeting, May 15, 1949, *FRUS, 1949,* 3:895–903.
60. Harrington, "American Policy in Berlin Crisis," 237–39.
61. Ibid., 239; Acheson to Truman, June 11, 1949, *FRUS, 1949,* 3:977–79.
62. Quoted in Harrington, "American Policy in Berlin Crisis," 243.
63. Ibid., 240, 245; documents regarding meetings of Council of Foreign Ministers in *FRUS, 1949,* 3:985.
64. Harrington, "American Policy in Berlin Crisis," 249–50 (quoting Acheson and American observer); DePorte, *Europe Between Superpowers,* 147, 149.
65. Davison, *Berlin Blockade,* xii–xiii. Davison argues that Berlin had held on for four intertwined reasons. First, most of the people wanted to withstand the blockade and therefore placed pressure on others to conform. Second, the city had capable political leaders who refused to capitulate to Soviet pressure. Third, these same political figures had control over influential groups—the police, political parties, trade unions, civil administrators, communications media. Fourth, the matériel brought in by air provided the foundation for resistance. Ibid., xiv.
66. Acheson memo of conversation with British Ambassador Sir Oliver Franks and Dean Rusk, assistant sec. of state, May 2, 1949, *FRUS, 1949,* 3:748–49.

TEN ■ TOWARD NEW DIRECTIONS IN THE COLD WAR

1. Jones, "*New Kind of War,*" 99; JCS 1798/1—"United States Assistance to Greece," Oct. 15, 1947, pp. 57–58, ABC-370.5 Greece-Italy, RG 107, War Dept.; JPS 858—Joint Staff Planners, Greek Situation Subcommittee Report, Oct. 16, 1947, pp. 1–2, 6–7, 9, P & O [Plans & Operations] 091 Greece (TS), sec. II-A, case 13, Army Staff Records, NA; JCS 1826/2, Jan. 29, 1948 —report by JSPC to JCS, "Outline Plans for the Dispatch on Short Notice of United States Forces to Greece and for Their Deployment in That Country," 33–35, approved by JCS on Feb. 24, 1948, ABC-370.5 Greece-Italy, sec. 1-B, RG 107, War Dept.; "Comments on Certain Courses of Action Proposed with Respect to Greece and Answers to Specific Questions Contained in the Memorandum by the Secretary of the National Security Council dated 24 February 1948," pp. 7–8, CD 6-1-21, Files of Sec. of Defense, NA.
2. The United States established the Joint U.S. Military Advisory and Planning Group in Dec. 1947 to provide operational advice to Greek soldiers. See Jones, "*New Kind of War,*" chap. 6.
3. Ibid., chaps. 4 and 5. Gen. Alexander Papagos led the way to victory after becoming commander-in-chief of the Greek armed forces in Jan. 1949. Ibid., 195.
4. Ibid., 117.

5. See ibid., chap. 8. See also Howard Jones, "The Diplomacy of Restraint: The United States' Efforts to Repatriate Greek Children Evacuated During the Civil War of 1946–49," *Journal of Modern Greek Studies* (May 1985): 65–85.
6. Jones, "*New Kind of War,*" 133–35; Djilas, *Conversations with Stalin,* 131–32, 181–82; Dedijer, *Battle Stalin Lost,* 68–69, 269–70; Svetozar Vukmanović-Tempo, *How and Why the People's Liberation Struggle of Greece Met with Defeat* (London, 1950), 3; Vladimir Dedijer, *Tito* (N.Y., 1953), 316–22; Dimitrios G. Kousoulas, "The Truman Doctrine and the Stalin-Tito Rift: A Reappraisal," *South Atlantic Quarterly* 72 (Summer 1973): 430–32; Elisabeth Barker, "Yugoslav Policy Towards Greece, 1947–1949," in Baerentzen, Iatrides, and Smith, eds., *Studies in History of Greek Civil War,* 273. For the opposing historians on the Truman Doctrine, see n. 30 of chap. 5. The writer cited in the text is William Taubman; see his study *Stalin's American Policy,* 151. Alexander Werth argues that in mid-1947 Stalin accepted the reality of Cold War after the advent of the Truman Doctrine, the Marshall Plan, and failed peace negotiations over Germany and Austria. See Werth, *Russia: The Post-War Years* (London, 1971), 142, 144.
7. Vladimir Dedijer, *Novi Prilozi za Josipa Broza Tita, Treci Tom* (Belgrade, 1984), 266–67, quoted in Barker, "Yugoslavs and Greek Civil War," 303. Barker believes that Dedijer's claims are probably accurate. See also Djilas, *Conversations with Stalin,* 131–32, 181–82; Kousoulas, "Truman Doctrine and Stalin-Tito Rift," 430–31; and Jones, "*New Kind of War,*" 135, 253 n. 7.
8. Jones, "*New Kind of War,*" 127, 136, 193, 217, 219, 223.
9. Ibid., 198, 214, 222–23.
10. Ibid., 133–35, 223–26. Few of the evacuated Greek children returned home after the war. Many of their parents were loyal to the guerrilla cause and themselves stayed out of the country as well. It is impossible to determine how many children were taken out of Greece involuntarily. Ibid., chap. 8 and 231–32; Jones, "Diplomacy of Restraint," 82–84.
11. Air Force, "Joint Military Mission for Aid to Turkey," pp. 2–3.
12. *Public Papers of Presidents: Truman, 1948,* 234; Hogan, *Marshall Plan,* 379–82, 391–92; Wexler, *Marshall Plan Revisited,* 185, 224 (quoting act to create Mutual Security Program), 241; Donovan, *Conflict and Crisis,* 290. Thomas G. Paterson likewise concludes that the Marshall Plan clarified the division in Europe, but his tone is condemnatory: "The Marshall Plan and the Soviet reaction to it divided Europe even more." Paterson, *On Every Front,* 60.
13. Sir John Balfour (of British embassy in Washington) to Michael Wright (of F.O.), Aug. 1, 1947, FO 371/61031, PRO; F. B. A. Rundall minute, Mar. 1, 1948, FO 371/68103B, PRO; Wexler, *Marshall Plan Revisited,* 209; Hogan, *Marshall Plan,* 53, 112–14, 117–18, 292, 366, 378, 439–40; Milward, *Reconstruction of Western Europe,* 62–63 (quoting Bevin on 62). See also Ireland, *Creating Entangling Alliance,* 164.
14. Hogan, *Marshall Plan,* 366–68, 378, 439; Wexler, *Marshall Plan Revisited,*

239–40, 244, 246–47; Ireland, *Creating Entangling Alliance,* 168–75; Arkes, *Bureaucracy, Marshall Plan, and National Interest,* 274. For the Schuman Plan, see Milward, *Reconstruction of Western Europe,* chap. 12.

15. The two writers are, respectively, Arkes, *Bureaucracy, Marshall Plan, and National Interest,* 323, and Milward, *Reconstruction of Western Europe,* esp. xv, 2, 54. See also Milward's penetrating analysis of Hogan's book on the Marshall Plan in a review article, "Was the Marshall Plan Necessary?" *Diplomatic History* 13 (Spring 1989): 231–53.

16. Wexler, *Marshall Plan Revisited,* 5, 197, 200–201, 207, 249–55; Donovan, *Conflict and Crisis,* 394; Mee, *Marshall Plan,* 262–63; Hogan, *Marshall Plan,* 425, 429–32, 444–45. Milward insists that Europe's recovery started in 1945 —before the Marshall Plan. In a highly questionable statement he declares that in the summer of 1949 the United States' attempt to reconstruct Western Europe was "a near-complete failure." Milward, *Reconstruction of Western Europe,* xv; see also 90–92, 282, chap. 14.

17. Donovan, *Tumultuous Years,* 98–99; Herken, *Winning Weapon,* 302–3; Yergin, *Shattered Peace,* 400; *Public Papers of the Presidents of the United States: Harry S. Truman, 1949* (Washington, D.C., 1964), 485.

18. Herken, *Winning Weapon,* 303; Kaplan, *U.S. and NATO,* 129; Ireland, *Creating Entangling Alliance,* 157; Donovan, *Tumultuous Years,* 99, 103; Trachtenberg, " 'Wasting Asset,' " esp. 6, 16; Vandenberg, *Private Papers,* 518.

19. Gaddis, *Strategies of Containment,* 99; Donovan, *Tumultuous Years,* 103–4 (quoting JCS, Strauss, and Lilienthal); Herken, *Winning Weapon,* 304, 306–7 (quoting Oppenheimer on 307), 314. The Soviet threat evoked at least two other responses, neither of which received widespread support: a return to isolationism and a resort to preventive nuclear war. Ibid., 327.

20. Donovan, *Tumultuous Years,* 104–5.

21. Ibid., 154–56 (quotations from 155–56); Gaddis, *Strategies of Containment,* 80–82; Lilienthal, *Journals,* 2:577.

22. Donovan, *Tumultuous Years,* 156–57; Yergin, *Shattered Peace,* 407; Herken, *Winning Weapon,* 322–23; LaFeber, *America, Russia, and Cold War,* 94–95; diary of Eben A. Ayers, Feb. 4, 1950 (quoting Truman), cited in Gaddis, *Long Peace,* 113n.

23. Gaddis, *Strategies of Containment,* 82, 95. For NSC-68, see "United States Objectives and Programs for National Security," Apr. 7, 1950, *FRUS, 1950,* vol. 1, *National Security Affairs; Foreign Economic Policy* (Washington, D.C., 1977), 235–92. In preparation of NSC-68, Acheson outmaneuvered Johnson (who had tried to do the same thing earlier with Acheson) and worked closely with Nitze. See Trachtenberg, " 'Wasting Asset,' " 11; Donovan, *Tumultuous Years,* 158–61; and LaFeber, *America, Russia, and Cold War,* 96–97. The existence of NSC-68 was not known until the 1970s, when it was accidentally declassified. Ibid., 96. For a penetrating discussion of the ways in which NSC-68 differed from Kennan's ideas on containment, see Gaddis, *Strategies of Containment,* chap. 4.

24. Donovan, *Tumultuous Years,* 160–61; Gaddis, *Strategies of Containment,* 82–83, 91–92, 97–98, 104, 106; Gaddis, *Long Peace,* 114; Yergin, *Shattered Peace,* 401–3.
25. Quoted in Gaddis, *Strategies of Containment,* 100–101. See also Bernard A. Weisberger, *Cold War, Cold Peace: The United States and Russia Since 1945* (N.Y., 1985), 96–103; and Taubman, *Stalin's American Policy,* 198–99. There were complications in securing such a program. Truman had repeatedly made public statements against increases in defense spending, and a feud had been growing between Acheson and Johnson that was personal as well as professional. The president ultimately forced Johnson's resignation. See Donovan, *Tumultuous Years,* 53, 62, 64–65, 159–60, 177, 265–67.
26. Trachtenberg, "'Wasting Asset,'" 11–16; Gaddis, *Strategies of Containment,* 106; Herken, *Winning Weapon,* 329.
27. Quoted in LaFeber, *America, Russia, and Cold War,* 98. See also Gaddis, *Strategies of Containment,* 109–10.
28. Quoted in Taubman, *Stalin's American Policy,* 201–2.

BIBLIOGRAPHY

PRIMARY MATERIALS

Acheson, Dean. Papers. Harry S. Truman Library, Independence, Mo.

———. *Present at the Creation: My Years in the State Department.* N.Y.: Viking, 1969.

Bailey, Thomas A. *The Marshall Plan Summer: An Eyewitness Report on Europe and the Russians in 1947.* Stanford: Hoover Institution Press, 1977.

Berle, Adolf. Papers. Franklin D. Roosevelt Library, Hyde Park, N.Y.

Bohlen, Charles E. *Witness to History, 1929–1969.* N.Y.: Norton, 1973.

Byrnes, James F. Papers. Clemson U., Clemson, S.C.

———. *Speaking Frankly.* London: Heinemann, 1947.

Cadogan, Sir Alexander. *The Diaries of Sir Alexander Cadogan, 1938–1945.* Edited by David Dilks. N.Y.: Putnam, 1972.

Churchill, Sir Winston, and Franklin Delano Roosevelt. *Churchill and Roosevelt: The Complete Correspondence.* Edited by Warren F. Kimball. 3 vols. Princeton: Princeton U. Press, 1984.

Clay, Lucius D. *Decision in Germany.* N.Y.: Doubleday, 1950.

———. *Germany and the Fight for Freedom.* Cambridge: Harvard U. Press, 1950.

———. *The Papers of General Lucius D. Clay, 1945–1949.* Edited by Jean Edward Smith. 2 vols. Bloomington: Indiana U. Press, 1974.

Clayton, William L. Papers. Harry S. Truman Library, Independence, Mo.

Clifford, Clark. Oral History Interview. Harry S. Truman Library, Independence, Mo.

———. Papers. Harry S. Truman Library, Independence, Mo.

Colville, John. *The Fringes of Power: Downing Street Diaries, 1939–1955.* London: Hodder & Stoughton, 1985.

Condit, Kenneth W. *The History of the Joint Chiefs of Staff.* 2 vols. Washington, D.C.: Historical Division, Joint Secretariat, Joint Chiefs of Staff, 1976.

Conway, Rose. File. Harry S. Truman Library, Independence, Mo.

Dalton, Hugh. Diary. London School of Economics, London.

Dedijer, Vladimir. *The Battle Stalin Lost: Memoirs of Yugoslavia, 1948–1953.* N.Y.: Viking, 1971.

Djilas, Milovan. *Conversations with Stalin.* N.Y.: Harcourt, Brace, 1962.

Dulles, John Foster. Papers. Princeton U., Princeton.

Elsey, George M. Oral History Interview. Harry S. Truman Library, Independence, Mo.

Forrestal, James V. Diaries. Princeton U., Princeton. Photocopies in Operational Archives. Naval History Division, Washington Navy Yard, Washington, D.C.

———. *The Forrestal Diaries*. Edited by Walter Millis. N.Y.: Viking, 1951.

———. Papers. Princeton U., Princeton.

Grigg, Sir Percy. Papers. Churchill College, Cambridge U., Cambridge.

Harriman, W. Averell, and Elie Abel. *Special Envoy to Churchill and Stalin, 1941–1946*. N.Y.: Random House, 1975.

Henderson, Loy. Author interview (Jones).

———. Oral History Interview. Harry S. Truman Library, Independence, Mo.

Hopkins, Harry. Papers. Franklin D. Roosevelt Library, Hyde Park, N.Y.

Howard, Harry N. *The Problem of the Turkish Straits*. Washington, D.C.: Government Printing Office, 1947.

Howley, Frank. *Berlin Command*. N.Y.: Putnam, 1950.

Jones, Jesse H. Papers. Library of Congress, Washington, D.C.

Jones, Joseph M. *The Fifteen Weeks (February 21–June 5, 1947)*. N.Y.: Viking, 1955.

———. Papers. Harry S. Truman Library, Independence, Mo.

Jones, Thomas. *A Diary with Letters, 1931–1950*. N.Y.: Oxford U. Press, 1954.

Kennan, George F. *Memoirs, 1925–1950*. Boston: Little, Brown, 1967.

Khrushchev, Nikita. *Khrushchev Remembers*. Translated and edited by Strobe Talbott. Boston: Little, Brown, 1970.

Krock, Arthur. *Memoirs: Sixty Years on the Firing Line*. N.Y.: Funk & Wagnalls, 1968.

Leahy, William D. Files. Records of Joint Chiefs of Staff. Modern Military Division, National Archives, Washington, D.C.

———. Papers. Library of Congress, Washington, D.C.

LeMay, Curtis E. *Mission with LeMay: My Story*. N.Y.: Doubleday, 1965.

Lilienthal, David E. *The Journals of David E. Lilienthal*. 7 vols. N.Y.: Harper & Row, 1964–83.

Lincoln, Francis F. Papers. Harry S. Truman Library, Independence, Mo.

McNaughton, Frank. Papers. Harry S. Truman Library, Independence, Mo.

Martin, Joseph W., Jr. *My First Fifty Years in Politics*. N.Y.: McGraw-Hill, 1960.

Morgenthau, Henry, Jr. Diaries. Franklin D. Roosevelt Library, Hyde Park, N.Y.

———. *From the Morgenthau Diaries*. Vol. 3, *Years of War, 1941–1945*. Edited by John Morton Blum. Boston: Houghton Mifflin, 1959.

Munkman, C. A. *American Aid to Greece: A Report on the First Ten Years*. N.Y.: Praeger, 1958.

Murphy, Robert. *Diplomat Among Warriors*. Garden City, N.Y.: Doubleday, 1964.

Nicolson, Harold. *Harold Nicolson, Diaries and Letters*. Vol. 2, *The War Years, 1939–1945*. Edited by Nigel Nicolson. N.Y.: Atheneum, 1967.

Patterson, Robert. Papers. Library of Congress, Washington, D.C.

Porter, Paul A. Papers. Harry S. Truman Library, Independence, Mo.
Public Papers of the Presidents of the United States: Harry S. Truman, 1947. Washington, D.C.: Government Printing Office, 1963.
Public Papers of the Presidents of the United States: Harry S. Truman, 1948. Washington, D.C.: Government Printing Office, 1964.
Public Papers of the Presidents of the United States: Harry S. Truman, 1949. Washington, D.C.: Government Printing Office, 1964.
Roosevelt, Franklin Delano, and Felix Frankfurter. *Roosevelt and Frankfurter: Their Correspondence, 1928–1945.* Edited by Max Freedman. Boston: Little, Brown, 1968.
Rusk, Dean. Author interview (Jones).
Schindler, Alfred. Papers. Harry S. Truman Library, Independence, Mo.
Schnabel, James F. "The History of the Joint Chiefs of Staff and National Policy" (Feb. 1979). MS in Modern Military Division, National Archives, Washington, D.C.
Smith, Walter Bedell. *My Three Years in Moscow.* Philadelphia: Lippincott, 1950.
Smothers, Frank, William H. McNeill, and Elizabeth D. McNeill. *Report on the Greeks: Findings of a Twentieth Century Fund Team Which Surveyed Conditions in Greece in 1947.* N.Y.: Twentieth Century Fund, 1948.
Stimson, Henry L. Diaries. Center for Research Libraries, Chicago, Ill.
Sulzberger, Cyrus L. *A Long Row of Candles: Memoirs and Diaries [1934–1954].* N.Y.: Macmillan, 1969.
Taft, Charles P. Papers. Library of Congress, Washington, D.C.
Taft, Robert A. Papers. Library of Congress, Washington, D.C.
Truman, Harry S. *Memoirs: Years of Trial and Hope, 1946–1952.* Garden City, N.Y.: Doubleday, 1956.
———. *Off the Record: The Private Papers of Harry S. Truman.* Edited by Robert H. Ferrell. N.Y.: Harper & Row, 1980.
———. Papers. Harry S. Truman Library, Independence, Mo.
United Kingdom. British War Cabinet, Records. Public Record Office, Kew.
———. Foreign Office, Records. Public Record Office, Kew.
———. *Parliamentary Debates.*
———. Prime Minister, Records. Public Record Office, Kew.
United Nations. General Assembly. *Official Records.*
United States. Air Force. "Joint Military Mission for Aid to Turkey, History 1947–June 1950." Simpson Library, Maxwell Air Force Base, Montgomery, Ala.
———. Army. Army Staff Records. Modern Military Division, National Archives, Washington, D.C.
———. Congress. *Congressional Record.*
———. Department of Defense. Files of Secretary of Defense. Modern Military Division, National Archives, Washington, D.C.

———. Department of State. *Foreign Relations of the United States, 1945: The Conference of Berlin (The Potsdam Conference).* 2 vols. Washington, D.C.: Government Printing Office, 1960.

———. Department of State. *Foreign Relations of the United States, 1946.* Vol. 5, *The British Commonwealth; Western and Central Europe.* Washington, D.C.: Government Printing Office, 1969.

———. Department of State. *Foreign Relations of the United States, 1946.* Vol. 6, *The Near East and Africa.* Washington, D.C.: Government Printing Office, 1970.

———. Department of State. *Foreign Relations of the United States, 1947.* Vol. 1, *General; The United Nations.* Washington, D.C.: Government Printing Office, 1973.

———. Department of State. *Foreign Relations of the United States, 1947.* Vol. 3, *The British Commonwealth; Europe.* Washington, D.C.: Government Printing Office, 1972.

———. Department of State. *Foreign Relations of the United States, 1947.* Vol. 5, *The Near East and Africa.* Washington, D.C.: Government Printing Office, 1971.

———. Department of State. *Foreign Relations of the United States, 1948.* Vol. 1, *General; The United Nations* (pt. 2). Washington, D.C.: Government Printing Office, 1976.

———. Department of State. *Foreign Relations of the United States, 1948.* Vol. 2, *Germany and Austria.* Washington, D.C.: Government Printing Office, 1973.

———. Department of State. *Foreign Relations of the United States, 1948.* Vol. 3, *Western Europe.* Washington, D.C.: Government Printing Office, 1974.

———. Department of State. *Foreign Relations of the United States, 1948.* Vol. 4, *Eastern Europe: The Soviet Union.* Washington, D.C.: Government Printing Office, 1974.

———. Department of State. *Foreign Relations of the United States, 1949.* Vol. 3, *Council of Foreign Ministers; Germany and Austria.* Washington, D.C.: Government Printing Office, 1974.

———. Department of State. *Foreign Relations of the United States, 1950.* Vol. 1, *National Security Affairs; Foreign Economic Policy.* Washington, D.C.: Government Printing Office, 1977.

———. Department of State. Records. National Archives, Washington, D.C.

———. House of Representatives. Committee on International Relations. *Foreign Economic Assistance Programs, Part 2: Extension of the European Recovery Program.* Vol. 4. Washington, D.C.: Government Printing Office, 1976.

———. House of Representatives. *Military Assistance Programs, Part 2: Assistance to Greece and Turkey.* Vol. 6. Washington, D.C.: Government Printing Office, 1976.

———. Senate. *Anglo-American Financial Agreement: Hearings Before the*

Committee on Banking and Currency. 79th Cong. 2d sess. Washington, D.C.: Government Printing Office, 1946.

———. Senate. *Legislative Origins of the Truman Doctrine: Hearings Held in Executive Session Before the Committee on Foreign Relations on S. 938: A Bill to Provide for Assistance to Greece and Turkey.* 80th Cong., 1st sess. Washington, D.C.: Government Printing Office, 1973.

———. State-War-Navy Coordinating Committee Case Files. Center for Research Libraries, Chicago, Ill.

———. War Department, Records. Modern Military Division, National Archives, Washington, D.C.

Vandenberg, Arthur H. *The Private Papers of Senator Vandenberg.* Edited by Arthur H. Vandenberg, Jr. Boston: Houghton Mifflin, 1952.

Vukmanović-Tempo, Svetozar. *How and Why the People's Liberation Struggle of Greece Met with Defeat.* London: Merritt & Hatcher, 1950.

Wallace, Henry A. Papers. U. of Iowa, Iowa City.

———. *The Price of Vision: The Diary of Henry A. Wallace, 1942–1946.* Edited by John Morton Blum. Boston: Houghton Mifflin, 1973.

Welles, Sumner. *The Time for Decision.* N.Y.: Harper, 1944.

White, Harry Dexter. Papers. Princeton U., Princeton.

Willkie, Wendell. *One World.* N.Y.: Simon and Schuster, 1943.

SECONDARY MATERIALS

Books

Alexander, George M. *The Prelude to the Truman Doctrine: British Policy in Greece, 1944–1947.* Oxford: Clarendon, 1982.

Alperovitz, Gar. *Atomic Diplomacy: Hiroshima and Potsdam.* N.Y.: Random House, 1965.

Ambrose, Stephen E. *Eisenhower and Berlin, 1945: The Decision to Halt at the Elbe.* N.Y.: Norton, 1967.

———. *Rise to Globalism: American Foreign Policy Since 1938.* 5th ed. N.Y.: Penguin, 1988.

Anderson, Terry H. *The United States, Great Britain, and the Cold War, 1944–1947.* Columbia: U. of Missouri Press, 1981.

Arkes, Hadley. *Bureaucracy, the Marshall Plan, and the National Interest.* Princeton: Princeton U. Press, 1972.

Armstrong, Hamilton Fish. *Tito and Goliath.* N.Y.: Macmillan, 1951.

Averoff-Tossizza, Evangelos. *By Fire and Axe: The Communist Party and the Civil War in Greece, 1944–1949.* New Rochelle, N.Y.: Caratzas Brothers, 1978.

Backer, John H. *The Decision to Divide Germany: American Foreign Policy in Transition.* Durham: Duke U. Press, 1978.

Baerentzen, Lars, John O. Iatrides, and Ole L. Smith, eds. *Studies in the History of the Greek Civil War, 1945–1949*. Copenhagen: Museum Tuscalanum Press, 1987.

Beitzell, Robert. *An Uneasy Alliance: America, Britain, and Russia, 1941–1943*. N.Y.: Knopf, 1972.

Best, Richard A. *"Co-operation with Like-minded Peoples": British Influences on American Security Policy, 1945–1949*. Westport, Conn.: Greenwood, 1986.

Bethell, Nicholas. *The Great Betrayal: The Untold Story of Kim Philby's Biggest Coup*. London: Hodder & Stoughton, 1984.

Borowski, Harry R. *A Hollow Threat: Strategic Air Power and Containment Before Korea*. Westport, Conn.: Greenwood, 1982.

Buhite, Russell D. *Decisions at Yalta: An Appraisal of Summit Diplomacy*. Wilmington, Del.: Scholarly Resources, 1986.

Bullock, Alan. *Ernest Bevin: Foreign Secretary, 1945–1951*. N.Y.: Heinemann, 1983.

———. *The Life and Times of Ernest Bevin*. 2 vols. London: Heinemann, 1960–67.

Burns, James MacGregor. *Roosevelt: The Soldier of Freedom, 1940–1945*. N.Y.: Harcourt Brace Jovanovich, 1970.

Burridge, Trevor D. *British Labour and Hitler's War*. London: Deutsch, 1976.

Carr, Albert Z. *Truman, Stalin and Peace*. Garden City, N.Y.: Doubleday, 1950.

Chandler, Geoffrey. *The Divided Land: An Anglo-Greek Tragedy*. London: Macmillan, 1959.

Churchill, Winston. *Triumph and Tragedy*. Boston: Houghton Mifflin, 1953.

Clemens, Diane Shaver. *Yalta*. N.Y.: Oxford U. Press, 1970.

Clements, Kendrick A., ed. *James F. Byrnes and the Origins of the Cold War*. Durham: Carolina Academic Press, 1982.

Cole, Wayne S. *Roosevelt and the Isolationists, 1932–1945*. Lincoln: U. of Nebraska Press, 1983.

Couloumbis, Theodore A. *The United States, Greece, and Turkey: The Troubled Triangle*. N.Y.: Praeger, 1983.

Couloumbis, Theodore A., and John O. Iatrides, eds. *Greek-American Relations: A Critical Review*. N.Y.: Pella, 1980.

Dallek, Robert. *Franklin D. Roosevelt and American Foreign Policy, 1932–1945*. N.Y.: Oxford U. Press, 1979.

Darilek, Richard E. *A Loyal Opposition in Time of War: The Republican Party and the Politics of Foreign Policy from Pearl Harbor to Yalta*. Westport, Conn.: Greenwood, 1986.

Davison, W. Phillips. *The Berlin Blockade: A Study in Cold War Politics*. Princeton: Princeton U. Press, 1958.

Dedijer, Vladimir. *Tito*. N.Y.: Simon and Schuster, 1953.

DePorte, A. W. *Europe Between the Superpowers: The Enduring Balance*. New Haven: Yale U. Press, 1979.

Divine, Robert A. *The Reluctant Belligerent: American Entry into World War II.* Rev. ed. N.Y.: Wiley, 1979.

———. *Roosevelt and World War II.* Baltimore: Johns Hopkins Press, 1969.

———. *Second Chance: The Triumph of Internationalism in America During World War II.* N.Y.: Atheneum, 1967.

Doenecke, Justus D. *Not to the Swift: The Old Isolationists in the Cold War Era.* Lewisburg, Pa.: Bucknell U. Press, 1979.

Donovan, Robert J. *Conflict and Crisis: The Presidency of Harry S Truman, 1945–1948.* N.Y.: Norton, 1977.

———. *Tumultuous Years: The Presidency of Harry S Truman, 1949–1953.* N.Y.: Norton, 1982.

Edmonds, Robin. *Setting the Mould: The United States and Britain, 1945–1950.* N.Y.: Oxford U. Press, 1986.

Eudes, Dominique. *The Kapetanios: Partisans and the Civil War in Greece, 1943–1949.* N.Y.: Monthly Review Press, 1972.

Feis, Herbert. *The Atomic Bomb and the End of World War II.* Princeton: Princeton U. Press, 1966. Originally published as *Japan Subdued* in 1961.

———. *Between War and Peace: The Potsdam Conference.* Princeton: Princeton U. Press, 1960.

———. *From Trust to Terror: The Onset of the Cold War, 1945–1950.* N.Y.: Norton, 1970.

Ferrell, Robert H. *George Marshall.* N.Y.: Cooper Square, 1966.

———. *Harry S. Truman and the Modern American Presidency.* Boston: Little, Brown, 1983.

Foot, Michael. *Aneurin Bevan: A Biography.* London: Atheneum, 1962.

Fitzsimmons, M. A. *The Foreign Policy of the British Labour Government.* Notre Dame: U. of Notre Dame Press, 1953.

Freeland, Richard M. *The Truman Doctrine and the Origins of McCarthyism.* N.Y.: Schocken, 1970.

Fulbright, J. William. *The Arrogance of Power.* N.Y.: Random House, 1966.

Gaddis, John L. *The Long Peace: Inquiries into the History of the Cold War.* N.Y.: Oxford U. Press, 1987.

———. *Russia, the Soviet Union, and the United States: An Interpretive History.* N.Y.: McGraw-Hill, 1990.

———. *Strategies of Containment: A Critical Appraisal of Postwar American National Security Policy.* N.Y.: Oxford U. Press, 1982.

———. *The United States and the Origins of the Cold War, 1941–1947.* N.Y.: Columbia U. Press, 1972.

Gardner, Lloyd C. *Architects of Illusion: Men and Ideas in American Foreign Policy, 1941–1949.* Chicago: Quadrangle, 1970.

George, Alexander L., and Richard Smoke. *Deterrence in American Foreign Policy: Theory and Practice.* N.Y.: Columbia U. Press, 1974.

Gilbert, Felix. *The End of the European Era: 1890 to the Present.* N.Y.: Norton, 1970.

Gilbert, Martin. *Winston S. Churchill*. Vol. 3, *Road to Victory, 1941–1945*. Boston: Houghton Mifflin, 1986.

Gimbel, John. *The American Occupation of Germany: Politics and the Military, 1945–1949*. Stanford: Stanford U. Press, 1968.

———. *The Origins of the Marshall Plan*. Stanford: Stanford U. Press, 1976.

Gottlieb, Manuel. *The German Peace Settlement and the Berlin Crisis*. N.Y.: Paine-Whitman, 1960.

Graebner, Norman A., ed. *The Cold War: A Conflict of Ideology and Power*. 2d ed. Lexington, Mass.: Heath, 1976.

Greenfield, Kent R. *American Strategy in World War II: A Reconsideration*. Baltimore: Johns Hopkins Press, 1963.

Grosser, Alfred. *Germany in Our Time: A Political History of the Postwar Years*. N.Y.: Praeger, 1971.

Hahn, Werner G. *Postwar Soviet Politics: The Fall of Zhdanov and the Defeat of Moderation, 1946–1953*. Ithaca, N.Y.: Cornell U. Press, 1982.

Hamby, Alonzo L. *Beyond the New Deal: Harry S. Truman and American Liberalism*. N.Y.: Columbia U. Press, 1973.

Harbutt, Fraser J. *The Iron Curtain: Churchill, America, and the Origins of the Cold War*. N.Y.: Oxford U. Press, 1986.

Hartmann, Susan M. *Truman and the 80th Congress*. Columbia: U. of Missouri Press, 1971.

Hathaway, Robert M. *Ambiguous Partnership: Britain and America, 1944–1947*. N.Y.: Columbia U. Press, 1981.

Haynes, Richard F. *The Awesome Power: Harry S. Truman as Commander in Chief*. Baton Rouge: Louisiana State U. Press, 1973.

Herken, Gregg. *The Winning Weapon: The Atomic Bomb in the Cold War, 1945–1950*. N.Y.: Knopf, 1980.

Herring, George C., Jr. *Aid to Russia, 1941–1946: Strategy, Diplomacy, the Origins of the Cold War*. N.Y.: Columbia U. Press, 1973.

Hogan, Michael J. *The Marshall Plan: America, Britain, and the Reconstruction of Western Europe, 1947–1952*. Cambridge: Cambridge U. Press, 1987.

Iatrides, John O. *Revolt in Athens: The Greek Communist "Second Round," 1944–1945*. Princeton: Princeton U. Press, 1972.

Ireland, Timothy P. *Creating the Entangling Alliance: The Origins of the North Atlantic Treaty Organization*. Westport, Conn.: Greenwood, 1981.

Isaacson, Walter, and Evan Thomas. *The Wise Men: Six Friends and the World They Made*. N.Y.: Simon & Schuster, 1986.

Jones, Howard. *"A New Kind of War": America's Global Strategy and the Truman Doctrine in Greece*. N.Y.: Oxford U. Press, 1989.

Kaplan, Lawrence S. *NATO and the United States: The Enduring Alliance*. Boston: G. K. Hall, 1988.

———. *The United States and NATO: The Formative Years*. Lexington: U. Press of Kentucky, 1984.

Kimball, Warren F. *The Most Unsordid Act: Lend-Lease, 1939–1941*. Baltimore: Johns Hopkins Press, 1969.

———. *Swords or Ploughshares? The Morgenthau Plan for Defeated Nazi Germany, 1943–1946*. N.Y.: Lippincott, 1976.

Kindleberger, Charles P. *Marshall Plan Days*. Boston: Allen & Unwin, 1987.

Kolko, Gabriel. *The Politics of War: The World and United States Foreign Policy, 1943–1945*. N.Y.: Random House, 1968.

Kolko, Joyce and Gabriel. *The Limits of Power: The World and United States Foreign Policy, 1945–1954*. N.Y.: Harper & Row, 1972.

Kousoulas, Dimitrios G. *The Price of Freedom: Greece in World Affairs, 1939–1953*. Syracuse, N.Y.: Syracuse U. Press, 1953.

———. *Revolution and Defeat: The Story of the Greek Communist Party*. London: Oxford U. Press, 1965.

Kuklick, Bruce. *American Policy and the Division of Germany: The Clash with Russia over Reparations*. Ithaca, N.Y.: Cornell U. Press, 1972.

Kuniholm, Bruce R. *The Origins of the Cold War in the Near East: Great Power Conflict and Diplomacy in Iran, Turkey, and Greece*. Princeton: Princeton U. Press, 1980.

Kurzman, Dan. *Day of the Bomb: Countdown to Hiroshima*. N.Y.: McGraw-Hill, 1986.

LaFeber, Walter. *America, Russia, and the Cold War, 1945–1984*. 5th ed. N.Y.: Knopf, 1985.

Larrabee, Eric. *Commander in Chief: Franklin Delano Roosevelt, His Lieutenants, and Their War*. N.Y.: Harper & Row, 1987.

Levering, Ralph B. *American Opinion and the Russian Alliance, 1939–1945*. Chapel Hill: U. of North Carolina Press, 1976.

Lincoln, Francis F. *United States' Aid to Greece, 1947–1962*. Germantown, Tenn.: Professional Seminars, 1975.

Lippmann, Walter. *The Cold War*. N.Y.: Harper & Row, 1947.

Louis, William Roger. *Imperialism at Bay: The United States and the Decolonization of the British Empire, 1941–1945*. N.Y.: Oxford U. Press, 1978.

Lundestad, Geir. *The American Non-Policy Towards Eastern Europe, 1943–1947: Universalism in an Area Not of Essential Interest to the United States*. N.Y.: Humanities, 1975.

McCagg, William O., Jr. *Stalin Embattled, 1943–1948*. Detroit: Wayne State U. Press, 1978.

McCoy, Donald R. *The Presidency of Harry S. Truman*. Lawrence: U. Press of Kansas, 1984.

McJimsey, George T. *Harry Hopkins: Ally of the Poor and Defender of Democracy*. Cambridge: Harvard U. Press, 1987.

McLellan, David S. *Dean Acheson: The State Department Years*. N.Y.: Dodd, Mead, 1976.

McNeill, William H. *The Greek Dilemma: War and Aftermath.* Philadelphia: Lippincott, 1947.

Martel, Leon. *Lend-Lease, Loans, and the Coming of the Cold War: A Study of the Implementation of Foreign Policy.* Boulder: Westview, 1979.

Mastny, Vojtech. *Russia's Road to the Cold War: Diplomacy, Warfare, and the Politics of Communism, 1941–1945.* N.Y.: Columbia U. Press, 1979.

Matthews, Kenneth. *Memories of a Mountain War, Greece: 1944–1949.* London: Longman, 1972.

May, Ernest R. *"Lessons" of the Past: The Use and Misuse of History in American Foreign Policy.* N.Y.: Oxford U. Press, 1973.

Mee, Charles L., Jr. *The Marshall Plan: The Launching of the Pax Americana.* N.Y.: Simon & Schuster, 1984.

———. *Meeting at Potsdam.* N.Y.: Evans, 1975.

Messer, Robert L. *The End of an Alliance: James F. Byrnes, Roosevelt, Truman, and the Origins of the Cold War.* Chapel Hill: U. of North Carolina Press, 1982.

Middleton, Drew. *The Struggle for Germany.* London: Allan Wingate, 1950.

Miller, Richard Lawrence. *Truman: The Rise to Power.* N.Y.: McGraw-Hill, 1986.

Miller, William J. *Henry Cabot Lodge: A Biography.* N.Y.: Heineman, 1967.

Milward, Alan S. *The Reconstruction of Western Europe, 1945–51.* London: Methuen, 1984.

Nelson, Daniel J. *Wartime Origins of the Berlin Dilemma.* University: U. of Alabama Press, 1978.

Neumann, William L. *After Victory: Churchill, Roosevelt, Stalin and the Making of the Peace.* N.Y.: Harper & Row, 1967.

Neustadt, Richard E. *Presidential Power: The Politics of Leadership.* N.Y.: Wiley, 1960.

O'Ballance, Edgar. *The Greek Civil War, 1944–1949.* N.Y.: Praeger, 1966.

Offner, Arnold A. *The Origins of the Second World War: American Foreign Policy and World Politics, 1917–1941.* N.Y.: Praeger, 1975.

Osgood, Robert E. *Alliances and American Foreign Policy.* Baltimore: Johns Hopkins Press, 1968.

Ovendale, Ritchie. *The English-Speaking Alliance: Britain and the United States, the Dominions and the Cold War, 1945–1951.* Boston: Allen & Unwin, 1985.

Page, Bruce, David Leitch, and Phillip Knightley. *The Philby Conspiracy.* Garden City, N.Y.: Doubleday, 1968.

Papandreou, Andreas. *Democracy at Gunpoint: The Greek Front.* Garden City, N.Y.: Doubleday, 1970.

Paterson, Thomas G. *On Every Front: The Making of the Cold War.* N.Y.: Norton, 1979.

———. *Soviet-American Confrontation: Postwar Reconstruction and the Origins of the Cold War.* Baltimore: Johns Hopkins Press, 1973.

Peterson, Edward N. *The American Occupation of Germany: Retreat to Victory.* Detroit: Wayne State U. Press, 1977.
Phillips, Cabell. *The Truman Presidency: The History of a Triumphant Succession.* N.Y.: Macmillan, 1966.
Pogue, Forrest C. *George C. Marshall: Statesman, 1945–1949.* N.Y.: Viking, 1987.
Price, Harry B. *The Marshall Plan and Its Meaning.* Ithaca, N.Y.: Cornell U. Press, 1955.
Randall, Stephen J. *United States Foreign Oil Policy, 1919–1948: For Profits and Security.* Montreal: McGill-Queen's U. Press, 1985.
Reynolds, David. *The Creation of the Anglo-American Alliance, 1937–1941: A Study in Competitive Cooperation.* Chapel Hill: U. of North Carolina Press, 1981.
Rhodes, Richard. *The Making of the Atomic Bomb.* N.Y.: Simon & Schuster, 1986.
Richter, Heinz. *British Intervention in Greece: From Varkiza to Civil War, February 1945 to August 1946.* London: Merlin, 1985.
Rogow, Arnold A. *James Forrestal: A Study of Personality, Politics, and Policy.* N.Y.: Macmillan, 1963.
Rose, Lisle A. *After Yalta.* N.Y.: Scribner, 1973.
Rothwell, Victor. *Britain and the Cold War, 1941–1947.* London: Cape, 1982.
Ruddy, T. Michael. *The Cautious Diplomat: Charles E. Bohlen and the Soviet Union, 1929–1969.* Kent, Ohio: Kent State U. Press, 1986.
Ryan, Henry Butterfield. *The Vision of Anglo-America: The U.S.-U.K. Alliance and the Emerging Cold War, 1943–1946.* Cambridge: Cambridge U. Press, 1987.
Sharp, Tony. *The Wartime Alliance and the Zonal Division of Germany.* Oxford: Clarendon, 1975.
Sherry, Michael S. *Preparing for the Next War: American Plans for Postwar Defense, 1941–1945.* New Haven: Yale U. Press, 1977.
Sherwin, Martin J. *A World Destroyed: The Atomic Bomb and the Grand Alliance.* N.Y.: Knopf, 1975.
Shlaim, Avi. *The United States and the Berlin Blockade, 1948–1949: A Study in Decision-Making.* Berkeley: U. of California Press, 1983.
Shulman, Marshall D. *Stalin's Foreign Policy Reappraised.* N.Y.: Atheneum, 1969.
Smith, Arthur L., Jr. *Churchill's German Army: Wartime Strategy and Cold War Politics, 1943–1947.* Beverly Hills: Sage, 1977.
Smith, Gaddis. *American Diplomacy During the Second World War, 1941–1945.* 2d ed. N.Y.: Knopf, 1985.
———. *Dean Acheson.* N.Y.: Cooper Square, 1972.
Smith, Jean Edward. *The Defense of Berlin.* Baltimore: Johns Hopkins Press, 1963.

Snell, John L., et al. *The Meaning of Yalta: Big Three Diplomacy and the Balance of Power.* Baton Rouge: Louisiana State U. Press, 1956.

Stoff, Michael B. *Oil, War, and American Security: The Search for a National Policy on Foreign Oil, 1941–1947.* New Haven: Yale U. Press, 1980.

Stoler, Mark A. *The Politics of the Second Front: American Military Planning and Coalition Warfare, 1941–1943.* Westport, Conn.: Greenwood, 1977.

Stueck, William. *The Road to Confrontation: American Foreign Policy Toward China and Korea, 1947–1950.* Chapel Hill: U. of North Carolina Press, 1981.

———. *The Wedemeyer Mission: American Politics and Foreign Policy During the Cold War.* Athens: U. of Georgia Press, 1984.

Sweet-Escott, Bickham. *Greece: A Political and Economic Survey, 1939–1953.* London: Royal Institute of International Affairs, 1954.

Taubman, William. *Stalin's American Policy: From Entente to Detente to Cold War.* N.Y.: Norton, 1982.

Theoharis, Athan G. *The Yalta Myths: An Issue in U.S. Politics, 1945–1955.* Columbia: U. of Missouri Press, 1970.

Thorne, Christopher. *Allies of a Kind: The United States, Britain and the War Against Japan, 1941–1945.* N.Y.: Oxford U. Press, 1978.

Truman, Margaret. *Harry S. Truman.* N.Y.: Morrow, 1973.

Tucker, Robert C. *The Soviet Political Mind: Stalinism and Post-Stalin Change.* Rev. ed. N.Y.: Norton, 1971.

Tusa, Ann and John. *The Berlin Airlift.* N.Y.: Atheneum, 1988.

Ulam, Adam B. *Expansion and Coexistence: Soviet Foreign Policy, 1917–1973.* 2d ed. N.Y.: Praeger, 1974.

———. *The Rivals: America and Russia Since World War II.* N.Y.: Viking, 1971.

———. *Stalin: The Man and His Era.* N.Y.: Viking, 1973.

———. *Titoism and the Cominform.* Cambridge: Harvard U. Press, 1952.

Ward, Patricia Dawson. *The Threat of Peace: James F. Byrnes and the Council of Foreign Ministers, 1945–1946.* Kent, Ohio: Kent State U. Press, 1979.

Watt, Donald Cameron. *Personalities and Policies: Studies in the Formulation of British Foreign Policy in the Twentieth Century.* Notre Dame: U. of Notre Dame Press, 1965.

Weisberger, Bernard A. *Cold War, Cold Peace: The United States and Russia Since 1945.* N.Y.: American Heritage, 1985.

Werth, Alexander. *Russia: The Post-War Years.* London: Robert Hale, 1971.

Wexler, Immanuel. *The Marshall Plan Revisited: The European Recovery Program in Economic Perspective.* Westport, Conn.: Greenwood, 1983.

Wheeler-Bennett, Sir John, and Anthony Nicholls. *The Semblance of Peace: The Political Settlement After the Second World War.* London: Macmillan, 1972.

Williams, William A. *The Tragedy of American Diplomacy.* N.Y.: World, 1959. Rev. ed. N.Y.: Dell, 1972.

Wilson, Theodore A. *The First Summit: Roosevelt and Churchill at Placentia Bay, 1941.* Boston: Houghton Mifflin, 1969.

———. *The Marshall Plan.* Headline Series No. 236. N.Y.: Foreign Policy Association, 1977.
Wittner, Lawrence S. *American Intervention in Greece, 1943–1949.* N.Y.: Columbia U. Press, 1982.
Woodhouse, Christopher M. *Apple of Discord: A Survey of Recent Greek Politics in Their International Setting.* London: Hutchinson, 1948.
———. *The Struggle for Greece, 1941–1949.* Brooklyn Heights, N.Y.: Beekman-Esanu, 1976.
Woods, Randall B. *A Changing of the Guard: Anglo-America, 1941–1946.* Chapel Hill: U. of North Carolina Press, 1990.
Xydis, Stephen G. *Greece and the Great Powers, 1944–1947: Prelude to the "Truman Doctrine."* Thessaloniki: Institute for Balkan Studies, 1963.
Yergin, Daniel H. *Shattered Peace: The Origins of the Cold War and the National Security State.* Boston: Houghton Mifflin, 1977.

Articles and Essays

Barker, Elisabeth. "Yugoslav Policy Towards Greece, 1947–1949." In Baerentzen, Iatrides, and Smith, eds., *Studies in History of Greek Civil War,* 263–95.
———. "The Yugoslavs and the Greek Civil War of 1946–1949." In Baerentzen, Iatrides, and Smith, eds., *Studies in History of Greek Civil War,* 297–308.
Bernstein, Barton J. "Roosevelt, Truman and the Atomic Bomb, 1941–1945: A Reinterpretation." *Political Science Quarterly* 90 (Spring 1975): 23–69.
Blum, Robert M. "Surprised by Tito: The Anatomy of an Intelligence Failure." *Diplomatic History* 12 (Winter 1988): 39–57.
Chandler, Harriette L. "The Transition to Cold Warrior: The Evolution of W. Averell Harriman's Assessment of the U.S.S.R.'s Polish Policy, October 1943–Warsaw Uprising." *East European Quarterly* 10 (Spring 1976): 229–45.
Clay, Lucius D. "Berlin." *Foreign Affairs* 41 (Oct. 1962): 47–58.
Diebold, William, Jr. "The Marshall Plan in Retrospect: A Review of Recent Scholarship." *Journal of International Affairs* 41 (Summer 1988): 421–35.
Divine, Robert A. "The Cold War and the Election of 1948." *Journal of American History* 59 (June 1972): 90–110.
Dorn, Walter L. "The Debate over American Occupation Policy in Germany in 1944–45." *Political Science Quarterly* 72 (Dec. 1957): 481–501.
Folly, Martin H. "Breaking the Vicious Circle: Britain, the United States, and the Genesis of the North Atlantic Treaty." *Diplomatic History* 12 (Winter 1988): 59–77.
Gaddis, John L. "The Corporatist Synthesis: A Skeptical View." *Diplomatic History* 10 (Fall 1986): 357–62.
Gimbel, John. "James F. Byrnes and the Division of Germany." In Clements, ed., *Byrnes and Origins of Cold War,* 89–91.
———. "On the Implementation of the Potsdam Agreement: An Essay on U.S. Postwar German Policy." *Political Science Quarterly* 87 (June 1972): 242–69.

Harbutt, Fraser J. "American Challenge, Soviet Response: The Beginning of the Cold War, February–May, 1946." *Political Science Quarterly* 96 (Winter 1981–82): 623–39.

Harrington, Daniel F. "Kennan, Bohlen and the Riga Axioms." *Diplomatic History* 2 (Fall 1978): 423–37.

Herring, George C., Jr. "Lend-Lease to Russia and the Origins of the Cold War, 1944–1945." *Journal of American History* 56 (June 1969): 93–114.

———. "The United States and British Bankruptcy, 1944–1945: Responsibilities Deferred." *Political Science Quarterly* 86 (June 1971): 260–80.

Hess, Gary R. "The Iranian Crisis of 1945–46 and the Cold War." *Political Science Quarterly* 89 (Mar. 1974): 117–46.

Hogan, Michael J. "Corporatism: A Positive Appraisal." *Diplomatic History* 10 (Fall 1986): 363–72.

———. "Revival and Reform: America's Twentieth-Century Search for a New Economic Order Abroad." *Diplomatic History* 8 (Fall 1984): 287–310.

———. "The Search for a 'Creative Peace': The United States, European Unity, and the Origins of the Marshall Plan." *Diplomatic History* 6 (Summer 1982): 267–85.

Iatrides, John O. "American Attitudes Toward the Political System of Postwar Greece." In Couloumbis and Iatrides, eds., *Greek-American Relations*, 49–73.

Jackson, Scott. "Prologue to the Marshall Plan: The Origins of the American Commitment for a European Recovery Program." *Journal of American History* 65 (Mar. 1979): 1043–68.

Jessup, Philip C. "Park Avenue Diplomacy—Ending the Berlin Blockade." *Political Science Quarterly* 87 (Sept. 1972): 377–400.

Jones, Howard. "The Diplomacy of Restraint: The United States' Efforts to Repatriate Greek Children Evacuated During the Civil War of 1946–49." *Journal of Modern Greek Studies* (May 1985): 65–85.

Kennan, George F. "Containment Then and Now." *Foreign Affairs* 65 (Spring 1987): 885–90.

[Kennan, George F.] "The Sources of Soviet Conduct." *Foreign Affairs* 25 (July 1947): 566–82.

Kimball, Warren F. "Lend-Lease and the Open Door: The Temptation of British Opulence, 1937–1942." *Political Science Quarterly* 86 (June 1971): 232–57.

Knight, Jonathan. "Russia's Search for Peace: The London Council of Foreign Ministers, 1945." *Journal of Contemporary History* 13 (Jan. 1978): 137–63.

Kousoulas, Dimitrios G. "The Truman Doctrine and the Stalin-Tito Rift: A Reappraisal." *South Atlantic Quarterly* 72 (Summer 1973): 427–39.

Lees, Lorraine M. "The American Decision to Assist Tito, 1948–1949." *Diplomatic History* 2 (Fall 1978): 407–22.

Leffler, Melvyn P. "The American Conception of National Security and the Beginnings of the Cold War, 1945–1948." *American Historical Review* 89 (Apr. 1984): 346–81.

———. "From the Truman Doctrine to the Carter Doctrine: Lessons and Dilemmas of the Cold War." *Diplomatic History* 7 (Fall 1983): 245–66.

———. "Strategy, Diplomacy, and the Cold War: The United States, Turkey, and NATO, 1945–1952." *Journal of American History* 71 (Mar. 1985): 807–25.

———. "The United States and the Strategic Dimensions of the Marshall Plan." *Diplomatic History* 12 (Summer 1988): 277–306.

Lukas, Richard C. "The Big Three and the Warsaw Uprising." *Military Affairs* 39 (Oct. 1975): 129–34.

McGhee, George M. "The Impact of Foreign Commitments upon the Coordinative Responsibilities of the Department of State." In *International Commitments and National Administration* (Charlottesville: Bureau of Public Administration, U. of Virginia, 1949), 39–55.

Messer, Robert L. "Paths Not Taken: The United States Department of State and Alternatives to Containment, 1945–1946." *Diplomatic History* 1 (Fall 1977): 297–319.

Milward, Alan S. "Was the Marshall Plan Necessary?" *Diplomatic History* 13 (Spring 1989): 231–53.

Paterson, Thomas G. "The Abortive Loan to Russia and the Origins of the Cold War, 1943–1946." *Journal of American History* 56 (June 1969): 70–92.

Pelling, Henry. "The 1945 General Election Reconsidered." *Historical Journal* 23 (June 1980): 399–414.

Pollard, Robert A. "Economic Security and the Origins of the Cold War: Bretton Woods, the Marshall Plan, and American Rearmament, 1944–50." *Diplomatic History* 9 (Summer 1985): 271–89.

Rappaport, Armin. "The United States and European Integration: The First Phase." *Diplomatic History* 5 (Spring 1981): 121–49.

Resis, Albert. "The Churchill-Stalin Secret 'Percentages' Agreement on the Balkans, Moscow, October 1944." *American Historical Review* 83 (Apr. 1978): 368–87.

Rosenberg, David A. "American Atomic Strategy and the Hydrogen Bomb Decision." *Journal of American History* 66 (May 1979): 62–87.

Rosenberg, J. Philip. "The Cheshire Ultimatum: Truman's Message to Stalin in the 1946 Azerbaijan Crisis." *Journal of Politics* 41 (Aug. 1979): 933–40.

Rourke, John T. "Congress and the Cold War." *World Affairs* 139 (Spring 1977): 259–77.

Rubel, Roberto. "Prologue to Containment: The Truman Administration's Response to the Trieste Crisis of May 1945." *Diplomatic History* 10 (Spring 1986): 141–60.

Siracusa, Joseph M. "The Meaning of Tolstoy: Churchill, Stalin, and the Balkans: Moscow, October 1944." *Diplomatic History* 3 (Summer 1979): 443–63.

Smith, Jean Edward. "General Clay and the Russians: A Continuation of the

Wartime Alliance in Germany, 1945–1948." *Virginia Quarterly Review* 64 (Winter 1988): 20–36.

Smith, Ole L. "Self-Defence and Communist Policy, 1945–1947." In Baerentzen, Iatrides, and Smith, eds., *Studies in History of Greek Civil War*, 159–77.

Trachtenberg, Marc. "A 'Wasting Asset': American Strategy and the Shifting Nuclear Balance, 1949–1954." *International Security* 13 (Winter 1988–89): 5–49.

Wala, Michael. "Selling the Marshall Plan at Home: The Committee for the Marshall Plan to Aid European Recovery." *Diplomatic History* 10 (Summer 1986): 247–65.

Wittner, Lawrence S. "The Truman Doctrine and the Defense of Freedom." *Diplomatic History* 4 (Spring 1980): 161–87.

Xydis, Stephen G. "The Secret Anglo-Soviet Agreement on the Balkans of October 9, 1944." *Journal of Central European Affairs* 15 (Oct. 1955): 248–71.

———. "The Truman Doctrine in Perspective." *Balkan Studies* 8 (1967): 239–62.

Dissertations

Green, Philip Earl. "Conflict over Trade Ideologies During the Early Cold War: A Study of Foreign Economic Policy." Duke U., 1978.

Harrington, Daniel F. "American Policy in the Berlin Crisis of 1948–49." Indiana U., 1979.

Hedlund, Richard P. "Congress and the British Loan of 1946." U. of Kentucky, 1978.

Knight, Wayne Stone. "The Nonfraternal Association: Anglo-American Relations and the Breakdown of the Grand Alliance, 1945–1947." American U., 1979.

INDEX